PACIFIC EXPOSURES

PACIFIC EXPOSURES

PHOTOGRAPHY AND THE AUSTRALIA–JAPAN RELATIONSHIP

MELISSA MILES AND ROBIN GERSTER

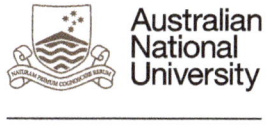

ASIAN STUDIES SERIES MONOGRAPH 11

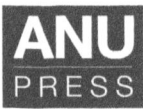

Published by ANU Press
The Australian National University
Acton ACT 2601, Australia
Email: anupress@anu.edu.au

Available to download for free at press.anu.edu.au

ISBN (print): 9781760462543
ISBN (online): 9781760462550

WorldCat (print): 1076493862
WorldCat (online): 1076494153

DOI: 10.22459/PE.2018

This title is published under a Creative Commons Attribution-NonCommercial-NoDerivatives 4.0 International (CC BY-NC-ND 4.0).

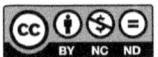

The full licence terms are available at creativecommons.org/licenses/by-nc-nd/4.0/legalcode

Cover design and layout by ANU Press.

Cover photograph: Ciaran Chestnutt, *My niece, enthralled by a geisha, strolling back from Senso-ji*, 2013.

This edition © 2018 ANU Press

CONTENTS

List of Figures vii

Acknowledgements xiii

Introduction 1

1. 'The Child of the World's Old Age': Photographing Japan in the Early Twentieth Century 11

2. 'White Australia' in the Darkroom: 1915–41 45

3. Shooting Japanese: Photographing the Pacific War 81

4. Japan for the Taking: Images of the Occupation 113

5. Through Non-Military Eyes: Developing the Postwar Bilateral Relationship 153

6. Cross-Cultural (Mis)Understandings: Independent Photography since the 1980s 187

7. Conclusion: Revising 'Us and Them' 227

Bibliography 235

LIST OF FIGURES

Figure 0.1. Untitled postcard, Wallaroo Mines c. 1915 2

Figure 1.1. Futaba and Co., *Untitled [Japanese Child]*, c. 1926. 12

Figure 1.2. Mortimer Menpes, *Advance Japan* 17

Figure 1.3. Leo Arthur Cotton, *Untitled [Japanese Children]*, c. 1926 19

Figure 1.4. George Rose, *Cherry Blossoms, Ueno Park, Tokyo, Japan*, c. 1890–1900. 21

Figure 1.5. Cavendish Morton, *L'Entente Cordiale* from the series 'Young Japan and Friends', c. 1905 27

Figure 1.6. Cavendish Morton, *Pals* from the series 'Young Japan and Friends', c. 1905 27

Figure 1.7. Cavendish Morton, *Two Handy Men* from the series 'Young Japan and Friends', c. 1905 28

Figure 1.8. Cavendish Morton, *That's How It's Done* from the series 'Young Japan and Friends', c. 1905 28

Figure 1.9. Anon., *The Motherland's Misalliance* 31

Figure 1.10. George Rose, Japanese schoolboys waiting to see soldiers bound for war. When the train arrives they all sing a war song and shout 'Bonzai' (good luck), c. 1904 34

Figure 1.11. Photographs of Mark Foy and family, including a trip to Japan in 1902. 37

Figure 1.12. Photographs of Mark Foy and family, including a trip to Japan in 1902. 38

Figure 1.13. Ruth Hollick, *Untitled [Child in Kimono]*, c. 1910–30 40

Figure 2.1. Harold Cazneaux, *Photographic Society Outing*, Sydney, c. 1915. 50

Figure 2.2. Attributed to Ichiro Kagiyama, *Untitled [Portrait of Japanese-Australian Family]*, c. 1915 51

Figure 2.3. Photographer unknown, *Mikado Farm*, Guildford, 1915 53

Figure 2.4. Attributed to Ichiro Kagiyama, *Untitled [White City]*, c. 1915 55

Figure 2.5. Attributed to Ichiro Kagiyama, *Untitled [White City]*, c. 1915 55

Figure 2.6. Monte Luke, *The Girl in the Kimona*. 58

Figure 2.7. Ichiro Kagiyama, *Untitled [Japanese Dancing Doll]* 58

Figure 2.8. Attributed to Ichiro Kagiyama, *Untitled [Parade]*, c. 1915. 59

Figure 2.9. Kiichiro Ishida, *A White Gum* 63

Figure 2.10. Kiichiro Ishida, *Mountain Decoration* 65

Figure 2.11. Stanley Eutrope, *Winter's Curtain*, c. 1922 66

Figure 2.12. Cover design for *The Home*, December 1921 69

Figure 2.13. Ichiro Kagiyama, 'Sydney—Seen Through Japanese Eyes' 71

Figure 2.14. Advertisement for NYK Line 73

Figure 2.15. Ichiro Kagiyama, *B.M.A Macquarie Street*, from
'Sydney—Seen Through Japanese Eyes' 74

Figure 3.1. George Silk, *Australian Soldiers with Japanese Dead after the Final Assault on Gona, Papua*, 17 December 1942 82

Figure 3.2. Norman Stuckey, *Troops of the 2/16th Australian Infantry Battalion Unearth a Dead Japanese Soldier*, Shaggy Ridge area, New Guinea, 27 December 1943 88

Figure 3.3. Unknown photographer, *Troops of 47th Australian Infantry Battalion with Dead Japanese by Enemy Pillbox*, Bougainville, 16 January 1945. 91

Figure 3.4. Unknown photographer, *Troops of the 2/17th Australian Infantry Battalion Search Japanese Bodies*, Brunei, North Borneo, 13 June 1945 91

Figure 3.5. Ronald Keam, *Australian Infantry Filling a Mass Grave with Japanese Dead*, Bougainville, 6 April 1945 93

Figure 3.6. George Silk, *Lieutenant John R. Greenwood, 2/14th Australian Infantry Battalion*, New Guinea, 23 November 1942 98

Figure 3.7. Unknown photographer, *Japanese Prisoner Known as 'Mickey Mouse', with Two Australians*, Morotai, c. 1945. 99

Figure 3.8. Unknown photographer, *Suspected Japanese War Criminals on Trial in Darwin*, March 1945 101

Figure 3.9. George Silk, *Wounded Japanese Carried by Australian Soldier*, c. 1942 103

Figure 3.10. Unknown photographer, *Two Japanese Prisoners Being Conveyed to Casualty Clearing Station*, c. 1944 105

Figure 3.11. Unknown photographer, *Military History Section Photographer Lance Sergeant Norman Stuckey (left) and an Australian Soldier with Japanese Prisoner*, New Guinea, 10 October 1943. 106

LIST OF FIGURES

Figure 3.12. Allan Cuthbert, *Japanese Schoolgirls Welcome Home Repatriated Prisoners-of-War*, Ujina (Hiroshima), 27 June 1946. 108

Figure 3.13. Unknown photographer, *Portrait of Lieutenant William Harry Freeman*, Official photographer, Hiroshima, 1947. 110

Figure 4.1. Lt Gaetano Faillace, *Emperor Hirohito and General MacArthur, at Their First Meeting, at the U.S. Embassy*, Tokyo, 27 September 1945 114

Figure 4.2. William Harry Freeman, *Members of BCOF Taking Photographs of 'Geisha Girls'*, Kyoto, August 1947 116

Figure 4.3. Unknown photographer, BCOF Public Relations, *Australian Soldier Shopping in Ginza*, Tokyo, c. 1946–48 122

Figure 4.4. Neil Town, 'Australia Is There—With Our Occupation Force in Japan', *Australasian*, 9 March 1946, 25 123

Figure 4.5. Unknown photographer, *Australian Soldiers in Hiroshima*, c. 1947. 127

Figure 4.6. Allan Cuthbert, *View South from Central Hiroshima*, 28 February 1946 129

Figure 4.7. Alan Queale, *Peace Festival, Hiroshima*, 6 August 1948 130

Figure 4.8. Phillip Hobson, *Australian Serviceman with a Group of Japanese Women, Japan*, c. April 1952 133

Figure 4.9. Alan Queale, *Venereal Disease Cases Discovered during a Medical Examination of Japanese Female Employees of BCOF*, Hiro, 26 September 1946 137

Figure 4.10. Ron Lovitt, *Pressmen Being Entertained*, Japan, date unknown. 138

Figure 4.11. Allan Cuthbert, *Japanese Shipyards Labourer*, Kure, 1948 . . .139

Figure 4.12. William Harry Freeman, *Emperor Hirohito on Tour*, Osaka, 1947. 143

Figure 4.13. Allan Cuthbert, *Soldiers of BCOF 65th Battalion, on Patrol*, Fukuyama Prefecture, 10 September 1946. .143

Figure 4.14. Phillip Hobson, *Grandmother Gardening with Granddaughter*, Kure area, c. Nov 1949. 145

Figure 4.15. Alan Queale, *Oysterman*, Kaitaichi, Hiroshima Prefecture, c. 1946–48 146

Figure 4.16. Claude Holzheimer, *Japanese Farming Family*, Hiroshima Prefecture, c. 1953 147

Figure 4.17. Phillip Hobson, *Australian Soldier Offering Money to Beggar*, Tokyo, 11 January 1955 148

Figure 4.18. Phillip Hobson, *Australian Soldier and Japanese Stand Guard at Ebisu Camp*, Tokyo, 8 August 1954 150

Figure 5.1. Stephen Kelen, *Hiroshima*, c. 1946–48, published in *I Remember Hiroshima* (Sydney: Hale & Iremonger, 1983), 18 154

Figure 5.2. Albert Tucker, *Three Boys Near Osaka*, 1947 158

Figure 5.3. Herbert Cole ('Nugget') Coombs, *Children in a Tokyo Street*, May 1946 158

Figure 5.4. Neville Govett, *Street Scene*, Hiroshima, c. 1947–49 160

Figure 5.5. Neville Govett, *Smokestack and Ventilator on the Hokkaido Ferry*, c. 1947–49 160

Figure 5.6. Frederick Frueh, *On the Road to the Railway Station*, Iwakuni, c. 1946 162

Figure 5.7. Brian and Cecilia McMullan, *Street Scene*, Kure, c. 1947–52 .. 163

Figure 5.8. Bruce Howard, *Murray Rose with his Japanese Rival Tsuyoshi Yamanaka after the 400m Freestyle Final at the 1956 Olympic Games*, Melbourne, 4 December 1956 165

Figure 5.9. Photographer unknown, *Prime Minister Menzies Greets Japanese Prime Minster Kishi at Essendon Airport*, Melbourne, 2 December 1957 170

Figure 5.10. Ellen Brophy, *'Memories of Japan'* (Album), Kobe-Osaka, 1957–60 174

Figure 5.11. Mark Strizic, *Monorail Viewed from Inside the Australian Pavilion, Expo '70*, Osaka, 1970 176

Figure 5.12. Mark Strizic, *Exterior of the Australian Pavilion, Expo '70*, Osaka, 1970 177

Figure 5.13. Photographer unknown, *Visitors and Crew Make a Toast*, Darwin Harbour 1961 180

Figure 5.14. George Lipman, *Matsue Matsuo Pays Her Respects to Her Son Lieutenant Keiu Matsuo*, Sydney Harbour, 29 April 1968 181

Figure 5.15. Cliff Bottomley, *Visiting Japanese Schoolchildren at an Australian Family Barbecue*, near Melbourne, 1963 183

Figure 5.16. Photographer unknown, *Gough and Margaret Whitlam with the Emperor and Empress of Japan*, Tokyo, 26 October 1963 186

Figure 6.1. Christopher Köller, *Untitled* from the series *Zen Zen Chigau*, 1984 195

Figure 6.2. Christopher Köller, *Untitled* from the series *Zen Zen Chigau*, 1984 197

Figure 6.3. Kristian Häggblom, *Yoyogi #11*, 2006 204

LIST OF FIGURES

Figure 6.4. Kristian Häggblom, *Kichijoji #6*, 2006 .204

Figure 6.5. Kristian Häggblom, *Aokigahara Jukai, Bible Translations*,
2000. 205

Figure 6.6. Kristian Häggblom, *Aokigahara Jukai, Donald Duck Badge*,
2000. 206

Figure 6.7. Matthew Sleeth, *12 Views of Mt Fuji #4 [Fujikyu Highland
Park]*, 2004. 208

Figure 6.8. Matthew Sleeth, *12 Views of Mt Fuji #43 [Shinjuku Southern
Tower Hotel]*, 2005 209

Figure 6.9. Matthew Sleeth, *12 Views of Mt Fuji #24 [Kawaguchiko]*,
2004. 210

Figure 6.10. Matthew Sleeth, *Kawaii Baby #15 [Tokyo]*, 2006 211

Figure 6.11. Matthew Sleeth, *Kawaii Baby #16 [Tokyo]*, 2006 212

Figure 6.12. Matthew Sleeth, *Millenario Lights, Marunouchi [Tokyo]*,
2006. 214

Figure 6.13. Matthew Sleeth, *North West from Shinjuku [Tokyo]*, 2005 215

Figure 6.14. Ciaran Chestnutt, *My Niece, Enthralled by a Geisha,
Strolling Back from Senso-ji*, 2013 219

Figure 6.15. Meg Hewitt, *Underwater Observatory, Katsuura*, from *Tokyo
is Yours*, 2016. 223

Figure 6.16. Meg Hewitt, *Tokyo is Yours*, 2015–17 .223

Figure 6.17. Meg Hewitt, *Tokyo is Yours*, installation view, Flinders Street
Gallery, Surry Hills 2017 225

Figure 7.1. Mayu Kanamori, *Untitled* from *You've Mistaken Me for
a Butterfly*, 2017–18. © Mayu Kanamori 2017 228

Figure 7.2. Mayu Kanamori, *Untitled* from *You've Mistaken Me for
a Butterfly*, 2017–18. © Mayu Kanamori 2017 228

ACKNOWLEDGEMENTS

Research for this book was funded by the Australian Research Council under its Discovery Projects scheme (DP140100039). Monash University's faculties of Arts and Art, Design and Architecture provided stimulating and supportive environments for this project. We are particularly grateful to Shane Murray, Kathie Barwick, Athena Bangara, Luke Morgan and Kristy Davidson, who provided encouragement and invaluable assistance at various stages along the way. Research assistants Viona Fung, Jessica Neath and Kate Warren helped with gathering literature, images and managing image permissions for this book at different stages throughout the research project. Kate Warren's commitment, attention to detail and efficiency in the final stages of this project are greatly appreciated. We also thank Anna Berry Fukuda and Basil Cahusac de Caux for their translations of Japanese language texts. Parts of this book adapt and expand on articles previously published in the journals *History of Photography*, *History Australia*, the *Journal of Australian Studies* and *Meanjin*, and we thank the publishers for permission to develop the work here.

At ANU Press, Craig Reynolds championed the original proposal through to publication. The thoughtful feedback offered by the anonymous peer reviewers enabled us to refine and consolidate our arguments, and Capstone Editing copyedited the final manuscript with great care. We are indebted to the photographers Kristian Häggblom, Mayu Kanamori, Matthew Sleeth, Meg Hewitt and Christopher Köller, whose work is featured in this book and who generously shared their time, work and impressive knowledge. We thank Noreen Jones for her time, thoughtfulness and for making her image archive available to us. In Japan, Keiko Okubora from the Hida-Takayama Australia-Japan Society, Kumiko Tango, Mutsumi Tsuda and Mr Tanaka provided invaluable help in sourcing information in private and public collections. Sincere thanks also to the Australian War Memorial, National Library of Australia, National Gallery of Victoria, Art Gallery of NSW,

State Library of NSW, State Library of Victoria, National Archives of Australia, Fairfax, Hiroshima Municipal Archives and the Takayama Machi Hakubutsukan for facilitating access to photographs and for providing reproductions. Finally, we thank our families for their tireless support and patience over the four years of this project.

INTRODUCTION

Sometime around 1915, a dozen Australian women paused for a photograph as they readied for a Japanese-inspired parade at Wallaroo Mines in Kadina on South Australia's remote Yorke Peninsula (see Figure 0.1). The women are dressed in homemade interpretations of kimonos and obis and wear chrysanthemums in their hair. Two of them hold Japanese umbrellas and one a painted fan. A young child clutches a Japanese doll and large paper chrysanthemum as she sits in a sedan chair decorated with flowers. The Japanese war flag, the ensign of the powerful Imperial Navy, flutters somewhat limply near the front of this little procession. Japan, for the time being, was an ally if not quite a friend. Its navy was protecting Australia's coastline and escorting Australian troopships to distant wars for and on behalf of Great Britain. This wartime connection is elsewhere apparent in the photograph. Towards the back of the pictured group, one woman has adorned her Japanese robe with the ribbon of the Australian Red Cross Society, formed in 1914 to provide comforts to serving soldiers overseas such as knitted socks, vests and chocolate bars.

This photographic performance of Australian conceptions of women's wartime duty using elements of Japanese culture speaks powerfully to the connections between Australian perceptions of Japan and photography at that time—connections that were to go through periods of rupture and reconciliation in the decades to come. Photography is an evocative means of crossing time and territory in imaginative and physical senses. The Wallaroo Mines photograph was likely taken as a memento of an Australia Day community pageant in 1915 in which participants demonstrated their imagined allegiance with the Allies by appearing in their national costumes. A group of so-called 'geisha girls' and 'Japanese ladies' received special mention in the local newspaper.[1] Japanese decorative arts and textiles, moreover, were *a la mode* in Australian homes and it was not unusual for Australian women to identify with their Japanese sisters to the far north by posing for photographs in which they

---

1 'Australia Day. Magnificent Kadina Pageant', *Kadina and Wallaroo Times*, 28 July 1915, 2.

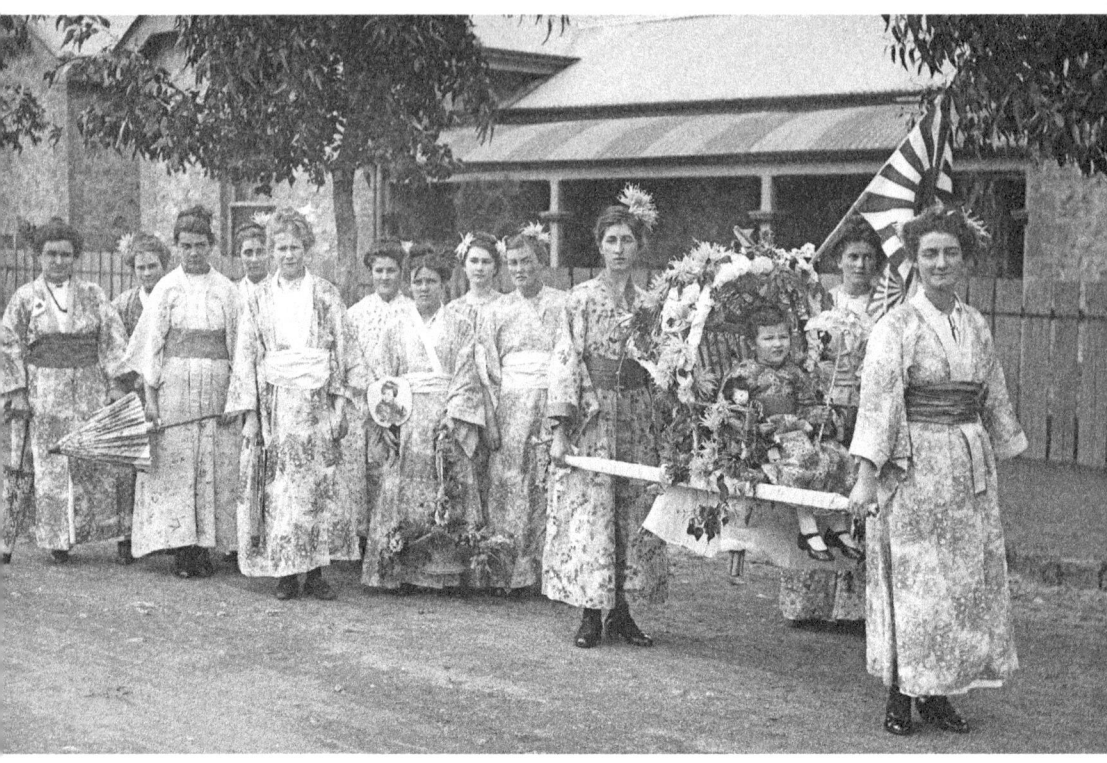

Figure 0.1. Untitled postcard, Wallaroo Mines c. 1915.
Source: National Library of Australia, PIC Album 1197/2 #PIC/15675/262.

interpret and adopt their dress at home.[2] Such imagined connections are heightened by the physical movement of the photograph across time and space. Not long after it was made, the Wallaroo Mines photograph travelled as a postcard connecting its writer with her brother, who lived 150 km away in Adelaide. Her message wished her brother good health and, in pointing out a special someone among the group, allowed the photograph to bring them emotionally closer to someone far away. After moving from one private collection to the next for almost a century, shifting from personal keepsake to collectable, the postcard acquired new value as an object of public cultural heritage when it entered the National Library of Australia collection in 2013.

This kind of complex, material and imaginative movement makes photography a valuable medium of historical analysis and cross-cultural interpretation. Photographs are highly adaptable objects of material culture that are equally at home in personal and public realms. Evident

---

2   Melissa Miles and Jessica Neath, 'Staging Japanese Femininity: Cross-Cultural Dressing in Australian Photography', *Fashion Theory* 20, no. 4 (2016): 545–73.

in their multitudes in immigration documents, government archives, the news media, postcards, tourism, advertising, art galleries and family albums, they also readily shift between and across these realms. Unbound by the limitations of written or spoken language, photographs are likewise well suited for moving between cultures. Their longevity means they can be revisited again and again, allowing them to acquire and shed meanings in often unpredictable ways. Yet, while they offer insight into the big questions of history—involving identity, place and conflict—there remains a quiet intimacy in historical photographs. When held in the hand, they offer a powerful material connection to other people, times and places.

Australia's historically ambivalent relationship with Japan—its oldest and arguably most significant regional partner—is fertile ground for analysing the critical nexus of photography, history and cross-cultural interpretation. While the connections between two such different countries should not be overstated, Australia and Japan share a certain geo-cultural commonality that lends itself to the kind of analysis that *Pacific Exposures* undertakes. Both Australia and Japan are uneasily located in the traditional East/West binary. One is ostensibly the most 'Western' country in the Asia-Pacific, and the other is in many ways the most Asian country in the 'West'. Crossing the vast Pacific in literal and figurative senses has represented a major cultural challenge to Australians—one that has been enabled by and reflected in photographs. From the fascination with all things Japanese in the early twentieth century through the bitter enmity of the Pacific War and the tortuous path to reconciliation in the postwar period and beyond, Australians have used photography to express a divided sense of conflict and kinship with Japan.

It is surely significant that Neville Meaney's comprehensive history of transformations in Australian–Japanese relations, *Towards a New Vision* (1999), was inspired by a pictorial exhibition, curated by the author, first shown in the New South Wales Parliament House in 1997. It is significant also that Meaney used a visual reference to signify the shifting points of view and perspectives of two countries thrown into an unlikely, enduring relationship.[3] Understanding the cultural process of response and reaction that characterises this relationship involves extending the

---

3   Neville Meaney, *Towards a New Vision: Australia and Japan through 100 Years* (East Roseville: Kangaroo Press, 1999).

interest in historical photographs beyond the events depicted, to also consider what photographs *do*. The photographs examined in *Pacific Exposures* indicate how Australians adopted an array of visual practices—including snapshots, lanternslides, art, news photographs and military public relations—to express their own experiences of international relations and their changing relationship to the past. As facilitators of encounters both real and imagined, as confronting images of battle, and as postwar reflections of rapprochement and anticipations of a fruitful mutual future, photographs have found an intimate place in Australian homes and also figured prominently in the public domain.

Pacific Exposures is, therefore, a story of transnational connection and movement—of people, ideas, labour, commodities and culture. It acknowledges that national histories are the products of relations with foreign countries, rather than merely an internalised vision of national uniqueness. The photographers examined in this book are not simply citizens, residents or public servants of Australia, they are also tourists, consumers, migrants, artists and workers who have forged their own emotional, material, aesthetic, familial and political links with Japan.[4]

In looking at these links, this book contributes to an existing body of research that examines Australia–Japan relations from the grassroots level to complement and extend histories structured around political, military and economic relations.[5] Further, it develops research on cross-cultural photographic relations. Modes of photographic encounter between Japan, Europe and the United States (US) have been the subject of numerous books and articles. Some historians have interpreted Anglo-European appetites for late nineteenth-century Japanese photographs as a sign of prevailing romantic impressions of Japan as an Oriental fantasia of cherry blossom, teahouses and geisha.[6] The thriving Yokohama trade in studio photographs has represented a particularly appealing subject

---

4   See Akira Iriye, 'The Making of the Transnational World', in *Global Interdependence: The World After 1945*, ed. Akira Iriye (Cambridge, MA: Harvard University Press, 2014).
5   See Paul Jones and Pam Oliver, eds., *Changing Histories: Australia and Japan* (Clayton: Monash Asia Institute, 2001); Michael Ackland and Pam Oliver, eds., *Unexpected Encounters: Neglected Histories Behind the Australia-Japan Relationship* (Clayton: Monash Asia Institute, 2007); Noreen Jones, *Number 2 Home: A Story of Japanese Pioneers in Australia* (Fremantle: Fremantle Arts Centre Press, 2002).
6   Lorraine Sterry, 'Constructs of Meiji Japan: The Role of Writing by Victorian Women Travellers', *Japanese Studies* 23, no. 2 (2003): 178; Gennifer Weisenfeld, 'Touring "Japan-as-Museum": Nippon and Other Japanese Imperialist Travelogues', *Positions: East Asia Cultures Critique* 8, no. 3 (Winter 2000): 757.

for historians, who have examined the production and consumption of these images in Europe, Britain, Australia and the US.[7] However, the ways in which Australians have used photography to express their responses to Japan, and more broadly their place in the Asia-Pacific region, has received far less critical attention. The photographs examined here not only provide new insight into the travels and experiences of individual photographers, they also contribute to photography history by revealing many other ways that photography serves as a medium for social and cultural connection.

While structured chronologically, *Pacific Exposures* is not simply an illustrated history of Australian–Japanese relations. It focuses on key moments when the practice of photography played crucial roles in Australian perceptions of and relations with Japan. Building on a body of scholarship on nineteenth-century photographs of Japan and their reception in Australia,[8] this book begins in a time of major change and ideological ferment in the two countries' histories. The interconnected issues of race, national identity and Australia's tenuous identification with its situation in the Asia-Pacific were hotly debated during the lead-up to Federation in 1901 and through to the interwar years. (Indeed, they have never really disappeared from the public conversation.) This period largely coincided with Japan's Meiji era, in which the formerly feudal society began ostensibly to 'Westernise' its social structures, economy and international relations. Significantly, Japan strenuously objected to the racially exclusionary immigration policy that came to be popularly known as 'White Australia' when it was enacted in 1901, not so much because of its fundamental inequity, but because they saw themselves as entitled to the same status as Europeans.[9]

---

7   Maki Fukuoka, 'Selling Portrait Photographs: Early Photographic Business in Asakusa, Japan', *History of Photography* 35, no. 4 (2011): 355–73; Luke Gartlan, 'Types or Costumes? Reframing Early Yokohama Photography', *Visual Resources* 22, no. 3 (2006): 239–63; Luke Gartlan, *A Career of Japan: Baron Raimund Von Stillfried and Early Yokohama Photography* (Leiden: Brill, 2016); Mio Wakita, *Staging Desires: Japanese Femininity in Kusakabe Kimbei's Nineteenth Century Souvenir Photograph* (Berlin: Reimer, 2013).
8   See for example Luke Gartlan, 'Japan Day by Day? William Henry Metcalf, Edward Sylvester Morse and Early Tourist Photography in Japan', *Early Popular Visual Culture* 8, no. 2 (2010); Gartlan, 'Types or Costumes?', 239–63; Isobel Crombie and Luke Gartlan, *Shashin: Nineteenth-Century Japanese Studio Photography* (Melbourne: National Gallery of Victoria, 2005).
9   See Neville Meaney, *The Search for Security in the Pacific* (Sydney: Sydney University Press, 1976), 111.

Chapter 1, '"The Child of the World's Old Age": Photographing Japan in the Early Twentieth Century', focuses on the significance attributed to photographs of children at this pivotal time. Although they are less well known than photographs of 'exotic' geishas, images of Japanese children were prevalent in women's magazines, newspapers, travel books, studio photographs and amateur photographic performances.[10] This chapter argues that the recurrence of this symbolic imagery reveals much about Australian perceptions of Japanese cultural traditions, its growing military strength, industrialisation and Australia's status as a British colony on the fringes of the Asia-Pacific. Popularly described in Australia, Britain and the US as 'the child of the world's old age', Japan was often personified as infantile—sometimes as an unpredictable, unmanageable *enfant terrible*. The international trade in commercially produced photographs of children, as well as postcards and tourist photographs, allowed these and other ideas about Japan to circulate widely in public culture and Australian homes. As photographs of children helped to reinforce conflicting conceptions of Japan as a children's paradise and a budding (and threatening) military and industrial powerhouse, they also offer new insight into Australian attitudes towards modernity and what it meant for the two nations.

Extending this discussion of how the Australia–Japan relationship was represented symbolically in photographs, Chapter 2, '"White Australia" in the Darkroom', addresses how aspects of this relationship were negotiated through direct, interpersonal relations between Australian and Japanese photographers in the 1910s through to the 1930s. The chapter looks at the contributions to Australian visual culture made by two Japanese photographers living and working in Sydney during the 'White Australia' era—Ichiro Kagiyama and Kiichiro Ishida. Japan's status as an enemy during World War II (WWII) has meant that much of the original photographic work examined in this chapter has been hitherto inaccessible and absent from historical analysis. Kagiyama's intriguing photographs of Sydney, its Japanese community and Japanese-inspired public spectacles have only recently been rediscovered—having spent

---

10   See Alison Broinowski, 'The Butterfly Phenomenon', *The Journal of the Asian Arts Society of Australia* 1, no. 3 (1992); Ofra Goldstein-Gidoni, 'Kimono and the Construction of Gendered and Cultural Identities', *Ethnology* 38, no. 4 (Autumn 1999); Mari Yoshihara, *Embracing the East: White Women and American Orientalism* (Oxford: Oxford University Press, 2003); Mikiko Ashikari, 'The Memory of Women's White Faces: Japaneseness and the Ideal Image of Women', *Japan Forum* 15, no. 1 (2003); Miya Elise Mizuta, '"Fair Japan": On Art and War at the Saint Louis World's Fair, 1904', *Discourse* 28, no. 1 (Winter 2006); Wakita, *Staging Desires*.

70 years in obscurity following the photographer's return to Japan amid escalating tensions in the lead-up to the Pacific War.[11] Additionally, many Japanese-inspired photographs produced by Australians in the first decades of the twentieth century are now known only in reproductions in magazines; the originals were lost, perhaps deliberately, at a time when to express sympathy with Japan was enough to be placed under official suspicion. As well as forming a compelling counterpoint to governmental and military attitudes towards Japan during this period, this chapter highlights how past political and military relations can shape historians' access to photographs and how the more secure bilateral relationship today affords a deeper investigation of these once neglected images of the interwar period.

Chapter 3, 'Shooting Japanese', discusses the Australian photography of the Pacific War from 1941 to 1945, which came to dominate and even define Australian relations with Japan long after the military conflict itself had ended. A large corps of official Australian photographers—working for both government and civilian agencies—expressed the racial ideology of a war fought against an opponent who was increasingly loathed as hostilities intensified. Their battlefield pictures of the Australian encounter with the Japanese, including graphic and often deliberately demeaning pictures of the dead or captured enemy, reflected the compulsions of wartime propaganda. At the same time, they also expanded on a body of visual and textual cultural references derived from decades of concern about the threat of invasion and revealed the national obsession with the battlefield as the ultimate arena for a contest of rival national masculinities. Australian photographers, including George Silk and others less well known, produced some remarkable pictures of the vicious conflict with the Japanese in the jungles and on the beaches of the Pacific islands. However, the enormous photographic archive has been largely ignored, except as a source of emotive illustrative material to popular and tendentiously patriotic histories of the campaign. This chapter delves deep into that archive to provide insights into national, cultural, military and geopolitical insecurities, as Australians sought to identify and produce purportedly definitive images of the Japanese bogeyman.

---

11   Melissa Miles, 'Ichiro Kagiyama in Early Twentieth Century Sydney', *Japanese Studies* 37, no. 1 (2017): 89–116.

Australia's enthusiastic participation in the US-led postwar military occupation of a defeated and temporarily demoralised Japan was a pivotal historical moment in its postwar relations with Japan, and with the Asia-Pacific region generally. Chapter 4, 'Japan for the Taking', examines how photography was the principal medium by which the Occupation of Japan was both officially recorded and circulated to the Australian people back home, a public that remained hostile to and deeply suspicious of its recent, bitter adversary. Phillip Hobson, Alan Queale and their colleagues formed a large cohort of official photographers charged with capturing the activities of the Australian military community in Japan—a force based largely in Hiroshima Prefecture, quite literally in the shadow of the atom-bombed city. Their images expressed the ambivalence of a force torn between the punitive control of a Japan still hated for the barbarities committed by its military against Allied prisoners of war and the well-intentioned governmental commitment to its positive reconstruction. The photography of the Occupation is analysed as a collective example of neo-colonialist visual representation. The images strategically produced to provide positive public relations for the occupying force betray a fundamental if illuminating contradiction. The postwar Japan they portrayed was dependent on the received imagery of the traditional, essentially rural Japan; the country was voided of ugly reminders of the war and pictured as timelessly 'picturesque', paradoxically so given that one of the major rationales for the Occupation was to revamp Japan into a forward-thinking, advanced nation. That the official photographers were so resistant to signs of the emerging Japan reflects a broader postwar Australian anxiety about the powerful modern nation it was in the process of becoming.

Chapter 5, 'Through Non-Military Eyes', looks at photography as a register of revisionary images of Japan in the late 1940s through to the epochal signing of the Basic Treaty of Friendship and Cooperation in Tokyo in 1976, when Australia sought to finalise conclusive links with Japan, economically, politically and culturally. Photography was a crucial tool of rapprochement in the rebuilding of the bilateral relationship in this period. For all their indulgence in the privileges of the conqueror, the men and women of the large Australian military community in Occupied Japan were the trailblazers of a new era of engagement with the Asia-Pacific region, later signified by the reoriented itineraries of Australian travellers and the belated embrace of Eastern cultures. Many of the private pictures taken in Occupied Japan identified a nation to which the official picture was blind—a country that was rapidly modernising and responding to outside influences while remaining true to its cultural roots. Post-Occupation, the photographic record of the Australians in Japan from the 1950s to the 1970s suggests a visual narrative of reinterpretation, in which the recently despised 'enemy' was humanised and revisioned as a potential 'friend' and ally. Beyond the pragmatic forging of diplomatic and trade links, photography was the most productive means by which Australians sought not merely to reconcile themselves to Japan but also to identify with it. An essentialised 'traditional' Japan was reframed into a dynamic society whose bright promise could bring benefit to Australia. Sources include both press and governmental images of interaction in fields such as trade, sport and forms of popular culture. These images of both momentous and mundane examples of cultural and political diplomacy are sometimes so contrived that they inadvertently suggest the tensions that continued to simmer beneath the smiling surface of bilateralism.

'Cross-Cultural (Mis)Understandings', the sixth and final chapter, considers how several Australian photographic artists since the 1980s have rejected the clichés of yesteryear and emphasised ambiguity, contradiction and even deliberate misapprehension in their interpretations of Japan. Seemingly in conflict with bland contemporary discourses of 'mutual understanding', these independent photographers have eschewed the official representational niceties of closer Australian–Japanese relations dominated by discussions of trade and security. Christopher Köller, Matthew Sleeth, Kristian Häggblom and Meg Hewitt use their cameras to ask more difficult questions at a time characterised by a more mutually confident bilateral relationship. In doing so, they have developed complex responses to Japan and Japanese people that speak to new possibilities of cross-cultural photographic interpretation. Their work suggests that Australia has arrived at a point in its responses to Japan when it is now no longer necessary to say—and photograph—the 'right thing'. Their images of today's Japan provoke us to re-examine the past and think critically about how we come to know it. Japan is no more seen reduced to 'the child of the world's old age', but a photographic subject both captivating and confounding, a place to build personal friendships and professional networks, and one open to multiple opportunities while at the same time frustratingly—but nonetheless fruitfully—uncapturable.

Pacific Exposures argues that photographs and photographic practices tell a compelling story of cultural production and response. Making, distributing and interpreting photographs are fundamentally cultural and political practices that show how people relate to one another and how they see themselves in the world. Whether made in times of peace or conflict, photographs both produce and are the products of relations. Therefore, the following chapters reveal not only how Australians have framed Japan over the decades, but also how they have defined their own place in the Asia-Pacific—through periods of heated social debate and political turbulence, vicious armed conflict, and social and economic changes that have been both dramatic and incremental—to arrive at today's era of bilateral cooperation and exchange. In seeking to represent and relate to Japan, Australians have revealed much about themselves.

1

'THE CHILD OF THE WORLD'S OLD AGE': PHOTOGRAPHING JAPAN IN THE EARLY TWENTIETH CENTURY

In 1926, while visiting Japan as a delegate to the third Pan-Pacific Science Congress in Tokyo, the Australian geologist Professor Leo Cotton purchased a series of lantern slides as mementos of his trip. Based at the University of Sydney, Cotton was the father of the celebrated modernist photographer Olive Cotton, who was just 15 years old when he made the trip. Along with photographs reflecting his research interests, including the crater rim of volcanic Mt Aso, Cotton collected photographs of Japanese children. One lantern slide produced by Futaba and Co. of Kobe features a joyful young child wearing a beautifully crafted silk vest and ceremonial kimono (see Figure 1.1). The distinctive blurred edged geometric pattern of the kasuri textile has been brightly hand coloured to accentuate the child's vitality and enhance the commercial appeal of the photograph. The child exuberantly waves the rising sun flag, which was adopted as the war flag of the Imperial Japanese Army in 1870 at the beginning of the Meiji era (1868–1912). Combining youth, innocence, artistic traditions and Japan's imperial might in one very appealing image, the photograph distilled many of Australia's impressions of Japan itself.

This chapter focuses on the ways in which Australian perceptions of Japan were visualised in photographs of children during a critical time in the two countries' histories. For Australia, the period from the lead-up to Federation in 1901 to the interwar years was one in which national identity and Australia's place in the Asia-Pacific were hotly debated. This period coincided with a time of radical change in Japan, during which

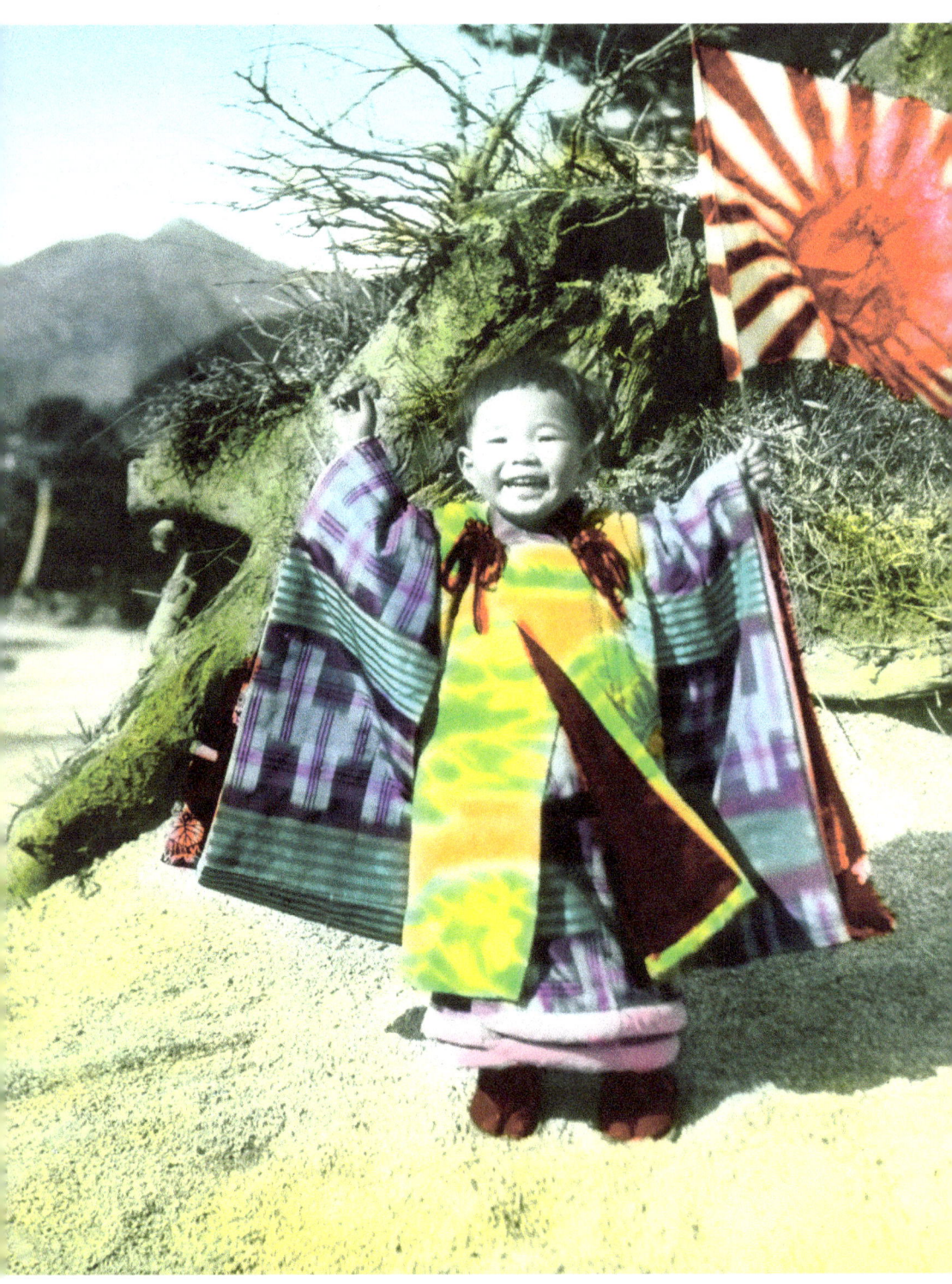

Figure 1.1. Futaba and Co., *Untitled [Japanese Child]*, c. 1926.

Source: National Library of Australia, 'Papers of Olive Cotton, approximately 1907–2003', MS Acc11.129.

its social structures, economy, military, industries and international relations were reshaped. Described popularly as 'the child of the world's old age', Japan was frequently personified in the Australian press and travel writing as essentially childlike, innocent or unruly. The symbolic dimensions of the child and the 'real' children who were photographed are inextricably linked in these photographs. Embodying views of Meiji Japan as a fledgling modern nation and an emergent partner in the Asia-Pacific region, photographs of children satisfied demand for images of Japanese culture as ancient yet forged through innocent artistic sensibilities.

Commercially produced photographs of children, like that purchased by Cotton, and postcards and tourist photographs affirmed these conceptions of Japan-as-child and allowed this imagery to find a place in Australian homes. Personal and public modes of cross-cultural encounter are intertwined in this process. The scale and light weight of photographs made them highly portable objects of material culture, and facilitated their movement across the seas with travellers or through the mail. Postcards, family photographs and photographs produced commercially were collected, assembled in albums and stored in the home where they also operated as a means of interpreting international relations and defining political and diplomatic networks. In these photographs, the domestic, diplomatic, industrial and imperial are enmeshed in fascinating ways.

Two Child Nations

It is not surprising that a commercially produced photograph of a Japanese child caught Cotton's eye during his travels. Beginning decades before Cotton's visit and extending many years beyond his return, the child was invoked symbolically and metaphorically in descriptions of Japan, Japanese culture and Japanese people in the Australian press. This language is evident in popular descriptions of the Japanese courts in Australian international exhibitions, which staged many Australians' first encounters with Japan. Art critic James Smith's description of the artisans at the Japanese court at the 1880 Melbourne exhibition reflects how the childlike innocence of the artist sat alongside conceptions of ancient Japan 'awakening' to the 'West':

In a word, the mind of the executant appears to be as young, as open to impressions from external phenomena, as receptive of lessons from every object he sees, and as capable of spontaneous, almost childlike, admirations, as if it belonged to the member of a race living in the infancy of civilisation; while the hand which fulfils the behests of that mind is the hand of an accomplished artificer, of a master craftsman, with all the dexterity and finesse capable of being acquired and exercised by one belonging to our 'wondrous mother age'. He is old in the technique of his art, but youthful in thought and feeling.[1]

Smith's comments encapsulate how childlike innocence became code for authenticity, in which 'authentic' Japan was grounded in artistic naiveté and ancient traditions.

Popular notions of Japan-as-child must, therefore, be distinguished from what eighteenth-century European commentators and missionaries commonly referred to as 'child races'. Underpinning this troubling concept is the belief that races are marked by a progression from infancy to maturity, as with individuals. 'Primitive' races were identified with the intelligence and innocence of children, deemed to lack rational thought and seen to become threatening if they reached adulthood too quickly. Recognition of Japan's ancient civilisation and artistic traditions meant that it was not viewed as a child race in these terms. Yet, there is a comparable desire to position Japan as the subordinate to Britain and Europe, which were implicitly cast as more developed and advanced.

The description of Japan as 'the child of the world's old age' provided a very popular means of reconciling this sense of ancient Japan with its Meiji-era modernity. This pervasive expression was popularised by Henry Norman's book, *The Real Japan* (1891), and was repeatedly used in the Australian press to describe Japan as 'young in years, but old in wisdom' during the first decades of the twentieth century.[2] The expression

---

1   James Smith, 'The Japanese Exhibits and Japanese Art', *Argus*, 5 March 1881, 4.
2   Henry Norman, *The Real Japan. Studies of Contemporary Japanese Manners, Morals, Administration, and Politics* (London: FT Unwin, 1891), 337. The phrase 'child of the world's old age' recurred throughout the press and popular culture. For example, 'The Anglo-Japanese Treaty', *Freeman's Journal*, 22 February 1902, 21; 'Hard Case of Japan', *Tasmanian News*, 22 December 1903, 2; 'Just Now in Little Japan. The Child of the World's Old Age', *Evening Telegraph*, 15 February 1904, 2; 'Japan. The Child of the World's Old Age', *Wyalong Advocate and Mining, Agricultural and Pastoral Gazette*, 2 March 1904, 4; 'Japanese Courage', *Newsletter*, 20 February 1904, 11; 'Some Reflections', *Geraldton Guardian*, 2 October 1913, 2; 'Japan', *Daily Examiner*, 29 April 1918, 2. Pastor and Mrs Greenaway, missionaries from Japan, toured offering lectures including one titled 'Japan! Child of the World's Old Age' in Brisbane in July 1938.

positioned Japan as a child of modernity, yet 'brought up by parents who lived through centuries of development and civilisation'.[3] Such newspaper and travel texts served as pre-reading for travellers to Japan, anticipating their search for 'authentic' Japan, shaping itineraries and informing their selection of photographic subjects. Photographs like Cotton's souvenir lantern slide reproduced that sense of authenticity for travellers, validating their experiences and reiterating impressions of Japan-as-child among family and friends when they returned.

Like Japan—but more so—Australia was perceived to be a fledgling nation. The Japanese political geographer Shiga Shigetaka personified Australia as a child in his book, *Current Affair in the South Seas*, written after his visit to Australia in 1886. In a section addressing Australia's potential for independence from Britain, Shiga likened the Australian colonies to a newly hatched egg evolving into an adult:

> The child is obviously now becoming an adolescent; as it begins to have a mind of its own, it is searching for its own national identity, distancing itself from its mother country Britain.[4]

Australia often represented itself in comparable terms. People born in Australian colonies—framed as a population yet to mature or find its own voice—became known as 'Young Australia' in the 1880s. After the New South Wales Government sent Australian troops to fight under British command in Sudan in 1885, Young Australia took the form of 'The Little Boy from Manly'. This character was named after a real boy who wrote to the government expressing his desire to join the troops. In political publications like the *Bulletin* and the *Melbourne Punch*, 'The Little Boy from Manly' was represented as a Fauntleroy-like boy clad in pantaloons, frilled shirt and flat peaked cap looking up to John Bull—the personification of British paternalism and authority.[5] Although Japan and Australia were both identified with children, this sense of a young British colony and emergent Australian identity differs significantly from representations of Japan-as-child, which were repeatedly linked to assumptions about Japan as a land of ancient artistic traditions.

---

3   'Japan', 2.
4   Shigetaka Shiga, *Nan'yō Jiji* (Tokyo: Maruzen, 1887), 41–45.
5   Ken Inglis, 'Young Australia 1870–1900: The Idea and the Reality', in *The Colonial Child*, ed. Guy Featherstone (Melbourne: Royal Historical Society of Victoria, 1981), 1–23.

A Paradise for Babies

P.L. Pham described how British and American commentators on Japan readily slipped between descriptions of Japanese children and ascribing childlike characteristics to the country itself.[6] This slippage is particularly evident in references to Japan as a 'paradise' for children and babies, a notion attributed to the British consul general in Japan, Rutherford Alcock, and his book, *The Capital of the Tycoon*.[7] Japan's reputation as a 'paradise of babies' was popularised in Australian, British and US travel writing through the late nineteenth and early twentieth centuries, and pervaded the Australian press from the 1890s to the 1920s.[8] These publications variously referred to the freedom enjoyed by Japanese children, their many opportunities for play and the love and patience that they were shown by their attentive mothers. An appreciation for artistic creativity and the natural world, as well as the love of play, were said to stay with Japanese children into adulthood as an essentially Japanese characteristic.

Although they proliferated in Australia during the early twentieth century, conceptions of childlike Japan have a much longer international history. Pierre Loti belittled the Japanese as a 'frivolous and childish people' throughout *Madame Chrysanthème*.[9] Mortimer Menpes, an Australian-born British painter who visited Japan in 1887 and 1896, also wrote of the 'almost childish simplicity of the Japanese woman' in *Japan: A Record in Colour*.[10] In a section on children, Menpes argued that the 'national artistic and poetic nature of the Japanese people'

---

6   P.L. Pham, 'On the Edge of the Orient: English Representations of Japan, Circa 1895–1910', *Japanese Studies* 19, no. 2 (1999): 170.
7   Rutherford Alcock, *The Capital of the Tycoon: A Narrative of a Three Years' Residence in Japan* (London: Longman, Green, Longman, Roberts & Green, 1863), 82.
8   William Elliot Griffis, *The Mikado's Empire* (New York: Harper and Brothers, 1895), 452; Henry T. Finck, *Lotus-Time in Japan* (New York: Charles Scribner's and Sons, 1895), 314; Douglas Sladen and Norma Lorimer, *More Queer Things About Japan* (London: Anthony Treherns and Co., 1905), xxi; James A.B. Scherer, *Japan Today* (Philadelphia and London: J.B. Lippincott Co., 1905), 94; 'A Children's Paradise', *Adelaide Observer*, 4 July 1896, 34; 'A Children's Paradise', *Evening Journal*, 4 July 1896, 3; 'The Children's Paradise', *Daily News*, 5 August 1899, 1; 'The Paradise of Children', *Armidale Express and New England General Advertiser*, 20 September 1901, 2; 'The Children's Paradise', *Adelaide Observer*, 30 May 1903, 8; 'The Children's Paradise', *Sydney Mail and NSW Advertiser*, 25 March 1903, 742; 'Japan. A Paradise for the Little Children', *Brisbane Courier*, 10 May 1911, 20; 'Child's Paradise. Sidelights on Japan', *Sydney Morning Herald*, 25 December 1923, 8; 'A Child's Paradise', *Advertiser*, 29 December 1923, 14.
9   Pierre Loti, *Madame Chrysanthème* (London: George Routledge and Sons, 1897), 44, 125, 182, 218, 308.
10 Mortimer Menpes, *Japan: A Record in Colour* (New York: Macmillan, 1901), 126.

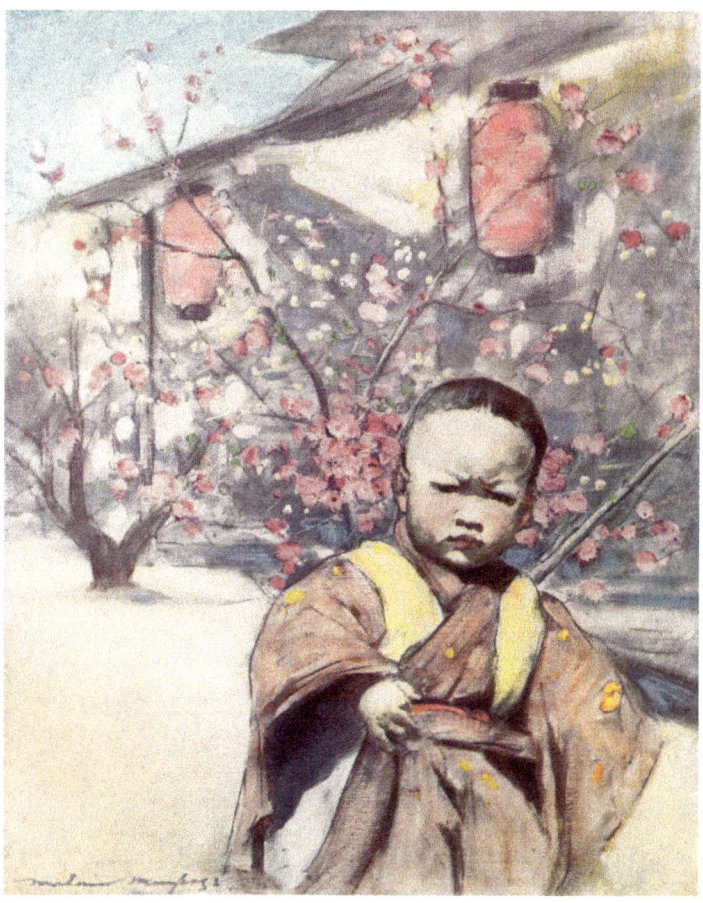

Figure 1.2. Mortimer Menpes, *Advance Japan*.
Source: Mortimer Menpes, *Japan: A Record in Colour* (New York: Macmillan, 1901).

is embodied in children. Looking forward to the ways in which photographs of Japanese children came to symbolise these qualities, some of Menpes's painted illustrations of children were given allegorical titles such as *Advance Japan* (see Figure 1.2) and *Young Japan*. Geo H. Rittner described 'artistic' Japan as a nation of people who never lose their love of play and childlike fascination for nature. His *Impressions of Japan* asked readers to:

> Imagine an aged gentleman with grey hair flying a kite for pure amusement, playing marbles, or spinning tops. We should term it second childhood, but in Japan that is unknown; they are born children, and die children.[11]

---

11 Geo Rittner, *Impressions of Japan* (New York: James Pott and Co., 1904), 112.

This sense of Japan as a land of adults who never lose their childhood innocence recurs in the Australian press during the late nineteenth and early twentieth centuries. Douglas Sladen's account of 'child life in Japan' proclaimed:

> It has been the lifelong prayer and advice of every Japanese parent for endless generations that their children, when they have reached the estate of men and women, should retain their child's hearts … Childhood certainly is the Golden Age in Japan, more than in any other country in the world.[12]

Other articles linked descriptions of the model behaviour of Japanese children to aspects of traditional culture such as festivals for children, lovingly made and gaily coloured children's kimonos, and even Japanese architecture.[13] Children accordingly became potent symbols of Japanese cultural traditions and the supposedly childlike qualities of the Japanese people more broadly. Photographs proved an ideal medium for reinforcing this image of Japan-as-child. As the photograph arrests time and fixes the child in an image forever, it dramatises the very idea of Japan as an eternal child.

Futaba and Co.'s commercially produced photograph of a child waving a flag in a glorious ceremonial kimono capitalises on this widespread international interest in children as symbols of Japan. Cotton's own appreciation of this imagery is also reflected in another item in his small collection of Japanese glass lantern slides. Taken by Cotton at Lake Chūzenji near the celebrated shrine site Nikko, it features a group of plump children in kimonos, including two small children who each carry a baby on their backs (see Figure 1.3). Cotton has framed the children quite tightly so they dominate the photograph, and the elderly woman accompanying them is cropped almost entirely out of the image. By crouching down to their level and photographing the two children on the left in profile, Cotton captured the full length of their little bodies and the relative scale of the babies they carried. In this practice, known in Japanese as *onbu*, babies were secured to the backs of their carers with a pair of crossed sashes. The practice offered babies a form of close contact with a loved one, deemed important for the socialisation of children, but to tourists and travel writers it had long attracted attention as a sign of Japanese exoticism.

---

12   Douglas Sladen, 'Child Life in Japan', *Brisbane Courier*, 15 October 1904, 13.
13   'The Children's Paradise', 1; 'Child's Paradise. Sidelights on Japan', 8; 'A Child's Paradise', 14; 'Japan. A Paradise for the Little Children', 20; 'The Paradise of Children', 1.

1. 'THE CHILD OF THE WORLD'S OLD AGE'

Western travellers viewed *onbu* with a mixture of admiration and scorn. To Menpes, the practice was evidence of the impressive deportment of Japanese children.[14] For others, it was a marker of these children's extraordinary sense of responsibility. In an article referring to Japan as a 'paradise for little children', a writer for the *Brisbane Courier* described how Japanese children between the ages of six and 10 learn to take responsibility in the household:

> As soon as a baby is born it is handed over to a sister, who takes care of it, and it is a common sight in Japan to see little girls of 6 or 7 with sleeping babies strapped to their backs like a knapsack … Hence when quite babies themselves they are taught to look after others.[15]

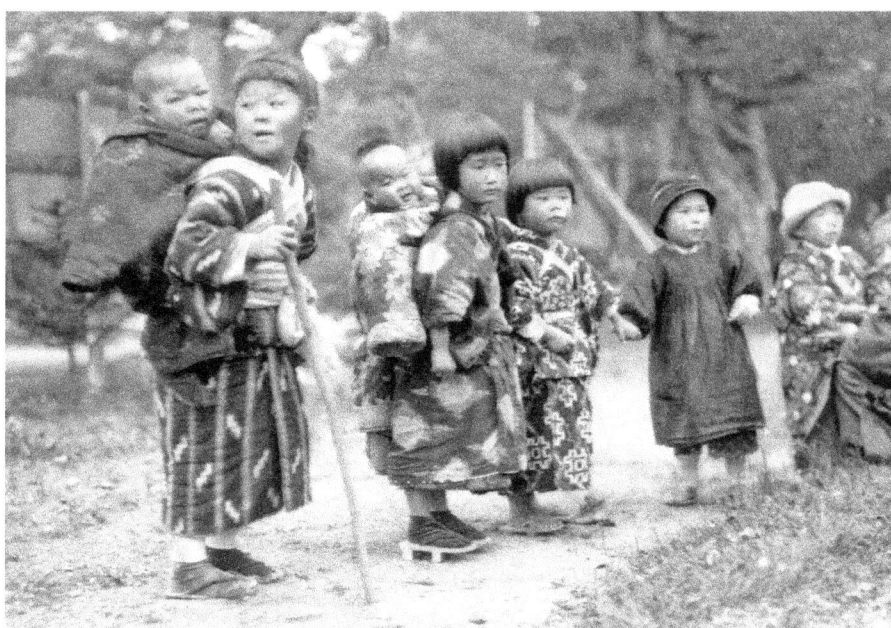

Figure 1.3. Leo Arthur Cotton, *Untitled [Japanese Children]*, c. 1926.
Source: National Library of Australia, 'Papers of Olive Cotton, approximately 1907–2003', MS Acc11.129.

---

14   Menpes, *Japan: A Record in Colour*, 140.
15   'Japan. A Paradise for the Little Children', 20. This article was published in several US newspapers in 1910, reflecting the international circulation of these ideas. See 'The Flowery Land', *Cook County Herald*, 18 March 1910, 14; 'Nippon Babies' Paradise', *Detroit Free Press*, 17 April 1910, 40; 'A Paradise of Babies', *Plymouth Tribune* 9, no. 31 (1910): 3.

Others were far more critical, arguing that this responsibility was harsh on the young carrier, a sign of lazy 'selfish, cruel' mothers and the cause of physical damage to young bodies.[16] It is interesting that Yanagawa Masakiyo, a shogunal envoy on the first Japanese mission to the US, found Western preferences for baby carriages just as shocking. He commented in a diary entry on 23 May 1860 that:

> In Washington and Philadelphia and all other American cities the mothers do not carry their babies on their backs or in their arms but put them in small baby carriages which are pushed by maidservants.[17]

Repeated references to *onbu* made it a potent signifier of Japanese traditions and conceptions of Japan-as-child. Photographs of women and children carrying babies on their backs, produced for the substantial international tourist market in Japan by studio photographers Felice Beato and T. Enami, helped to reinforce this interest. An enterprising Melbourne photographer, George Rose, circumvented the need for Australian collectors of Japanese photographs to take the long journey to Japan. During his visit to Japan in 1904, Rose produced many photographs of the Japanese people and countryside. He also made an arrangement with Enami to publish his photographs in Australia and distribute them through the Rose studio.[18] Alongside Rose's many stereographs of pretty geishas and gardens filled with cherry blossoms are several photographs of children. *Cherry Blossoms, Ueno Park, Tokyo, Japan* (see Figure 1.4) features Japanese women carrying babies on their backs, while *The Perambulators of Japan* depicts Japanese babies being carried on the backs of their older sisters.[19]

Stereography added to the experience of these images. Commercialised in the 1850s and 1860s, stereographs were immensely popular in the United Kingdom, the US, Europe and Australia from this period through to the early twentieth century. Stereography was thought to be particularly suited to the depiction of foreign sites because of the

---

16   Connie Keat, ed. *Amy's Diaries: The Travel Notes of Elizabeth Amy Cathcart Payne 1869-1875* (Morwell: LaTrobe Valley U3A, 1995), 57. 'Child Nursing in Japan', *Darling Downs Gazette*, 27 June 1907, 2; Douglas Sladen, *Queer Things About Japan* (1904; repr., London: Kegan Paul, Trench, Trübner & Co., 1913), 16–17.
17   Lizbeth Halliday Piel, 'The Ideology of the Child in Japan 1600–1945' (PhD diss., University of Hawaii, 2007), 28.
18   Ron Blum, *George Rose: Australia's Master Stereographer* (Oaklands Park: Ron Blum, 2008), 65–68.
19   US Marine Joe O'Donnell's moving photograph of a young Japanese boy standing erect with a lifeless, slumped baby strapped to his back at a crematory in Nagasaki in 1945 decades later became a powerful image of lost innocence in the wake of the atomic bombing.

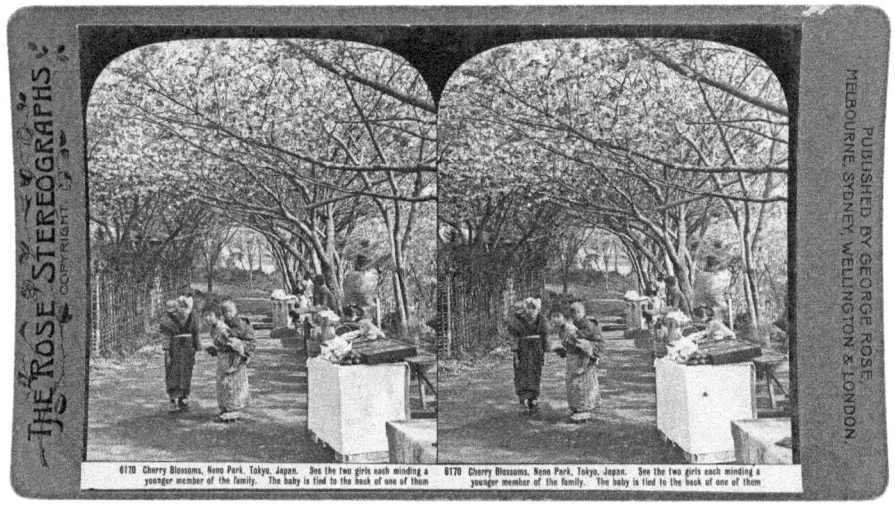

Figure 1.4. George Rose, *Cherry Blossoms, Ueno Park, Tokyo, Japan*, c. 1890–1900.
Source: State Library of Victoria. Accession no: H83.125/88.

illusion of three dimensions it created.[20] In the closed viewing field of the stereoscope, which was held right up to the face, stereographs offered a highly accessible form of simulated travel within the home, especially appealing to those without the means of travelling themselves. The Rose Stereograph Company's employment of six staff is indicative of the high demand that these photographs generated in Australia. Photographs of foreign countries occupy a significant proportion of Rose's catalogue, with Japan being the subject of over 200 stereographs.

In contrast to the private viewing space of the stereoscope and the intimate familial enjoyment of photo albums, lantern slides, like those purchased and produced by Cotton, afforded the display of the photograph on a larger scale for collective spectatorship. Slides were viewed with the use of a projector for public entertainment, educational lectures or in the home among family and friends.[21] Public lantern slide lectures on Japan were also offered in Australia at this time, including one given by Professor Arthur Sadler who taught Oriental Studies at the University

---

20 Joan M. Schwartz, 'The Geography Lesson: Photographs and the Construction of Imaginative Geographies'. *Journal of Historical Geography* 22, no. 1 (1996): 16; Pauline Stakelon, 'Travel through the Stereoscope: Movement and Narrative in Topological Stereoview Collections of Europe', *Media History* 16, no. 4 (2010): 407–15.
21 Joy Sperling, 'From Magic Lantern Slide to Digital Image: Visual Communities and American Culture', *The Journal of American Culture* 31, no. 1 (2003): 1.

of Sydney.²² Such lectures offered a kind of armchair travel that was entertaining, public and communal. Popular conceptions of Japan-as-child helped to incorporate the fragmentary impressions offered by the photographs into a unified experience for both the traveller and viewer.²³

Child Labour and Education

One of the consequences of the repeated recycling of these ideas was that modernity and Japan's Meiji-era industrial growth were framed as both the source of Japan's youth and the cause of its potential corruption. Geo Rittner accordingly lamented that 'formerly every man, woman, and child in that country was a born artist, but through the change it has undergone, much of the artistic feeling has been destroyed'.²⁴ This sense of the damaging power of modernisation and industrialisation is particularly evident in discussions of Japanese child labour. Japanese industrial expansion from the 1880s saw a growth in child labour outside of the home. Work in factories manufacturing cigarettes, textiles, shoes and matches proved a more cost-effective alternative for families to child labour within the home because it provided families with much needed cash. As child workers were paid around one-quarter of the rate of adults, it also provided Japanese manufacturers with a significant advantage over foreign competitors in international markets. In the early twentieth century, Australian newspapers commented critically on these child labour practices as a source of corruption for the 'child's paradise'. More sensational commentaries referred to 'child slaves of Japan', 'Japan, the child devourer' and 'factory prisoners'.²⁵ Criticism of child labour was concentrated particularly heavily in workers' publications. One article quoted Walter Kingsley from *World's Work*, who described the Japanese capitalist as 'the most remorseless devourer of little ones the world has ever known'. Contrasting Meiji Japan with an imagined pre-modern ideal, the article noted that children:

---

22   'Japan. Country Life', *Sydney Morning Herald*, 4 July 1923, 16; 'Lecture on Japan', *Mercury*, 14 January 1909, 3; 'Lecture on "Through Japan"', *Brisbane Courier*, 18 October 1912, 9.
23   Elizabeth Edwards, 'Postcards—Greetings from Another World', in *The Tourist Image: Myths and Myth Making in Tourism*, ed. T. Selwyn (Chichester: John Wiley and Sons, 1996), 201.
24   Rittner, *Impressions of Japan*, 138–39.
25   'Child Slaves of Japan', *Truth*, 4 March 1911, 9; 'Japan the Child Devourer', *Worker*, 9 January 1908, 18; 'The Child Slaves of Japan', *Worker*, 11 February 1911, 2.

do not laugh as blithely as in the old days. Happiness was their heritage then, but now the nation demands that the little ones go to work at a time of life regarded in England as infancy. In the manufacturing cities like Osaka there are no longer seen thousands of boys and girls playing in dainty, many-colored costumes like gorgeous butterflies on the grass of temples. You will find them in coarse dull clothing, working like pathetic dolls in the factories. These babes toiling for a few pennies a day form a vast and sorrowful army.[26]

International concerns over child labour during this period extended well beyond Japanese child factory workers and became an important feature of the early history of social documentary photography in the US. American photographer Lewis Hine hoped that his photographs of children working in mines, factories, textile mills and canneries would bring about an end to the exploitation of child labour in his home country, but it took many years before changes to child labour practices had an impact.

The immense popularity of photographs and texts that locate Japanese children in an idyllic, pre-industrial context is indicative of international resistance to the roles children played in Japan's industrialisation. This criticism of Japan's supposed transformation from a child's paradise to Dickensian nightmare can be seen in part as a reaction to Japan's sizable exports of cheap textiles, produced for costs with which Australia and Britain could not compete. It was also informed by Australian shifts in ideologies of childhood from Victorian notions of its essential innocence to ideals of childhood health supported by the rise of the infant welfare movement and the professionalisation of childcare. Australian women in the early twentieth century were increasingly 'instructed in the science of motherhood' as a mode of progressive thought justified in terms of humanitarianism and the growth of the modern nation.[27] The criticism of Japanese child labour helped Australians to define their own modernity in terms of the vigour, strength and promise of youth.

In Meiji Japan, approaches to childhood were also being redefined in relation to the needs and ambitions of the modern nation. Industrialisation, the movement towards universal education and greater investment in childhood development led to new ideologies of the

---

26   'Japan the Child Devourer', 18.
27   Judith Raftery, '"Mainly a Question of Motherhood": Professional Advice-Giving and Infant Welfare', *Journal of Australian Studies* 19, no. 45 (1995): 67.

child in the twentieth century. Compulsory elementary education was introduced in 1872 'with the goal of preparing Japan's future generations for "civilization and enlightenment" (*bunmei kaika*)'. The dilemma for the Meiji government was that while it valued education, it also sought to protect its industries and resist 'taking actions that would raise the cost of production, such as restricting the availability of low-wage child workers'.[28]

Lizbeth Halliday Piel has pointed out that the higher ratio of girls to boys in factories correlated with the lower ratio of girls to boys in schools.[29] Yet, the education of girls was deemed especially important. The Japanese ideal of *ryōsai kenbo* or 'good wives and wise mothers' gained momentum in the late nineteenth century and played an important role in the redesign of Meiji-era education for girls. The ideal combined Japanese traditions of feminine restraint with British conceptions of the Victorian woman. This Victorian ideal of motherly virtue was also evident in other nations undergoing processes of modernisation. As 'good wives and wise mothers', Japanese women helped to advance the nation by building a workforce capable of competing with the West, acting as helpmates to their husbands and teachers to their sons. Piel argued that:

> With the exception of a handful of protesters such as Ueki Emori and Yokoyama Gennosuke, concern over child labor [in Japan] was not driven by sentimentality or sympathy for children. It was driven by the Meiji Government's agenda for mass indoctrination through schools, as well as by the army's need for fit soldiers.[30]

Infant Prodigy and *Enfant Terrible*

Meiji Japan's military and diplomatic advances were another important context in which notions of Japan-as-child were contested and re-evaluated. Japanese writers took exception to Western representations of childlike Japan. In 'Misunderstood Japan', published in *The North American Review* in 1900, Ozaki argued that such 'misconceptions were corrected' by Japan's victory in the Sino-Japanese War (1894–95). He lamented that, in early 1894, 'Japan was regarded as a spoiled child,

---

28   Piel, 'The Ideology of the Child in Japan 1600–1945', 95, 103.
29   Ibid., 100. In 1877, an estimated 55.97 per cent of boys were enrolled in school compared to 22.48 per cent of girls. Some 20 years later (in 1895), the number of girls enrolled in school had doubled to 43.87 per cent, but still lagged behind the number of boys at 61.24 per cent.
30   Ibid., 107.

wantonly bent on amusing herself with her newly devised toy army and navy'. Yet, by mid-1895, in foreign eyes Japan had become 'a formidable military power … a deadly menace to the peace of the Far East'.[31] Some of Ozaki's sentiment is echoed in Kakuzo Okakura's book, *The Awakening of Japan*, published in English in 1905. Like Ozaki, this Japanese scholar remarked that 'until recently the West has never taken Japan seriously … We are both the cherished child of modern progress and a dread resurrection of heathendom—the Yellow Peril itself!'[32] At least one Australian commentator agreed that the dramatic growth of Japan's military power meant that it had left its childhood behind:

> Japan has been described by somebody as the 'child of the world's old age', and if that were ever true of Japan in the past it only requires a brief practical experience of the present condition of the 'Land of the Rising Sun' to convince the most sceptical that it is now developing rapidly into a vigorous manhood.[33]

These comments highlight the gendered quality of these discourses of Japan-as-child. Whereas Meiji-era Japan's growing military and industrial strength were typically identified with boys, conceptions of Japan as artistic, traditional and eternally childlike were commonly feminised. Despite such commentaries about Meiji Japan's impending maturity, the view of Japan as 'the cherished child of modern progress' was ultimately not displaced by Japan's growing military strength. Instead, the Japan-as-child motif became a means of symbolically containing its 'vigorous manhood' as diplomatic relations were tested in the early twentieth century.[34]

A series of commemorative postcards titled *Young Japan and Friends* is indicative of how images of children were used to symbolically manage diplomatic and military relationships between Japan, Britain and Australia. Produced by the London-based company Raphael Tuck and Sons, these postcards centre on hand-coloured photographs by the British photographer, actor and art director Cavendish Morton. The series features an English and Japanese boy in various poses in front of British and Japanese flags. These postcards, and other products by Raphael Tuck and Sons, were advertised extensively in the Australian press and found an eager market in Australia.[35] *Young Japan and Friends* was likely

---

31 Y. Ozaki, 'Misunderstood Japan', *North American Review* 171, no. 527 (1900): 567.
32 Kakuzo Okakura, *The Awakening of Japan* (New York: The Century Co., 1905), 4.
33 'The Awakening East', *Bendigo Independent*, 28 November 1906, 6.
34 Ibid.
35 This particular series of was advertised in 'Raphael Tuck and Sons', *Daily News*, 16 October 1905, 8.

produced to commemorate the first Anglo-Japanese Alliance, which was negotiated in response to the threat of Russian expansion in Asia. The Alliance was signed in London on 30 January 1902 by Lord Lansdowne (the British foreign secretary) and Hayashi Tadasu (the Japanese minister in London), and was renewed and expanded in 1905 and 1911. At first glance, Morton's photographs appear to capture the spirit of friendship between the two nations. In one image, the boys adopt a common diplomatic pose, facing partly towards the camera and partly to each other as they shake hands to seal their partnership (see Figure 1.5). Captioned *L'Entente Cordiale*, this postcard also alludes to a series of agreements signed on 8 April 1904 between the United Kingdom and France that saw a significant improvement in Anglo–French relations.

Although Britain and Japan are both represented by children in this series to symbolise the young Alliance, the boys are posed in a manner that suggests an unequal relationship. The English boy, dressed in a sailor suit, is notably taller than his Japanese counterpart. It also is pertinent that the Japanese child is shown wearing a kimono, rather than European dress. The Japanese emperor and empress actively promoted European clothing at this time, reflecting their desire to embrace modern European technologies, infrastructure and partnerships. The couple were often photographed for official portraits wearing European dress, including Uchida Kuichi's official portrait of the Meiji emperor of 1873. In contrast, the Japanese child's traditional dress in this postcard recalls contemporary conceptions of Meiji Japan as the modern offspring of essentially ancient parents. It is telling that Australian newspapers repeatedly referred to Japan as the 'child of the world's old age' in accounts of its naval victories, alongside Japan's 'courage', 'fighting spirit', 'readiness for war' and the 'pluck of the Japanese soldier'.[36] However, at times that child took on menacing qualities. One account in the *Daily Mail*, quoted in several Australian outlets in 1904, used the phrase 'the child of the world's old age' to describe the Japanese soldier 'and the spirit which animates him'. The author referred to Japan as an 'infant prodigy' as 'poor old China … learnt to her exceeding cost', and an 'enfant terrible'

---

36   'Hard Case of Japan', 2; 'Japanese Courage', 11; 'Japanese Readiness for War. A Proud and High-Spirited People', *Evening Journal*, 29 January 1904, 2; F.J. Norman, 'The Japanese Army', *Geelong Advertiser*, 9 January 1904, 4.

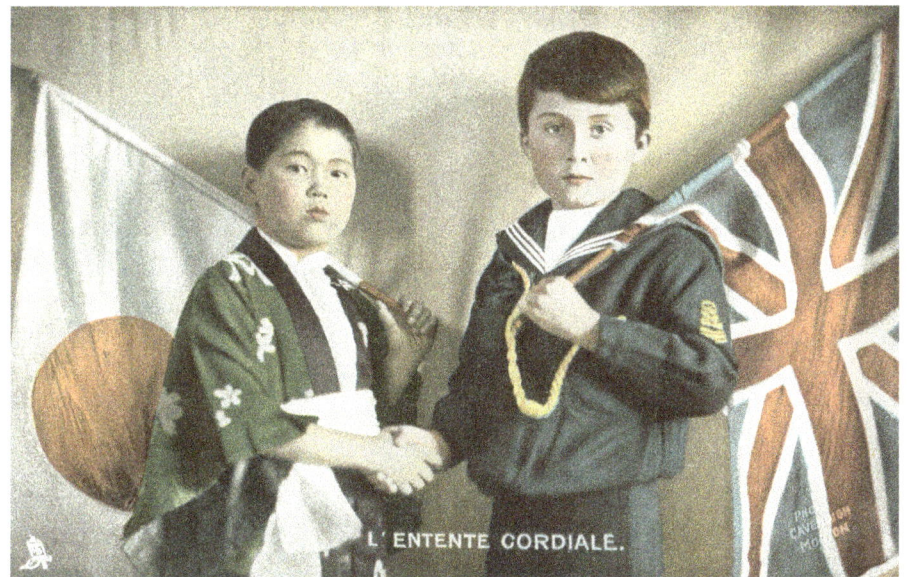

Figure 1.5. Cavendish Morton, *L'Entente Cordiale* from the series 'Young Japan and Friends', c. 1905.

Source: State Library of Victoria. Accession no: H99.166/199.

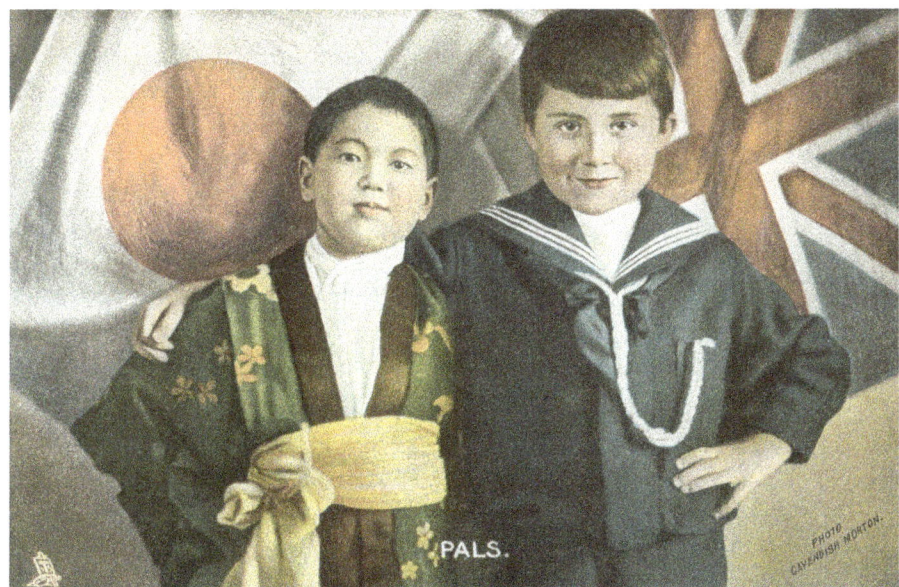

Figure 1.6. Cavendish Morton, *Pals* from the series 'Young Japan and Friends', c. 1905.

Source: State Library of Victoria. Accession no. H99.166/198.

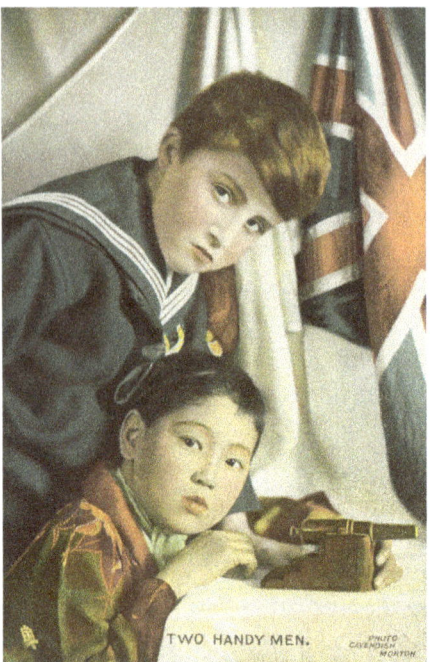
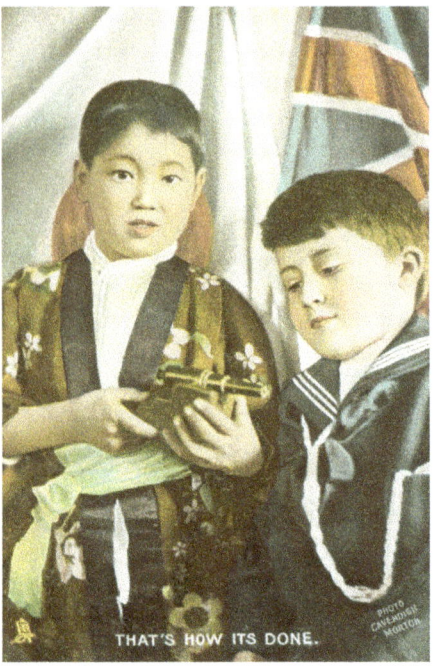

Figure 1.7. Cavendish Morton, *Two Handy Men* from the series 'Young Japan and Friends', c. 1905.
Source: State Library of Victoria.
Accession no. H99.166/202.

Figure 1.8. Cavendish Morton, *That's How It's Done* from the series 'Young Japan and Friends', c. 1905.
Source: State Library of Victoria.
Accession no. H99.166/200.

as experienced by Russia.[37] Accordingly, the notion of the troublesome child helped to represent conceptions of Japan as 'a misfit in the assumed patterns of East-West power relations'.[38]

That misfit is brought under the control of a protective big British brother in Morton's postcards. The postcard titled *Pals* shows the English boy with a protective arm around the smaller Japanese boy's shoulder while his other hand is placed authoritatively on his hip (see Figure 1.6). They both smile for the camera as though perfectly happy with this arrangement. The construction of an unequal power relationship becomes more pronounced in *Two Handy Men* (see Figure 1.7). Here, the English boy looks to the camera with a very stern expression while standing over the seated Japanese boy who holds a toy cannon on the table in front of him. The Japanese boy hunches forward, seemingly overwhelmed by the towering English sailor.

---

37   'Japan. The Child of the World's Old Age', 4. This material was also reported in 'Just Now in Little Japan. The Child of the World's Old Age', *Telegraph*, 15 February 1904, 7; 'The Child of the World's Old Age', *Geelong Advertiser*, 27 February 1904, 6.
38   Tomoko Akami, 'Frederic Eggleston and Oriental Power, 1925-1929', in *Relationships: Japan and Australia*, ed. Paul Jones and Vera Mackie (Melbourne: University of Melbourne, 2001), 103.

As evinced by the 1904 headline in the *Sydney Morning Herald* declaring the Japanese Navy 'The Child of Great Britain',[39] Japan was represented as a diligent student but, nonetheless, junior to Britain. Readers of this article were told that the Japanese naval fleet was not only modelled on its British counterpart but also benefited from the strategic advice of British officers. *Two Handy Men* gives form to this relationship by positioning the English child as the teacher and supervisor of the Japanese boy. Nonetheless, Morton's postcards do not represent this relationship as entirely dominated by Britain. *That's How it's Done* shows the English boy seated with his hands passively in his lap as he looks at the toy cannon being held firmly in the hands of the standing Japanese boy (see Figure 1.8). The Japanese child is here in the position of authority as he teaches the British boy the art of warfare.

Postcards were an especially effective means of promoting ideas about these diplomatic relationships. Raphael Tuck and Sons' distribution of these postcards in Australia coincided with a period of postcard mania. The craze for collecting postcards gained momentum after 1905 when the Australian Postal Service permitted postcards to be divided on the back, allowing the address and message to be put on one side and the pictorial image to take up the whole of the other side. The Raphael Tuck and Sons range was highly collectable and incredibly varied, and included many postcards of war scenes, British and foreign military men, and idyllic Japanese village scenes and landscapes. Such postcards, like photographs acquired and produced through travel, helped Australians to reimagine their own place in relation to Britain and Japan. Postcards trigger a form of imaginative travel and help to maintain connections with loved ones overseas.[40] However, postcards like these had another important function. As they were collected, handled, posted or arranged in scrapbooks, they allowed these international political relationships to become part of the social space in the home. These objects helped

---

39   'The Japanese Navy. The Child of Great Britain', *Sydney Morning Herald*, 13 February 1904, 11.
40   Konstantinos Andriotis and Misela Mavric, 'Postcard Mobility: Going Beyond Image and Text', *Annals of Tourism Research* 40 (2013): 21; Julia Gillen and Nigel Hall, 'The Edwardian Postcard: A Revolutionary Moment in Rapid Multimodal Communications', paper presented at the British Educational Research Association Annual Conference, University of Manchester, 2–5 September 2009; Julia Gillen and Nigel Hall, 'Any Mermaids? Early Postcard Mobilities', in *Mobile Methods*, ed. Monika Buscher, John Urry and Katian Witchger (London and New York: Routledge, 2010), 20–35.

collectors to feel connected to a world beyond Australian shores, to locate their own identities within that world and to affirm their individual positions in relation to the Anglo-Japanese Alliance.

Although Australia was imagined and imaged as a child in its colonial relationship to the British motherland, it was noticeably absent from Morton's *Young Japan and Friends*. Here, Australia was implicitly cast as a passive onlooker to and consumer of the Alliance forged by the 'big boys' on the other side of the world. This perception of Australia's position (or lack thereof) in the Anglo-Japanese Alliance was a source of frustration.[41] A contributor to the *Freeman's Journal* complained in 1902 that the treaty was 'made without any reference to, or consultation with, the Commonwealth Government. Australia was ignored—though Australian interests are gravely touched by the terms of the treaty'.[42] At the heart of the issue were two main concerns: that the Anglo-Japanese Alliance undermined Australia's exclusionary immigration laws and that it posed a threat to Australian security. The *Immigration Restriction Act 1901*, commonly known as the 'White Australia' policy, was one of the first pieces of legislation to pass the newly formed federal government. Although it was written in response to a desire to protect the nation's labour market, the Act was informed by racial ideologies. It placed restrictions on the immigration of 'coloured races' to Australia by requiring non–Anglo Europeans to sit a convoluted dictation test in any European language. Restrictions on Japanese immigration were eased in 1904 when laws were changed to allow tourists, students and merchants from Japan to enter for one year on passports without being subject to the dictation test.

By this time, substantial communities of Japanese workers had already developed around the pearl shell industries in Queensland and Western Australia. The abovementioned contributor to the *Freeman's Journal* found cause for concern in the presence of Japanese labourers in Queensland. After commenting on the exceptional 'precocity' of Japan as the 'child of the world's old age', the author complained that the Anglo-Japanese Alliance resulted in a 'clash' of competing interests.[43] The 'phases of the Japanese civilization which charmed the world' were contrasted with the presence of labourers and prostitutes in Queensland, which

---

41 Peter Lowe, 'The British Empire and the Anglo-Japanese Alliance 1911–1915', *History* 54, no. 181 (1969): 212–25; I.H. Nish, 'Australia and the Anglo-Japanese Alliance, 1901–1911', *Australian Journal of Politics and History* 9, no. 2 (1963): 201–12.
42 'The Anglo-Japanese Treaty', *Freeman's Journal*, 22 February 1902, 21.
43 Ibid.

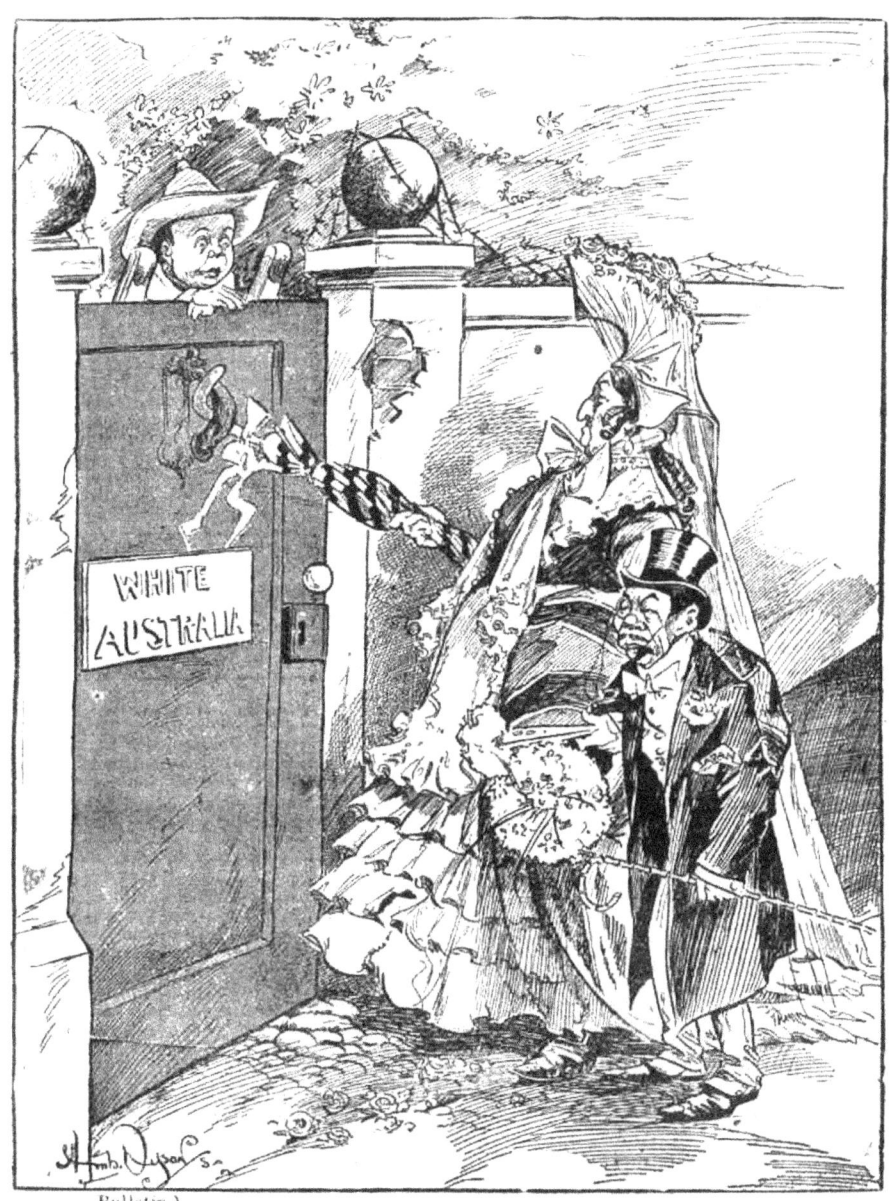

Figure 1.9. Anon., *The Motherland's Misalliance*.
Source: *Bulletin*, 1 March 1902.

were seen as 'inimical to European labour, and inimical to Australian morality'. It was feared that Australia may 'pay the price of the treaty in the admission of the Japanese hordes, and the establishment and maintenance of Japanese morals on Australian shores'.[44] Reflecting this anxiety, a cartoon published the following week in the political magazine the *Bulletin* personified Australia as a frightened young boy, clearly nervous about the 'marriage' between Britannia and her new Japanese groom (see Figure 1.9). Defined here by its relationship to Australia, Britain is no longer personified as a child but as a very large, imposing, matronly mother. Titled *The Motherland's Misalliance*, the cartoon shows Britannia knocking on the door of 'White Australia' announcing: 'Now my good little son. I've married again. This is your new father. You must be very fond of him'. The stooped, ancient Japanese groom is dwarfed by his bride and presented in ill-fitting European clothing including a top hat, monocle and oversized tail coat. This representation of the Japanese groom ultimately places him in a subservient position to the enormous Britannia and young Australia—his imperialist ambitions have been symbolically cut short. Despite the Motherland's instructions to young Australia, who is himself too immature to marry, the boy is still able to stand guard at his very high, exclusionary fence and gate.

Unsurprisingly, Australia's immigration policy caused diplomatic offence in Japan and was a source of ongoing dispute between the two countries. Alison Broinowski noted that 'eminent Japanese described Australian migration policy as "selfish and impolitic", "an offence against humanity", and "an insulting piece of legislation"'.[45] The Japanese Government was affronted by Japan's categorisation as a 'coloured race', rather than the racial ideology underpinning the legislation itself. Hisakichi Eitaki, the Japanese consul in Sydney, explained his country's position in a letter to Edmund Barton, Australia's first prime minister, in 1901:

---

44 Ibid.
45 Alison Broinowski, 'About Face: Asian Representation of Australia' (PhD diss., The Australian National University, 2001), 107.

> The Japanese belong to an Empire whose standard of civilization is so much higher than that of kanakas, negroes, Pacific Islanders, Indians, or other Eastern peoples, that to refer to them in the same terms cannot but be regarded in the light of a reproach, which is hardly warranted by the fact of the shade of the national complexion.[46]

Japan did not disagree with the broader racial hierarchy that it identified with the policy, but challenged where Japan should sit within it.

Japanese officials also remarked that Australia had caught *kyōnichibyō* (fear of Japan illness) in the wake of the Russo-Japanese War.[47] The Japanese Navy's defeat of the Russians at Tsushima received extensive attention in the Australian press in 1905.[48] A Sydney paperboy in his youth, Frank Clune, recalled earning four times his usual profit from sales of the *Evening News* and the *Star* on the day of Japan's victory at Tsushima.[49] Three weeks after the Battle of Tsushima, soon-to-be Prime Minister Alfred Deakin expressed his concern that Australia was within 'striking distance of no less than sixteen foreign naval stations', noting that the strongest was Yokohama.[50] Deputy Prime Minister in the Reid Government, Allan McLean, similarly warned:

> It must be apparent to every thinking man, that sense of security we have always considered we derived from our great distance from the bases of all the great military or naval powers of the world has now been removed. We now find one of the great naval and military powers of the earth within a very short distance of our shores … It is fortunate for us that the great Power that has recently arisen in the East is an ally of the Empire. Of course, that condition of things might not always continue, and we must be prepared for what might happen.[51]

In this context, representations of Japan-as-child took on new connotations. Imagery invoking Japan as a precocious military force and bottomless source of aspiring young soldiers began to emerge.

---

46   H. Eitaki, 'Japanese Invasion: View of the Consul', *Brisbane Courier*, 3 July 1901, 7. For more on the Japanese response to the White Australia policy see Yuichi Murakami, 'Australia's Immigration Legislation, 1893–1901: The Japanese Response', in *Relationships: Australia and Japan*, ed. Vera Mackie and Paul Jones (Parkville: University of Melbourne, 2001), 45–70.
47   Broinowski, 'About Face: Asian Representation of Australia', 107.
48   See for example 'The Battle of Tsushima', *Morning Bulletin*, 30 June 1905, 3; 'Togo's Tsu-Shima Triumph', *Mercury*, 24 June 1905, 11; 'Tsushima and Its Lessons', *Brisbane Courier*, 1 June 1905, 4.
49   Robin Gerster, *Travels in Atomic Sunshine* (Melbourne: Scribe, 2008), 37.
50   'Important Statement by Mr Deakin. A Call to Action', *Daily Telegraph*, 15 June 1905, 5.
51   'Mr Mclean's View. Old Sense of Security. It Exists No Longer. A Serious Situation', *Herald*, 13 June 1905, 3.

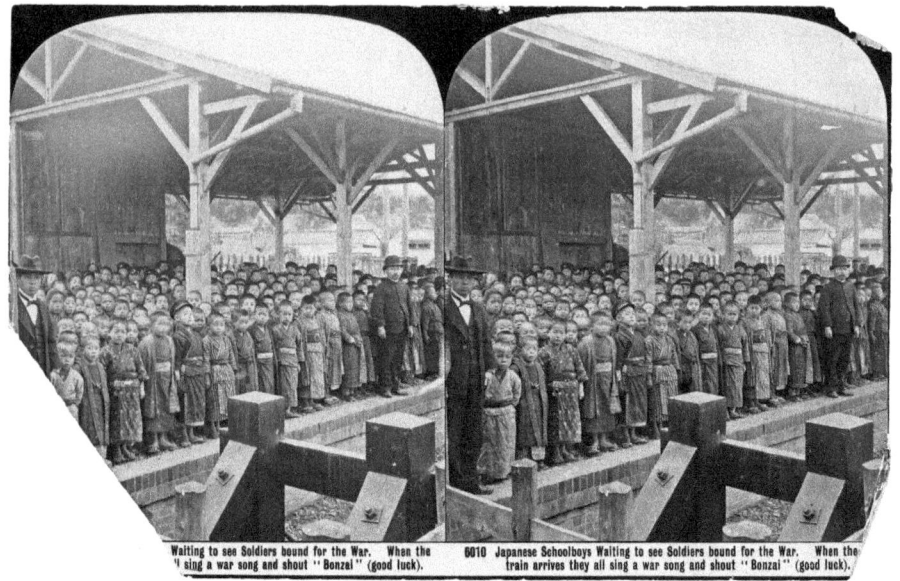

Figure 1.10. George Rose, Japanese schoolboys waiting to see soldiers bound for war. When the train arrives they all sing a war song and shout 'Bonzai' (good luck), c. 1904.
Source: State Library of Victoria. Accession no. H96.160/941.

Boy Soldiers

Rose's catalogue of Japanese stereographs acknowledged the market for this military-inspired child imagery. One stereograph shows a large group of Japanese school children waiting on a train platform to farewell soldiers leaving for the Russo-Japanese War (see Figure 1.10). Many of the children are looking at the camera and the child wearing a hat in the centre front is standing sharply to attention as though expressing his own military aspirations. Although there are also girls on the crowded platform, it is telling that the caption refers only to boys: 'Japanese schoolboys waiting to see soldiers bound for war. When the train arrives they all sing a war song and shout "Bonzai" (good luck)'. This marginalisation of the girls reflects the gendered character of representations of Japanese children—diplomatic and military relations were the domain of boys.

Rose's visit to Japan coincided with the Russo-Japanese War, but his photograph responded to an older Australian interest in the young age at which military training began for Japanese boys. Australian newspapers linked Japan's success in the First Sino-Japanese War (1894–95) in part to the military training of Meiji-era children.[52] Comparable reports proliferated during the Russo-Japanese War. An article in the *Geelong Advertiser* in 1905 attributed the stamina, strength and courage shown by the Japanese in the 'recent war' to the discipline that boys acquire in school: 'A portion of the school gymnastics consists of military drill. The school boys desirous of showing they can be more than toy soldiers, practice long marches. The Government encourages them by providing them with real rifles and bayonets'.[53] Another article on Japan's military strength, with strong xenophobic overtones, emphasised the nation's boundless young human resources:

> Japan is in no danger of race suicide. The mothers are not shirking maternity as in other lands, and the result is that we can spare half a million men a year for an indefinite number of years and not miss them … When the time comes Japan will guide the yellow whirlwind and direct the yellow storm, and I am prone to think that certain nations will find it a veritable sirocco … The spirit which won the world's great battles is the spirit with which modern Japan, the Child of the World's Old Age, will go into action on sea and on land.[54]

The reference to 'race suicide' alludes to contemporary concerns about Australia's own declining birth rate, which was the subject of a New South Wales royal commission in 1903–04. Fears of military defeat to growing Asian armies merged with anxieties about race suicide in the mind of the bishop of the Riverina, who described the declining birth rate in Australia as a 'wilful shirking of responsibilities'. To the bishop, the increasing birth rates in China and Japan meant that the 'East' was growing 'stronger and stronger, and is becoming conscious of her strength. Are the Christian nations refusing their inheritance, and by a wanton race suicide surrendering the sceptre to the East?'[55]

Rose's stereograph gave such anxieties visual form. Through the stereoscope, Australian viewers could study the faces of the school children gathered to support the Japanese army. The children wait

---

52 'The China-Japan War', *Capricornian*, 3 November 1894, 18; 'The War in China', *Scone Advocate*, 31 December 1894, 2.
53 'Japan's Secret. How Her Victories Were Won. Training the Child. Interesting Details of Japanese School Life and Methods', *Geelong Advertiser*, 18 November 1905, 8; 'Japan's Secret. How Her Victories Were Won. Training the Child. Interesting Details of Japanese School Life and Methods', *Sunday Times*, 12 November 1905, 4.
54 'Japan. The Child of the World's Old Age', 4.
55 'Race Suicide', *Daily Standard*, 17 September 1913, 4.

under the watchful eye of a stationmaster and a male teacher dressed impeccably in a three-piece suit, hat and bow tie. Unlike the child in Cotton's lantern slide, whose expression of glee undermines the potential threat posed by the war flag that he waves, none of the children in Rose's photograph are smiling. Many of the boys frown at the camera, while others look at it sideways, as though out of suspicion. Although they all wear kimonos, many also wear the military-style school caps adopted in the Meiji era that reinforce the sense that these children were being prepared to take over from the previous generation of soldiers.

Importantly, the circulation of this type of commercial imagery in Australian homes not only shaped perceptions of Japan in Australia but also informed the perceptions and photographic practices of Australians who had the means to travel through Japan. The travel photographs of Mark Foy and his family are indicative of this process. Foy was an owner of the family-run Foy's department store in Sydney, which traded between 1885 and 1980. The Foys were regular visitors to Japan and frequently commented on Japanese issues in the Australian press.[56] On their trips, the family collected commercially produced photographs of scenery and tourist sites and produced their own photographs capturing their encounters with Japanese people. Individually sold, mass-produced photographs were commonly placed alongside family photographs in personal travel albums, which became sites in which commercial visions of Japan were merged with personal imagery and memories.[57] Photographs from a Foy family trip in 1902 feature several photographs of local children that reflect prevailing Australian impressions of Japan, including a photograph of three children pumping water from a well with babies strapped to their backs.

A particularly striking group of photographs focus on militarised schoolboys. One of these photographs centres on a group of boys emerging from long grass on a hillside (see Figure 1.11). Their military-inspired attire reflects the interrelationships between citizen making, education and military training in the Meiji era. Originally designed as a junior version of the late nineteenth-century Japanese army uniform—

---

56 'Back from Japan', *Sydney Morning Herald*, 10 January 1918, 8; 'War Items', *Armidale Express and New England General Advertiser*, 15 January 1918, 4; 'Eleven Trips to Japan', *Daily Standard*, 11 February 1936, 2; 'Japan More Progressive Than Australia, Says Businessman', *Telegraph*, 1 March 1938, 3.
57 See for example Margaret Preston's photograph album held in the Powerhouse Museum, registration number 2009/104/5.

1. 'THE CHILD OF THE WORLD'S OLD AGE'

modelled on French and Prussian military dress—these school uniforms were widely adopted from 1879. The overexposure at the top right of Foy's photograph creates the impression that these schoolboys are moving en masse towards the camera from outside its frame. Some boys in the distance can be seen walking towards the camera, while others in the mid ground stand still with startled or quizzical expressions on their faces. The photograph is composed to focus attention on a particular boy seen slightly left of the centre grimacing fiercely at the camera. His feet are spread in a firm stance as he pretends to point a gun at

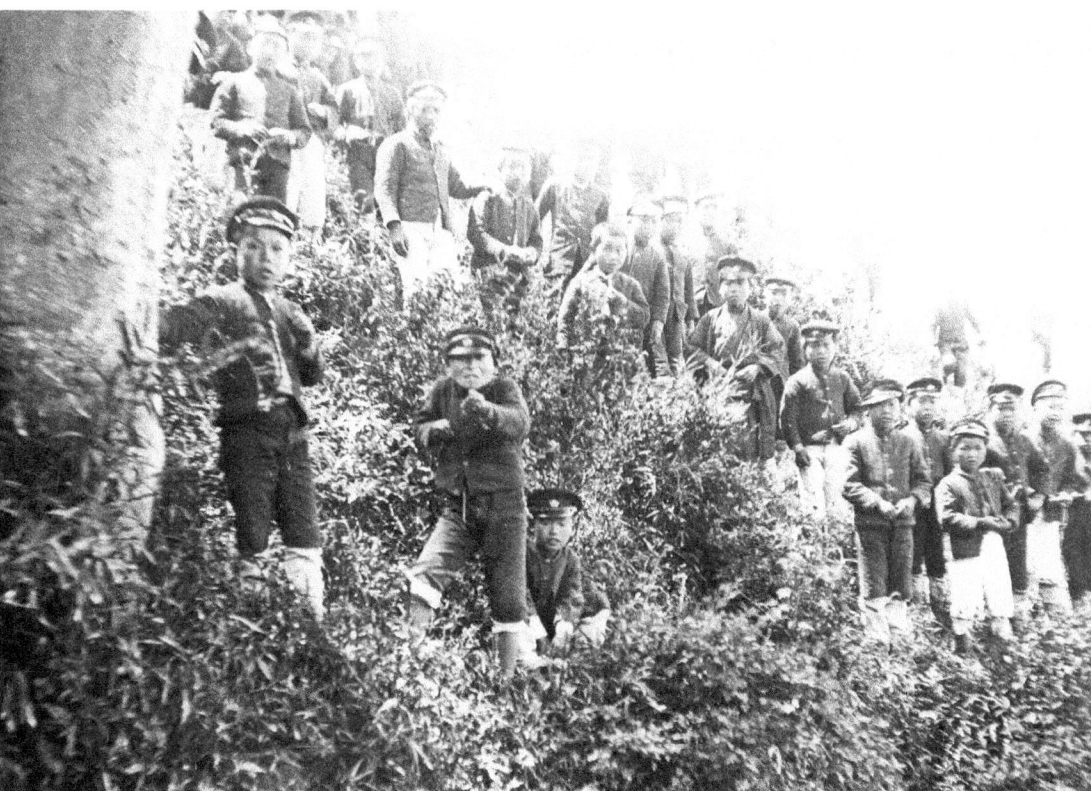

Figure 1.11. Photographs of Mark Foy and family, including a trip to Japan in 1902.
Source: State Library of New South Wales. Accession no. PXD 1199.

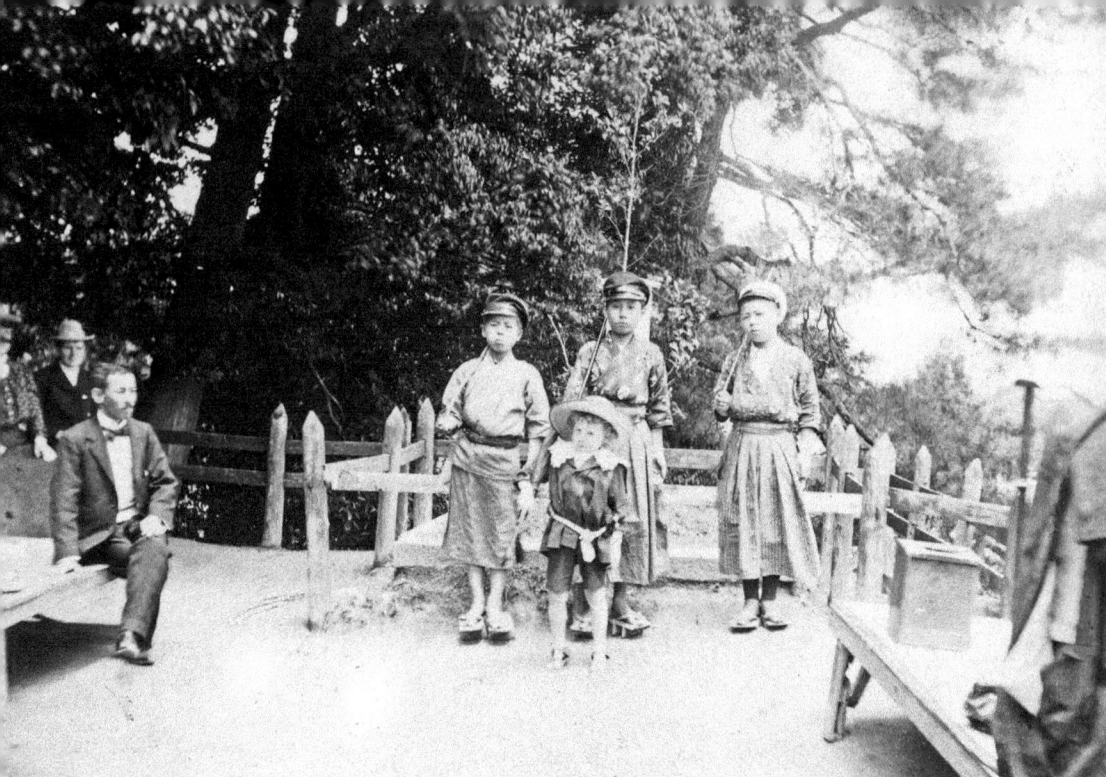

Figure 1.12. Photographs of Mark Foy and family, including a trip to Japan in 1902.
Source: State Library of New South Wales. Accession no. PXD 1199.

the photographer, while a younger boy crouches at his feet as though enjoying his protection. Although the absence of a weapon makes it clear that the child is just miming an attack, to Australian viewers familiar with newspaper reports about Japan's training of young soldiers the photographs may have assumed more menacing qualities. Such military associations may have been implicit when the Foys viewed their travel photographs at home or showed them to family and friends, but no doubt merged with commentaries describing their personal recollections of this encounter with the children.

This crossover between the world of international relations and personal or familial recollections is also strongly suggested in another Foy photograph that shows militarised Japanese children standing with a young blonde Australian boy (see Figure 1.12). The blonde boy is most likely Mark Francis Foy, who accompanied his parents to Japan along with his baby sister Elizabeth. In this photograph, the three Japanese boys wear Japanese dress with military-style school caps. They stand to attention in a neat row, holding rods over their shoulders like rifles, while adult members of the Foy party and a Japanese man in a European suit look on. Two of the boys have very serious expressions and the other looks at the camera with curiosity and a slightly cocked head. The three boys mark a sharp contrast to the much younger Australian boy who stands in front of them attempting to mimic their stance with what appears to be an umbrella over his shoulder. While the Japanese boys represent the epitome of Meiji military boyhood—disciplined, orderly and strong— the soft blonde curls of the Foy child, his bonnet, pleated tunic and large lace collar reflect remnants of the Victorian ideals of the 'innocent saintly child' embodied popularly by Hodgson Burnett's *Little Lord Fauntleroy* (1886).[58] Ideologies of the 'saintly child' drew on Christian iconography and Enlightenment and Romantic philosophies to perpetuate belief in the supposedly 'natural' goodness of children in nineteenth-century England. Although the image was also popular in Australia during the late nineteenth century and informed representations of 'The Boy from Manly', by the early twentieth century, 'Fauntleroy-like "cissies"' were being overpowered in popular culture with representations of the 'hardy little mischief maker', later embodied in the comic book character Ginger Meggs.[59] The Foy photograph seemingly stages a meeting of Young Australia and the 'child of the world's old age' in a humorous photograph for the family travel album.

Such patterns of recycling, layering and building representations of Japan resonate with Jørgen Ole Bærenholdt, Michael Haldrup, Jonas Larsen and John Urry's discussion of the 'imaginative mobilities' of tourism. Although their focus is on contemporary tourism, the authors' analysis may be extended to the Foy photograph. Imaginative mobilities acknowledge that tourism does not occur in a vacuum but, instead, involves the anticipation, performance and remembrance of travel at home and abroad.[60] As the children in the Foy photograph pose for the camera, they enact a performance that has already been refined and scripted in commercial photographs, cartoons, news articles, international diplomacy and meanings of childhood. This performance of Australian–Japanese relations may have continued when the Foys returned home, as they used their photographs to repeat narratives of their Japanese encounters among family and friends. The Foy's famous department store became yet another forum for staging encounters

---

58   Jan Kociumbas, 'The Spiritual Child: Child Death and Angelic Motherhood in Colonial Women's Writing', *Journal of the Royal Australian Historical Society* 85, no. 2 (1999): 86.
59   Ibid., 92; Inglis, 'Young Australia 1870–1900', 1–24.
60   Jørgen Ole Bærenholdt et al., *Performing Tourist Places* (Aldershot: Ashgate, 2004), 10, 70.

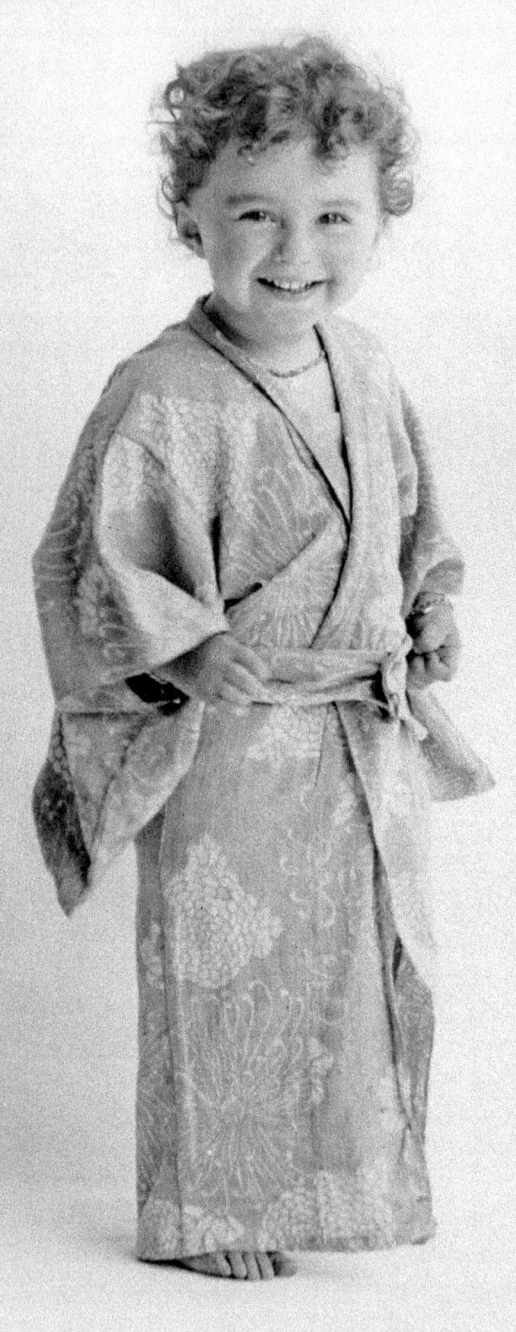

Figure 1.13. Ruth Hollick, *Untitled [Child in Kimono]*, c. 1910–30.
Source: State Library of Victoria. Accession no. H2004.61/418.

between Australia and Japan, this time for Sydney's public. The store not only stocked Japanese goods such as silks and flower pots, its official publication, the *Magnet*, included a full page dedicated to photographs of a Japanese teahouse in its June 1910 issue. Through the purchase of Japanese goods, Australian consumers could also participate in these patterns of anticipating and performing encounters with Japan without leaving home.

From Japan-as-Child to Australian-Child-as-Japan

Japanese goods were used in other photographic representations of Australian–Japanese encounters during the early twentieth century. Here, notions of Japan-as-child were transformed into the Australian-Child-as-Japan. Across the country, in school performances, backyard plays, photographers' studios and fancy dress parties, Anglo-Australian children adopted Japanese costumes and posed for the camera. Reflecting the popularity of this practice, Australian state library collections feature many photographs of Anglo-Australian children in Japanese costume and newspaper social pages regularly published photographs of children posing in Japanese costume for fancy dress parties.[61] Other photographs, like Ruth Hollick's portrait of an unnamed curly haired child (see Figure 1.13), were produced professionally in the studio. This Melbourne-based photographer is best known for her portraits of women and children, many of which were made at her home studio in Moonee Ponds and, later, in her Collins Street studio. Hollick's high society portraits featured in newspapers and *The Home* magazine in the early 1920s, making her a highly sought after portraitist. We can only speculate why the parents of this child dressed her in a kimono for her portrait session. The girl also wears a tiny bead necklace with a *manji* pendant—a symbol associated with Japanese Buddhism—and a silver bracelet. Although kimonos were readily available in Australia, it is likely that the pendant was bought in Japan, perhaps by the girl's parents. The girl's bare feet also allude to conceptions of the feminine Japanese child as innocent and close to nature.

---

61 'Children's Fancy Dress Ball at the Sydney Town Hall', *Sydney Mail*, 7 October 1899, 864; 'At the Children's Hospital Ball', *Queenslander*, 15 August 1903, 23.

An admiration for Japanese children, along with the concurrent fashion for Japanese goods, no doubt helped to foster the trend for photographing Anglo-Australian children in Japanese-inspired dress. Throughout the first two decades of the twentieth century, Australian newspapers regularly published articles about idealised Japanese children. Japanese children, it was argued, were experts of self-control, rarely crying or throwing temper tantrums, and were always quiet, gentle, polite and obedient.[62] Such reports about the behaviour of children must be distinguished from symbolic references to an unmanageable *enfant terrible* to describe the imperialist nation. One reporter noted:

> Travellers in Japan are unanimous in their praise of the gentleness, courtesy, and charm of the Japanese child, whose quaint, old-fashioned manners, curious garb, and still more curious play, is an unfailing source of interest to all lovers of children who visit the Land of the Chrysanthemum and the Cherry Blossom.[63]

Another article praising the extraordinarily good behaviour of Japanese children was republished across the country repeatedly between 1905 and 1919.[64] It seemed as though Australians did not tire of hearing about well-behaved Japanese children. Piel has suggested that Western perceptions of Japanese children as universally polite and well behaved may be as much to do with the fact that Westerners encountered children typically as outsiders to the family, or as guests, strangers or customers in Japanese businesses. The Japanese custom of keeping up appearances in front of strangers and reserving their true feelings for members of their inner circle may have given many Westerners a distorted view of Japanese family life.[65]

Likewise, women's magazines published photographs and articles about selfless Japanese mothers and their angelic children. An issue of *New Idea* accompanied an article by Pierre Loti with a full-page montage of five photographs taken by Miss Nell Brownlow Cole from Brisbane of a little Anglo-Australian girl dressed in a kimono. The girl was photographed variously posing cross-legged, holding a fan and making tea in front of a Japanese screen. She is seemingly composed, innocent and disciplined,

---

62 Sladen, 'Child Life in Japan', 13.
63 'The Boys and Girls of Japan', *Geelong Advertiser*, 28 November 1908, 9.
64 See for example 'Japanese Child Life', *Benalla Standard*, 26 June 1917, 1; 'Japanese Child Life', *St Arnaud Mercury*, 9 February 1916, 1; 'Japanese Child-Life', *Burrowa News*, 3 March 1905, 1; 'Japanese Child-Life', *Ovens and Murray Advertiser*, 15 July 1905, 5; 'Japanese Child-Life', *Fitzroy City Press*, 12 July 1919, 2.
65 Piel, 'The Ideology of the Child in Japan 1600–1945', 50.

suggesting that Australian mothers could similarly align these qualities with their own children by staging such photographs. Several scholars have addressed the adoption of Japanese dress by adults in the US, Britain and Europe during the late nineteenth and early twentieth century.[66] This body of work has tended to frame cross-cultural dressing as a symptom of Western Orientalism, fantasies of power and a combination of fear and desire for the 'other'.[67] However, rather than simply reflecting fantasies of the distant and exotic East, photographs of Anglo-Australian children in Japanese costume may be better understood as practices that responded to complex and contradictory conceptions of childhood and both countries' places as emerging nations in the Asia-Pacific. Underpinning these photographs are decades of discussion about Japanese children and Japan-as-child, informed by concerns about international diplomacy, immigration, industry and perceptions of Japan's imperialist ambitions.

These and the other photographs examined in this chapter represent the accumulation of many years of anticipation, performance and remembrance of Australian encounters with Japan through newspapers, commercial photographs and tourist photographs. The apparent innocence of these images of children and their circulation in homes belies the important political role that conceptions of Japan-as-child played. Australian experiences of modernity and impressions of Japanese children were shaped by a variety of debates about industrialisation, modernisation, immigration and security. By staging, seeking out or purchasing these visions of Japanese childhood, Australians consumed and reproduced a series of conflicting views of Japan as a naïve artistic child and *enfant terrible*. As the twentieth century wore on, photography was to become an increasingly significant medium for reproducing and reconciling antithetical perceptions of both Japan and the Japanese.

---

66   Mari Yoshihara, *Embracing the East: White Women and American Orientalism* (New York: Oxford University Press, 2003); Terry Castle, *Masquerade and Civilization: The Carnivalesque in Eighteenth-Century English Culture and Fiction* (Stanford: Stanford University Press, 1986); Christine M.E. Guth, 'Charles Longfellow and Okakura Kakuzo: Cultural Cross-Dressing in the Colonial Context', *Positions: East Asia Cultures Critique* 8, no. 3 (2000): 605–35; Mary Roberts, 'Cultural Crossings: Sartorial Adventures, Satiric Narratives, and the Question of Indigenous Agency in Nineteenth-Century Europe and the near East', in *Edges of Empire*, ed. Jocelyn Hackforth-Jones (Malden: Blackwell, 2005); Tara Mayer, 'Cultural Cross-Dressing: Posing and Performance in Orientalist Portraits', *Journal of the Royal Asiatic Society* 22, no. 2 (2012); Marie-Cecile Thoral, 'Sartorial Orientalism: Cross-Cultural Dressing in Colonial Algeria and Metropolitan France in the Nineteenth Century', *European History Quarterly* 45, no. 1 (2015).
67   Castle, *Masquerade and Civilization*, 62. See also Mayer, 'Cultural Cross-Dressing', 281–98; Christine Riding, 'Travellers and Sitters: The Orientalist Portrait', in *The Lure of the East*, ed. Nicholas Tromans (London: Tate Gallery, 2008), 48–81.

2

'WHITE AUSTRALIA' IN THE DARKROOM: 1915–41

In his review of the 1922 Photographic Society of New South Wales (NSW) exhibition for the *Australasian Photo Review*, critic Alek Sass alluded to some of the incongruities associated with Australian–Japanese photographic relations in the interwar period. While praising the two Japanese exhibitors, Sass commented wryly that their participation in the local photography scene ran counter to the racially exclusionary aims of Australian immigration policy:

> By way of diversion, the White Australia policy in the dark-room seems to be in danger; I refer to the work of Messrs. K. Ishida and K. Yama. They have eyes to see and things to say, those men … Very thoughtful work, gentlemen.[1]

Kiichiro Ishida and Ichiro Kagiyama were among the approximately 300 Japanese living in NSW during this period.[2] These two men were active members of the Photographic Society of NSW and regularly exhibited and published their work alongside leading Australian photographers at a time when the 'White Australia' policy was testing diplomatic relations with Japan. Sass's review and the exhibition itself highlight how the political and personal photographic relations between Australia and Japan tell quite

---

1   Alek Sass, 'Old Friends and New: A Ramble through the Exhibition of Camera Pictures by the Photographic Society of New South Wales', *Australasian Photo Review* 29, no. 11 (1922): 356.
2   There was an increase in Japanese residents in NSW from 126 (118 male and seven female) in 1911 to 308 (289 male and 19 female) in 1921, largely due to the growth of Japanese merchants in Sydney (H.A. Smith, *The Official Year Book of New South Wales 1922* (Sydney: NSW State Government, 1924), 246). For more on Kagiyama see Melissa Miles, 'Through Japanese Eyes: Ichiro Kagiyama and Australian-Japanese Relations in the 1920s and 1930s', *History of Photography* 38, no. 4 (2014): 356–58.

distinct, even incompatible stories. While Australian politicians concerned about perceived Japanese military and economic threats sought to limit Japanese immigration and photographic activity, Japanese photographers developed thriving practices and social relationships in Australia.

Extending the previous chapter's discussion of how Australians interpreted the Australia–Japan relationship symbolically in photographs, this chapter examines how conflicting aspects of this relationship were negotiated up close through interpersonal relations and the creative practices of Anglo-Australian and Japanese photographers in the pre–World War I (WWI) and interwar period. Several Japanese photographers developed thriving businesses and practices in different parts of the country from the late nineteenth century to WWII, including in the remote West Australian town of Broome.³ By focusing largely on the work of two Japanese photographers in Sydney, this chapter examines how their commercial, personal and artistic practices were also entangled with international trade, diplomacy and fashion.

Japanese Photographers and 'White Australia'

Kagiyama's and Ishida's entries into 'White Australia' differed significantly. The absence of arrival documents for Kagiyama clouds his early years in Australia in mystery. Although some historians suspect that Kagiyama landed in Sydney illegally as a teenager in 1906 or 1907,⁴ Kagiyama provided a very different story to immigration officials in 1934. In a statutory declaration, Kagiyama noted that he was born in Gifu Prefecture in 1890 and that he came to Thursday Island as an infant when his father took work in the pearl shell industry.⁵ Kagiyama described being taken to live with family friends in Mackay on the eastern coast of Queensland after his father's death in 1897 or 1898. At this time, many of Queensland's 3,247 resident Japanese were encouraged to move south from Thursday Island to Queensland's sugar growing regions, including

---

3   Melissa Miles and Kate Warren, 'The Japanese Photographers of Broome: Photography and Cross-Cultural Encounter', *History of Photography* 41, no. 1 (2016): 3–24.
4   Pam Oliver, 'Japanese Relationships in White Australia', *History Australia* 4, no. 1 (2007): 5.6; Yuri Mitsuda, *Modernism/Japonism in Photography 1920s–40s. Kiichiro Ishida and Sydney Camera Circle* (Tokyo: Shoto Museum of Art, 2002), 21; Beth Hise and Pam Oliver, 'Kiichiro Ishida', *Insites*, Summer 2003, 4.
5   NSW Branch Department of Immigration, 'Ichiro Kagiyama [Applicant for Exemption from the Dictation Test under the Immigration Act and for Admission of His Wife into the Commonwealth], 1934–5', National Archives of Australia (NAA) SP42/1 C1934/4618.

around Townsville and MacKay, where employment opportunities were more plentiful.⁶ It is telling that, when Japan established its first consulate in Australia in March 1896, it chose to locate it in Townsville in the region favoured by Japanese immigrants and indentured labourers. Kagiyama claimed that he spent 14 years in Mackay before moving to Adelaide for one year, and then Sydney around 1913, where he remained resident until he returned to Japan in 1941 amid rising tensions between his homeland and the Allies.

The disparity in arrival dates between those suggested by historians and that described by Kagiyama is significant; Japanese people were subject to a very different set of immigration laws in Australia in the mid-1890s and 1907. The time that Kagiyama claimed he and his father arrived at Thursday Island coincided with a period of relatively relaxed travel requirements, when the movement of individual indentured labourers was not well documented. During the mid to late 1890s, anxieties about Japanese control over the pearl shelling industry were growing and some Queenslanders feared that Thursday Island was in danger of becoming a Japanese colony.⁷ After 1898, no Japanese were permitted to land in Queensland without a passport. The Immigration Restriction Act imposed more stringent restrictions on Japanese immigration, described in the previous chapter, including requiring non–Anglo Europeans to sit a complicated European language dictation test. Further changes in the law in 1904 allowed Japanese tourists, students and merchants to enter for one year on passports without being subject to the dictation test. Applications could be made for a Certificate of Exemption from the Dictation Test (CEDT), which allowed Japanese people to stay in Australia for up to three years.⁸ Kagiyama's 1934 interview and statutory declaration were part of his application for a CEDT—the first such application from him on record—which coincided with his first return trip to Japan.

The absence of immigration documents for Kagiyama's initial arrival in Australia, and current restrictions on accessing personal family records in Japan that could verify the time and place of death of

---

6   J. Armstrong, 'Aspects of Japanese Immigration to Queensland before 1900', *Queensland Heritage* 2, no. 9 (1979): 4.
7   Henry Frei, *Japan's Southward Advance and Australia* (Carlton: Melbourne University Press, 1991), 80–81; 'Pearlshell and Beche-De-Mer. Report on the Fishers', *Brisbane Courier*, 24 November 1897, 5.
8   George Reid, 'Japanese Tourists and Merchants', *Sydney Morning Herald*, 26 September 1904, 6.

Kagiyama's father, make it impossible to confirm the veracity of his story. A descendant of one of Kagiyama's friends in Takayama, where he returned after WWII, suggested that he arrived in Australia illegally as a young man. Whether it was a carefully planned fabrication designed to obscure his illegal entry into Australia or the truth, Kagiyama's explanation of his time in Australia satisfied immigration officials enough to allow him to remain resident.[9]

Ishida had a very different experience, arriving in Sydney in 1919. As an employee of the Okura Trading Company (a subsidiary of the large *Okura-gumi*), Ishida was one of a 'new breed of company men' who were sent to work in branch offices in ports around the Asia-Pacific.[10] Japanese firms such as Kuwahata, Kanematsu, Nakamura and Iida all had offices in Sydney, and their senior merchants were well connected with the Japanese consul and Sydney society. The nature of Ishida's work meant that he lived in Sydney for a relatively short period between 1919 and 1923. Cremorne and the adjoining north shore suburb of Mosman became popular homes for Japanese merchant families. Kagiyama's environment was not as salubrious as that enjoyed by Ishida and his fellow merchants. During the mid-1910s, he worked as a laundry worker, presser and dyer in Cowper Street, Waverley, later starting his own commercial photography studio in Woollahra. Yet, the two men found common ground through their shared love of photography and became valued members of the Photographic Society of NSW. Although neither man left behind written accounts of their perspectives on Australia and its photography, their photographs and those of their peers offer valuable insight into the complexity of the Australia–Japan relationship in this era.

Personal Photographic Encounters

As a member of the Photographic Society of NSW from around 1914, Kagiyama refined his skills by working with some of Sydney's most accomplished practitioners, including Harold Cazneaux and Monte Luke. The society was established in 1872 in response to the growing popularity of photography among amateurs. As its name suggests, it was driven by social interaction between photographers. Members exchanged photographs, gained feedback on their work and attended monthly meetings at which they would 'receive hints and otherwise improve

---

9 NAA SP42/1 C1934/4618.
10 Frei, *Japan's Southward Advance and Australia*, 118.

their knowledge of the art'.[11] At this time, the Photographic Society of NSW was heavily focused on pictorialism. This mode of photography was popularised in Europe, the US and Britain in the 1890s and soon gained a wide following in Australia. Motivated by the desire to fulfil the artistic potential of photography, pictorialists used control processes including bromoil, carbon pigment, oil prints or gum bichromate to subdue details, lower or raise tone and strengthen highlights in their photographs. Although pictorialism has now become synonymous with aesthetic qualities such as low-tone and soft, romantic 'fuzzy' effects, in early twentieth-century Australia the term referred more broadly to the art of photography.[12]

The society also organised social gatherings and excursions to the beaches, parks and bush surrounding Sydney so that members could practice their craft and consider questions of lighting, subject matter and composition together. A photograph taken by Cazneaux on one of these excursions around 1915 shows a young, dapper Kagiyama posing among a large group of members with their photographic equipment in tow (see Figure 2.1). Kagiyama also took photographs of his fellow photographers during these outings and kept these photographs in his (recently rediscovered) personal album, indicating that the social aspect of such excursions was as important to him as the opportunities they afforded to photograph new subjects.[13] Other photographs assembled in this rare album capture Sydney's York Street, the Queen Victoria Market, the Art Gallery of NSW, the Domain, Hyde Park, the University of Sydney and St Mary's Cathedral, and collectively create the impression of a roving photographer eagerly exploring the city. These city views stand in contrast to the 'tourist gaze' described by John Urry as a means of controlling the unfamiliar world from afar and 'combining detachment and mystery'.[14] As a resident of Sydney, Kagiyama was no tourist. His photographs demonstrate that he was thoroughly immersed in the city, part of the crowd on a curbside, in a park or amid the throngs in Central Station.

---

11   'Amateur Photographic Society of NSW', *Sydney Morning Herald*, 20 July 1872, 7.
12   Francis Ebury, 'Making Pictures: Australian Pictorial Photography as Art 1897–1957' (PhD diss., University of Melbourne, 2001); Gael Newton, *Silver and Grey: Fifty Years of Australian Photography 1900–1950* (Sydney: Angus and Robertson, 1980); Melissa Miles, *The Language of Light and Dark: Light and Place in Australian Photography* (Montreal: McGill Queen's University Press, 2015).
13   The album was found by the authors in Takayama, Japan in the possession of a descendant of one of Kagiyama's friends, who inherited it upon Kagiyama's death.
14   John Urry, *The Tourist Gaze*, 2nd ed. (London: Sage, 2002), 147.

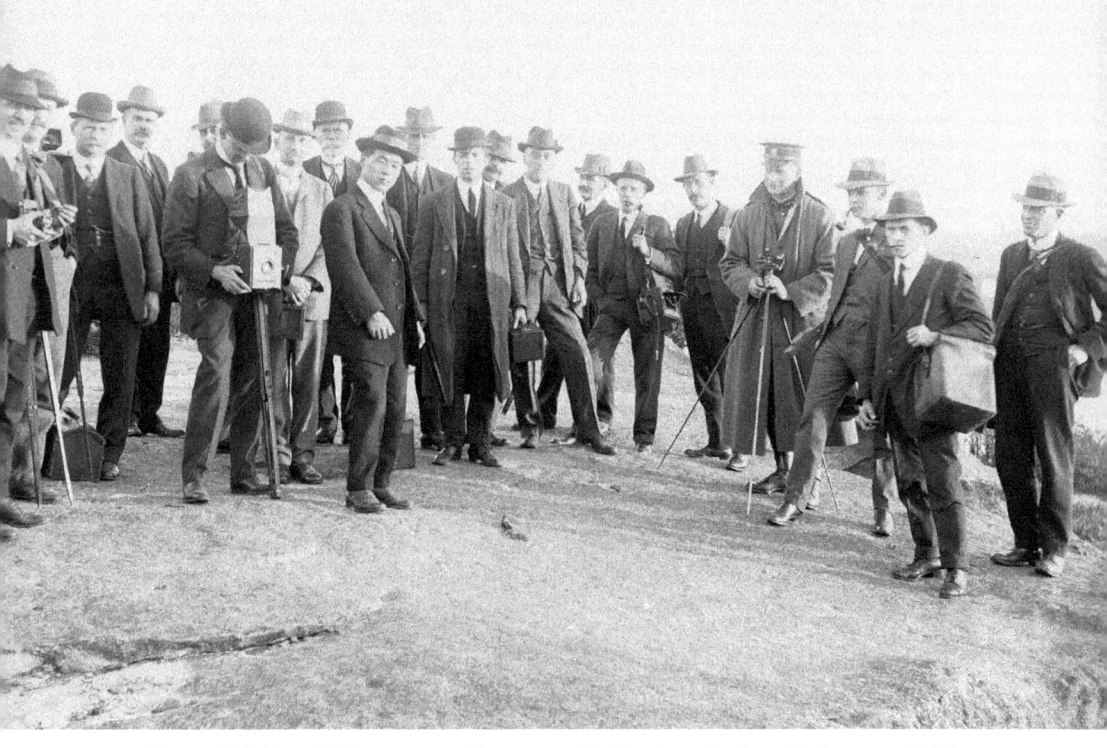

Figure 2.1. Harold Cazneaux, *Photographic Society Outing*, Sydney, c. 1915.
Source: National Library of Australia, PIC P1067/209 LOC Cold Store PIC HCF.
Printed from a negative.

Kagiyama's personal photographs also capture the intercultural friendships and relationships that flourished in Sydney and highlight the way that photography operated as a medium for building social connections.[15] Relationships between Anglo-Australian women and Japanese men were not uncommon in Sydney in the early to mid-twentieth century.[16] Kagiyama himself married an Anglo-Australian woman named Cicelia Howard Walker in 1916. Cicelia was 19 years old and Kagiyama was still working as a cleaner and presser at the time of their marriage. The couple had a daughter who died in infancy and then a son, Harno, who was born in 1920. Some of Kagiyama's photographs depict other unnamed Japanese men, their Australian wives and their children (see Figure 2.2), or show Anglo-Australian and Japanese people picnicking together in a national park. The act of huddling together as a social or familial unit and posing for the camera was part of the social activities that connected Kagiyama to his sitters.

---

15   Melissa Miles, 'Ichiro Kagiyama in Early Twentieth Century Sydney', *Japanese Studies* 37, no. 1 (2017): 89–116.
16   Oliver, 'Japanese Relationships in White Australia', 5.16.

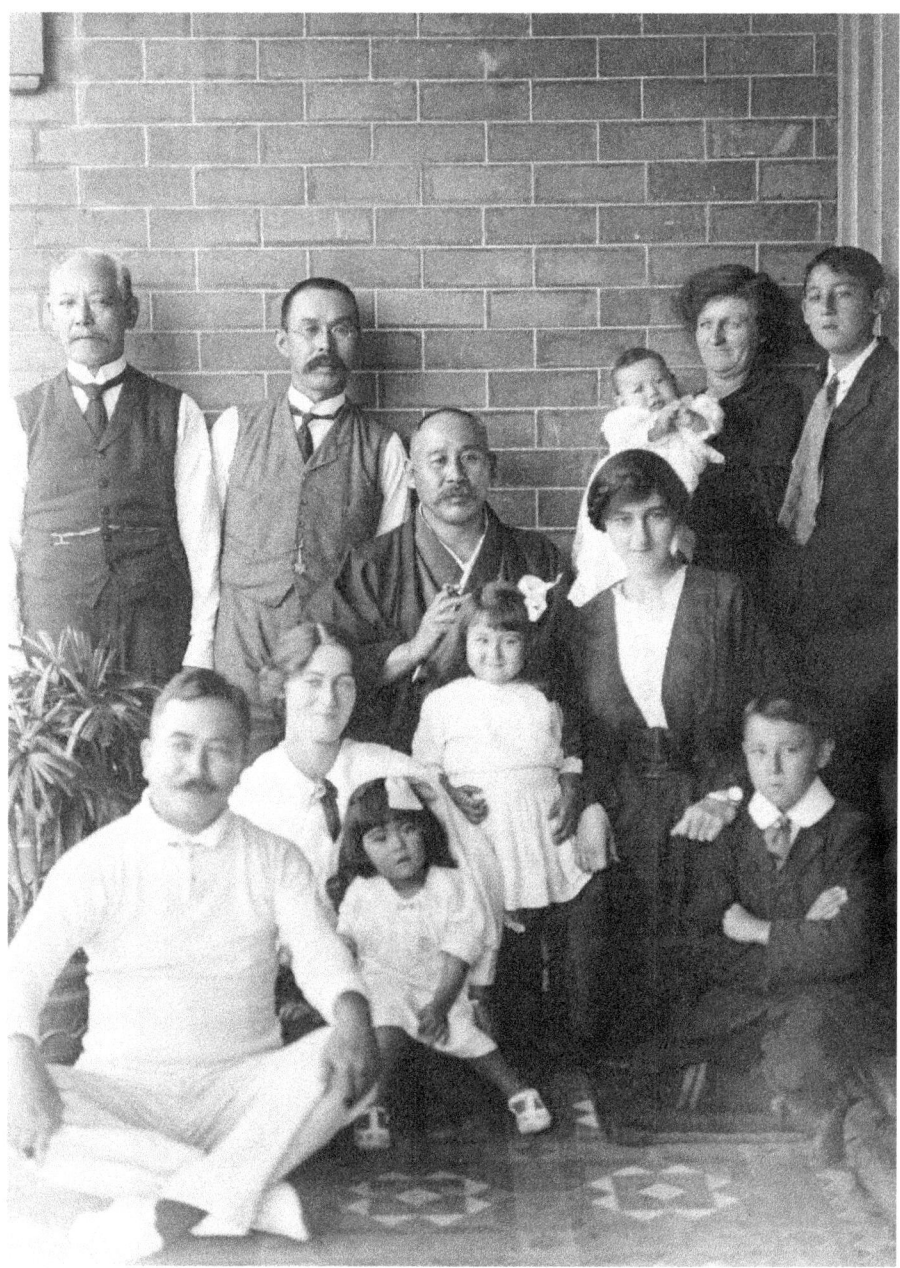

Figure 2.2. Attributed to Ichiro Kagiyama, *Untitled [Portrait of Japanese-Australian Family]*, c. 1915.
Source: Private Collection.

In 1915, Kagiyama photographed Hideo Kuwahata, his English-born Australian wife Mary, their sons Thomas and Frederick, and other unknown Japanese guests at the family home, Mikado Farm. After Kuwahata came to Australia in 1888, he established a small import business in Sydney. He soon expanded the business to supply shipping companies Nippon Yusen Kaisha and Osaka Shosen Kaisha and the Japanese Navy. Mikado Farm in Guildford, NSW, became Kuwahata's home in 1908. It also operated as a nursery specialising in Japanese plants. The farm was an important social space for Japanese residents and visitors to Sydney who would visit Kuwahata's home for weekends of fishing, photography and picnics. According to Pam Oliver, 'over 80 per cent of sailors off Japanese ships at Sydney and Newcastle before 1920 gave this farm as their shore address'.[17] As well as being behind the lens, Kagiyama appears with the family in some of his photographs of Mikado Farm, suggesting a personal relationship. One photograph featuring Kagiyama, Hideo and Mary Kuwahata and an unidentified guest has been hand coloured in an effort to communicate some of the vibrancy of Kuwahata's gardens (see Figure 2.3). Although the result is somewhat crude, the use of this time-consuming process to colour the flowers, grass, trees, bridge, greenhouse and clothing worn by the sitters speaks to the value that this place held for Kagiyama.

Photography and *Japonisme*

Compellingly, these cross-cultural social relationships flourished amid a public culture in which Japanese racial stereotypes ran deep. Kagiyama lived and worked in a city enamoured of things Japanese. Described today as part of a European trend known as *Japonisme*,[18] the fashionable presence of Japanese-inspired decorative arts, kimono, floral arrangements and silks in Sydney's shops and visual culture provided inspiration to several local photographers and shaped the reception of Kagiyama's work. The popularity of Japanese art and goods from the mid-1910s to the mid-1930s followed an earlier wave of *Japonisme*, which was fostered by the enthusiastic reception of the Japanese courts and products at the

---

17   Pam Oliver, 'Interpreting "Japanese Activities" in Australia, 1888–1945', *Journal of the Australian War Memorial* (online), no. 36 (May 2002), unpaginated.
18   For more on *Japonisme* see Lionel Lambourne, *Japonisme: Cultural Crossings between Japan and the West* (London and New York: Phaidon, 2005); Toshio Watanabe, *High Victorian Japonisme* (Berlin and New York: Peter Lang, 1991).

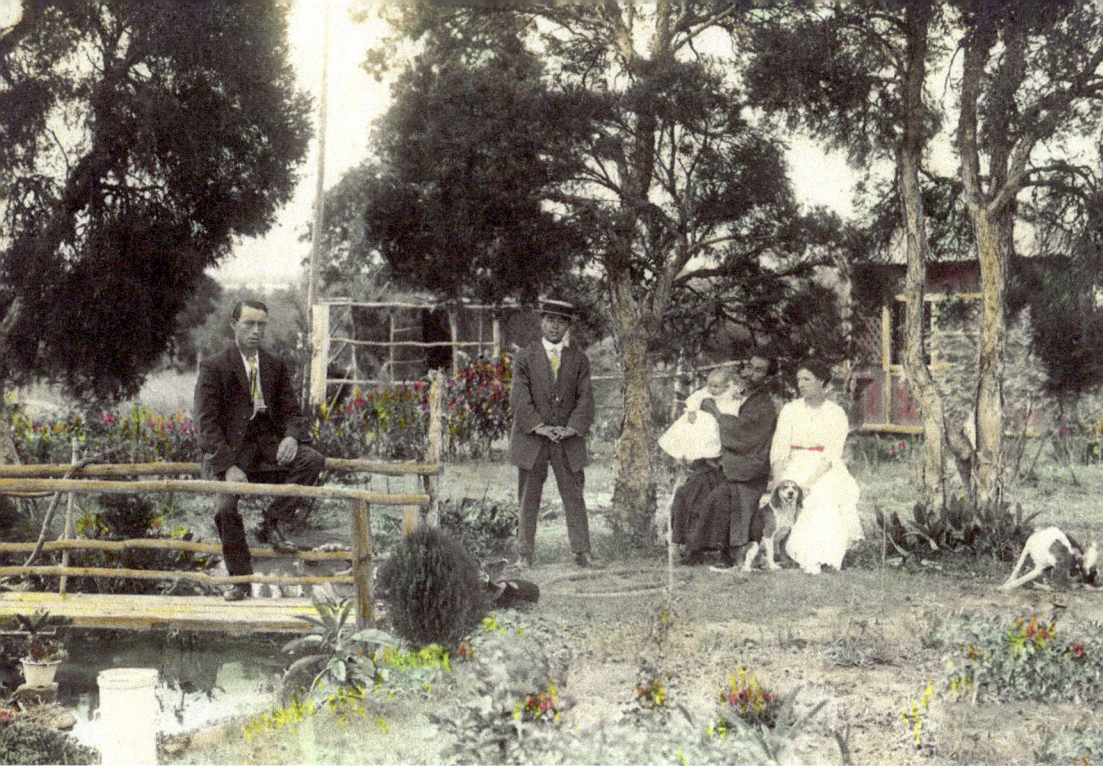

Figure 2.3. Photographer unknown, *Mikado Farm*, Guildford, 1915.
Source: Private Collection.

Sydney and Melbourne International and Intercolonial exhibitions of 1875, 1877, 1879 and 1880. The ready availability of Japanese goods in Australian stores further fed this burgeoning market, and Japanese motifs and aesthetics soon found their way into Australian art, such as Charles Condor's paintings *Bronte Beach* (1888) and *A Holiday at Mentone* (1888), and Tom Roberts's portrait *Mrs L. A. Abrahams* (1888). The second wave of *Japonisme* in the early twentieth century was the product of several additional factors including increased Australian tourism to Japan and strengthening political, military and trade relations.

This trend was strongly evident in Sydney's photography culture. From 1911, the Sydney-based publication *Harrington's Photographic Journal* often included illustrated articles on the delights promised by Japan as a travel destination for the photographer and the latest Japanese photography journals and books that could be purchased.[19] The British

---

19 See for example 'From all Quarters', *Harrington's Photographic Journal*, 22 February 1911, 59; Rita Broughton, 'Snapshots in Japan', *Harrington's Photographic Journal*, 22 April 1911, 110; Neville A. Tooth, 'A Camera in Japan', *Harrington's Photographic Journal*, 22 December 1911, 380–81; 'New Books', *Harrington's Photographic Journal*, 22 August 1919, 258; C. Taylor, 'Snapshots on Japan', *Harrington's Photographic Journal*, 22 April 1914, 119, 132; 'Our Illustrations', *Harrington's Photographic Journal*, 20 August 1919, 242, 249.

annual *Photograms of the Year* disseminated the work of Japanese photographers internationally from 1914. Read eagerly in Australia, this publication also routinely featured the work of Australian pictorialists including members of the Photographic Society of NSW. The Japanese photographs selected for publication were dominated overwhelmingly by imagery of bathhouses, pagodas, geishas, bamboo and idyllic rural scenes. These clichés were so entrenched that in 1915 they inspired a protest by photographer H. Yahagi in one of his regular written contributions to *Photograms of the Year*:

> I would like to preface my remarks about the pictorial photography of Japan by drawing attention to the fact that we, as a nation, deeply regret the misunderstanding that exists with regard to Japan and its people. It seems strange that in these days of travel, when the nations of the world are linked together by steamboats and Continental railways, there should still be a lingering idea in the world that Japan is only a half-civilised land, the principal attraction of which is the questionable Geisha, the old dreamy pagoda rearing its head above the pines, the Ronin of a bygone age, and the feathery bamboo groves—sure symbols of a primitive people. Such are to be seen, but they do not constitute the things that enable one to get to the heart of modern Japan.[20]

Yahagi went on to cite the many admirable qualities of modern Japan, including its education system, respect for modern science and interest in international affairs. However, his plea fell on deaf ears, as *Photograms of the Year* continued to publish photographs based on a very limited range of stereotypes for decades to come.

Not only did Kagiyama encounter such stereotypes on spectacular display in Sydney, he also turned them into subjects for his own photographs. In 1915, Kagiyama took three photographs of the Japanese Village in the White City amusement park, which operated in the Sydney suburb of Rushcutters Bay between 1913 and 1917 (see Figures 2.4 and 2.5). Sydney's White City was one of dozens of similarly named amusement parks established in the US, Britain and Australia. Inspired by the White City and Midway Plaisance sections of Chicago's World's Columbian Exhibition of 1893, White Cities typically combined entertainment with 'educational' displays and experiences such as a 'native village'.

---

20   H. Yahagi, 'Pictorial Photography in Japan', *Photograms of the Year 1915* (London: Dawbarn & Ward, 1916), 27.

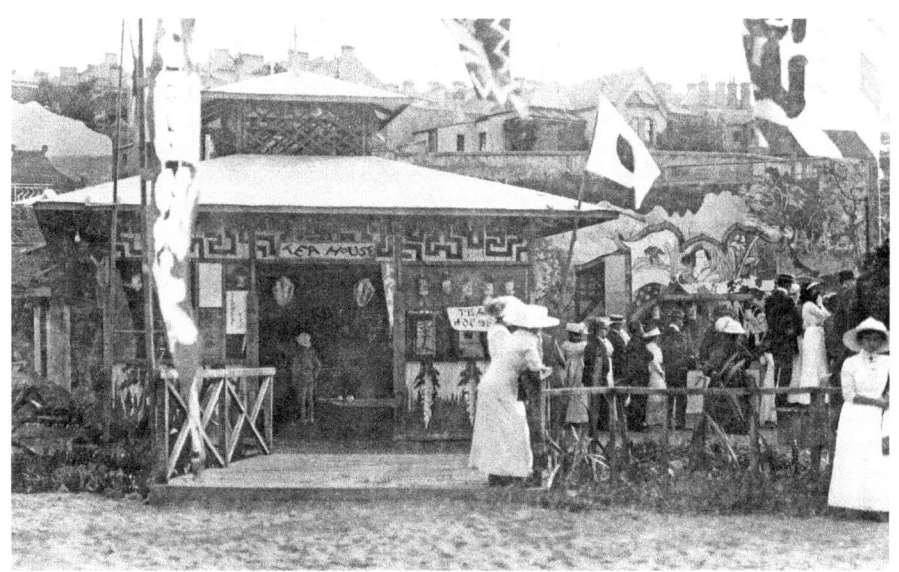

Figure 2.4. Attributed to Ichiro Kagiyama, *Untitled [White City]*, c. 1915.
Source: Private Collection.

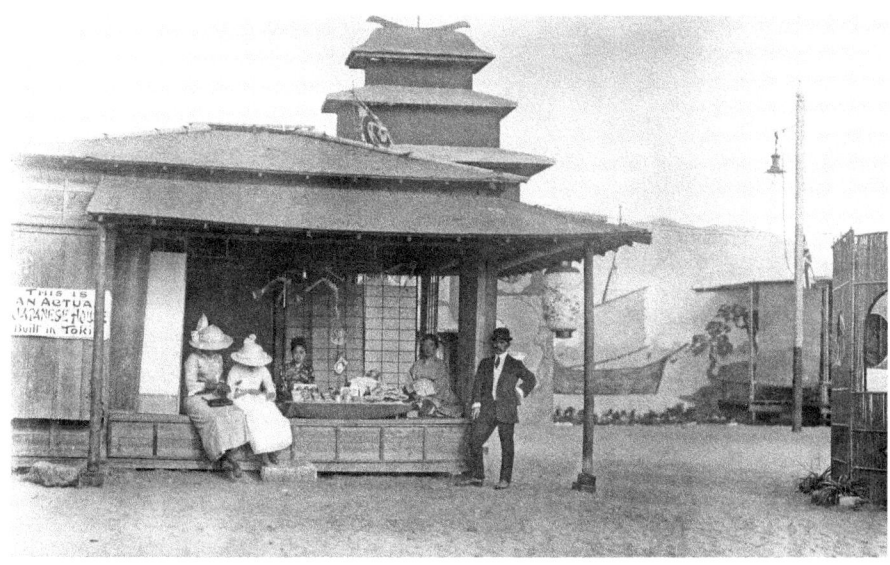

Figure 2.5. Attributed to Ichiro Kagiyama, *Untitled [White City]*, c. 1915.
Source: Private Collection.

55

The promise of a 'real' Japanese encounter recurred in press coverage of Sydney's White City. The *Truth* promoted the Japanese Village as one of the most interesting attractions:

> There has been no attempt at artifice in the creation of this model village—everything is real and directly imported. Real Japanese houses, flower gardens, museums, temples, workshops, lily ponds, and the innumerable crazy, curved, and twisted bridges, without which no Japanese picture would be correct.[21]

The presence of acrobats, contortionists, sword swallowers and 'Samurai sword-dualists' did not dampen enthusiasm for the supposed realism of the village.[22]

Kagiyama's photographs of the Japanese Village suggest that this supposedly 'authentic' cultural encounter was underpinned by familiar stereotypes. The photographs show the large crowds of Anglo-Australians who flocked to the Japanese Village, its teahouse, kimono-wearing women attendants, Japanese garden and pond, decorative bridge, and buildings adorned with flags and lanterns. Murals crudely interpreting Japanese prints, and screens depicting a sailboat and a figure with irises, form evocative backdrops. It is intriguing to imagine how Kagiyama made sense of this spectacle. His photographs seem to treat the village and its hordes of visitors as a curiosity; they are photographed in a somewhat stark manner, rather than as a subject for creative expression to be artfully composed. One photograph (Figure 2.5) centres on a house in which kimono-clad Japanese women sell fans, bowls and mobiles to visitors. Kagiyama deliberately includes the large sign proclaiming 'this is an actual Japanese House built in Tokio', which could have easily been cropped out of the photograph. He perhaps found these claims for authenticity amusing.

Australian stereotypes of a feminine, artistic and childlike Japan were perpetuated in the press, and in turn shaped the experiences of other visitors to the village. In the 'Woman's Page' in the *Freeman's Journal,* a writer described the village as 'very fascinating' and 'truly Japanese':

---

21   'The White City', *Truth*, 28 December 1913, 3. See also 'A New Amusement Centre for Sydney', *Sunday Times*, 19 October 1913, 6.
22   'The White City', *Freeman's Journal*, 18 December 1913, 25.

Several Japanese families are in actual residence there, and one may wander through the quaint little houses and carry on a conversation with the inmates … There is a tea-house where a charming Madame Butterfly dispenses tea in truly Japanese fashion, whilst her little son, six or even seven years old, talks to the visitors and begs them to come again with a perfectly delightful accent.[23]

The author's reference to Madame Butterfly underscores the importance of theatre in propagating impressions of Japan. David Belasco's play *Madame Butterfly: A Tragedy of Japan* toured Australia early in the century, while Puccini's opera, which was based on the same story, made its Australian debut in 1910. Other immensely popular Japanese-inspired performances of this period include *The Mikado*, *The Geisha*, *Moonlight Blossom*, *The Japanese Nightingale* and *The Darling of the Gods*.[24] These performances helped to cement romantic notions of Japan as a feminine and artistic land in the minds of many Australians.

Some of these stereotypes informed the work of Kagiyama's peers in the Photographic Society of NSW. Monte Luke's photograph *The Girl in the Kimona* (c. 1919) was published in *Harringtons' Photographic Journal* in 1919 (see Figure 2.6). Now known only through this magazine reproduction, this full-length portrait of an Anglo-European woman wearing a sumptuous embroidered kimono diverges from Luke's more well-known landscape photographs and portraits. Wearing chrysanthemums in her hair and clutching an arrangement of chrysanthemums and wheat, *The Girl in the Kimona* embodies contemporary perceptions of Japan as the delicate, feminine and exotic 'Land of the Chrysanthemum', made famous decades earlier in Pierre Loti's book *Madame Chrysanthème* (1888). The dramatic stance of Luke's model mirrors the posture of popular Japanese dolls sold as tourist souvenirs and collectables, and photographed later by Kagiyama (see Figure 2.7). So familiar were audiences with these highly stylised signifiers of Japan that they crystallised as truth; the editors of *Harringtons' Photographic Journal* proclaimed that Luke's model's 'bend of the knees gives the true Japanese effect'.[25]

---

23 'Woman's Page', *Freeman's Journal*, 1 January 1914, 29.
24 Darryl Collins, 'Emperors and Musume: China and Japan "on the Boards" in Australia, 1850s–1920s', *East Asian History* 7 (June 1994): 67–92.
25 'Our Illustrations', 242.

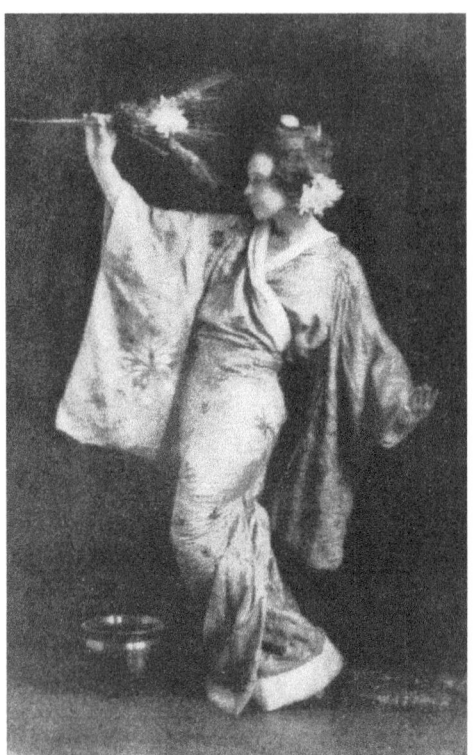 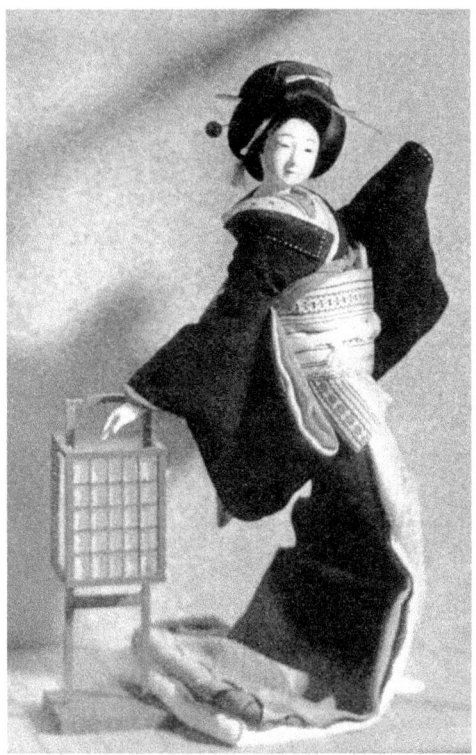

Figure 2.6. Monte Luke, *The Girl in the Kimona*.
Source: *Harrington's Photographic Journal*, 20 August 1919, 249.

Figure 2.7. Ichiro Kagiyama, *Untitled [Japanese Dancing Doll]*.
Source: *The Home*, July 1940, 46.

Wartime Ambivalences

While these Japanese-inspired photographs and the enthusiastic public reception of White City's Japanese Village suggest broad public support for Japan, behind the scenes Japan's growing military might and participation in WWI generated significant political anxiety and diplomatic tension. Kagiyama was a keen observer at Sydney's public celebrations of Japan's military capacity. Six photographs in his personal album focus on military parades in which Japanese flags decorate the city among the flags of other Allied nations. One of these captures the celebrations as crowds watch a passing convoy of cars decorated with Japanese national flags, naval flags and flowers (see Figure 2.8). Kagiyama stood in the thick of the parade, at street level between the procession and long line of spectators. The exaggerated perspective that results heightens the atmosphere so that we can almost hear the cars rattle and rumble past the cheering crowd.

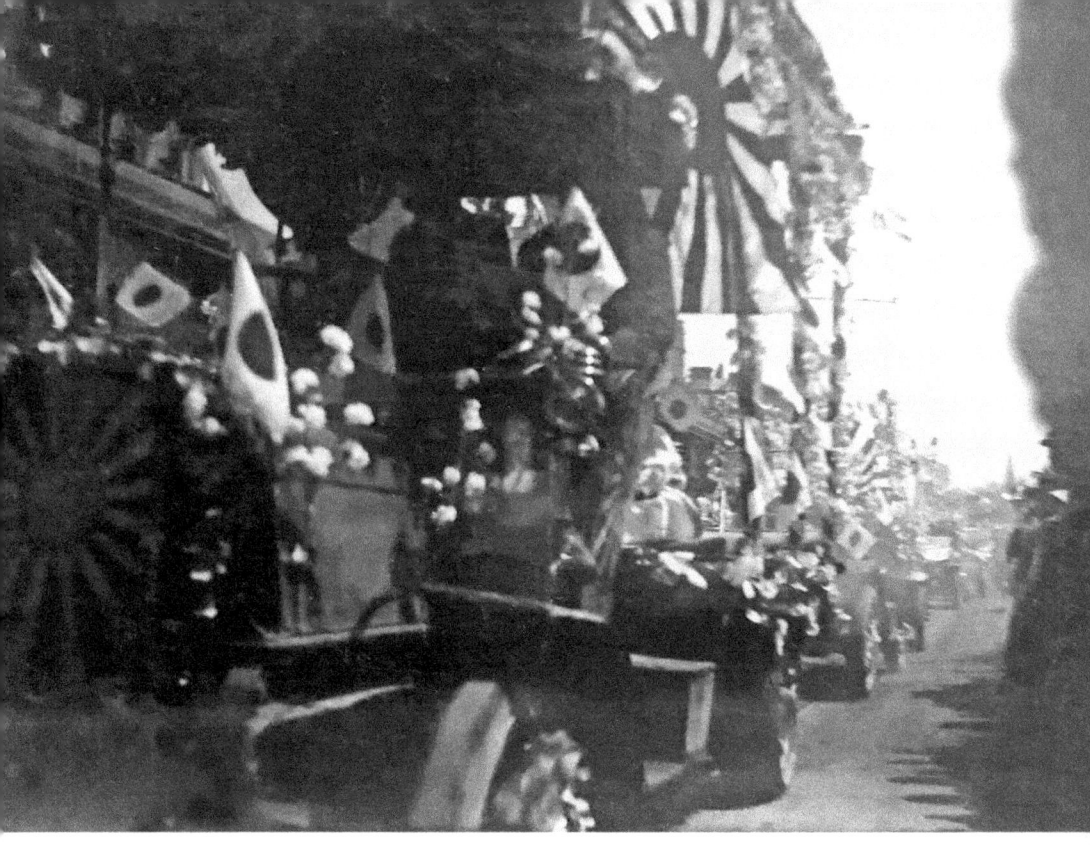

Figure 2.8. Attributed to Ichiro Kagiyama, *Untitled [Parade]*, c. 1915.
Source: Private Collection.

However, news reports in the Japanese press about its future southward expansion and ongoing diplomatic disputes about Australia's efforts to limit Japanese immigration fuelled official concerns about Japan's motives for supporting Britain during WWI.[26] One fear was that Japan would seek rewards for its wartime service and pressure the Commonwealth to allow its citizens to enter Australia freely. The Australian government was also troubled that Japan could secure former German territories in the Pacific, leaving Australia vulnerable to future attacks from the north. Japanese Consul General Shimizu urged his audience at a gathering in Sydney in 1915 to 'most earnestly disabuse your minds of the suspicion that we have an ulterior or sinister objective in view'.[27] However, those suspicions continued to rise, and were reinforced by a major Naval

---

26 L.F. Fitzhardinge, 'Australia, Japan and Great Britain, 1914–18: A Study in Triangular Diplomacy', *Historical Studies* 14, no. 54 (1970): 250–59; Neville Meaney, *Australia and World Crisis 1914–1923* (Sydney: Sydney University Press, 2009), 124–30.
27 'Japan's Loyalty', *Western Champion*, 29 April 1915, 29.

Board survey of Japan's status as a strategic threat.[28] One Japanese diplomat commented on the effects of this atmosphere on Japanese photographers: 'If they see our tourists taking photographs in the streets, they immediately think that they are spies. They fear Japan in the way you fear a bogeyman in the dark'.[29]

In the aftermath of WWI, the cumulative success of Japan's military and its seemingly inevitable place as one of the world's great powers exacerbated anxieties about maintaining a 'White Australia'. Japanese photographers were again placed under suspicion. Captain Longfield Lloyd, a member of Army Intelligence commented:

> The use of cameras by Japanese ship officers is proverbial, and indicates either a most remarkable liking for photography on the part of the Japanese, or a careful and consistent encouragement in the use of the camera by their Government.

Lloyd described how, at the end of the war, there was 'an epidemic of photography by the officers of Japanese vessels in Sydney'. These officers were typically placed under surveillance, and if they were seen photographing within the Port of Sydney the *War Precautions Act 1914* was invoked to seize their cameras, destroy their negatives and forward their empty cameras to the Japanese consul general with a written reprimand for the captain and crew. Lloyd was concerned that:

> With constant photography on the part of almost every Japanese officer who comes to the port, some negatives at least would be valuable to an Intelligence Bureau engaged in building up a complete system of local knowledge.[30]

According to Henry Frei, 'Australian Japanophobia rose to a crescendo' at the Paris Peace Conference of 1919, the year that Ishida arrived in Sydney.[31] Prime Minster Hughes fought to quash Japan's proposed racial equality clause in the League of Nations preamble, resist Japan's claims to the German possessions in the south-west Pacific and secure those islands as what the *Weekly Times* described as 'White Australia's Bulwarks'

---

28   See Navy Department Reports 'The Japanese Danger', 'Problems of Pacific Defence' and 'Post-Bellum Naval Policy for the Pacific', October 1915, Papers of William Morris Hughes, National Library of Australia MS 1538/156/7 and AAMP1049/1 file 14/0285.
29   D.C.S. Sissons, 'Australian Fears of Japan as a Defence Threat 1895–1971', Papers of D.C.S. Sissons, National Library of Australia MS 3092, Series 1, Box I, Folder 2.
30   Longfield Lloyd, 'Japan Espionage – General', NAA A981/1, JAP 55, 137–39.
31   Frei, *Japan's Southward Advance and Australia*, 109.

2. 'WHITE AUSTRALIA' IN THE DARKROOM

against Japan.[32] Suspicion of Japanese intentions towards Australia escalated, so much so that during celebrations for the emperor's birthday at the Japanese Consulate in Sydney in 1920 a senior political dignitary, R.W. Caldwell, made an apology to the acting consul general in front of the assembled politicians, diplomats, businessmen and military men:

> I avail myself of this opportunity to express my deep regret and shame at the recrudescence of anti-Japanese prejudice, which has taken place in Australia since the conclusion of the late war. So many of the prognostications of anti-Japanese prophets were disproved by the faithful performance of her treaty obligations by Japan during the great struggle that her detractors have had to take a new position. They deny that Japan did anything at all during the war, or assert that, if she did, she did it from interested motives.[33]

Tensions were exacerbated by a postwar naval arms race between the US and Japan that raised renewed fears of war on Australia's doorstep. However, the situation changed at the Washington Conference of 1921–22. The resultant Four Power Treaty between the US, Japan, the British Empire and France involved an agreement to respect one another's possessions and dominions in the Pacific, while the Five Power Treaty eased the pressure of the arms race by limiting naval construction until 1936. The conference ushered in a new period of optimism and confidence towards Japan.[34] In the wake of this event, Defence Minister George Pearce declared in parliament that Australia was beginning a new era of peaceful relations with the 'Far North'. Pearce noted that while 'Australians were Europeans in race they were geographically in Asia', and that it was therefore critical that peace in the Pacific was maintained.[35]

Aesthetic Relations Between the Wars

Despite the tensions of the Peace Conference, Ishida received a warm welcome into Sydney's photography community after arriving in 1919. Ishida brought a camera with him so that he could send snapshots home to his parents, but took up photography seriously after meeting Kagiyama

---

32 'White Australia's Bulwarks', *Weekly Times*, 8 February 1919, 29.
33 'Japan. The Emperor's Birthday. Relations with Britain', *Sydney Morning Herald*, 1 November 1920, 8.
34 D.C.S. Sissons, 'Attitudes to Japan and Defence, 1890–1923' (MA thesis, University of Melbourne, 1956), 101–24.
35 'Washington Conference. Speech by Senator', *West Australian*, 28 July 1922.

and receiving some lessons from his new friend. Kagiyama invited Ishida to join the Photographic Society of NSW and by 1920 Ishida was successfully entering his photographs in national and international competitions, exhibitions and salons including the 1920 London Salon. President of the Photographic Society of NSW, D.J. Webster, encapsulated Ishida's dramatic rise to prominence when he described him in 1922 as 'that photographic meteorite from the East that swooped down in our midst with hurricane suddenness'.[36] In another article dedicated to Ishida, published the same year in *Harrington's Photographic Journal*, Webster wrote glowingly of the photographer:

> I do not know of one who is more versatile or more consistently prolific … He is keen, enthusiastic and receptive, with an aesthetic temperament, that I am sure will carry him even higher up the pictorial ladder.[37]

Ishida quickly mastered the control processes that the pictorialists admired, especially bromoil. This technique allowed practitioners to limit their photographs' tonal range and eliminate detail, leaving a soft, matt surface. Ishida's work so impressed Sydney's leading photographers that in 1921 he was invited to become a member of the exclusive Sydney Camera Circle. It is telling that Australian journalists covering the 1922 and 1923 London Salons of Photography described Ishida as one of the Australian exhibitors.[38] Practically and aesthetically, he was an Australian photographer. Ishida learned about composition and lighting from members of the Photographic Society and Sydney Camera Circle, and on group outings they photographed beach scenes, pastoral idylls and bush landscapes. Ishida's photographs unsurprisingly bear similarities to the work of his peers. *A White Gum* (c. 1922) (see Figure 2.9), which Ishida presented in the 1922 Photographic Society of NSW exhibition, reflects the popularity of photographing single, majestic gum trees in Australian pictorialism. Such photographs were often given patriotic titles, such as John Kauffmann's *The Battler*, *The Survivor* and *Victory* (all published in his 1919 monograph *The Art of John Kauffmann*), Eutrope's *Guardian Gum* (c. 1920–30) and Eaton's *In Stately Splendor* (1929). Although Ishida did not opt for such a title, he similarly framed *A White Gum* in

---

36 D.J. Webster, 'Photographic Society of New South Wales', *Harrington's Photographic Journal*, 1 November 1922, 14.
37 D.J. Webster, 'Mr K. Ishida', *Harrington's Photographic Journal*, 1 September 1922, 23.
38 'Salon of Photography', *Northern Star*, 10 September 1923, 5; 'Salon of Photography', *Examiner*, 10 September 1923, 4; 'General Cable News', *West Australian*, 10 September 1923, 7; 'Photography. Australians' Good Work', *Daily Herald*, 16 September 1922, 5.

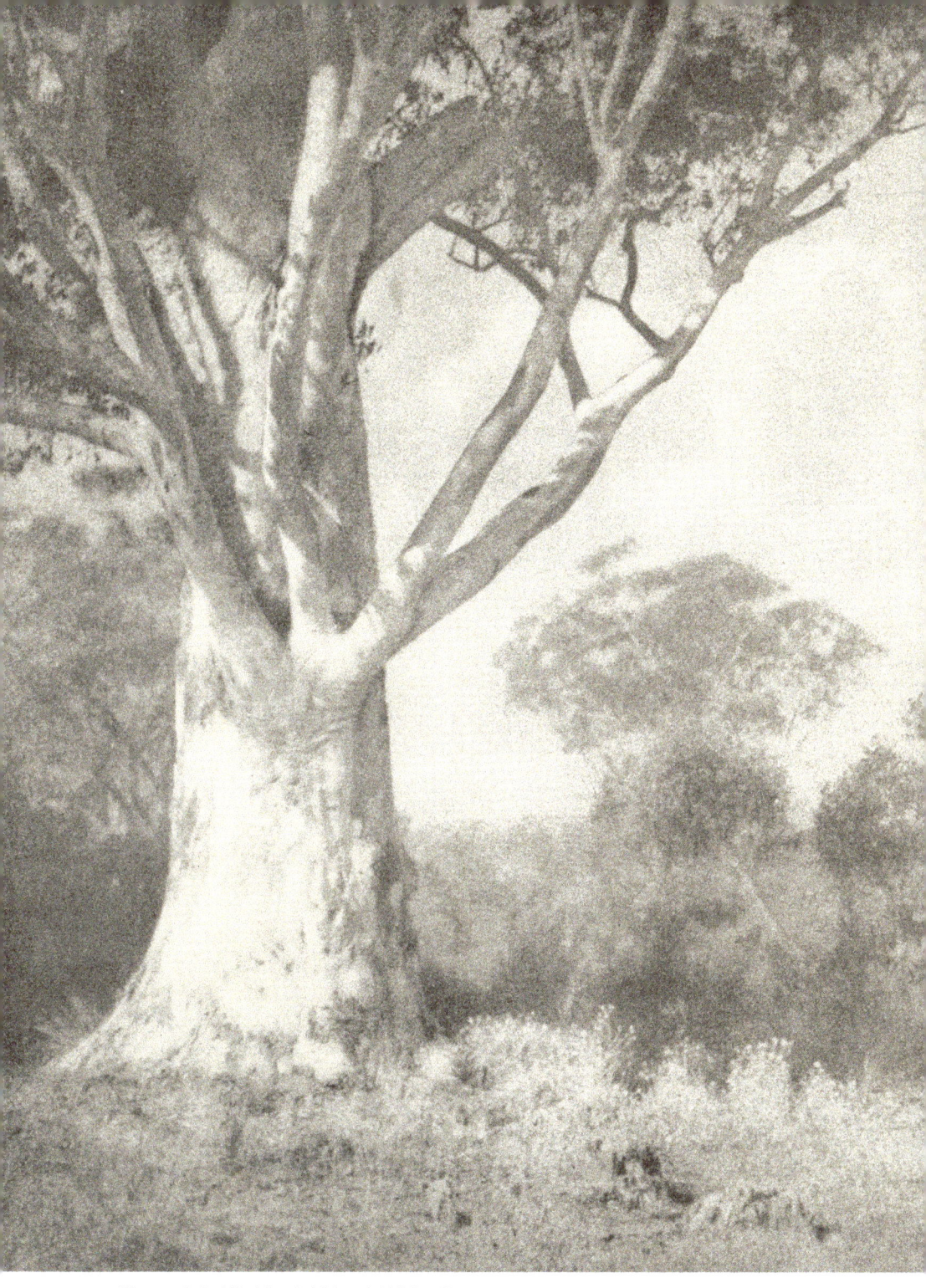

Figure 2.9. Kiichiro Ishida, *A White Gum*.
Source: *Catalogue of an Exhibition Camera Pictures by the Photographic Society of N.S.W., 1922* (Sydney: Photographic Society of New South Wales, 1922), plate V.

a manner that monumentalises the tree. The use of bromoil to soften the scrubby undergrowth accentuates the pictorial authority of the tree and emphasises its thick trunk and enormous branches.

Looking at the variety of Ishida's work from this period, which included photographs of industrial workers, city scenes, portraits, landscapes and still life, it is not surprising that Webster described him as 'one of Australia's leading Pictorialists'. Webster continued, 'when we consider that Australia has such camera artists as Cazneaux and Smith, of Sydney, Kauffman and Temple Stephens, of Adelaide, this is a great compliment to our little friend from Japan'.[39] Webster's description of Ishida as 'our little friend from Japan' will likely be jarring to contemporary readers. Although Ishida was respected by the photography community in Sydney as one of its own, Webster's allusion to stereotypes of the childlike Japanese highlights how old, entrenched racial prejudices can nonetheless seep into supposedly positive, personal and artistic relations.

As well as sharing characteristics of Australian pictorialism, the work of Ishida and some his Anglo-Australian peers reveal evidence of a common interest in Japanese compositional devices. As seen in *ukiyo-e* woodblock prints, Ishida's *Mountain Decoration* (see Figure 2.10) features branches and foliage that act as a screen through which the distant landscape is viewed. Ishida's use of light, shade and contrast also works to reduce the Australian mountain range to a series of imbricated planes in a manner that recalls Japanese *sumi-e* black ink scroll paintings. It is not clear whether Ishida was consciously imaging the Australian landscape using Japanese composition or applying photography lessons that he learned in Australia. Cazneaux's landscape *The Bidding of Spring* (later retitled *Spring Time*) (c. 1919), Kauffmann's *Thro' the Fog* (c. 1919) and Stanley Eutrope's *Winter's Curtain* (c. 1922) (see Figure 2.11) affirm that Australians were experimenting with the Japanese 'photography of hanging branches'[40] before and after Ishida's arrival in Australia. Eutrope used bromoil in *Winter's Curtain* to dissolve some of the detail of the distant river and bridge, and flatten and radically simplify the pictorial plane. Seen through the 'curtain' of weeping winter foliage, the view and its watery reflection seem to merge into one space. Ishida may

---

39   Webster, 'Photographic Society of New South Wales', 14.
40   F.C. Tilney, 'American Work at the London Exhibitions', *American Photography* 21, no. 12 (December 1927): 666.

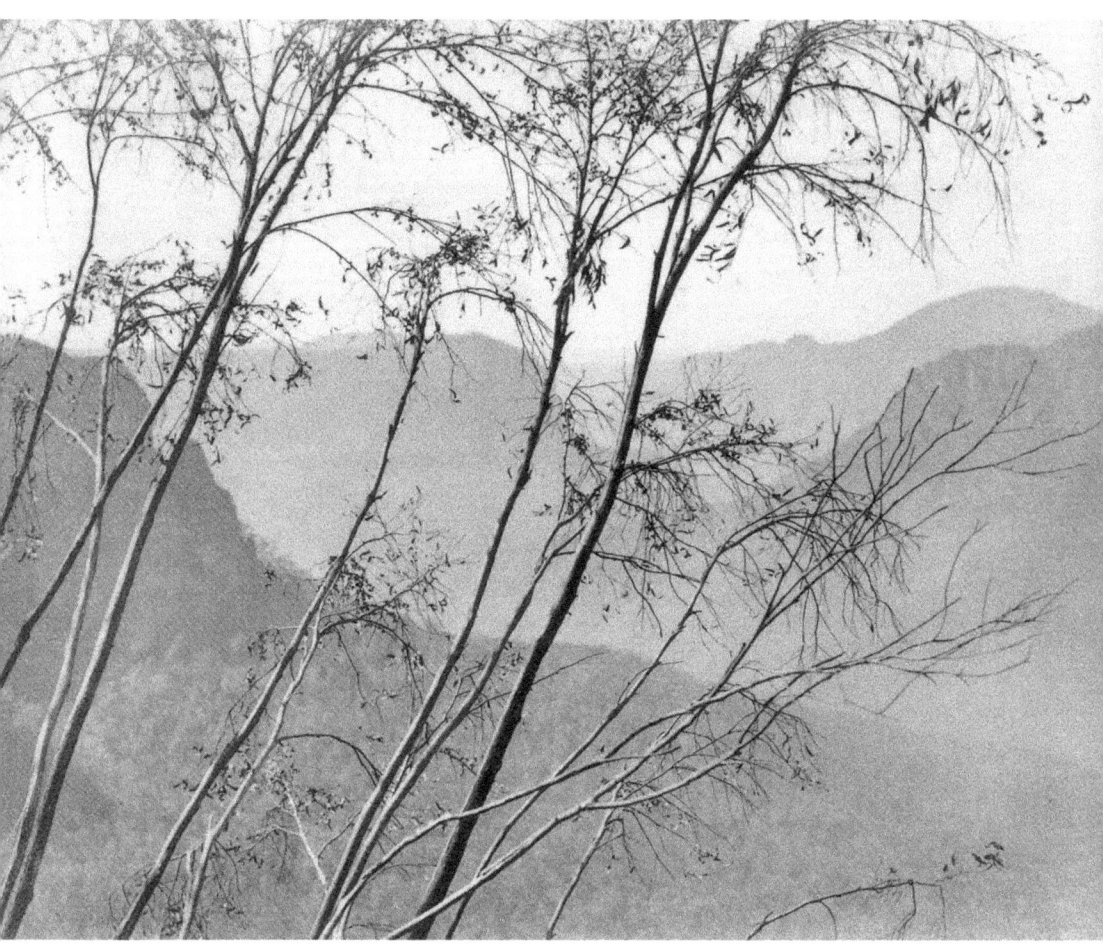

Figure 2.10. Kiichiro Ishida, *Mountain Decoration*.
Source: *Photograms of the Year 1923* (London: Iliffe & Sons Ltd, 1924).

Figure 2.11. Stanley Eutrope, *Winter's Curtain*, c. 1922.
Source: Gallery of Modern Art, Brisbane.

have also seen these techniques in *Photograms of the Year*, particularly in US photographer Rupert Lovejoy's own *Mountain Decoration* published in 1919.

Although today's curators and commentators have noted these links between modernist Australian photographs and Japanese prints, when Cazneaux's and Eutrope's photographs were originally published and exhibited in Australia their nods to Japanese art went unmentioned.[41] J.T. Farrell, editor of *Harringtons' Photographic Journal*, described Cazneaux's *The Bidding of Spring* in 1919 as 'a creation of the fancy, with delicate tone values and light tracery symbolical of the artist's conception of the impression of Spring'.[42] Similarly, when Eutrope's photograph was published in *Cameragraphs of the Year 1924*, Cazneaux praised the bromoil for its rendition of the 'tender passage of light' and made no mention of a Japanese influence.[43] The fact that this two-way exchange of Australian and Japanese compositional devices was unremarkable at the time suggests they were part of a relaxed and open exchange of pictorial ideas and images that were not necessarily fixed to national identities or clearly delineated patterns of cross-cultural appropriation.

The creative and interpersonal exchange between Ishida, Kagiyama and Sydney's leading photographers continued after Ishida's departure in December 1923. Before he left, Ishida donated 10 pounds to the Sydney Camera Circle and asked that in return each of its members give him some prints as a memento. Ishida took 25 of their prints back to Japan, along with prints by Kagiyama, and exhibited 15 of them at the Shiseido Gallery in Ginza in March 1924 with 31 of his own photographs. The exhibition was highly praised and works by Sydney Camera Circle members were subsequently published in the Japanese periodical *Asahi Camera* in 1926 and 1927. A Japanese translation of a profile on Monte Luke written by US photographer and critic Sigismund Blumann was also published in *Asahi Camera* alongside examples of Luke's work in May 1926, exposing Japanese audiences to the work and reputation of this Australian.[44]

---

41 For example, see the discussion of Cazneaux's *Spring Time* in Judy Annear, 'Kiichiro Ishida and the Sydney Camera Circle', *Look*, December 2003, 19.
42 J.T. Farrell, 'Our Illustrations', *Harrington's Photographic Journal*, 15 October 1919, 312.
43 Harold Cazneaux, 'A Review of the Pictures', in *Cameragraphs of the Year 1924*, ed. Cecil W. Bostock (Sydney: Harringtons, 1924).
44 Sigismund Blumann, 'Monte Luke. An Artist Who Illuminates Australia's Fame', *Asahi Camera*, May 1926, 120.

The Home and the 1930s

The open exchange between Kagiyama, Ishida and the amateur photographic society in the 1920s contrasts with the fetishisation of Kagiyama's Japanese vision in his early contributions to *The Home*. Before Kagiyama took work with *The Home* in 1935, the magazine developed an established record for promoting Japanese-inspired art and design to its readers as the height of modern fashion. Produced in Sydney by the artist, publisher and high profile figure in the Australian art world, Sydney Ure Smith,[45] *The Home* aimed to raise the tastes of Australians by presenting the best products and people using the best production values.[46] The cover of the first issue of *The Home* in 1920 featured a woman holding a Japanese umbrella, and was followed by several cover designs in the coming years inspired by Japanese woodblock prints.[47] The cover of the summer 1921 issue, designed by Bertha Sloane, draws on the simplicity, crisp outlines and bright colours of Japanese woodblocks to image a stylishly dressed Australian woman enjoying time at the beach with her children (see Figure 2.12). She sits beneath a bamboo-framed Japanese umbrella decorated with colourful blossoms, which occupies the central focal point of the composition. Readers of *The Home* were also able to witness the impact of Japanese woodcuts on Thea Proctor's fashion illustrations and fan designs, and on Margaret Preston's still life paintings.[48]

Other issues throughout the 1920s and 1930s featured photographs by Max Dupain and Spencer Shier of Australian society ladies and models wearing kimonos or clutching sprigs of cherry blossom, and articles promoting the art of Japanese floral arrangement or design.[49] Cazneaux took a number of jobs for *The Home* in the 1920s and 1930s in which he photographed the homes of significant figures in Australia–Japan relations. In the late 1920s, he travelled to Mikado Farm to photograph Hideo Kuwahata's gardens. Cazneaux's photographs of Kuwahata's bonsais featured in the same issue as his photograph of the iris pond

---

45   Although Ure Smith sold *The Home* to John Fairfax & Sons Ltd in 1934, he continued to act as editor until 1938.
46   Sydney Ure Smith, 'The Story of the Home', *The Home*, March 1930, 60.
47   Other Japanese-inspired covers were featured in the February 1920, December 1921, December 1922 and January 1932 issues of *The Home*.
48   See *The Home*, March 1923; June 1934; December 1934.
49   *The Home* February 1926; July 1935; April 1937; May 1932.

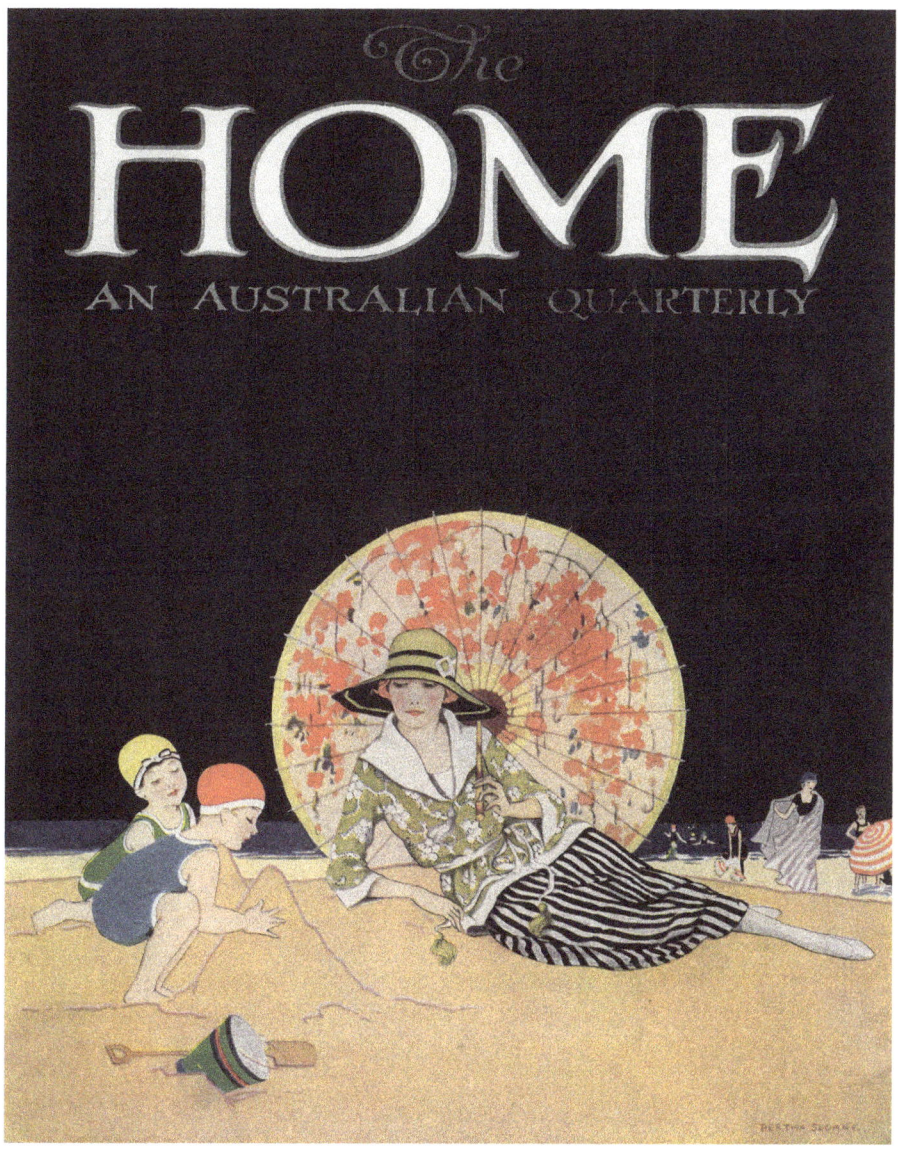

Figure 2.12. Cover design for *The Home*, December 1921.

at 'Rivenhall', the Japanese-inspired home and garden of Arthur Sadler in the upper north shore suburb of Warrawee.[50] Sadler was professor of Oriental Studies at the University of Sydney between 1922 and 1947, and known for his collection of Japanese art.[51]

The prevalence of Japanese motifs in *The Home* was complemented by articles and photographic portraits of Japanese dignitaries, including Madame K. Inoue, the wife of the former Japanese consul general in Australia; Count Kato, the prime minister of Japan; Japan's new princess Shigeko, Teru-no-Miya; and Iemasa Tokugawa, the first Japanese minister to Canada and his family.[52] This promotion of Japan reflects Ure Smith's longstanding interest in Japanese culture. The publisher was a supporter of the Australia-Japan Society and socialised with Sydney's Japanese merchants, diplomats and Japanophiles.[53] As a guest at Japanese consul events, including official celebrations of the emperor's birthday in 1930, 1931 and 1932, Ure Smith mixed with the consul general and senior Japanese merchants of Sydney, as well as figures like Sadler. In 1935, Ure Smith also undertook discussions 'with a Japanese authority' in the hope of leading to an exchange of Japanese and Australian art exhibitions.[54]

It is likely that Ure Smith's interest in Japan led him to hire Kagiyama as a photographer for *The Home*. By this stage, Kagiyama had opened his own studio, counting as clients the *Sydney Morning Herald* and the Atlantic Union Oil Company among other firms. Although Kagiyama's photographs of contemporary Sydney contrasted with the Japanese-inspired imagery that pervaded *The Home*, the fashionable interest in Japan initially framed the publication of his work. A spread of photographs of shrines, temples and bustling streets in contemporary Tokyo—taken in 1934 during Kagiyama's first return trip to Japan since arriving in Australia—was included in the May 1935 issue. Kagiyama's first contribution of photographs of Sydney was published in November that year. Despite living and working in Sydney for well over 20 years, Kagiyama's photographs were presented as a foreign encounter under the headline 'Sydney—Seen Through Japanese Eyes' (see Figure 2.13).[55]

---

50 Cazneaux's photographs of Sadler and his wife in their Japanese home and garden appeared in the February 1928 and July 1932 issues.
51 'Reception by the Japanese Consul', *Sunday Times*, 4 May 1930, 16; 'Emperor of Japan', *Sydney Morning Herald*, 30 April 1932, 14.
52 *The Home*, August 1922; May 1926; June 1926; November 1931.
53 'Relations with Japan. New Society Formed', *Sydney Morning Herald*, 26 October 1928, 12.
54 'National Art Gallery', *Sydney Morning Herald*, 24 September 1935, 4.
55 Ichiro Kagiyama, 'Sydney Through Japanese Eyes', *The Home*, November 1935, 38–39.

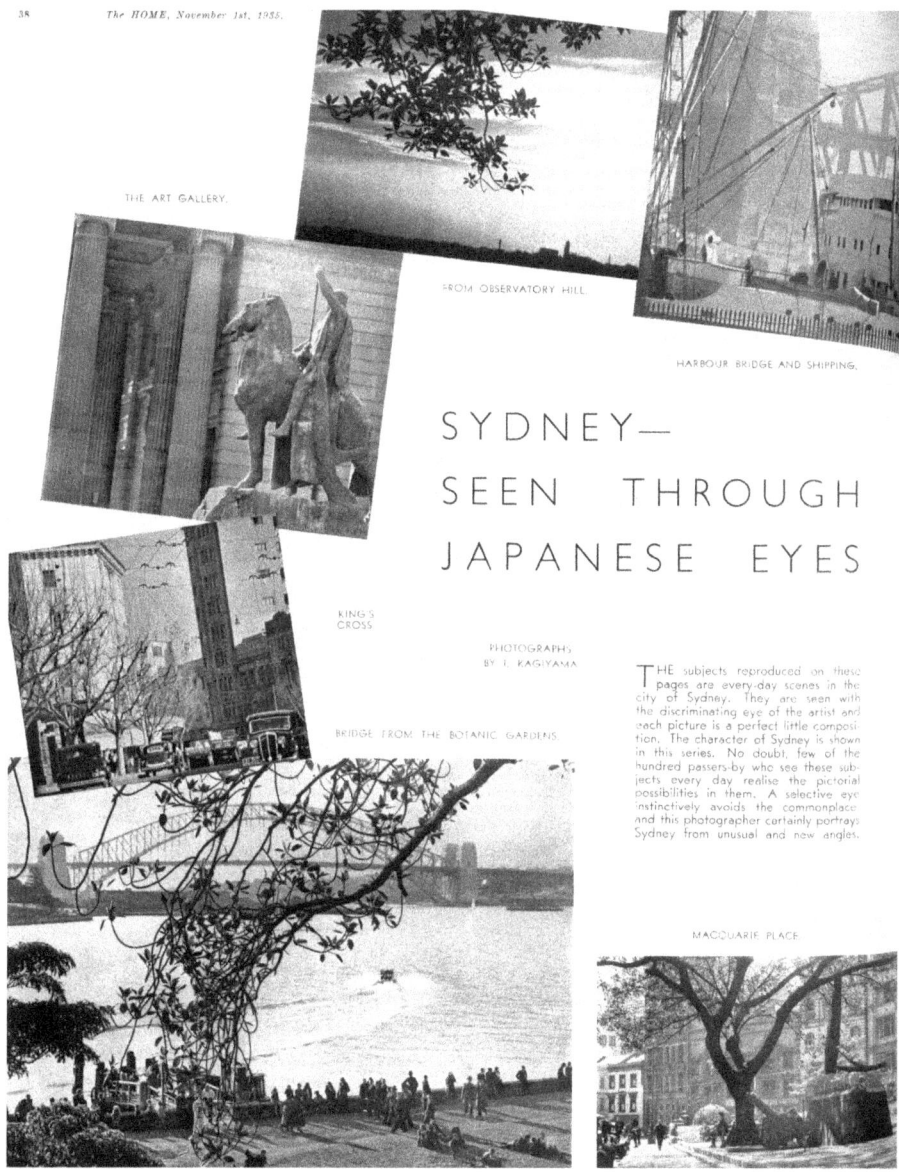

Figure 2.13. Ichiro Kagiyama, 'Sydney—Seen Through Japanese Eyes'.
Source: *The Home*, November 1935, 38–39.

Apart from the spread's attention-grabbing headline, the brief introductory text made no mention of Kagiyama's Japanese heritage or its potential impact on his view of Sydney. Kagiyama's photographs were praised for capturing the true 'character of Sydney' and described as the result of 'the discriminating eye of the artist and each picture is a perfect little composition'.[56] The phrase 'perfect little composition' recalls the tendency to describe the Japanese and Japanese culture as little, dainty, artistic or delicate, as in the description of Ishida as our 'little friend from Japan'. Other allusions to stereotyped visions of Japan were evident in the selection and placement of Kagiyama's photographs. The largest photograph at the bottom of the first page and another placed prominently at the centre top offer views of the city framed by hanging branches from a Morton Bay fig tree. This compositional device would have been familiar to readers as a signifier of quintessential Japan seen in tourist advertising and contemporary photographs inspired by Japan. Indeed, there is a striking compositional similarity between Kagiyama's photograph of Sydney Harbour Bridge and the image of 'Japan the Fascinating' in an NYK Line travel advertisement published in *The Home* earlier the same year (see Figure 2.14).

There is nothing particularly Japanese about Kagiyama's vision of Sydney in the other 12 crisp, sharply focused black and white photographs included in the spread. The photographs are a salute to modern Sydney, its iconic Harbour Bridge, shipping industry and bustling city. There is dynamism and energy in these images. Cars rush through busy streets lined with high-rise buildings, while electric tramlines mirror the sweep of the road overhead. The most dramatic photograph is on the second page: Kagiyama's study of the British Medical Association building on Macquarie Street, completed in 1930 (see Figure 2.15). Kagiyama accentuates the soaring vertical lines and geometric finishes of the Art Deco architecture by framing it at a diagonal, which creates the impression of the building surging skywards. A window washer dangles precariously from a rope midway down as though the building is dragging him along for the ride. It seems as though the views through hanging branches were selected by the editors for the first page of the spread to accentuate the impression of an essentially Japanese vision.

---

56   Ibid., 38.

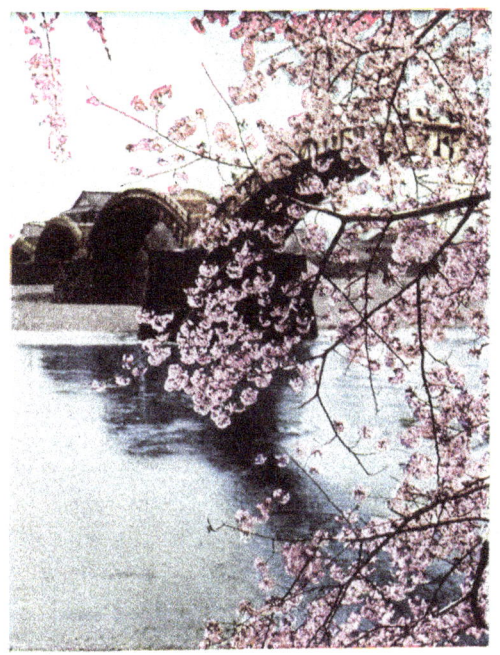

Japan the fascinating.

VISIT THE COLOURFUL ORIENT BY N.Y.K. LINE

The colourful Orient with its modern tourist facilities well deserves the distinction of being the pleasantest of recreation lands affording unending interest and indescribable charm to foreign visitors.

ROUND TRIP FARES:
To Yokohama £90
To Hong Kong £76
(NO EXCHANGE)

Monthly sailings by
ATSUTA MARU, 8,000 tons
KAMO MARU, 8,000 tons
KITANO MARU, 8,000 tons

BURNS, PHILP & CO. LTD.
Managing Agents in Australasia

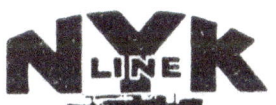

Sydney, Brisbane, Townsville, Thursday Island, Auckland, Wellington.

NIPPON YUSEN KAISHA, HEAD OFFICE, TOKYO
Dalgety & Co. Ltd., Melbourne.   McIlwraith McEachern Ltd., Adelaide.

Figure 2.14. Advertisement for NYK Line.
Source: *The Home*, July 1935.

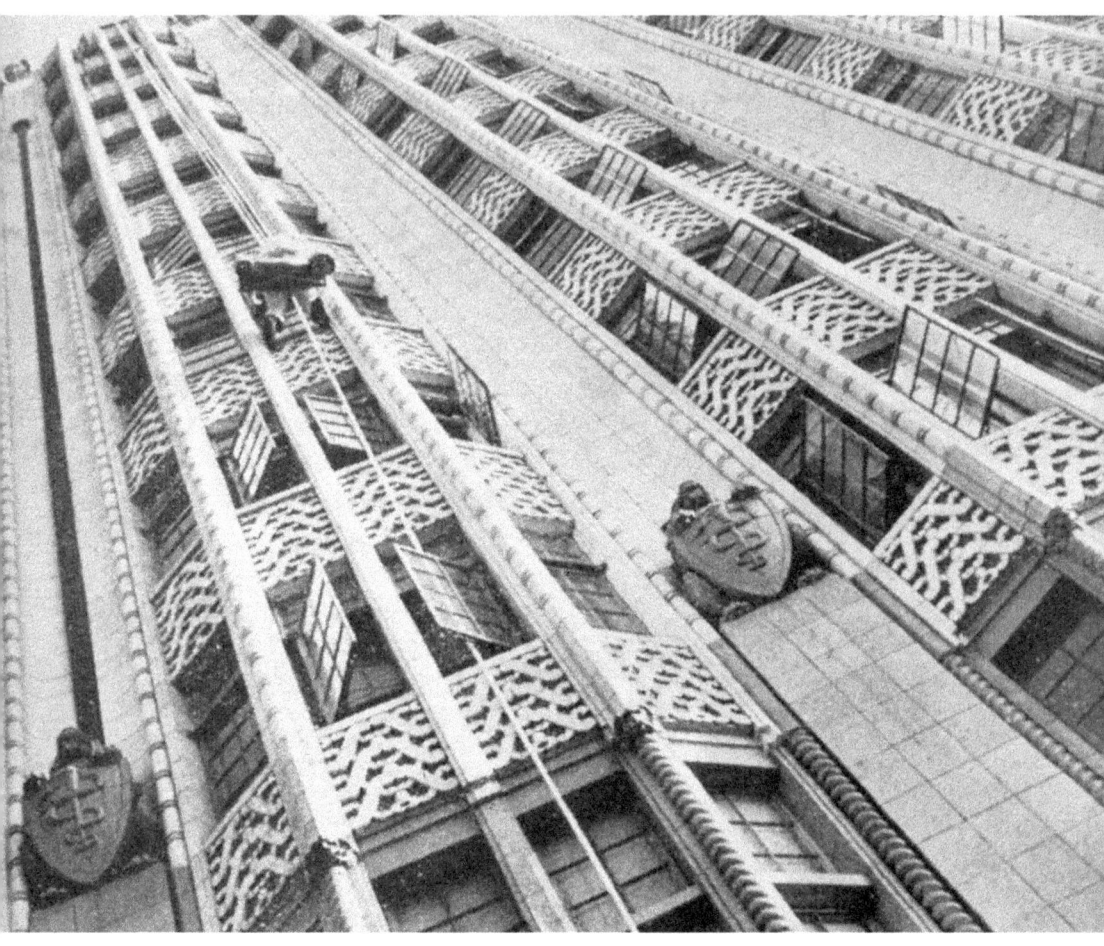

Figure 2.15. Ichiro Kagiyama, *B.M.A Macquarie Street*, from 'Sydney—Seen Through Japanese Eyes'.
Source: *The Home*, November 1935, 38–39.

However, soon after Kagiyama appears to be treated like any other photographer. Over the following three years, *The Home* published many of Kagiyama's photographs of Sydney and its suburbs, the Australian bush and the properties of well-known graziers without mention of his 'Japanese vision'. The soft pictorialism seen in Kagiyama's work from the 1920s had been replaced with crisp, clear photographs of Sydney and its people. In several photo essays, Kagiyama represented well-known Australian myths including the landscape tradition and the role of the bronzed lifesaver as a symbol of masculine, albeit Sydney-centric, nationhood in the 1930s.[57] A survey of 16 of Kagiyama's photographs of Sydney's modernist apartment buildings, which accompanied the article 'Modernity in Flats', reveal Kagiyama's interest in working with different viewpoints, cropping and unusual angles in architectural photography.[58] Night-time photography is his subject in 'The Night Falls on King's Cross Sydney', in which he used car headlights snaking along wide city streets lined with neon signs, and the glow emanating from Art Deco shop fronts, bars and cafes to create the impression of an exciting, vibrant capital.[59] Together, these photographs document a vibrant time in Sydney's development.

As well as being a time for developing his profile as a photographer, the 1930s was a period of personal change for Kagiyama. His marriage to Cicelia ended in 1932 and their divorce was finalised in 1934.[60] During his seven-month trip to Japan in 1934, Kagiyama married a woman from Takayama named in Australian immigration documents as both Sadako and Sata.[61] Immigration restrictions meant that she was not permitted to accompany her husband on his trip back to Australia or to stay indefinitely. A 1905 amendment to the Immigration Restriction Act removed the provision for wives and children of non-Europeans residing in Australia to join their spouses, but exceptions could be made on a case-by-case basis for Japanese people who applied through the consulate.[62] Upon Kagiyama's return to Australia, the Japanese consul applied on Kagiyama's behalf to have his new wife exempted from the dictation test. The request was granted in 1935. Kagiyama paid a substantial bond of 100 pounds as part of this process and, thanks to his connections to the Japanese trading networks, an unnamed 'reputable Japanese merchant of Sydney' accepted surety for that bond.[63] His new wife eventually landed in Australia in August 1939, just two weeks before Great Britain declared war on Germany, bringing Australia as a British nation into WWII.[64]

---

57   'The March to Nationhood', *The Home*, March 1938, 33, 36.
58   'Modernity in Flats', *The Home*, February 1936, 22–25.
59   'The Night Falls on King's Cross Sydney', *The Home*, August 1936, 37–40.
60   'In Divorce' 1932, 10; 'In Divorce', 1933, 5; 'In Divorce', 1934, 8, NSW State Archives and Records 1127/1932 and 73/1933.
61   NAA A12508 32/128 and NAA C123 9904.
62   Immigration Restriction Amendment 1905 s 4c; Oliver, 'Japanese Relationships in White Australia', 5.5.
63   NAA SP42/1 C1934/4618.
64   NAA A12508 32/128.

The Home featured fewer articles and editorials about Japan from late 1937. As news reports of Japanese atrocities in the Second Sino-Japanese War spread throughout Australia from late September 1937, anti-Japanese sentiment began to rise. Torao Wakamatsu, the consul general of Japan who arrived in Australia in February 1937 to help finalise the details of the Japan–Australia trade arrangement, discussed his disappointment at Australia's reaction to 'the unfortunate China Incident'. He took issue with what he described as propaganda, false reports and misunderstandings published in the Australian press, including notorious photographs reportedly showing Japanese soldiers using the bodies of Chinese prisoners for bayonet practice. These photographs were discussed in Australian newspapers in late September 1937 and published around the world including in London's *Daily Mirror*. In his farewell speech to the Japan-Australia Society, Wakamatsu was critical of how this coverage resulted in 'public movements to boycott Japanese goods, in refusals by wharf labourers to load Japanese ships, and in other forms that threatened to disturb the friendship between the two countries'.[65]

While the Sino-Japanese War continued, Japan went on the offensive. In June and July 1940, an exhibition of Japanese decorative arts toured Sydney and Melbourne, organised by the Australia-Japan Society, the Society of International Cultural Relations and the Japan Foreign Trade Federation. The exhibition was opened in Sydney by the Japanese consul general, Akiyama. Media coverage of the exhibition emphasised the 'ancient crafts', pretty dolls, 'exquisite' tea sets, fabrics, bonsai, kimonos and cultured pearls.[66] Also featured was a large map of Japanese tourist sites including those in Japanese territories in China occupied as a result of the Sino-Japanese War. Kagiyama covered this exhibition for *The Home* as his final contribution in July 1940. His photographs of an ancient Japanese warrior figurine, dancing geisha doll, bamboo hand bag and shell-shaped cooking pot reinforced the message of the exhibition of Japan as ancient, doll-like, artistic and therefore non-threatening. Two months later, in late September 1940, Japan joined the enemy Axis Powers, Italy and Germany, in a formal Tripartite Pact.

---

65 Torao Wakamatsu, *Farewell Message to Australian People* (Sydney: New Century Press, c. 1938), 2–12.
66 'Japanese Industrial Arts Show in Sydney', *Telegraph*, 4 June 1940, 15.

Rising Suspicions and Looming War

By the late 1930s, the Australian Department of Defence was keeping a close eye on Japanese activities in Australia. Surveillance activities increased exponentially from 1937. The names of Japanese residents of NSW were collected; Japanese social groups, clubs and businesses were scrutinised; and individuals were increasingly shadowed. Department of Defence documents reveal how Japanese photographers were of particular interest.[67] Kagiyama was placed under surveillance in 1938. Although Kagiyama had photographed several sites that were later to become especially sensitive, including the Port at Newcastle, Fort Denison, Bradley's Head and the navy base at Garden Island—the site where the HMAS Kuttabul was sunk by a Japanese submarine in May 1942—it was not his photography that attracted the attention of security officials. Instead, Kagiyama became the focus of an investigation after a neighbour who operated a tobacco kiosk under Kagiyama's Kings Cross flat reported some unusual activities. Between October and December 1938, Kagiyama reportedly left a parcel on his doorstep each morning between 8 and 8.10 am. Another man collected that parcel between 8.45 and 9 am the same day. Containing wax cylinders for sound recordings supposedly of radio broadcasts from Tokyo, the contents were deemed to be cause for no further action. The Australian security report conceded that there was a possibility that coded messages were being exchanged through the cylinders, but noted that they were powerless to prevent it.[68] There is anecdotal evidence that Kagiyama was 'approached by the Japanese army to work as a spy and this he did'.[69] However, gaining access to additional evidence that could either confirm or refute this assertion is currently impossible.

As tensions between Japan and the Allies escalated, including the US Government's freezing of Japanese assets in retaliation for Japanese incursions into French Indochina, many Japanese merchants and diplomats returned to Japan. Kagiyama left Australia with his new wife

---

67 See 'NSW Security Service file – Pre war Activities of Japanese and training of Interpreters', NAA C320 J240; 'NSW Security Service file – Police Observation of Japanese Movements in the City', NAA C320 J70; 'NSW Security Service file – Japanese firms in Australia', NAA C320 J78; 'NSW Security Service file – Japanese Society of Sydney', NAA C320 J79; 'NSW Security Service file – Japanese Organization in Sydney', NAA C320 J208.
68 NAA SP42/1 C1934/4618.
69 Mitsuda, *Modernism/Japonism in Photography 1920s–40s*, 31.

on 15 August 1941 on board the Japanese repatriation ship the *Kashima Maru*, taking his photographs with him.[70] Had the couple remained in Australia, they would have been arrested and interned in one of several internment camps where those classified as 'enemy aliens', including thousands of men, women and children of Japanese, German and Italian origin, where detained until the end of the war.[71] Back in Takayama, Kagiyama was able to capitalise on the language and photography skills that he had developed in Australia. He worked as an interpreter for the forces of the American-led military Occupation of postwar Japan, in which Australia played a substantial role. The former mayor of Takayama, Shūzō Tsuchikawa, described Kagiyama as a significant support during these years:

> He was a gentle, earnest person with a strong sense of responsibility. The fact that the city of Takayama was well-liked by the Occupying Forces, and got by with no problems, was entirely thanks to this one man's beautiful, passionate interpreting. I will never forget him.[72]

Kagiyama also gave a presentation to the city council, presidents of neighbourhood associations, school staff and the head of the Ladies' Association in Takayama regarding what to expect from the Allied occupying forces and how to interact with them, given their cultural differences.

The work of Kagiyama and Ishida in Sydney, and the cultural interest in Japan among their Anglo-Australian contemporaries, highlight some of the complexities of Australia–Japan relations in the interwar period. Australia's relative proximity to Japan, and the ebbs and flows of international politics and diplomacy, ensured that Australian representations of Japan and responses to the work of these Japanese photographers were nuanced and transcended Orientalist clichés. Although stereotypes of diminutive, feminine, ancient and artistic Japan endured over time, they were reinvented and adapted continually with reference to specific political events, changing cultural values and the interpersonal relations among photographers. The dramatic fluctuations in Australian attitudes to Japan—from perceived threat to WWI ally,

---

70 NAA SP1148/2. In this 'Passenger List – Outgoing Passengers' document, the ship's name is misspelled as Kasima Maru.
71 Yuriko Nagata, *Unwanted Aliens: Japanese Internment in Australia* (St Lucia, Brisbane: University of Queensland Press, 1996).
72 Shūzō Tsuchikawa, 'Episodes from the War's End (Shusen Kobanashi)', *Hida Shunju*, August 1978, 434.

trading partner to bitter battlefield enemy—meant that these stereotypes took on divergent meanings in the first decades of the twentieth century. The belittling caricatures of Japanese men, used to infantilise Japan in conservative defences of 'White Australia', were just as likely to be invoked as a term of endearment to describe 'our little friend' Ishida, or to praise Kagiyama's 'perfect little compositions'. This process of reinterpreting and adapting familiar stereotypes gave Australian national identities a degree of porosity, allowing aspects of Japanese visual culture, and these two Japanese photographers themselves, to be viewed as both Australian and foreign. Yet, such simplistic ways of understanding racial and cultural differences also amounted to a form of symbolic violence that misrecognised the dynamic and complex character of individuals, societies and their modes of representation. Whether they were linked to friendship or enmity, the very persistence of these stereotypes ultimately gave them a longevity that continued through WWII and well beyond.

3

SHOOTING JAPANESE: PHOTOGRAPHING THE PACIFIC WAR

Anonymous Japanese lie dead in the kunai grass at Gona in Papua New Guinea in December 1942, sprawled before a semi-circle of 10 Australian 'diggers' brandishing their weapons for the camera (see Figure 3.1). One of the Australians looks away, grinning sheepishly. Three-quarters of a century later, George Silk's photograph is one of the signature photographs of a remorseless war fought with a racially charged viciousness. It first came to public notice in the overheated atmosphere of the conflict itself, in *War in New Guinea* (1943), an official photographic collection published by the Australian Government's chief propaganda agency, the Department of Information (DOI). Over the years since, it has often appeared in both popular and scholarly histories of the Pacific War.

The image partakes of a long tradition of wartime 'trophy pictures', of victors displaying their dead or humiliating their captive enemy—a tradition that reached its nadir in 2004, with the publication of digital images of American military personnel mockingly torturing Iraqi detainees in Abu Ghraib prison outside Baghdad.[1] The diggers in the photograph resemble big game hunters, posing proudly with their kill. In a struggle often described in the press of the day as a kind of hunt,

---

1   It is strongly reminiscent, for instance, of the grainy photographs of heavily armed American soldiers clustered around the corpses of Lakota Indians in the aftermath of the Wounded Knee massacre in South Dakota in 1890. *Burial of the dead after the massacre of Wounded Knee*, 17 January 1891. Northwestern Photo Co. Library of Congress Prints and Photographs Division, Reproduction Number: LC-USZ62-44458. For an account of military trophy pictures, see Janina Struck, *Private Pictures: Soldiers' Inside View of War* (London: I.B. Tauris, 2011), 18.

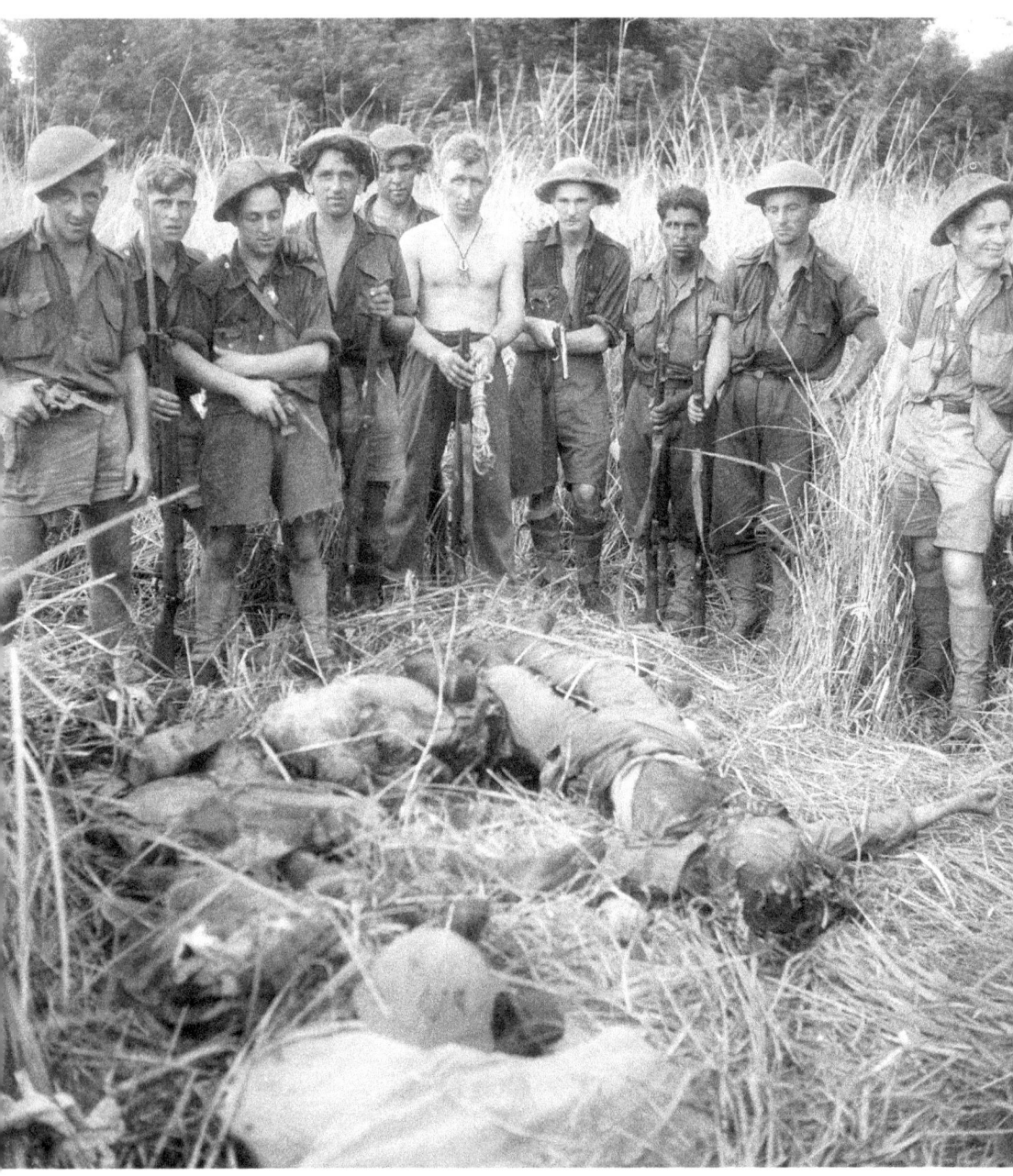

Figure 3.1. George Silk, *Australian Soldiers with Japanese Dead after the Final Assault on Gona, Papua*, 17 December 1942.
Source: Australian War Memorial (AWM) 013881.

with the Japanese as the quarry, perhaps this is not surprising. In January 1943, reporter for the *Argus* Geoffrey Hutton wrote of remnants of retreating enemy being 'hunted down' by Australian patrols. Later that year, Hutton gave a verbal picture of the intense fighting taking place in thick, trackless jungle. This, he wrote, was 'rather a manhunt than a battle', with the Japanese 'in full flight'. Ironically, given that Australian reportage customarily emphasised the superior virtuosity of Australian troops in their confrontation with the enemy, the caption to the photograph in *War in New Guinea* reports that the five Japanese had been killed by a single grenade. The diggers so flamboyantly parading their kill were enjoying a little vicarious fame.[2]

The 'Pacific War' is oxymoronic enough, without taking into account the mutual loathing of the antagonists. It was a deeply racialised encounter, which both suspended notions of common humanity and pitted contrasting modes of male military behaviour in and out of battle. In his study of the nexus of race and power that characterised the conflict, *War Without Mercy*, John Dower noted that both Allied commanders and common soldiers routinely used 'exceedingly graphic and contemptuous' imagery to denigrate a 'uniquely contemptible' foe. The revered American war correspondent Ernie Pyle expressed the common view that, while the European enemies were 'people', the Japanese were 'something subhuman and repulsive', likening them to cockroaches and mice.[3]

The Australians could be at least as brutal in expressing their aversion. In his study of their responses to their adversaries, *Fighting the Enemy*, Mark Johnston quoted the diary of a veteran of the fighting in North Africa, who exhibited 'very humane' attitudes to his Axis opponents in that theatre. Killing Japanese was different. To destroy 'such repulsive looking animals', he asserted, 'was not murder'.[4] This was a view encouraged by the military leadership. In an interview carried on the front page of the *New York Times* in January 1943, the commander of

---

2   Department of Information, *War in New Guinea* (Sydney: F.H. Johnston Publishing, 1943), n.p. Hunt references Geoffrey Hutton, 'Papuan Fight Drawing to a Close', *Argus*, 21 January 1943, 1; Geoffrey Hutton, 'Hunting Japs in the Jungle', *Argus*, 14 October 1943, 2; See also Geoffrey Hutton, 'Hunting Japs on slopes of Satelberg', *Argus*, 16 November 1943, 4.
3   Ernie Pyle, *The Last Chapter* (New York: Henry Holt, 1945), 5, quoted in John Dower, *War Without Mercy: Race & Power in the Pacific War* (New York: Pantheon Books, 1986), 9, 78.
4   Mark Johnston, *Fighting the Enemy: Australian Soldiers and their Adversaries in World War II* (Cambridge: Cambridge University Press, 2000), 87.

the Australian forces, General Sir Thomas Blamey, observed: 'We are not dealing with humans as we know them … Our troops have the right view of the Japs. They regard them as vermin'. A few months earlier, giving a pep talk to his exhausted troops at the base camp outside Port Moresby, Blamey reportedly described the enemy as a 'subhuman beast' who was 'a cross between the human being and the ape'. Warming to his theme, Blamey invited his men to take a journey deep into the 'miasmic' jungle and into the heart of darkness: 'We must exterminate the Japanese', he exhorted.[5]

This ethos of extermination seems to have permeated the corps of cameramen covering the Australian campaigns in the sweltering jungles and beachheads of New Guinea and neighbouring islands such as Borneo, Bougainville and the Bismarck Archipelago. A large corps of official photographers shooting for both government and military agencies expanded on an established frame of cultural reference created by longstanding national anxieties over the prospect of 'White Australia's' vulnerability to Asian invasion. These anxieties were cultural and psychological as much as military and geopolitical. The Pacific War realised the racial fears that had for decades marked Australian responses to Japan. The late nineteenth-century male stereotypes of the quaintly charming Mikado and the self-sacrificing samurai, followed by the ambitious imperialist on a prolonged campaign of regional annexation in the first three decades of the new century, evolved into a terrifying new hybrid: the homicidal maniac of the 1940s.

Institutional resources were ploughed into photographing a threat to Australia itself after the fall of Singapore voided the region of British power and turned the isolated nation into a 'bastion of the white race'.[6] A new military Directorate of Public Relations (DPR) was formed in February 1942, augmenting and at times competing with the DOI, whose photographic teams comprised accredited civilians such as George Silk. A rebadged Military History Section (MHS) comprised photographers who were attested members of the armed services to provide an official pictorial record of what was an immense national

---

5   *New York Times*, 9 January 1943, 1; Blamey quoted in George H. Johnston, *The Toughest Fighting in the World* (New York: Duell, Sloan and Pearce, 1943), 207, 227–28.
6   'Lesson of Singapore', *Argus*, 13 February 1942, 2. In seeking parliamentary approval for declaring war on Japan after Pearl Harbor, Prime Minister John Curtin invoked upholding the 'principle of a White Australia' (quoted in Peter Dennis et al., *The Oxford Companion to Australian Military History* (Melbourne: Oxford University Press, 1995), 323).

crisis. By the end of 1944, the New Guinea–based MHS had no fewer than nine teams shooting the war with Japan. Official photography was integral to the operations and public relations of other branches of the armed forces as well. A corps of up to 200 officially accredited photographers and cinematographers, supplemented by internally appointed unit photographers, covered the war.[7]

The Australian photographers were unequivocally 'official', with an identity intrinsically bound up with the national armed forces. Their affiliation came at a cost. Australian military and civilian agencies had fixed ideas about which of their pictures were deemed suitable for distribution; it was as if nothing life-threatening could be seen to have happened to Australians on the battlefield. The autocratic policies of the DOI were largely instrumental in the departure of the two most famous members of its photographic cohort, the New Zealand–born Silk and the celebrated, ill-fated Damien Parer, to work for independent American outlets. In Silk's case, the move was prompted in part by the suppression of his Christmas Day 1942 photograph of a wounded, blindfolded Australian being tenderly escorted by a 'Fuzzy Wuzzy Angel', the Kiplingesque term applied to the Papua New Guineans who aided the Australians. The DOI apparently considered the picture a touch too distressing; snapped up by *Life* magazine and published in March 1943, it became one of the most famous images of the war.[8]

---

7   Shaune Lakin, *Contact: Photographs from the Australian War Memorial Collection* (Canberra: Australian War Memorial, 2006), 105, 137, 140. Lakin noted that some MHS photographs were misattributed to the DOI when published in Australian newspapers. The MHS was formed from the existing Military History and Information Service. On the institutional complexities surrounding the photography of the war, including conflict between the DPR and the DOI, and more broadly between the army, government and agencies themselves, see Ian Jackson, '"Duplication, Rivalry and Friction": The Australian Army, the Government and the Press during the Second World War', in *The Information Battlefield: Representing Australians at War*, ed. Kevin Foster (North Melbourne: Australian Scholarly Publishing, 2011), 74–85.
8   George Silk's photograph of the Australian soldier 'Dick' Whittington being helped by the Papuan Raphael Oimbari at Buna, Papua New Guinea, 25 December 1942: AWM 014028. Subsequently, Silk resigned from the DOI to photograph for *Life* full-time. Out of solidarity with his colleague and disenchanted with the department over what he perceived as its parsimonious attitude to the payment of expenses, Parer soon followed suit, joining the US news organisation Paramount News. On the issue of censorship and Silk's frustration at the department's opposition to releasing his photographs of Australian casualties at Buna in New Guinea in late 1942, see also Lakin, *Contact*, 144, 156. For an account of the Silk/Parer resignations, see Niall Brennan, *Damien Parer: Cameraman* (Carlton: Melbourne University Press, 1994), 144–56.

Frustration with bureaucratic interference did not prevent the Australian photographers, Silk and Parer included, from expressing the animus of the battlefield to a degree that went well beyond the obligation to produce effective propaganda. Reviewing *War in New Guinea*, the *Sydney Morning Herald* significantly complimented his courage in moving to the 'vanguard' of the fighting, 'heedless of danger', to record 'with sympathy' the 'heroic performance' of the soldiers. The photographers shared the soldiers' travails as well as their triumphs. In 1943, Damien Parer wrote that the Australians showed 'no beg-pardons' to an enemy increasingly loathed as reports of battlefield savagery and treatment of prisoners spread throughout both the war zones and the home front. 'The Jap', Parer opined, 'is a fanatic with a subnormal, animal cunning', who was no match for the Australian 'diggers', whose 'greatness as infantrymen' was confirmed each time he went into battle to film them.[9] Bloodied, spreadeagled or quietly decomposing, the Japanese was considered fair photographic game.

Capturing the Japanese Dead

Some 6,000 Australian soldiers are known to have died fighting the Japanese in the Pacific campaign. However, there is very little evidence of this heavy toll in the published oeuvre of official Australian photography. In the US, the censors working for the American counterpart of the DOI, the Office of War Information, at first also routinely suppressed pictures of men killed in action, on the grounds that they would sap national morale. However, in 1943, the American administration decided that complacency was even more dangerous than demoralisation, and images of the national dead began to emerge, beginning with George Strock's famous picture of American marines washed up on Buna Beach in New Guinea, published in *Life* in September 1943. By contrast, the DOI's intransigence on this issue lasted right through to the end of the war, and the policy has continued up to and including the war in Afghanistan.[10]

---

9 'Silk is not soft', *Sydney Morning Herald*, 15 May 1943, 6; Damien Parer, typed manuscript, Australian War Memorial PR84/389, published as 'The Cameraman Looks at the Digger', Foreword to Neil McDonald and Peter Brune, *200 Shots: Damien Parer, George Silk and the Australians at War in New Guinea* (St Leonards, NSW: Allen & Unwin, 1998), ix.
10 See Kevin Foster, 'Deploying the Dead: Combat Photography, Death and the Second World War in the USA and the Soviet Union', *WLA: An International Journal of the Humanities* 26 (2014): 7; Fay Anderson, 'Chasing the Pictures: Press and Magazine Photography', *Media International Australia* 150, no. 1 (February 2014): 50.

Squeamish about the publication of images of dead Australians, the censors were far less fussy when it came to the taking and distribution of pictures of dead Japanese. Military photography has long sought to boost morale by circulating pictures of enemy casualties. In *Regarding the Pain of Others*, Sontag cited the case of a photograph of unburied British dead taken after the Boers' victory at Skion Kop in 1900, published to great British indignation. 'To display the dead', she wrote, 'is what the enemy does'.[11] Yet the preponderance of photographs of dead Japanese is striking. As Shaune Lakin noted in his superbly detailed study of Australian military photography, *Contact*, this is at odds with the relative scarcity of pictures of European casualties in campaigns against the Germans and Italians in North Africa.[12] This revealing disparity can be attributed to the increasingly poisonous hatred of the Japanese as the Pacific War dragged on, which exacerbated cultural views of them as somehow less than fully human.

Certainly, the intensity of the fighting contributed to the representational contempt for the Japanese. In a late 1942 report on the Allied offensive on the Japanese beachheads of Buna-Gona on the north coast of New Guinea, the leading reporter (and future novelist) George Johnston described the encounter as 'coldly animal'. When machine guns and mortars did not do the job, the fighting became personal. Men wrestled to the ground, strangling or stabbing each other to death. After several terrible days the Australians were emerging the stronger, and 'the piles of Japanese dead' were 'mounting higher'.[13]

The omnipresence of death hardened hearts and minds in soldier and photographer alike. Melbourne-born Norman Stuckey, a member of the MHS, was a brave and fastidious photographer. Shooting the Australian advance on Shaggy Ridge in New Guinea in December 1943, he got so close to the action that a blast shattered the glass in his camera. In the aftermath of this successful assault, Stuckey photographed Australians unearthing and examining enemy dead. A bloodied Japanese corpse is dragged out of what looks like some kind of dugout or 'foxhole' as such defensive positions were called (see Figure 3.2). As Shaune Lakin observed, the 'shocking' frankness of the photograph is accentuated by

---

11 Susan Sontag, *Regarding the Pain of Others* (New York: Picador/Farrar, Straus and Giroux, 2003), 57.
12 Lakin, *Contact*, 143.
13 George H. Johnston, 'Kill or Be Killed at Buna', *Argus*, 9 December 1942, 2.

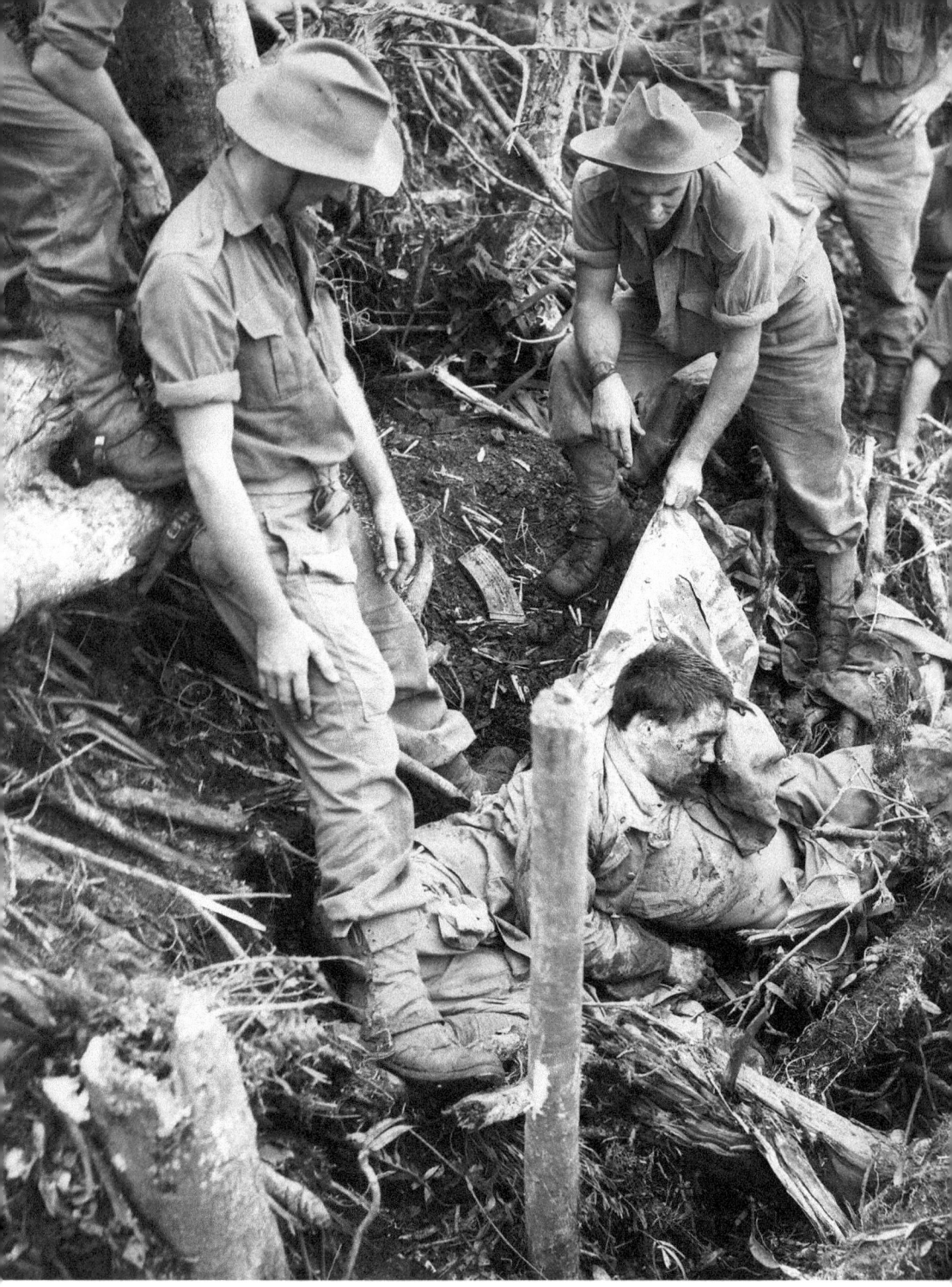

Figure 3.2. Norman Stuckey, *Troops of the 2/16th Australian Infantry Battalion Unearth a Dead Japanese Soldier*, Shaggy Ridge area, New Guinea, 27 December 1943.

Source: AWM 062305.

Stuckey's point of view, looking down on the dead man from the edge of the trench.[14] Perhaps more shocking is that this is actually one of at least two pictures Stuckey took of the scene; another, taken a little further away, shows the Australian dragging the body by his other hand and the onlookers are positioned slightly differently. The grisly ritual had been repeated for the photographer's benefit.

Taking evidence of Nazi depravity at newly liberated Bergen-Belsen in April 1945, the English photographer George Rodger was so ashamed at arranging the chaos of dreadful carnage into a pleasing composition in the viewfinder that he temporarily gave up photographing war altogether.[15] Yet, it would be unfair to attribute callousness to Stuckey or indeed any of the Australian cameramen. As an MHS operative, it was his professional duty to document the process of frisking enemy casualties for whatever information they might hold. As John Taylor noted in *Body Horror*, the camera itself and the process of framing pictures distances the photographer from the subject matter, however horrifying.[16] Nonetheless, Stuckey's recomposition of the scene, and the scant respect for the identity of the dead soldier, reveals the deliberateness with which the Australian photographers went about their business— and their attitude towards the Japanese.

Little respect was afforded to the corpses by either their adversary or their photographer. In one photograph, Australian troops in Bougainville in January 1945 are pictured with a mutilated Japanese corpse, with one of the Australians about to enjoy a celebratory cigarette (see Figure 3.3). Perhaps the men were directed by the anonymous photographer to point their weapons so melodramatically at the body, but their gesture is gratuitous, for he is well dead. Yet, at least the casualty, lying face down on the jungle floor, is unidentifiable. Anonymity, as Paul Fussell has remarked, is a convention in Allied photography of the war; in Strock's picture of the dismal scene at Buna Beach, the corpses lie 'ostentatiously'

---

14 Lakin, *Contact*, 143. See F.R. Peterson, 'Cameraman in Thick of Fight', *Herald*, 8 February 1944, 8. See Stuckey photograph, AWM 062304.
15 See interview with George Rodger in *Dialogue with Photography*, eds. Paul Hill and Thomas Cooper (New York: Farrar, Straus and Giroux, 1979), 59–60; quoted in Zelizer, *Remembering to Forget*, 88–89.
16 John Taylor, *Body Horror: Photojournalism, Catastrophe and War* (New York: New York University Press, 1998), 13. The *Life* photographer Margaret Bourke-White, who accompanied the forces into the murder camps, has written of a 'protective veil' that came over her while photographing the carnage. Margaret Bourke-White, *Portrait of Myself* (New York: Simon and Schuster, 1963), 160, quoted in Zelizer, *Remembering to Forget*, 88.

face down in the wet sand. By the time of the D-day landings in June 1944, photographs of dead GIs appeared regularly in American news magazines, but always prone, shrouded or with their heads turned away from the camera. 'This is a dignity', Sontag observed of the brazen photographic display of the dead from 'exotic' places, 'not thought necessary to accord to others'.[17]

Certainly, respect for the enemy's basic human dignity is not one the Australians routinely afforded the Japanese. In June 1945, on Labuan Island off the coast of Borneo, a Japanese sniper was shot by Australian troops while senior officers, including Allied Supreme Commander General Douglas MacArthur, were touring the area. A photographer took several pictures of the body from different angles and distances, including one of the general himself by the corpse. The final photograph is a disturbingly intimate portrait of the bloodied death face of a young man perhaps no more than 20 years old. On occasion, the photographers went out of their way to highlight the identity of the fallen opponent. In one photograph, two Australian soldiers—brothers from Sydney—search the bodies of dead Japanese in Brunei, North Borneo (see Figure 3.4). One of them roughly holds up the head of one of them to face the photographer. This brutal image does not reflect well on the official photographer, who would have directed the soldier to lift the limp head of the deceased for the benefit of the camera.[18]

The cumulative impression provided by the host of images of Japanese war dead is that they had been overwhelmed by a superior opponent. Clearly that was the perception of the popular Sydney-based weekly photo magazine *Pix*, an important outlet for the official photographs.

---

17 See Paul Fussell, 'The War in Black and White', in *The Boy Scout's Handbook and Other Observations* (New York: Oxford University Press, 1982), 234, 235; Sontag, *Regarding the Pain of Others*, 70.
18 Anonymous photographs, Labuan, 10 June 1945, AWM 109148. See also AWM 109145, AWM 109146, AWM 109147. The two Australians in the picture are identified as Private G.B. Creber and Lance Corporal J.H. Creber. The WWII Nominal Roll lists their birthdates as 2 December 1921 and 3 November 1921 respectively, but both with the same mother. It is likely that the former put up his age upon enlistment in June 1941 (to be able to do so); the inscription on his gravestone in the cemetery at Bellingen, New South Wales, indicates that he was born in 1924. The contemptuous close-up of Japanese corpses was not confined to the still photographers. In her discussion of Damien Parer's newsreel *Assault on Salamua* (1943), Keiko Tamura remarked how his 'close and steady shots' of dead Japanese, contrasted with his 'fast and moving' footage of the actual fighting, expresses Parer's 'unforgiving' attitude towards the enemy. See Keiko Tamura, 'Shooting an Invisible Enemy: Images of Japanese Soldiers in Damien Parer's New Guinea Newsreels', *The Journal of Pacific History* 45, no. 1 (2010): 130.

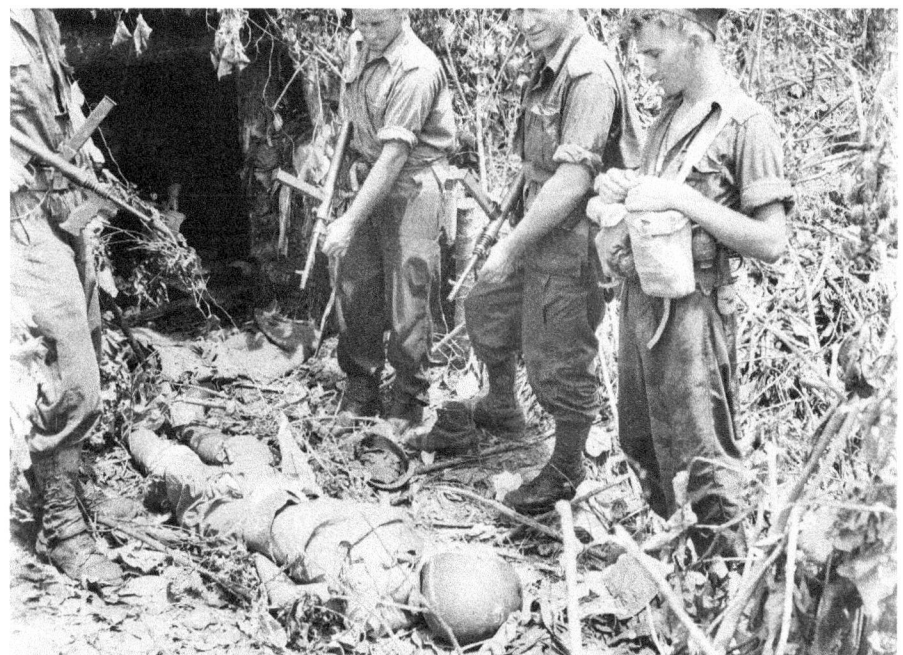

Figure 3.3. Unknown photographer, *Troops of 47th Australian Infantry Battalion with Dead Japanese by Enemy Pillbox*, Bougainville, 16 January 1945.
Source: AWM 078485.

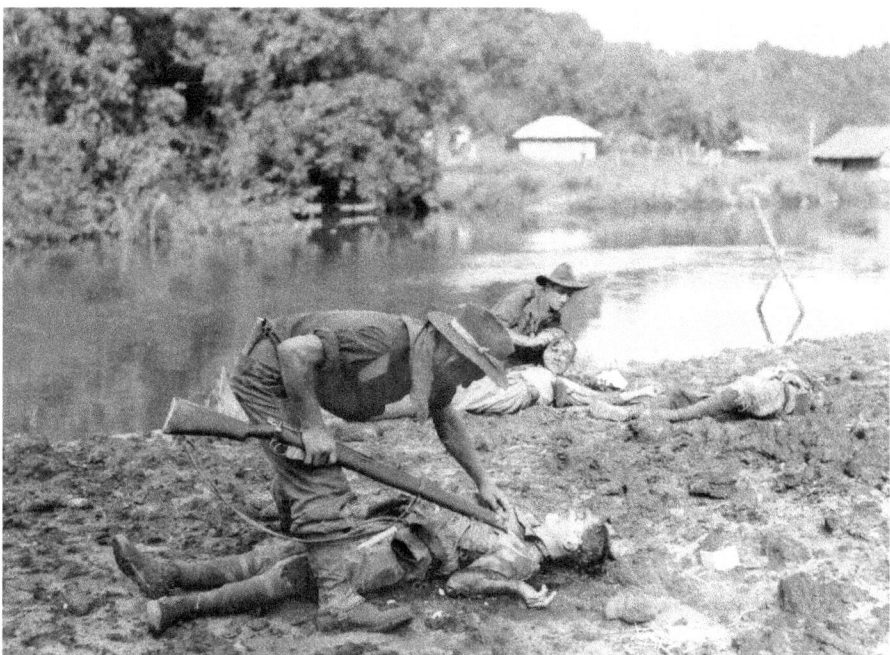

Figure 3.4. Unknown photographer, *Troops of the 2/17th Australian Infantry Battalion Search Japanese Bodies*, Brunei, North Borneo, 13 June 1945.
Source: AWM 109317.

'Aussies Beat Japs in Jungle Fight', published in October 1943, was illustrated with images of Australians assisting wounded comrades, along with the testimonial of US paratroopers said to be 'amazed' by their courage. Supplied by the DOI, these pictures include a photograph of an identifiable Japanese corpse. He had been killed near Lae, in a bloody skirmish in which Australian casualties were claimed to be 'extraordinarily light'.[19]

Not all photographs of dead Japanese were considered suitable for circulation. One such case is the MHS photographer Ronald Keam's image of a mass grave dug for Japanese casualties after an unsuccessful assault on an Australian position in Bougainville in April 1945 (see Figure 3.5). In its digitised archive of photographs, the Australian War Memorial captions the image by suggesting that Australian troops were 'placing' the Japanese into the grave, but the image reveals that the troops were simply hurling the bodies into the trench. Of course they were engaged in a ghastly task, not one to dither over, and the Australians were performing a humane service by not leaving the corpses to rot in the jungle, to be consumed by rats and bugs. Nonetheless, it was not an image that invited public exposure at the very time when the liberation of the Nazi death camps had brought to public notice scences of mass killings. Australian newspapers were full of Holocaust horror stories, but photographs from the camps were used sparingly.[20] However, in May 1945 *Life* magazine published selected work by the posse of photographers accompanying the invading Allied armies into the concentration camps, dreadful images of decomposing corpses and other horrors that created an outcry. Thus, there was a powerful impediment to the dissemination of photographs revealing the Allies' own hand in mass death. Agonising over the relentless firebombing of Japanese cities in the early months of 1945—but just a matter of weeks before the nuclear destruction of Hiroshima and Nagasaki—US Secretary of War Henry Stimson had worried about 'the United States getting the reputation for outdoing Hitler in atrocities'.[21] For their part, the Australians did not want to appear to be heartless mass killers, even of the Japanese military. Victory had to be seen as moral as well as military.

---

19   *Pix*, 30 October 1943, 5.
20   Anderson, 'Chasing the Pictures', 50.
21   'Atrocities', *Life*, 7 May 1945, 32–37; Stimson quoted in Monica Braw, *The Atomic Bomb Suppressed: American Censorship in Japan 1945–1949* (Tokyo: Liber Forlag, 1986), 141.

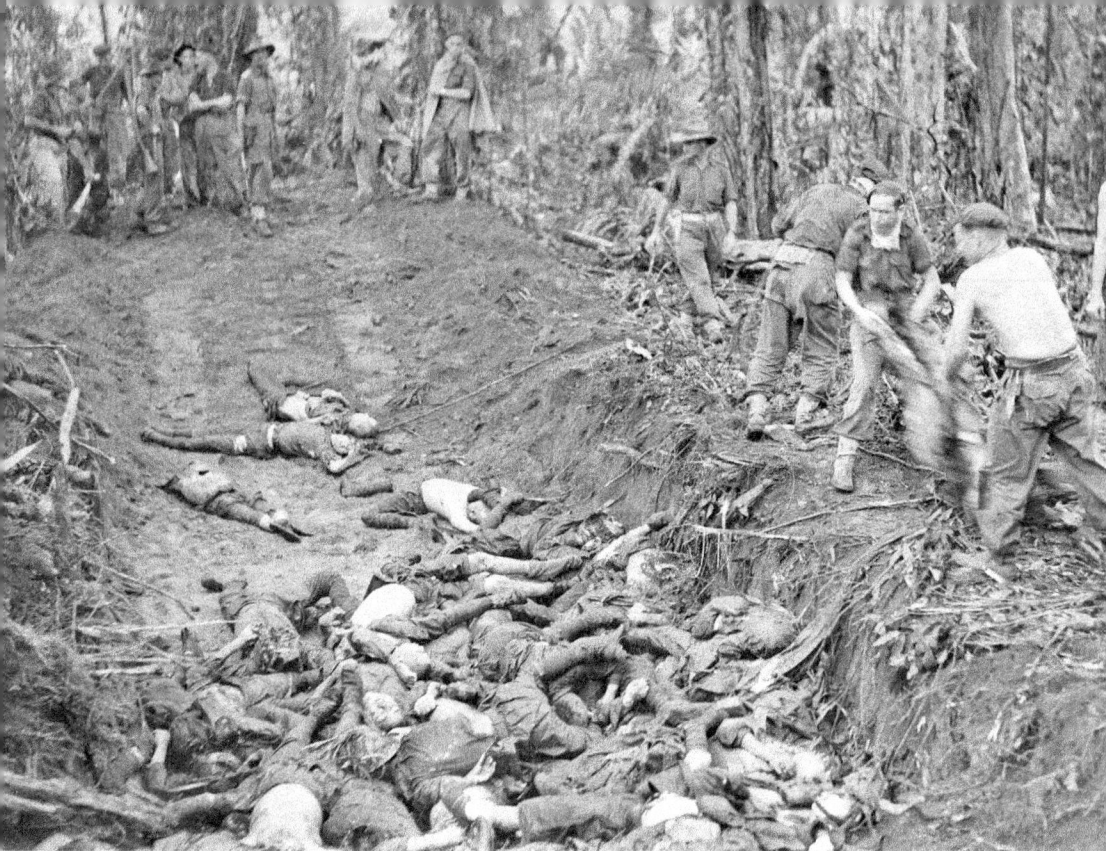

Figure 3.5. Ronald Keam, *Australian Infantry Filling a Mass Grave with Japanese Dead*, Bougainville, 6 April 1945.
Source: AWM 090380.

Man to Man

The Australian photographers were capturing not only the 'battle for Australia', but also a contest of competing races. More specifically, the acute hostility to the Japanese in the official photography suggests that the war was envisaged as a battle of rival codes of manhood, conceptualised over decades of Australian trepidation at the military ambitions of Japan. Punning on the language of photography, with its jargon of 'loading', 'aiming' and 'shooting', Sontag long ago described the camera as a phallic 'sublimation of the gun'.[22] This is an assertion that can be usefully applied to the photographic representation of the ferocious conflict in the Pacific.

---

22   Susan Sontag, *On Photography* (1977; repr., New York: Anchor Books Doubleday 1990), 13–14.

The history of Australian fear of the Japanese bogeyman needs to be understood if, in turn, the photography of the war is to be appreciated. In March 1942, the DOI sought to stiffen Australian resolve in the face of the unnervingly rapid Japanese southward thrust by mounting a propaganda campaign titled 'Know Your Enemy'. The campaign was short lived but virulent: a two-week flurry of posters, articles and news releases, supported by radio broadcasts on the national broadcaster each evening, advertised by provocative two-minute messages broadcast throughout the day. The principal aim was to debunk the opponent's reputation as a 'super-fighter', largely through volleys of racial abuse. The Japanese were variously 'little monkey-men of the North'; a 'bespectacled ape-like race that lent colour to the theory of evolution'; and 'semi-civilised savages, ready to aid and abet the grossest indecencies and the most bestial animalism'. A series of newspaper advertisements concluded with the words 'We've always despised them—NOW WE MUST SMASH THEM!' The 'we' is identified as 'every White Australian'.[23]

In fact, Australians had not 'always despised' the Japanese. The capricious cruelty of Japan's military during the war exposed the 'glorious chivalric code' of *bushido* as a self-serving myth, wrote the war correspondent Rohan Rivett, a survivor of the Burma-Siam Railway, in the *Argus* in September 1945.[24] Yet there was a time, around the turn of the century as Japan began its rise to regional military pre-eminence, when *bushido* was viewed with admiration in Australia. In 1904, an Adelaide newspaper, the *Register*, praised the precepts of the code as 'a powerful moral force' akin to chivalry, though the analogy was 'inadequate, for bushido rises to a loftier moral elevation'.[25] In the wake of the Japanese Navy's impressive defeat of Tsarist Russia's fleet at Tsushima in 1905, a Melbourne politician, George Swinburne, recommended the implementation of a local version of the Japanese warrior code, and the Melbourne *Punch* published a jaunty verse comparing the trivial pursuits of sports-mad urban Australians with the sterner disciplines on display from martial Japan: 'There's common sense and wisdom, as the Japanese can show/In Ju Jitsu and straight shooting and hard-hitting "Bushido"'.[26]

---

23 See Lynette Finch, 'Knowing the Enemy: Australian Psychological Warfare and the Business of Influencing Minds in the Second World War', *War & Society* 16, no. 2 (October 1998): 80; 'Every One a Spy…Every One a Killer…', *Sydney Morning Herald*, 25 March 1942, 10.
24 Rohan D. Rivett, 'It is Bushido to Torture the Sick', *Argus*, 20 September 1945, 2.
25 'Bushido', *Register*, 22 November 1904, 4. See also W.A.M., 'Bushido', *Morning Post* (Cairns), 16 February 1905, 4.
26 'Bushido', *Punch*, 17 May 1906, 7.

Meiji Japan was a new imperial power that Australia could relate to and learn from. Overlooking the oppression that attended Japan's annexation of Formosa and Korea, the *Register* in 1905 lauded its 'entirely peaceful and beneficent' influence on the 'decadent communities' of the Far East. Japanese colonialism was paid the ultimate compliment by being said to exhibit 'the virtues of Anglo-Saxondom'. Referencing the Gilbert and Sullivan light opera that had popularised Japan in Western culture, the *Register* described 'The Mikado' as 'a highly civilized monarch'. The conduct of his military garrisons was exemplary and there were 'no signs' that his subjects 'have the slightest ambition to become bloodthirsty despoilers of foreign territories'.[27]

Not all Australians took such a sanguine view. Japan's muscle flexing was met with foreboding in a country that had for several decades grappled with the spectre of being swamped by Asian migration. In the years before WWI, several fictions fantasised about the prospect of Japanese invasion, and in terms that saw the coming war as a test of national manhood. Discussing works such as C.H. Kirmess's novel *The Australian Crisis* (1909), David Walker wrote: 'Japan had an elaborately codified warrior tradition in bushido. Warrior Japan created a powerful case for an answering tradition of defiant masculinity in Australia'. In these imaginary wars, 'the man-to-man encounter with the Japanese was presented as central to Australia's future'.[28] In *The Australian Crisis*, a Japanese invasion of the nation's vulnerable, sparsely populated north is challenged by a volunteer 'White Guard' of hardy pioneering types— 'typical Australians' who were fighting for 'Aryan ideals'. Outnumbered, these 'sturdy sons of the Bush' have to fall back and the government grudgingly cedes the Japanese-occupied territory to the nominal control of the British.[29]

Invasion novels such as *The Australian Crisis* reflect a sense that urbanising Australia was losing its rural-derived virility, the source of so much of its national myth making. Kirmess suggested that Japanese merchants and travellers to Australia, including the naval squadrons that visited major Australian ports in the first decade of the new century after Japan's

---

27 'Japan as a Civilizing Agent', *Register*, 14 June 1905, 4.
28 David Walker, 'Shooting Mabel: Warrior Masculinity and Asian Invasion', *History Australia* 2, no. 3 (December 2005): 89.9.
29 C.H. Kirmess, *The Australian Crisis* (Melbourne: George Robertson, 1909), 146, 149–50. The novel originally appeared in serial form in 1908 in the magazine *Lone Hand*, with the title *The Commonwealth Crisis*.

signing of an alliance with Britain, must have observed 'all the symptoms of indolent culture, love of play, indulgences in luxuries and careless national pride'.[30] Belligerently committed to the maintenance of 'White Australia', the nationalist journal the *Bulletin* had supported Russians in the war with Japan. When a Japanese naval training squadron called on Australian ports in 1906, a *Bulletin* editorialist lampooned the enthusiasm created by the visit of the 'Jap sailor-men', derisively labelling it 'a circus'. After all, what was Japan but a comic opera of a country, whose soldiers 'fought with curios' and with 'fans for shields'?[31]

The *Bulletin*'s disdain for the 'feminine fuss' surrounding the visitors goes beyond instinctive racism. The Japanese were a sexual threat and sexual competitor. David Walker referred to T.R. Roydhouse's obscure 1903 novel *The Coloured Conquest* in which an Australian strikes a Japanese naval officer who had undiplomatically made advances to his fiancée at a civic reception in honour of a training squadron's visit to Sydney in May 1903.[32] The Australian's gesture is futile; the Japanese eventually invade Sydney and take possession of the women as well. Significantly, the Japanese aggression in China in the 1930s and, in particular, what soon became known as the Rape of Nanking, was widely reported in Australia as a welter of sexual violence and sadism. In February 1938, the *Argus* specified 'outrageous brutalities' committed against Chinese nurses and nuns in Nanking hospital, and elsewhere of drunken rape and murder at a girls' school and the beheading of catechists at Roman Catholic missions.[33] Later that year, *Pix* ran a photo spread of Japanese atrocities in Nanking and elsewhere, pictures purportedly taken for pleasure by Japanese soldiers and secretly developed and circulated by Chinese printers. The article was titled 'Killing For Fun!'[34]

Therefore, in the dark days of early 1942, when Japanese invasion seemed a distinct possibility, it was predictable that such a nightmare invoked the havoc that would be wrought on Australian women as a result.[35] As the nation braced itself for battle, cartoons ironically titled

---

30   Ibid., 148–49.
31   'The Japanese Welcome', *Bulletin*, 24 May 1906, 6.
32   Walker, 'Shooting Mable', 89.3.
33   'Outrages by Japanese', *Argus*, 23 February 1938, 1.
34   *Pix*, 10 December 1938, 3–5.
35   Recent scholarship has revealed that the upper echelons of the Japanese military never seriously contemplated an invasion of Australia. See for example Steven Bullard, 'A Japanese Invasion?', *Wartime*, no. 77 (Summer 2017): 44–49.

'Bushido' in Melbourne's *Argus* and Sydney's *World's News* showed monstrous Japanese ogres having their way with white womanhood.[36] The war was a definitive challenge to Australian manhood. In *The Australian Crisis*, a truce is called until '1940 A.D.', by which time the nation had to 'get ready' to reclaim the land in the country's north lost to the marauding Japanese and so 'save the purity of the race by sweeping the brown invaders back over the coral sea'.[37] History laced with Australian military mythology was to prove the novel prescient. A nation under siege was to be defended by racial stock reinvigorated by the experience of WWI. The men of the Second Australian Imperial Force (AIF) were following in the footsteps of their fathers in the earlier war. They were the 'Anzacs'—the acronym ascribed the men of the Australian and New Zealand Army Corps—whose elan at Gallipoli in Turkey in 1915 seemed to partake of the legendary heroism of the Homeric warriors at nearby Troy. In January 1940, the *Argus* juxtaposed a photograph of the men of the new AIF marching off to war through Melbourne streets with a similar one of its famous predecessor parading through the same streets in 1914. 'A generation separates the two forces', the caption stated, 'but the race remains the same'.[38] The analogy was made not merely through juxtaposition but also through an intertextual referencing of pictures of the fresh generation of Anzacs to well-known images from WWI.

Many photographs of the Pacific campaign present distinctive Australian military types who bear the Anzac imprint—amiable rogues who pose cheerfully for the camera without self-consciousness or arrogance. However, sometimes the priorities of DOI propaganda overrode professional good sense. In 1941, Silk's picture of a trio of smiling diggers (evacuees from Crete photographed in Alexandria) featured prominently in army recruitment posters. In a colloquial tribute to a late nineteenth-century bushranger, the photograph is captioned 'They're still as game as Ned Kelly'. Yet Silk's publicity photograph of Lieutenant John R. Greenwood, taken in the Kokoda area in November 1942, owes more to the imagery of the Wild West in popular Hollywood films than to anything peculiarly Australian (see Figure 3.6). With his elegant moustache, bare chest, headband and firm hand upon his Tommy gun, the figure's stance

---

36 Mick Armstrong, cartoon, *Argus*, 12 March 1942, 2; Stuart Peterson, 'Bushido', cartoon, *World's News*, 28 March 1942, 3.
37 Kirmess, *Australian Crisis*, 335.
38 'To-day Echoes the Marching of Anzac Feet', *Argus*, 16 January 1940, 1; see Lakin, *Contact*, 102.

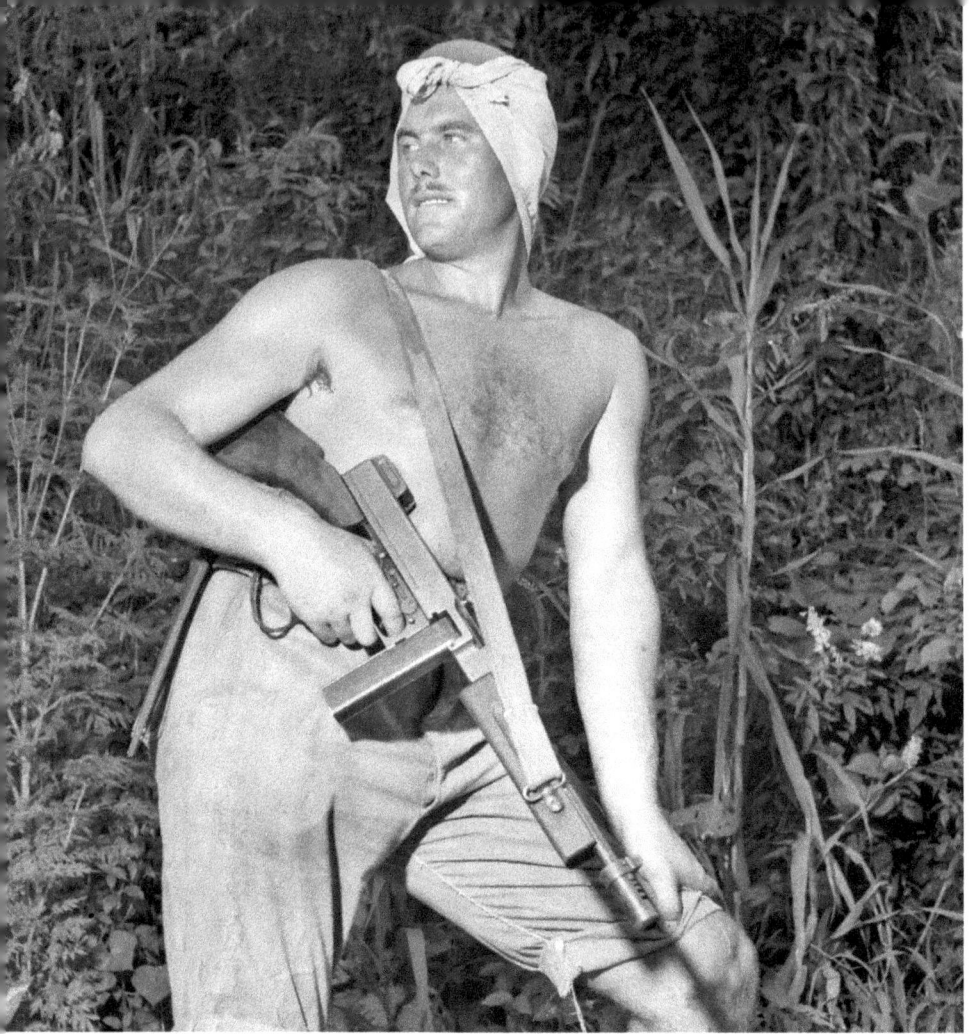

Figure 3.6. George Silk, *Lieutenant John R. Greenwood, 2/14th Australian Infantry Battalion*, New Guinea, 23 November 1942.
Source: AWM 013622.

is of a movie star more than a soldier engaged in the ugly flesh-and-blood saga being enacted in New Guinea.. Facially, the soldier looks uncannily like the publicity photographs of the character played by the Australian-born Errol Flynn in the popular 1939 western *Dodge City*.[39] There is something desperate about the photograph. In addition to its surely unintended tincture of homoeroticism, the photograph betrays a certain insecurity, of the kind detected by the enormously respected

---

39   See Silk photograph, June 1941, AWM 007786; Recruitment poster, AWM ARTV04332. Hollywood's Wild West seemed to have been on Australian minds in New Guinea. George Johnston likened a Papuan comrade's habit of collecting military insignia of Japanese he had personally killed to 'gunmen of the Wild West' putting notches in the revolver butts to signify their victims. See Johnston, *Toughest Fighting in the World*, 143.

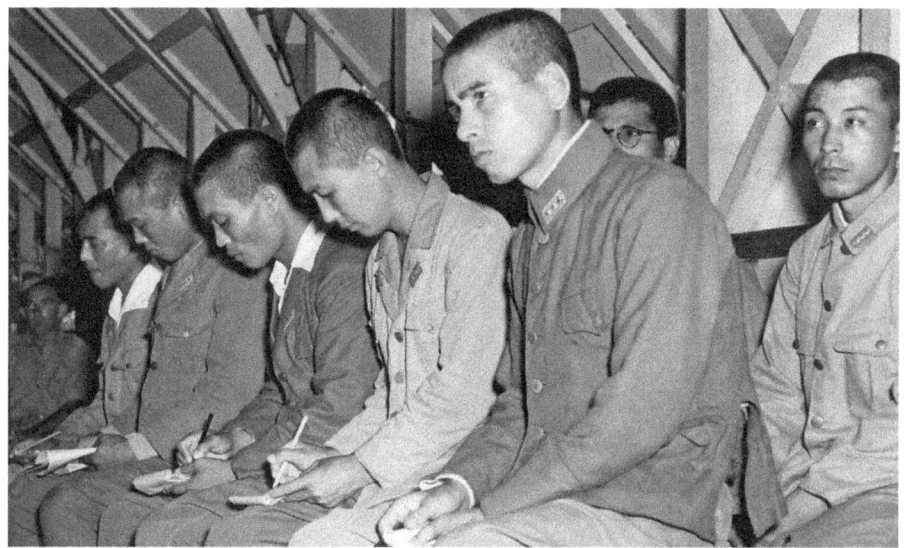

Figure 3.8. Unknown photographer, *Suspected Japanese War Criminals on Trial in Darwin*, March 1945.
Source: *Argus* Newspaper Collection of Photographs, State Library of Victoria. Accession no. H99.203/418.

Siffleet photograph as published in *Life* labels it 'Exhibit No. 5' and lists the name of a member of the Australian Army's corps of war crimes' investigators, Captain V.A.R. Chapple.

Evidentiary photographs produced, authorised and circulated by the DOI also found their way into the press at the time. One of the most notable, of men released from a hospital in Singapore's Changi, was published in *Sydney Morning Herald* under the unequivocal heading 'Evidence of Suffering in Prison Camp'.[43] In March 1946, the *Argus* published photographs of a military trial taking place in Darwin (see Figure 3.8). The stern-faced Australian members of the court are juxtaposed against an image of the Japanese accused of atrocities against their countrymen. Listening intently or diligently taking notes while the charges against them are read, the accused do not look particularly humbled and contrite. Nonetheless it must have been consoling to see the Japanese being brought to account. Yet the image would hardly have quelled the public outrage created by the photographs of the brutalised Australian survivors in internment camps that regularly appeared in national newspapers in the weeks and months after the war's end. These

---

43   *Sydney Morning Herald*, 14 September 1945, 4.

illustrated accounts of the atrocities perpetrated by the Japanese military throughout the Pacific as journalists and photographers entered camps from Singapore to Yokohama and documented the stories of the men.[44]

The Australian treatment of captured Japanese was presented by contrast as a model of humanity. An anti-Japan diatribe filed from Tokyo by the *Sydney Morning Herald* journalist William Marien in early September 1945 is accompanied by a photograph of Japanese POW hospital patients in the Australian compound at Morotai, as they enjoy an unlikely lunch of 'chicken, potatoes and salad, followed by rice and cream custard'. In case readers miss the point, the caption stresses how well cared for they are, 'in contrast to the brutality of the Japanese in their treatment of war prisoners'.[45] The DOI collection *War in New Guinea* juxtaposes images of Japanese dead after the bloody fighting at Gona with pictures of wounded or exhausted prisoners being tended by the Australian victors.

The DOI was determined to promote the image of the humane victor and the magnificently effective antagonist. Numerous photographs were taken of Australians providing succour to injured or starving Japanese. Put simply, they were 'good propaganda', in the phrase used by George Silk to describe his image of a Queensland private piggybacking a stricken Japanese back to camp, to be treated and tended (see Figure 3.9).[46] Use was made of such uplifting photographs during the war in the Australian Military Forces' frankly propagandist (published by the Australian War Memorial) *Jungle Warfare: With the Australian Army in the South-west Pacific* (1944). Tellingly, they continue to illustrate contemporary accounts of the Pacific campaign as appealing testimony to Australian humanity—photographs of Japanese prisoners drinking from an Australian's water bottle appear in two identically titled popular blockbusters published in 2005, Peter FitzSimons' *Kokoda* and Paul Ham's *Kokoda*.[47]

---

44   *Argus*, 5 March 1946, 1. For horrifying stories see, for example, George H. Johnston, 'Brutality of Jap Guards: Pathetic Stories Told by Australian POW's', *Argus*, 1 September 1945, 1; 'Japanese Hands Sword to Australian General', *Sydney Morning Herald*, 10 September 1945, 1; Jack Percival, 'Prisoners Beaten to Death: Grim Accounts from Japan', *Sydney Morning Herald*, 5 September 1945, 1; Graham Jenkins, 'Six Australians of 1800 Survive Borneo Horror', *Argus*, 22 September 1945, 1.
45   William Marien, 'The Barbarian of Last Week Is the Shy, Smiling Jap To-day', *Sydney Morning Herald*, 3 September 1945, 2.
46   Silk quoted in McDonald and Brune, *200 Shots*, 118. See the sequence of a distressed Japanese prisoner being cared for by Australian stretcher bearers: AWM 026822, AWM 026824, AWM 026825, AWM 026827; see also AWM 026839, AWM 013455.
47   Peter FitzSimons, *Kokoda* (Sydney: Hodder Headline, 2005), 368–69; Paul Ham, *Kokoda* (Sydney: Harper Collins, 2005), 318–19.

At times, the Australians overplayed their hand in presenting themselves as beneficent captors. In early July 1944, a photographer working for the propaganda and field intelligence unit, the Far Eastern Liaison Office (FELO), took a series of photographs of robust Japanese prisoners playing baseball at the POW camp in Cowra, New South Wales.[48] Part of FELO's brief was to undermine morale in Japanese-held parts of the south-west Pacific theatre by producing leaflets that were printed and air dropped by the million. It was for this purpose that the scenes of the Cowra idyll were taken. The camp buildings are neat and evidently commodious and the playing fields wide and inviting. Surely this was an attractive option to starvation and probable death in a fetid, claustrophobic jungle.

This was wishful thinking that did not take into account the acute sense of dishonour attached to surrender by the Japanese. Though there had been rumours of trouble brewing at the Cowra camp, the FELO photographer could not have anticipated the mass escape of more than a thousand Japanese POWs in the early hours of 5 August 1944. In what has become known as the 'Cowra Breakout', four Australians and well over 200 Japanese died,

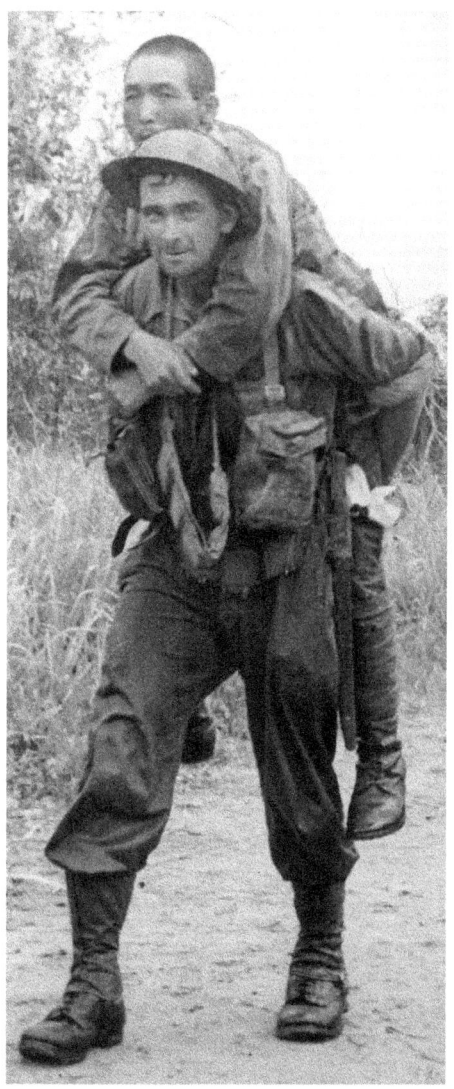

Figure 3.9. George Silk, *Wounded Japanese Carried by Australian Soldier*, c. 1942.

Source: *Argus* Newspaper Collection of Photographs, State Library of Victoria. Accession no. H98.103/4006.

---

48   Cowra camp photographs, 1 July 1944: AWM 06717; AWM 067179; AWM 067187; AWM 067188.

many shot dead while armed only with primitive weapons, including baseball bats. Disturbed by the implications of the breakout, Australian Government censors imposed severe restrictions on media reports of the episode. The Cowra camp principally housed Japanese and Italian POWs, but no specific identification of the nationality of the escapees was to be made. Sydney's *Sunday Telegraph* was deemed to have defied the ban by mentioning that some escapees had been discovered in 'foxholes', thereby alerting a readership familiar with reportage of the New Guinea campaign that they were Japanese. The newspaper's editor was rebuked by both the wartime Minister for Information Calwell and Prime Minister Curtin for putting the lives of Australians then in Japanese hands at risk.[49] Such was the fear of an enemy that did not play by the rules (and had not signed the Geneva Convention on the treatment of POWs). Of the Japanese dead, over 30 committed suicide, many by hanging. Two escapees lay on the train tracks and were run over by the morning train from Sydney. A cornered escapee was photographed still clutching the knife he had used to sever his own throat so deeply that he had nearly succeeded in decapitating himself. The picture, a disturbing revelation of the kind of enemy who would do anything to win and anything to avoid capture, was never published.[50]

The Japanese may have had other reasons for refusing to surrender on the battlefield, for despite their own projected image as kindly captors, the Australians had acquired a reputation for mercilessness. Prisoners were a burden, and many did not make it to camp or compound. The summary shooting of wounded Japanese (and some who were not wounded) was not uncommon, if conspicuously unpublicised. The official war artist Ivor Hele's charcoal drawing of the calm execution of stricken Japanese at Timbered Knoll in New Guinea in 1943 was long suppressed. Daien Parer, who was in the area at the time, chose not to film these episodes, though he did take some photographs of dead Japanese in their foxholes.[51] While the Australian treatment of its surviving captives was generally in accordance with regulations, it

---

49 See letters from Calwell and Curtin, quoted in John Hilvert, *Blue Pencil Warriors: Censorship and Propaganda in World War II* (St Lucia, Brisbane: University of Queensland Press, 1984) 189–90; Cowra breakout files in the National Archives of Australia, NAA SP195/1 73/23/32.
50 See AWM P02567.006. For a detailed account of the breakout see Steve Bullard, *Blankets on the Wire: The Cowra Breakout and its Aftermath* (Canberra: Australian War Memorial, 2006).
51 Neil McDonald, *The Story of Damien Parer* (Port Melbourne: Lothian 1994), 210–11. On the killing of Japanese captives see Tom O'Lincoln, *Australia's Pacific War: Challenging a National Myth* (Melbourne: Interventions, 2011), 84–86.

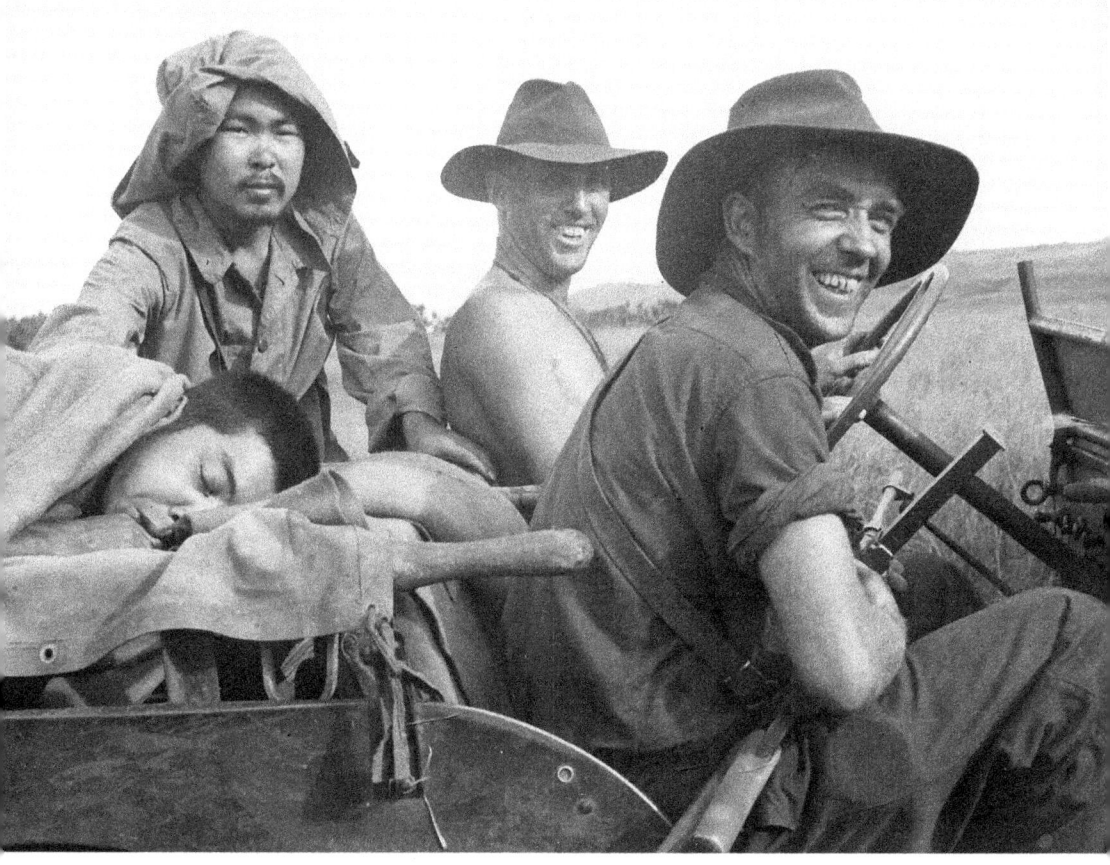

Figure 3.10. Unknown photographer, *Two Japanese Prisoners Being Conveyed to Casualty Clearing Station*, c. 1944.

Source: *Argus* Newspaper Collection of Photographs, State Library of Victoria. Accession no. H98.103/4005.

was touched by an ugly triumphalism that sought to humiliate and demean. A picture supplied to the *Argus* captures two injured and ailing Japanese being brought into camp on the back of a jeep driven by two diggers—teeth bared in jubilation—looking like they have been out on a particularly productive kangaroo shoot (see Figure 3.10).

Photographing the process of capture became an exercise in ritual humiliation. In a sequence of pictures of the capture of an unnamed Japanese prisoner in New Guinea in May 1943, Norman Stuckey himself participated in the documentation of the prisoner's degradation. Stuckey photographed the prisoner being brought into camp. Later, several photographs taken by both himself and two colleagues working for the DOI show the Japanese alongside his smirking captors. Finally, Stuckey had a photo taken of himself with the prisoner and an Australian guard, holding a drawn bayonet menacingly by the captive's face (see Figure 3.11). The sequence hardly plumbs the debased level of digital

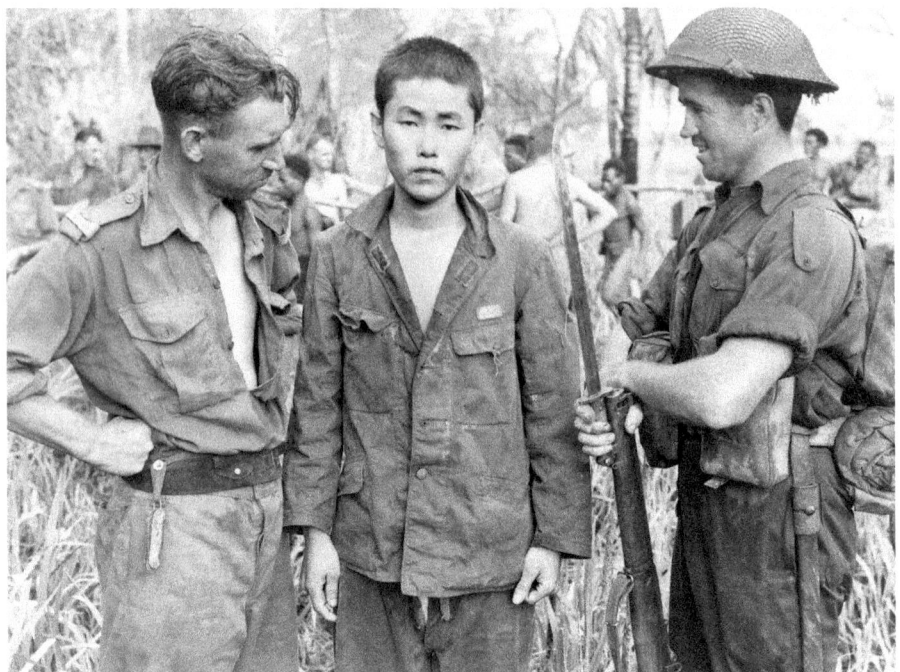

Figure 3.11. Unknown photographer, *Military History Section Photographer Lance Sergeant Norman Stuckey (left) and an Australian Soldier with Japanese Prisoner*, New Guinea, 10 October 1943.
Source: AWM 058653.

images (made by amateurs) of vile abuse inflicted on Iraqi prisoners at Abu Ghraib, taken in late 2003. Nonetheless, it transgresses the specifications of the MHS photographer's professional requirement to document with objectivity. The MHS director John Treloar was a firm advocate for impersonality in the creation of photographic records, believing that the identity of the photographer should be lost in the photograph's factual historicity. Indeed, when MHS photographs were published, the specific photographer's identity (and even the section itself) was usually concealed. One wonders whether the presence of the camera encouraged Stuckey's exhibitionism and, thus, contributed to the prisoner's mistreatment. Here, the Japanese prisoner's face bears the imprint of humiliation and abject disgrace—having his picture taken, with the possibility the image might be seen by his family back home, is itself a form of torture.[52]

---

52 On the MHS strictures of impersonality and impartiality, see Lakin, *Contac*t, 113, 140. Photographs, Dumpu New Guinea, 5 May 1943, AWM 058654; AWM 058651; AWM 016310; AWM 016314. The two colleagues were the photographers Gordon Short and Harold Dick. (Dick was later killed in an air accident in Queensland.) See also a George Silk sequence of photographs of the capture process, taken in the Oivi-Kokoda area in November 1942: AWM 151093; AWM 151094; AWM 151095.

The greater misery of national defeat was one that every Japanese serviceman had to bear. Many took it personally. Looking back at 1945, one middle-aged veteran recalled that losing the war for Japanese men meant 'losing their balls'.⁵³ Defeat was exacerbated by returning home to a country taken over and occupied by their antagonists, and a booming sexual commerce between Japanese women and foreigners. Approximately 8 million Japanese military personnel were either repatriated from overseas theatres or demobilised from the Japanese Home Forces. Having joined the American-led Occupation of Japan as part of the British Commonwealth Occupation Force (BCOF), Australian military personnel had already processed several hundred thousand Japanese repatriates by mid-1946. Much of this activity took place in Hiroshima Prefecture, where the Australian forces were largely based. One of the centres for the reception and demobilisation of returning Japanese was located at Hiroshima's port, Ujina. From 1894, when Japan's Supreme Imperial Headquarters moved to the Hiroshima Castle compound, the city was a major staging base, and soldiers were sent off from Ujina to the various military ventures that Japan embarked on over the ensuing decades. Ujina also housed the *Gaisenkan*, 'The Hall of Victorious Return', built to welcome home the nation's all-conquering armies, outside of which stood two ancient stone lions plundered from China. The defeated Japanese returnees from the Pacific had to re-enter Japan through it—a bitter irony that would not have been lost on them.

Australian military photographers were waiting in Occupied Japan to capture the dejected homecoming. Allan Cuthbert, the first photographer appointed to MHS BCOF, photographed schoolgirls dutifully greeting a returning POW upon his belated arrival in June 1946 as he casts a rueful, almost furtive sideways glance at the camera (see Figure 3.12). It is a moment of supreme bathos. The decades of Japanese militarism—so damaging to untold peoples in the region and so catastrophically self-destructive—had come to an ignominious end. The Japanese were still wending their way home in August 1947, two years after the surrender,

---

53 Koga Takeshi, 'Rikugan danshoku monogatari' ('A Tale of Male Eroticism in the Army'), published in the homoerotic pulp magazine *Fuzoku kitan*, November 1973, 168, quoted in Mark McLelland, *Queer Japan from the Pacific War to the Internet Age* (Lanham, MD: Rowman and Littlefield, 2005), 61–62. For an incisive account of this issue see Christine de Matos, 'Occupation Masculinities: The Residues of Colonial Power in Australian Occupied Japan', in *Gender, Power and Military Occupations: Asia Pacific and the Middle East since 1945*, ed. Christine de Matos and Rowena Ward (New York: Routledge, 2012), 23–42.

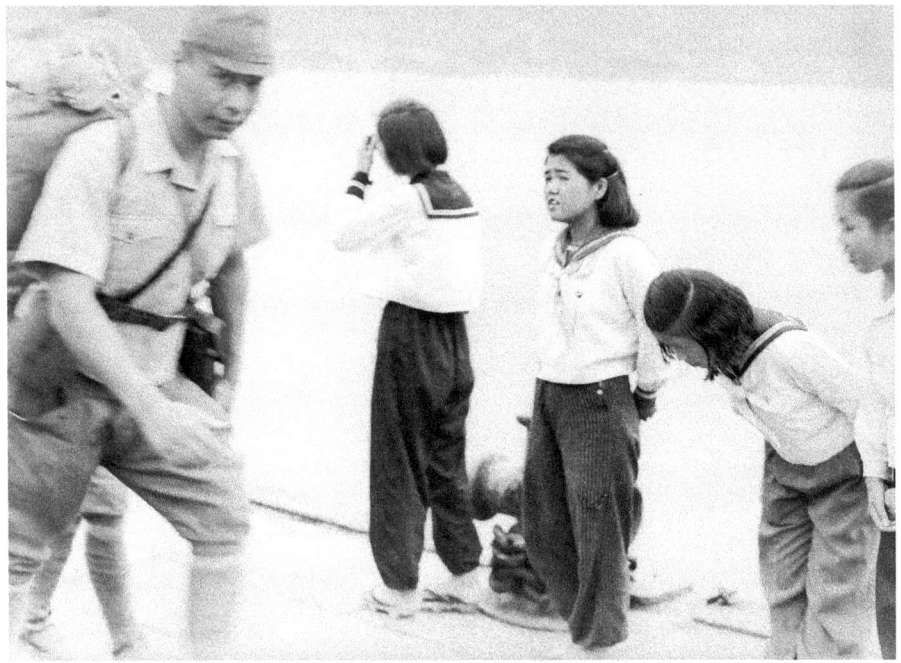

Figure 3.12. Allan Cuthbert, *Japanese Schoolgirls Welcome Home Repatriated Prisoners-of-War*, Ujina (Hiroshima), 27 June 1946.
Source: AWM 131647.

when *Pix* ran a photo spread of Australian troops processing the stragglers. *Pix* could not help itself. A picture of soldiers being deloused was captioned 'Big Vermin have Little Vermin'.[54]

Photographic Overkill

Australia can be proud of the achievements of its photographers of the war against the Japanese in the Pacific. In an environment bristling with danger, they faced the formidable challenge of transporting and maintaining photographic equipment in a tangled, boggy and humid landscape, and shooting in the dim light of the jungle.[55] Characterised by their determination to get close to the action, the Australian combat

---

54 'Jap Troops Go Home', *Pix*, 16 August 1947, 24.
55 'Until a photographer has tried to work in the jungle', Damien Parer remarked in September 1943, 'he can have no idea how greedily the heavy foliage of the tropics eats up light'. As told to A.H. Chisholm, 'Frontline Cameraman', *Herald*, 23 September 1943, 7.

3. SHOOTING JAPANESE

cameramen of WWII made a significant contribution to the evolution of the war photographer into the dynamic figure so familiar in the contemporary media landscape—the heroic warrior photojournalist, embedded in the military and dodging the same bullets. The signed photograph of the MHS's William 'Harry' Freeman, bestriding the rubble of Hiroshima with his trusty camera, is palpably grandiloquent—it is almost he who had laid waste to the enemy, and not the atomic bomb (see Figure 3.13). Here, we see the camera's increasing importance as a destructive tool of war, in a sense complicit in the violence it documents.

This triumphant image also suggests the enduring importance of photography to Australian representation and remembrance of the war against the Japanese. The persistent republication of tendentious official pictures in essentially nationalistic retrospectives of the Pacific War supports a discourse that propagates anachronistic myths of Australian military potency and diminishes the Japanese as degraded as well as defeated. Damien Parer's staged publicity picture of a dashing digger posing with a Bren machine gun appears in a photomontage on the front cover of *Kokoda*, produced by the Australian Government in 2012 to mark the seventieth anniversary of the New Guinea campaign. This publication was specifically intended for the teaching of history in Australian secondary schools.[56] Fiction is being taught as fact.

The strategic public use of photographs perpetuates wartime animosities beyond their historical context. Seventy years after the event, the picture of Len Siffleet's execution lives on as a memorialised reminder of Australian suffering and Japanese fanaticism. In Canberra's Australian War Memorial, the photograph is on permanent display in its own glass cabinet right by the entrance to the gallery dedicated to the Australian New Guinea offensives of 1943 and 1944, which helped turn the tide of the Pacific War. The repugnant image of the Japanese executioner is the first thing visitors see, providing a kind of moral as well as circumstantial context for the subduing of the Japanese threat. Moreover, it provides a potent personification of the threat itself. In the age of ISIS terror and

---

56   *Kokoda: Exploring the Second World War Campaign in Papua New Guinea* (Canberra: Commonwealth of Australia Department of Veterans' Affairs, 2012). See AWM 013285. McDonald and Brune described the staging of the incident from which this widely circulated photograph was taken, see *200 Shots*, 23.

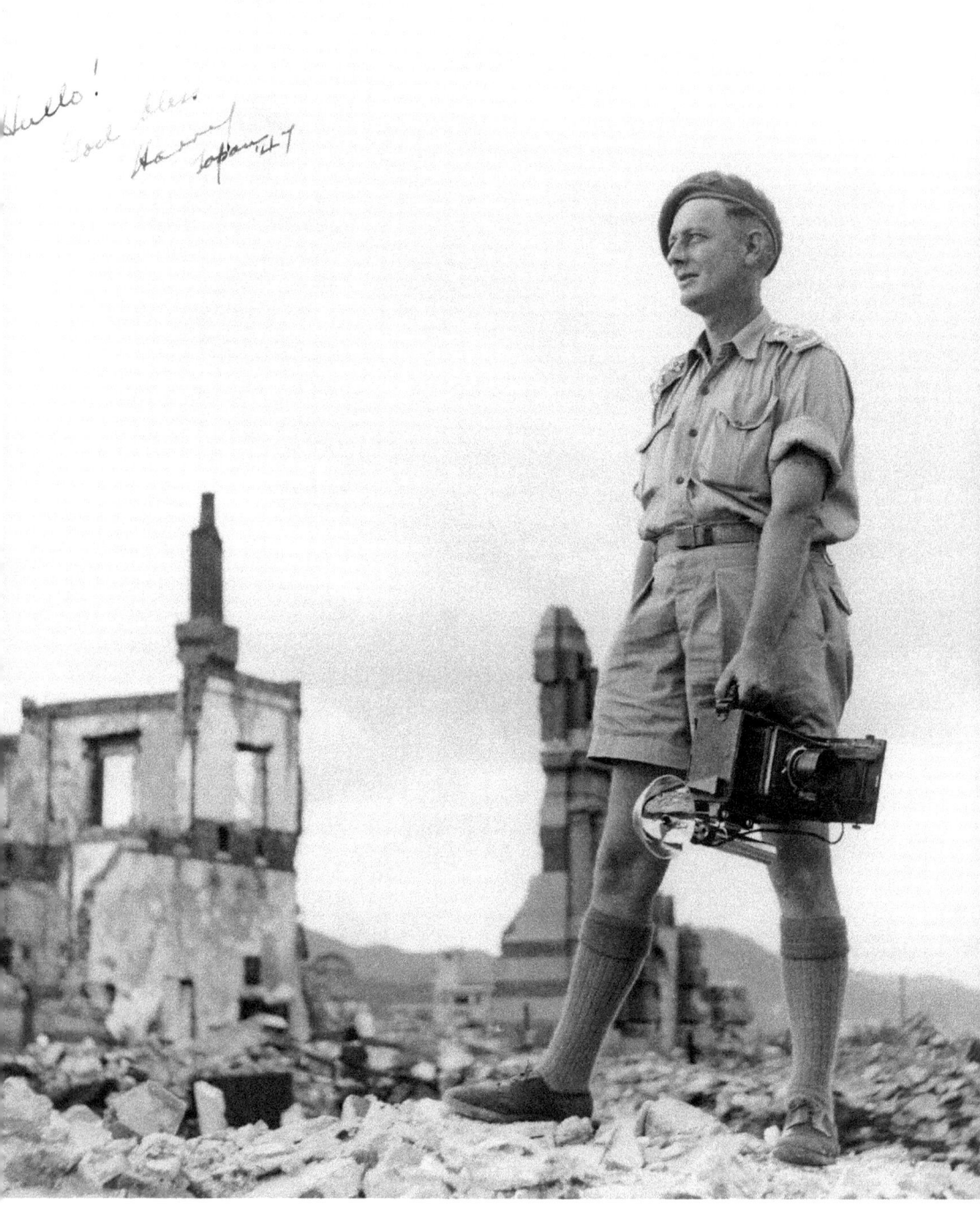

Figure 3.13. Unknown photographer, *Portrait of Lieutenant William Harry Freeman*, Official photographer, Hiroshima, 1947.
Source: AWM P10753.001.

the digitised mass circulation of gruesome executions and beheadings produced and disseminated by murderous jihadists, it is a highly emotive image.[57]

The Japanese character was fixed in the national consciousness for decades by the Australian military photographs taken in the Pacific in the early 1940s. The war remained a constant visual reference point, against which the Japanese people were continually assessed and, as old enmities faded, reassessed and reimaged. The long road to postwar reconciliation was signposted by photography. It began in Japan itself, with the several thousand Australian soldiers—many of them festooned with their cameras, feasting on the foreign spectacle—who journeyed to Japan to participate in a military occupation that lasted longer than the bloody conflict that preceded it.

---

57   Photograph of execution of Private Reharin, 24 October 1943, AWM 101100.

4

JAPAN FOR THE TAKING:
IMAGES OF THE OCCUPATION

The public perception of Japan's place in the postwar world, observed Karen M. Fraser in *Photography and Japan*, was informed by a 'single photograph'.[1] Six weeks after the atomic destruction of Hiroshima and Nagasaki, the totality of Japan's defeat was signalled by an image taken in late September 1945 by Lieutenant Gaetano Faillace, a member of the American Camera Corps. The occasion was the historic first meeting of General Douglas MacArthur, the supreme commander of the Allied Occupation, with Emperor Hirohito. According to MacArthur's biographer, Hirohito was 'trembling' when he arrived at the US Embassy in Tokyo, close by the imperial palace; the general tried to calm him by proffering an American cigarette, which was accepted with a shaky hand.[2] The diminutive emperor, swaddled in formal frock coat, cravat and striped pants, stands stiffly by the American, just two feet to his right but a good foot taller (see Figure 4.1). By contrast, McArthur is the at-home host, unsmiling but disarmingly relaxed, nonchalant even, dressed casually in khaki, hands in his pockets. It was the only time during the six years of the Occupation that MacArthur deigned to be photographed with any Japanese, let alone the emperor. He made sure Faillace's photograph was published in Japanese newspapers the next day. One devastating image had reduced Japan's living god to a nervous, slightly absurd visitor in his own country—a country now ruled by the US with

---

1   Karen M. Fraser, *Photography and Japan* (London: Reaktion Books, 2011), 68.
2   William Manchester, *American Caesar: Douglas MacArthur 1880–1964* (New York: Dell Publishing, 1978), 577.

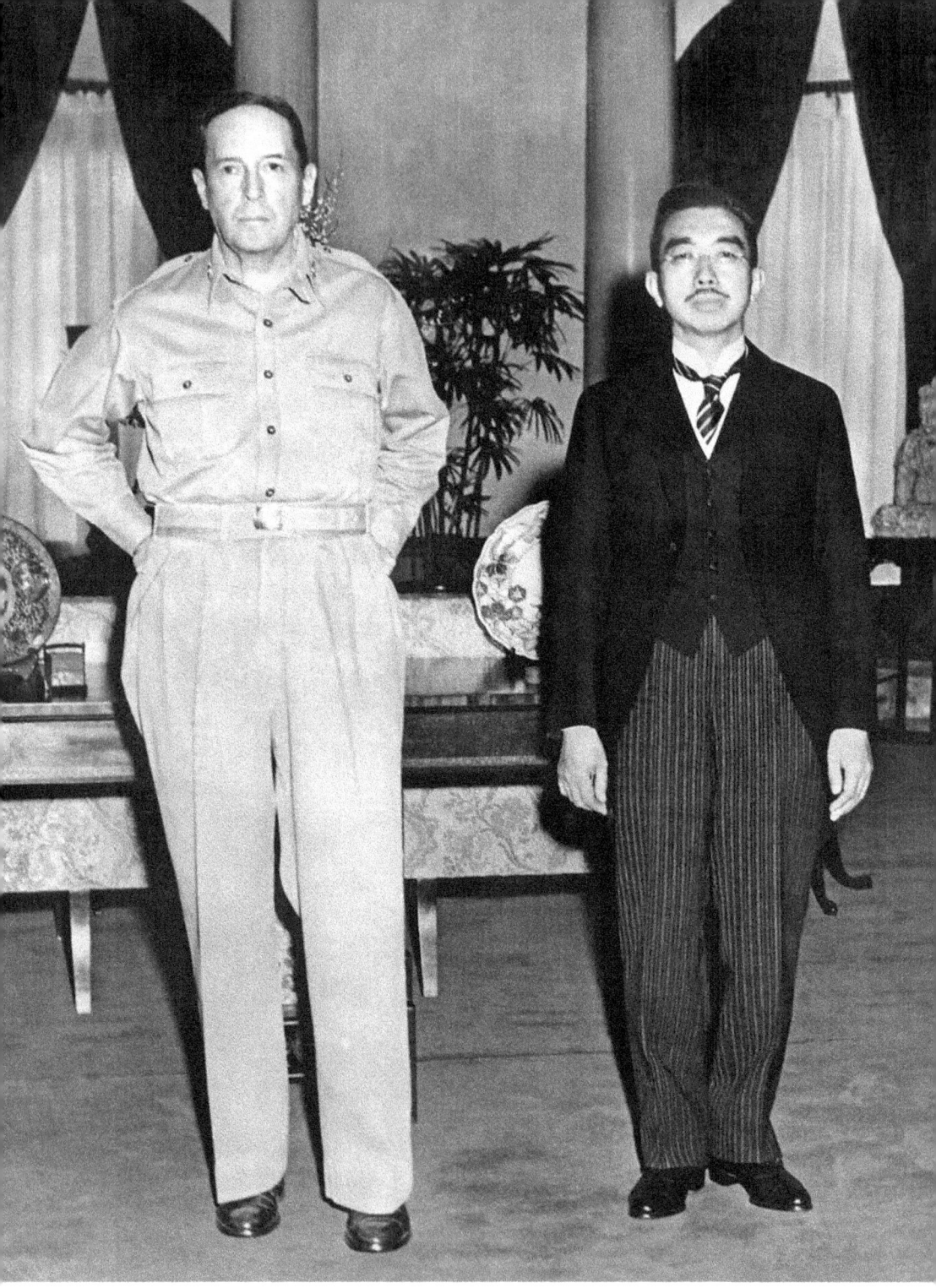

Figure 4.1. Lt Gaetano Faillace, *Emperor Hirohito and General MacArthur, at Their First Meeting, at the U.S. Embassy*, Tokyo, 27 September 1945.
Source: United States Army Photograph.

help from the British Commonwealth Occupation Force (BCOF), made up of Australians, British, New Zealanders and Indians, of which the Australians provided the leadership and the largest contingent.

Perhaps Fraser is overstating the influence of one purportedly definitive image; nevertheless, it is true to say that few military events have been as marked by photography as the Occupation of Japan. Just as the predatory 'chopper' is a symbol of the Vietnam War, the essence of the Occupation is represented by an iconic material object, the camera. As an observer quipped in 1949, 'the Army of Occupation is extensively armed—with Kodaks, Leicas and Speed Graphics'.[3] Perhaps this was especially true of the Australians, many of whom were on their first overseas trip and determined to document the experience. In the permanent display dedicated to the Occupation in the Australian War Memorial, the event is fittingly represented by the iconography of tourism, including a suitcase, a leave pass, a battered booklet entitled *Japanese in 3 Weeks* and a few conventional Japanese souvenirs such as a black-ribbed Agfa Box 45, used in Japan by the Australian BCOF serviceman Frank Lawrence. It is an appropriate collection of relics, for the Australians were relentless sightseers and ardent photographers. Off duty (and sometimes on it), they rarely ventured anywhere without a camera slung over their shoulders.

As the Occupation wore on, the chances were that more and more of their cameras were made locally. Photography was a booming enterprise in Occupied Japan. The local camera and optical industries grew quickly, catering in the main to the influx of foreigners—the Americans alone numbered up to 350,000. At up to 20,000, the Australian contingent was tiny by comparison, though still a significant number. Germany, the previous dominant power in photographic equipment, was in ruins, with much of what was left of its industry located in the eastern zone, dominated by Russia. Established Japanese camera companies such as Nikon and Canon took advantage of financial and technical support by the Americans to meet the market for locally made copies of German models, a market boosted in 1950 by the arrival of a large press corps stopping off in Japan en route to the new war that had broken out in

---

3   Lucy Herndon Crockett, *Popcorn on the Ginza: An Informal Portrait of Postwar Japan* (London: Victor Gollancz, 1949), 99. Quoted in Morris Low, 'American Photography during the Allied Occupation of Japan: The Work of John W. Bennett', *History of Photography* 39, no. 3 (August 2015): 265.

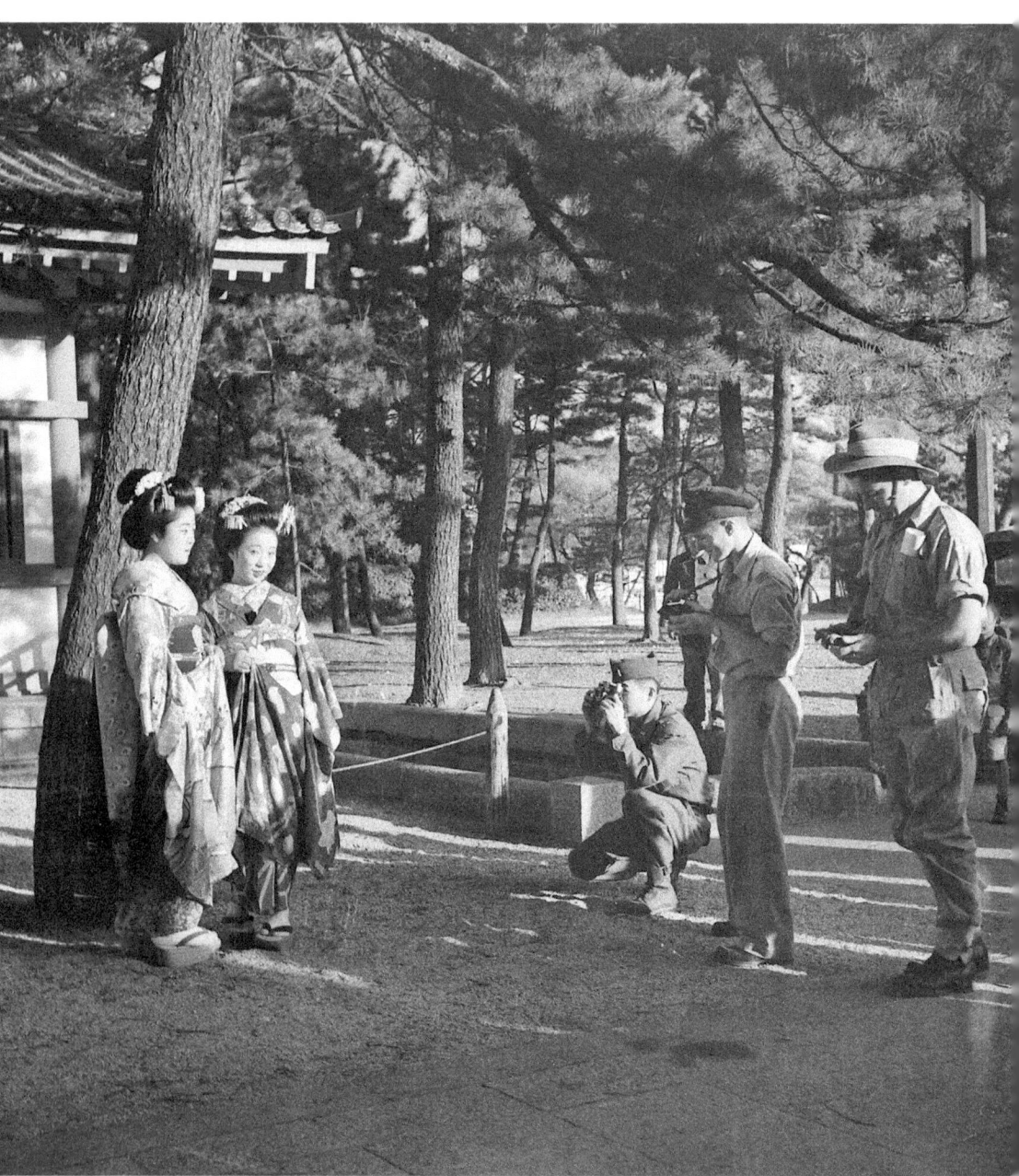

Figure 4.2. William Harry Freeman, *Members of BCOF Taking Photographs of 'Geisha Girls'*, Kyoto, August 1947.
Source: AWM 133125.

Korea.⁴ Sightseeing and photography became inextricably intertwined, one activity feeding off the other. The dedication to taking pictures was habitual and, in many cases, slightly obsessive. One Australian paid homage to the activity by taking an image of a Kodak processing store in the town of Bofu, a major BCOF air force station.⁵ Many servicemen took photographs of their comrades and were themselves caught in the act of taking pictures, or awaiting the next shot.⁶

The flurry of photographic activity in Occupied Japan became a subject of choice for the official cohort of photographers assigned to cover what was a unique episode in Australian military history—the first time Australia had formally occupied a nation defeated in war. Photographers working for the Directorate of Public Relations (DPR) attached to both the army and the air force made attractive images designed to appeal to a sometimes sceptical public back home, while the Military History Section (MHS) documented the Occupation for posterity, with an eye to the historical record and an official history that never saw the light of day. Together, their pictures often reveal a kind of professional self-reflexivity, as in the DPR's Douglas Lee's image of army photographers shooting the farewell parade for the Australian commander of BCOF, Lieutenant General Robertson, in Kure in November 1951.⁷ In August 1947, Harry Freeman of the MHS photographed soldiers in turn photographing 'geisha girls' (so says the caption) in Kyoto (see Figure 4.2).⁸ The image is telling, for in a sense the Occupation was not only officially documented by photography, but also by the presentation of an almost absurdly redundant view of an untouched, timeless Japan that deflected from the damage the pitiless Allied bombing had wrought on the country.

Most members of the official Australian photographic cohort, including leading practitioners such as Alan Queale of the MHS and Phillip Hobson of the DPR, came fresh from the military that had just fought in the conflict. Several were still on active service and answerable to

---

4   See Robert White, *Discovering Cameras, 1945–1965* (London: Shire Discovering, 1968), 13. Marked 'Made in Occupied Japan', cameras figured prominently in the nation's export trade in the immediate postwar period, garnering foreign currency and stimulating the economy. The importance of the camera industry to Japan's economic recovery is illustrated by the section dedicated to postwar Japan in Tokyo's Edo-Tokyo Museum prominently featuring a Konica 35 mm camera.
5   Frank Lees, photograph of Kodak store, Bofu. AWM P06206.012.
6   See for example Lindsay Poore, *Grandmummasan*, c. 1947–1949, State Library of Victoria H2009.14/165.
7   Lee AWM LEEJ0013.
8   Freeman AWM133125.

a command that tended to see the Occupation as the last phase of a long military campaign, they maintained a deep dislike of the Japanese.⁹ Their professional obligations did not easily accommodate a nuanced personal response to Japan or new ways of picturing the country, despite the process of radical transformation they were there to record. They remained tied to the framing of a traditional Japan that was both bucolic and ultra-refined, and above all photogenically alluring—the Japan, indeed, of postcards of geisha and teahouses. This was 'the land of the picturesque' delighted in by the Australian traveller James Hingston in the 1870s, who likened the place to a pre-modern version of Britain 'in the days of old, when there were maypoles and morris-dancers, and caps with bells to them'.¹⁰ It was a fanciful vision way back then, in the initial phases of Japan's process of modernisation in the early Meiji era; it was even more outmoded after the ravages of the recent war, which scarred the country physically and affected it socially and culturally.

The dependence on redundant imagery of a pristine Japan derived, in part, from the established institutions of Australian war photography. The DPR had sprung from the wartime Department of Information, whose pictures of soldiers on leave or training in the Middle East had drawn on the tourist and ethnographic aspects of photographs of their predecessors in Oriental locales in WWI.¹¹ However, it also reveals the persistent influence of the decorative Japonisme that swept Australia in waves from the 1880s to the 1930s, which distinguished the 'real', significantly feminine and childlike Japan, from the modernising and militaristic nation that Australia went to war against.¹² This idealised Japan emerged most blatantly in the pictorial motifs of tourism. Both before and after WWI, during which Japan was an Australian ally, the Sydney shipping and trading company Burns Philp used photographs of geisha, temples and sumptuous mountainscapes to illustrate its in-house publication *Picturesque Travel*, hoping to lure customers to its cruises to

---

9   The Treaty of Peace with Japan was not signed until September 1951 and did not come into force until the following year.
10 James Hingston, from *The Australian Abroad* (1879–1880), in *Hotel Asia*, ed. Robin Gerster (Ringwood: Penguin, 1995), 33.
11 See Shaune Lakin, *Contact: Photographs from the Australian War Memorial Collection* (Canberra: Australian War Memorial, 2006), 102, 105. The Department of Information originated in the pre-WWI Department of External Affairs, one of whose roles was to produce attractive photographic images of Australia to encourage tourism to the country.
12 On the influence of Japonism in Australia, see Melissa Miles, 'Through Japanese Eyes: Ichiro Kagiyama and Australian-Japanese Relations in the 1920s and 1930s', *History of Photography* 38, no. 4 (2014): 368.

Japan and the Orient aboard the Japanese steamship company Nippon Yusen Kaisha.[13] In this, they anticipated the propaganda of the Japanese National Board of Tourist Industry in the 1930s, which attempted to encourage foreign tourism as an aggressively expansionary Japan sought to convey a sympathetic impression of itself to the world. A 'carefully cultivated image of picturesqueness' marked the promotional booklets produced by the board and even the sophisticated photo journal *Nippon*, produced in several European languages for foreign consumption, which was anxious to present Japan as a technologically advanced trading nation the equal of any in the West.[14]

Many of these tourist trailblazers to Japan would have followed the advice of the Australian photographer Nevil A. Tooth, in a piece on Japan published in *Harrington's Photographic Journal* in 1911: 'take a camera'.[15] WWII temporarily halted this early tourist traffic to Japan and destroyed the idealised country Australian travellers had coveted. Conditioned to see Japan in certain ways, BCOF photographers sought to validate a set of images that the war had made obsolete and that the Occupation was designed to revise. They documented a force charged with rebuilding Japan, but uncomfortable with the social and political volatility reconstruction had unleashed. An act of recreation, of remaking feudal Japan into a self-reliant and pluralistic modern nation, was visually realised as a regressive exercise in control.

The Allied mission in Japan, led by the imperious MacArthur, lasted twice as long as the Pacific War that preceded it. For all its benevolent modernity in facilitating Japan's transition from militarism to a functioning democracy, it was an enterprise that was both anachronistic and neo-colonialist. BCOF was one of the last collective armed gestures of a moribund empire as Britain began its retreat from Asia. In noting its historically familiar exercise of the white conqueror's privilege over the conquered Asiatic, both American and Japanese historians have likened the Occupation to the British Raj in India. John Dower, in *Embracing Defeat*, applied Rudyard Kipling's euphemism for imperial hegemony, labelling it 'the last immodest exercise in the colonial conceit

---

13 The first issue of *Picturesque Travel* appeared in 1911 and the last in 1925. Burns Philp pioneered the Pacific cruise and the packaging of tours in Asia for Australians, monopolising the trade for decades.
14 See Gennifer S. Weisenfeld, 'Touring "Japan-As-Museum": Nippon and Other Japanese Imperialist Travelogues', *Positions: East Asia Cultures Critique* 8, no. 3 (Winter 2000): 788.
15 Nevil A. Tooth, 'A Camera in Japan', *Harrington's Photographic Journal*, 22 December 1911, 381.

known as "the white man's burden'".¹⁶ In Occupied Japan, the 'white man's burden' was one borne lightly, for the country lay prostrate and apparently accommodating. The camera became both an instrument of power and a neo-colonial medium of framing places and peoples, and the Occupation itself a new paradigm of the historical nexus of photographic appropriation, tourism and military colonisation.

Atomic Tourists

Japan was in ruins when the first Australian Occupationnaires arrived in early 1946. Sixty of its cities had been pulverised and incinerated by a saturation bombing campaign that included the prodigious use of napalm. Up to 100,000 citizens of Tokyo perished in a single night in March 1945, 'scorched and boiled and baked to death', in the phrase of the campaign's chief strategist Major General Curtis ('Bombs Away') Le May.¹⁷ The postwar homeless numbered more than 8 million, people were dying of malnutrition and orphans scrounged in gutted buildings and blackened streets. Prostitution was the only thing to thrive in the wreckage. From April 1946, Australians settled into a cluster of camps in and around the heavily bombed Inland Sea port of Kure, just down the coast from Hiroshima. The following year saw the arrival of the wives and children of many servicemen, housed in purpose-built residential colonies, amply serviced by Japanese domestic staff—a practice that reminded the visiting Australian travel writer Frank Clune of the British garrison towns in Imperial India.¹⁸

Yet, the manifest misery and squalor of postwar Japan hardly registers in the official Australian photography. In 1948, BCOF's Australian commander-in-chief, Lieutenant-General Horace Robertson, presented

---

16 John Dower, *Embracing Defeat: Japan in the Aftermath of World War II* (Harmondsworth: Penguin, 2000), 23. Written in response to the American colonisation of the Philippines, a prize of the Spanish–American War, Kipling's landmark poem 'The White Man's Burden' (1899) urged the United States to take up the noble cause of empire formerly borne by European nations, most notably by the British Raj in Imperial India. The reference is singularly apt, for the first military governor of American-occupied Manila was none other than General Arthur MacArthur, father of Douglas. The Japanese historian of the Occupation, Eiji Takemae, drew a similar parallel with the British Raj. See Eiji Takemae, *The Allied Occupation of Japan*, trans. Robert Ricketts and Sebastian Swann (New York: Continuum, 2003), 75.
17 Le May quoted in John W. Dower, *War Without Mercy: Race and Power in the Pacific War* (Pantheon Books: New York, 1986), 40–41.
18 Frank Clune, *Ashes of Hiroshima* (Sydney: Angus & Robertson, 1950), 56.

eight handsome, personally inscribed photograph albums to the serving Australian Prime Minister, Ben Chifley.[19] The albums contained the work of the photographers attached to the DPR; one can assume that this was considered a representative collection of its endeavours. Somewhat alarmingly for the photographic record of a force entrusted with the serious mission of assisting the Americans in neutering Japan as a future threat and turning it into a responsible ally, it resembles a highly polished selection of the prized photographs of a family on its dream trip abroad. Servicemen are revealed in several stylised touristic poses, such as living it up in glamorous leave resorts, playing golf with snow-capped Fujisan looming majestically in the background, and negotiating the famous stepping stones across the pond at the Heian shrine in Kyoto (trying not to drop their cameras into the water). The wives and children of BCOF personnel are also there, picnicking and cavorting on the beaches of the Inland Sea, having the time of their lives.

One photograph in the collection, less staged than the others, stands out. It reveals a slouch-hatted young Australian 'digger' on leave in Tokyo's Ginza, shopping at one of the street markets that cropped up in Japanese cities in the early postwar years (see Figure 4.3). Trying his hand at an accordion, the occupying soldier is the tourist consumer self-consciously partaking of the passing pleasures that come his way, in an environment in which such things are his for the taking. Meanwhile, the Japanese bric-a-brac vendor, clothed in military remnants of the late war, stares vaguely in the direction of the camera, bristling and humiliated, awaiting, though not indulging, the Australian's pleasure.[20] The DPR photographer has inadvertently identified the nature of human exchange in Occupied Japan, in which military domination and control extended beyond the subjugation of a people defeated in war, penetrating and corrupting all aspects of human interaction.

---

19   Photographs of BCOF clubs, churches, leave resorts and hospitals, photographed and compiled by Public Relations Section, HQ, BCOF, Japan. 30446636 PIC Albums 525–528, 530–533. See esp. album 528.
20   The photograph anticipates by at least three years Ken Domon's well-known 1951 picture of postwar Japanese abjection, *ShoiGunjin, Ueno*, in which a maimed, cap-wearing Japanese war veteran turned street beggar dolefully plays a squeezebox. The photograph is discussed in Julia Adeney Thomas, 'Power Made Visible: Photography and Postwar Japan's Elusive Reality', *The Journal of Asian Studies* 67, no. 2 (May 2008): 365–94, and features on the cover of the issue.

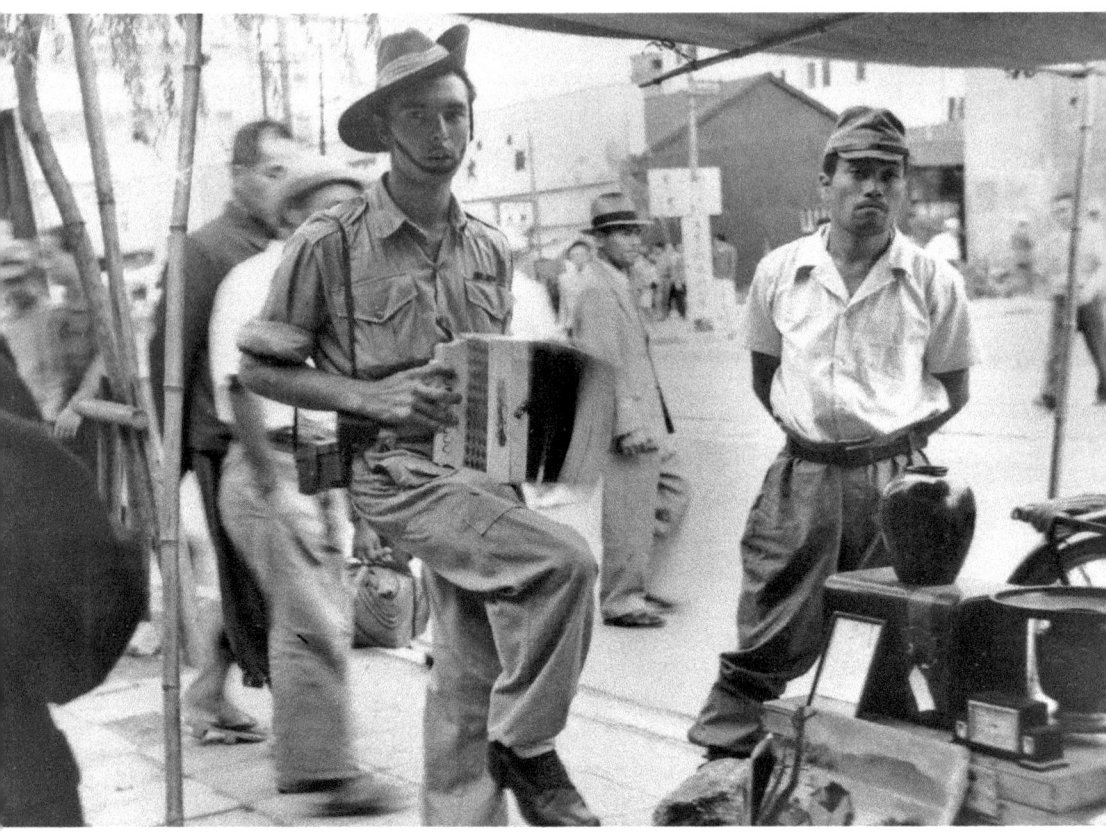

Figure 4.3. Unknown photographer, BCOF Public Relations, *Australian Soldier Shopping in Ginza*, Tokyo, c. 1946–48.
Source: National Library of Australia, 3044336, Album 528.

The imagery of tourism dominated Australian photography of the Occupation from virtually the first Australian landfall in Japan. In March 1946, a few weeks after Australian troops had started arriving in Kure, Australia's longest-running weekly picture magazine, the *Australasian*, published an extensive photo story trumpeting this historic event. Taken by Neil Town, the staff photographer for the *Australasian* while still enlisted in the Royal Australian Air Force, the images illustrated an article with the title 'Australia Is There', reminiscent of the jingoistic bluster that attended national participation in the remote theatres of WWI.[21] In the main photograph, a group of Australian soldiers saunter out of a destroyed Hiroshima shrine, via the *torii*, or entrance gate (see Figure 4.4). Though the caption does not identify it, this was the

---

21   'Australia Will Be There' was a popular patriotic song written in response to Australia's entry into WWI. It was written in 1915 by the songwriter Walter Skipper Francis.

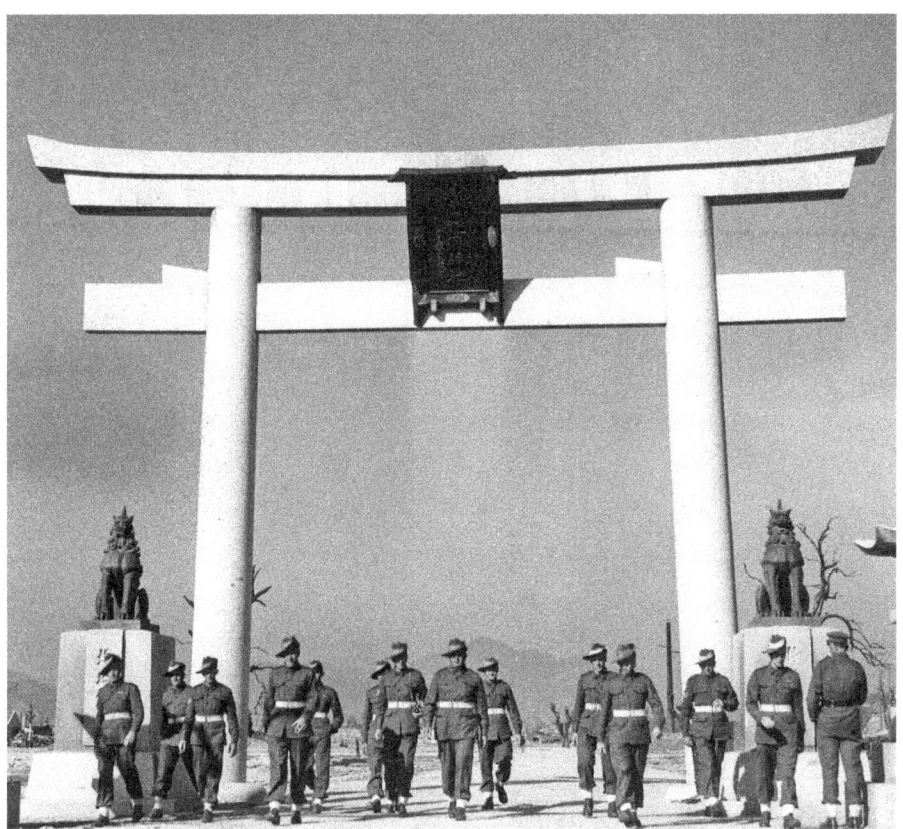

Figure 4.4. Neil Town, 'Australia Is There—With Our Occupation Force in Japan', *Australasian*, 9 March 1946, 25.

Source: *Argus* Newspaper Collection of Photographs, State Library of Victoria. Accession no. H98.104/565.

only *torii* of three local 'Gokuku' shrines to survive the blast of 6 August 1945. Gokuku shrines are dedicated as places of worship honouring those who have died in war; the Hiroshima version commemorated local victims of the civil war in the late 1860s between the Tokugawa shogunate and the imperial forces. The *torii* symbolically marks the transition from the profane to the sacred—or the other way round if one is exiting. It would be asking too much for this information to be conveyed to the unknowing Australian audience. Yet, at the same time, Town's image captures the mix of arrogance and blithe ignorance with which the Australians went to Japan. The diggers had arrived in Japan and were in command; the sacred *torii* is turned into a triumphal arch.

The photograph conjures something else besides military swagger. The group of soldiers look like tourists in khaki; as the caption states, they appear to be on a 'sightseeing tour'. The formal architecture of the *torii* throws the casualness of the Australians into relief; even for the notoriously 'unmilitary' Australian soldiers, they are well out of step. In the text accompanying the pictures, co-written by the noted war correspondent (and future eminent novelist) George Johnston, who had covered the Japanese surrender in Tokyo Bay the previous September, Neil Town insisted the Australians were 'not in Japan as tourists', but understood 'the serious international implications of their tasks'. Yet, Town also talked about soldiers in Hiroshima 'scratching through the debris looking for souvenirs'. This unappealing image is supported by one of Town's own photographs showing two Australian soldiers doing just that (and photographing themselves doing it), published a couple of weeks earlier in the Melbourne daily broadsheet the *Argus*, the stablemate of the *Australasian*, for whom he also provided pictures. The day before, the *Argus* ran what must have been a disconcerting picture to civilian Australians in 1946—Town's image of a soldier being fitted out in a kimono in a Japanese store, attended by two admiring Japanese female assistants.[22]

Neil Town was not alone among newspaper photographers and journalists in drawing attention to the touristic aspects of the enterprise. Recruitment literature exploited the imagery of travel to lure men into the occupying force in the first place, and the press coverage played up the sightseeing nature of the event.[23] The 'FIRST PICTURES OF AUSTRALIAN TROOPS IN JAPAN', unveiled on the front page of the *Sydney Morning Herald* in late February 1946, revealed a posse of smiling soldiers promenading across a Hiroshima bridge and buying fruit from local vendors.[24] Around the same time, the respected journalist Massey Stanley, writing in the *Daily Telegraph*, recommended the tour of duty to members of the Australian Imperial Force (AIF) as a chance to visit 'fascinating' Japan, 'one of the loveliest countries on earth', where soldiers could readily access 'an abundance of supplies and luxuries beyond the dreams' of civilian Australia.[25] Stanley's article was titled 'AIF

---

22 Neil Town and George H. Johnston, 'Australia Is There—With Our Occupation Force in Japan', *Australasian*, 9 March 1946, 31; *Argus*, 20 February 1946, 13; *Argus*, 19 February 1946, 1.
23 See Prue Torney-Parlicki, *Somewhere in Asia: War, Journalism, and Australia's Neighbours 1941–75* (Sydney: UNSW Press, 2000), 139.
24 *Sydney Morning Herald*, 19 February 1946, 1.
25 Massey Stanley, 'AIF Should Like Japan', *Daily Telegraph*, 17 February 1946, 47.

Should Like Japan'. As if to prove its validity, a photographic feature on the Occupation published in July 1946 in *Pix*—a reliable outlet for propaganda pictures during the Occupation as in the war—reveals the female proprietor of a Japanese hotel on the island of Shikoku bowing deeply before two Australian military visitors. Accompanying pictures show Australians' attempts with chopsticks, being entertained by geisha, disporting themselves in a hot tub and visiting a local castle.[26]

These pleasures and privileges were enacted in the shadow of Hiroshima. The city exercised a somewhat perverse fascination for the Australians. Partly this was due to proximity, for Hiroshima was quite literally down the road. As well, the city was sensationally topical and many Australians made a beeline for the place—its nuclear notoriety made it a must see on the tour of duty. On day trips or family outings, they went there heedless of the potential risk, for the official guidebook *Know Japan* provided to the troops never once mentioned the word 'radiation'. By 1946, the fledgling beginnings of a tourism industry were already in evidence in Hiroshima. Bomb debris was being peddled to tourists, mostly household items remoulded in the tremendous heat caused by the explosion. Australians were enthusiastic clients, buying (or looting) pieces of rubble from around the hypocentre of the explosion on 6 August 1945, ground zero, to take back home.

'The damage is far greater than any photographs can show', wrote the first foreigner to report from the devastated city, the Australian journalist Wilfred Burchett, in early September 1945. Burchett was trying to convey the colossal material damage and the suffering of the survivors, who died 'mysteriously and horribly'.[27] In fact, the photographs taken by Australians say a great deal about the death of a city and its rebirth. Equally importantly, they provide a self-reflexive view of the way Australians perceived postwar Japan. Photographing Hiroshima, more than any other site in the country, was the means through which they negotiated the ethical and perceptual confusions of an Occupation that was part indulgently vengeful and punitive and part an exercise in reconciliation and reconstruction.

26   *Pix*, 12 July 1947, 6–9. See also a feature on Australian servicemen enjoying themselves at the Kawana Hotel, 'Aussies in Swank Japan Hotel', *Pix*, 9 August 1947, 3–5.
27   Wilfred Burchett, 'The Atomic Plague', *Daily Express*, 5 September 1945, 1, quoted in Burchett, *Shadows of Hiroshima* (London: Verso, 1983), 34–36. Burchett's report led to the enforcement of a *cordon sanitaire* around Hiroshima by the American occupying authority, enforced as much by the determination to keep prying eyes away from the city as by concern about visitors being exposed to radiation.

In distant Australia, relief at the end of the war was tempered by inarticulate trepidation at the power the science of mass destruction had unleashed.[28] Photography filled a representational vacuum. Members of the Australian advance party of BCOF were struck dumb by the sight of Hiroshima upon their arrival in the country in February 1946. The men 'had no word to describe it, which is unusual for Australian soldiers', stated a brief report published in the Melbourne *Argus*.[29] The *Argus* article is dwarfed by photographs taken by the newspaper's staff photographer. These include a panorama of the extensive damage in the centre of the city, highlighting the skeletal structure of what was to become the iconic symbol of both Hiroshima and the nuclear age itself, the A-Bomb Dome; another wide-angle shot of the bombed harbour at Kure; and a carefully contrived counter to the images of destruction—a scene of a genial Australian soldier interacting with adoring Japanese women and children. In the publicly circulated photography of the early days of the Occupation, the military might of the conquering force was balanced by an imagery of benignity. The Allies had won the war with ruthless technological efficiency and were now rebuilding Japan, helping it to mend its militaristic ways and nurturing its future. In one photograph (see Figure 4.5), a group of crisply uniformed diggers stroll past the A-Bomb Dome with a conqueror's cocky self-assurance. The symbol of the city's nuclear destruction serves as a decorative backdrop—the Australians' eyes are firmly fixed ahead—and the picture suggests a force free of self-doubt or moral qualms.[30]

The landscape of devastation surveyed in these early photographs from Hiroshima is pleasantly free of signs of human suffering. This was both calculated and shameless.[31] Anxious not to disturb what it politely called 'public tranquillity', MacArthur's headquarters imposed a strict code of press censorship in September 1945 as one of its first disingenuous acts to democratise totalitarian Japan. This systematically silenced the *hibakusha*, the survivors of Hiroshima and Nagasaki who had lived to tell

---

28 A Gallup Poll of Australians taken in September 1945 revealed that 83 per cent thought their use justified ('Use of Atom Bomb on Japs Approved', *Australian Gallup Polls*, nos 294–303 (September–October 1945)).
29 'New Era', editorial, *Courier Mail*, 8 August 1945, 2; 'Atom Bomb Ruin Staggers Australians in Japan', *Argus*, 18 February 1946, 20.
30 See for example *Argus* Newspaper Collections of Photographs, State Library of Victoria, H98.104/563, H98.100/172.
31 Wilfred Burchett, 'The Atomic Plague', *Daily Express*, 5 September 1945, 1, quoted in Burchett, *Shadows of Hiroshima*, 34–36.

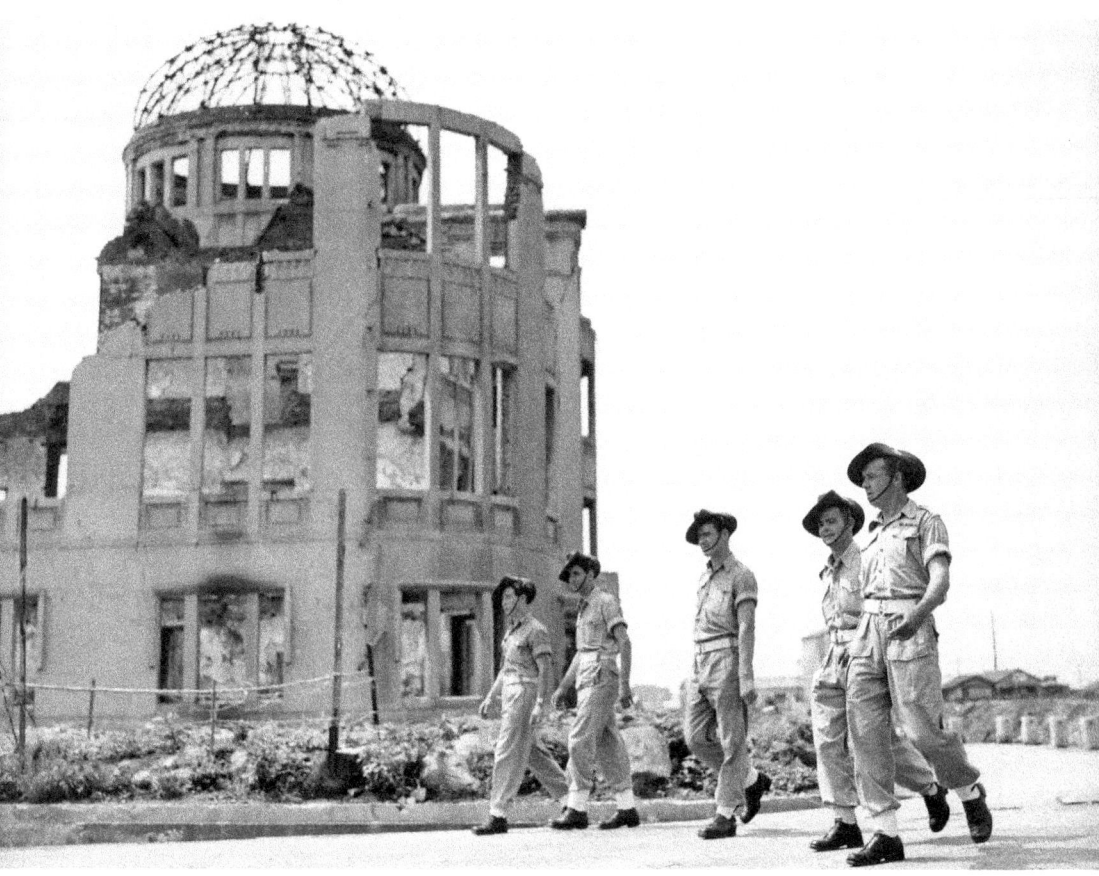

Figure 4.5. Unknown photographer, *Australian Soldiers in Hiroshima*, c. 1947.

Source: *Argus* Newspaper Collection of Photographs, State Library of Victoria. Accession no. H98.100/282.

the tale. Years later, the Hiroshima poet Sadako Kurihara remembered her frustration: 'We were not allowed to write about the atomic bomb during the Occupation. We were not even allowed to say that we were not allowed to write about the atomic bomb'.[32] The portrayal of the misery inflicted by the bombings was strictly the privilege of the foreigner and could only be communicated to foreign audiences. *Hiroshima* (1946), by the American news correspondent John Hersey and first published as a single issue in the *New Yorker*, was enormously influential and was extracted in the service newspaper the *British Commonwealth Occupation*

---

32   See Monica Braw, *The Atomic Bomb Suppressed: American Censorship in Japan 1945–1948* (Tokyo: Liber Forlag, 1986), 14. Kurihara interviewed in 1978 by the author.

News (*BCON*), which subtitled its story 'A US Writer Tells What Really Happened at Hiroshima'.³³ Of course, Hersey was not himself actually there; his book is built on interviews. It was forbidden for Japanese survivors to tell the story in their own words.

The ban applied to photographs and the written word. Ostensibly it was latent Japanese resentment that the Occupation wanted to contain. However, there was another, deeper reason; at stake was the prestige of the US and allies like Australia as a collective beacon of enlightened humanity. Documentary images of grotesquely burned corpses or massed remains would not do. Macarthur's administration prohibited the publication of ground-level photographs capturing the horror of the immediate atomic aftermath, including the handful of pictures of Hiroshima taken by local photographer Yoshito Matsuhige and those of Nagasaki taken by Yosuke Yamahata. These harrowing images were not published in the US until *Life* magazine presented them in a photo spread in September 1952, after the implementation of the Peace Treaty formally ended the Occupation. In their official absence, explicit images of the destruction circulated on the black market in the form of postcards (with titles such as 'Terrible Sight'), many of which were acquired by BCOF servicemen.³⁴ Photographic imagery of the atomic bomb came to be monopolised by the uncensored sight of the mushroom cloud spiralling high into the sky, conveniently camouflaging the horrors down below.³⁵

The MHS's Alan Cuthbert produced several panoramic photographs of Hiroshima that provide an impressive visual register of the immensity of the nuclear devastation, but which obscure the intimacies of human suffering that pervaded the city. Soon after arriving in Japan in

---

33   See 'Death Came Swiftly With the Atomic Bomb—And Lingers', *BCON*, 12 October 946, 5.
34   See 'When the Atom Bomb Struck—Uncensored', *Life* 33, no.13, 29 September 1952, 19–25. Some images, including those of Yamahata, had been published before the ban was introduced in September 1945 and a few appeared on rare occasions later, especially after it was relaxed in 1949. For example, the BCOF newspaper *BCON* published photographs of radiation and burn victims in March 1949. The suppression of the colour film footage of US military crews and black and white Japanese newsreel shot in Hiroshima and Nagasaki was even more draconian; the American military footage would remain hidden until the early 1980s and has never been fully aired publicly. See Greg Mitchell, 'The Great Hiroshima Cover-up—And the Greatest Movie Never Made', Japan Focus, 8 August 2011. apjjf.org/2011/9/31/Greg-Mitchell/3581/article.html.
35   See Robert Hariman and John Louis Lucaites, 'The Iconic Image of the Mushroom Cloud and the Cold War Optic', in *Picturing Atrocity: Photographs in Crisis*, ed. Geoffrey Batchen, Mick Gidley, Nancy K. Miller and Jay Prosser (London: Reaktion, 2012), 135–45. See also Robin Gerster, 'Bomb Sights in Japan: Photographing Australian-occupied Hiroshima', *Meanjin* 74, no. 4 (2015): 88–103.

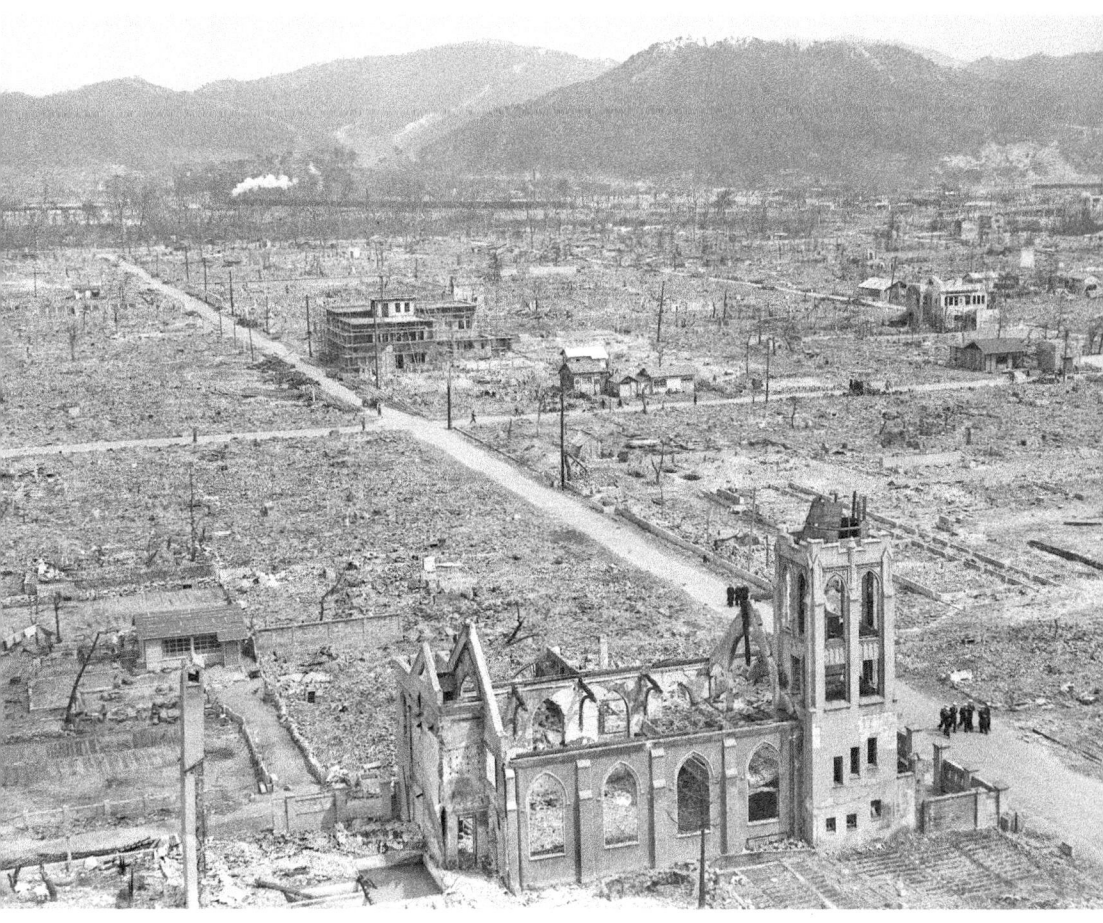

Figure 4.6. Allan Cuthbert, *View South from Central Hiroshima*, 28 February 1946.
Source: AWM 131583.

February 1946, he photographed from the roof of the *Chugoku Shinbun* building, in which over 100 employees perished on the sunny morning of 6 August (see Figure 4.6). The elevated vantage point reveals a landscape virtually devoid of people, save a few anonymous figures walking along the crossroads and two small clusters of uniformed personnel in the foreground, by the shell of the Jesuit church that served Hiroshima's small Christian congregation. Clinical and methodical, Cuthbert's vista of absence and annihilation is reminiscent of the photographs taken by the 'Physical Damage Division' of the *Strategic Bombing Survey* (1946) commissioned by the US Government after the war to assess the effectiveness of the aerial campaigns in Germany and Japan, with

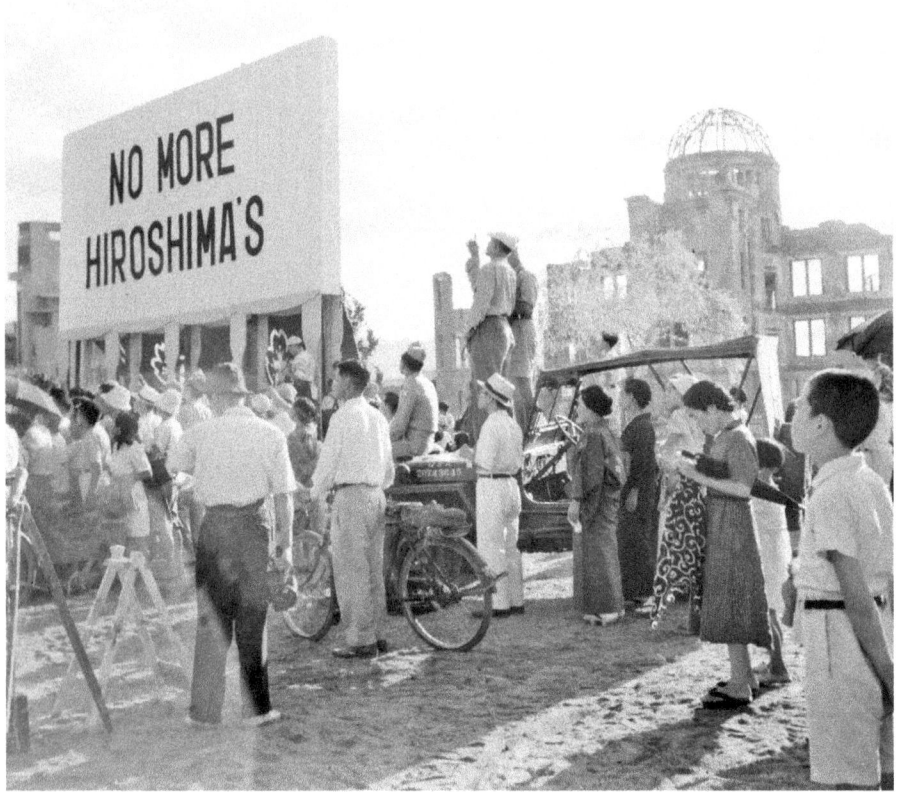

Figure 4.7. Alan Queale, *Peace Festival, Hiroshima*, 6 August 1948.
Source: AWM 145724.

a view to informing the future civil defence architecture of the US.[36] The panorama conveys an impersonal and even sanitised picture of the atom-bombed city; what it does not reveal is the pervasive misery and persistent sickness of a traumatised population.

By 1946, as Cuthbert's image suggests, much of the debris had been cleaned up and the streets were neat and tidy; only picturesque ruins remain of what was Hiroshima. Its reconstruction was to be symbolic as well as pragmatic, and it was on the way to becoming the 'place of pilgrimage for pacifists' anticipated by Frank Clune in his travel book *Ashes of Hiroshima* (1950), the product of a trip to BCOF areas in

---

36 See 'Hiroshima: Ground Zero 1945', International Center of Photography (New York City), accessed 14 July 2015, www.icp.org/browse/archive/collections/hiroshima-ground-zero-1945-may-20-august-28-2011.

1948.³⁷ The making of Hiroshima as a self-styled 'Mecca for World Peace' had begun almost immediately, with the formation in January 1946 of the Hiroshima Reconstruction Bureau. The creation of what we now know as 'Peace Park', with its host of commemorative facilities including Kenzo Tange's museum, was just a few years away. In 1948 the slogan 'No More Hiroshimas' was applied to a local campaign to make the city a focus for the advocacy of world peace. It has stuck as an anti-nuclear catchcry ever since, paradoxically linking the city forever with the historical fact of its destruction.

'No More Hiroshima's' [sic] made its first appearance on a large banner at the second of the official annual Peace Festivals, held on the third anniversary of the bombing, 6 August 1948. Cuthbert's colleague Alan Queale was on hand to document the event (see Figure 4.7). In what has since become a ritual at this solemn event, doves were sent fluttering into the summer sky, bells tolled and poets recited commemorative odes. BCOF Commander Horace Robertson, Gallipoli veteran and hero of the North African campaign in WWII, then strode to the podium. In 1946, Robertson had demonstrated his goodwill by offering the services of Australian engineers and town planners to rehabilitate Hiroshima as 'a city dedicated to the idea of Peace', a gesture vetoed by MacArthur. However, on this special day, he chose to tell the assembled citizens, many of them young children who would have lost beloved family members in the blast, that it was their own fault. The bomb was a 'punishment' handed to the city as 'retribution' for Japanese militarism. To emphasise his point, he had detailed a squadron of Mustang fighters to fly low over the ceremony—an ear-shattering reminder of the bolt from the blue exactly three years earlier. Perhaps that is what prompted the Japanese man standing on the jeep in Queale's picture to point skyward.³⁸ So much for 'Peace'.

---

37   Frank Clune, *Ashes of Hiroshima: A Post-War Trip to Japan and China* (Sydney: Angus & Robertson, 1950), 103.
38   See Clune's interview with Robertson, *Ashes of Hiroshima*, 148–49; Donald Richie interview with Robertson, *Pacific Stars and Stripes*, c. September 1948, 13–14. See also American criticism of the speech, 'Hotfoot in Hiroshima', *Time*, 16 August 1948,www.time.com/time/archive/preview/0,10987,798930,00.html. A short film of the occasion, made by the Military History Section, is held by the Australian War Memorial, F07474.

Spoils of War

Writing in the *Sydney Morning Herald* in April 1952, soon after the historic decision to permit the Japanese brides of Australian servicemen to enter Australia, former BCOF serviceman Stephen Kelen dissociated these female 'New Australians' from the warmongers who had terrorised the region for years. 'After all', he wrote, 'it is never women who wage wars—they only suffer, and pay for man's folly no matter to what race or country they belong'.[39] Kelen echoed the pervasive BCOF view that Japanese women and men were two distinctively different types, and that the females suffered unduly in a male-dominated society. To the MHS's Alan Queale, the women were 'shy, demure, very feminine', the men 'vicious, violent, ugly'.[40]

Yet, sympathy for Japanese women was not entirely disinterested. Japan was for the taking in every sense. Sexual rapacity was an abiding aspect of the Occupation, indulged in by members of all the Allied forces. Among Neil Town's 'first pictures' of the arrival in Japan of the Australians in February 1946 was an image of two soldiers purchasing souvenirs. Their eyes are fixed firmly on two comely, sweetly smiling young women purveying the curios, and they cannot contain their smirks.[41] Many Australian men considered Japan's vulnerable, desperately penurious women among the spoils of war. As the BCOF interpreter Allan Clifton observed in his memoir *Time of Fallen Blossoms* (1950), most of the men on the first shipments of Occupationnaires had been fighting in the tropics, cut off from feminine society for long periods, and some 'made no secret of what they wanted, or of their readiness, willingness and ability to recover lost ground'. Their indiscriminate desires are suggested by the generic name given the women in and around the Kure encampments—'moose', a bastardisation of the Japanese *musume*, or girl. The women, Clifton wrote, were 'quarry in a great game hunt'.[42] As the metaphor implies, this mating ritual was an essentially coercive form of human exchange, even when outright assault was not involved.

---

39 See Stephen Kelen, 'New Australians—From Japan', *Sydney Morning Herald*, 12 April 1952, 6.
40 Alan Queale, 'Japan Diary', *As You Were: A Cavalcade of Events with the Australian Services from 1788 to 1947* (Canberra: Australian War Memorial 1947), 190.
41 *Argus*, 19 February 1946, 1.
42 Allan S. Clifton, *Time of Fallen Blossoms* (London: Cassell, 1950), 21–22.

Fantasies of the prospect of available Japanese women had inspired some men to enlist in the first place. Early publicity images of local women fawning on Australian men were a calculated lure to recruitment into the force; this was one remove from what would now be called sex tourism. The DPR saw the sexual possibilities arising from occupying Japan. Phillip Hobson's photograph (see Figure 4.8) of an unidentified but immensely self-satisfied Australian serviceman, draped as was customary with a camera, surrounded by a bevy of radiant Japanese women in traditional attire, is testimony to the way the tour of duty came to be seen and promoted by the military. Seven women for one man—a ratio guaranteed to make Australian friends back home green with envy.

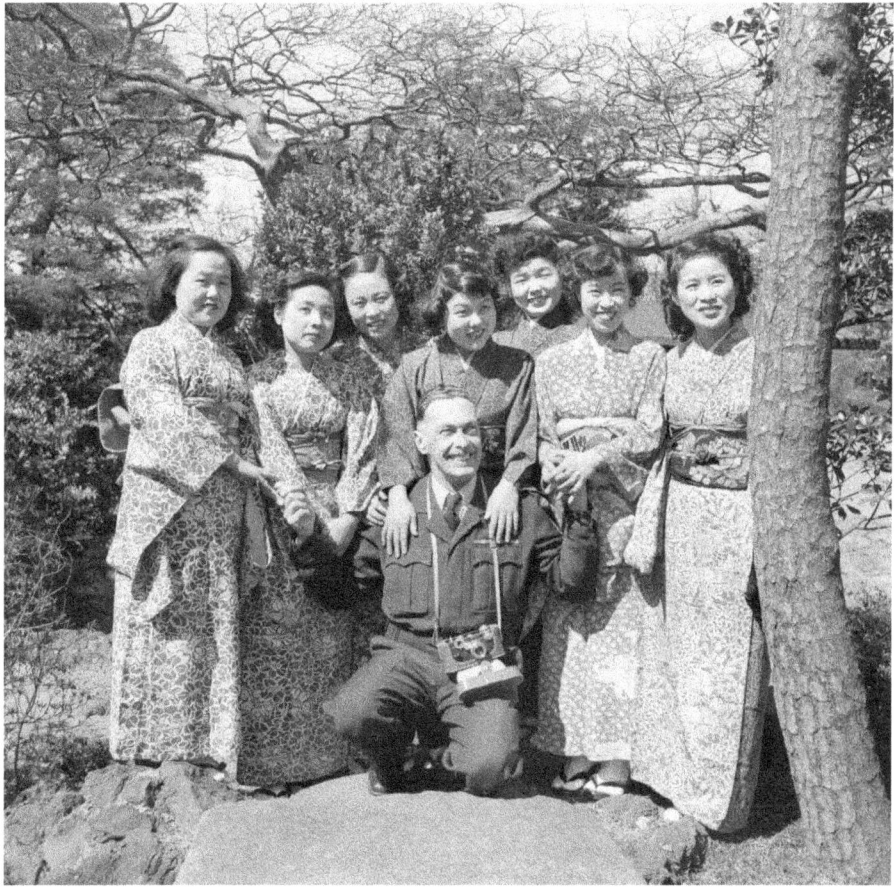

Figure 4.8. Phillip Hobson, *Australian Serviceman with a Group of Japanese Women, Japan*, c. April 1952.
Source: AWM HOBJ2914.

Yet, Hobson's photograph is decorous enough; nothing overly suggestive is portrayed and delicate Australian sensibilities back home would not be offended. There were dangers in sexualising the Occupation too overtly, for the DPI's target audience was female as well as male, domestic as well as military. Hedonistic imagery did not wash well with the general Australian community, which considered that nothing good could come from anything other than an armed encounter with the Japanese. The Australians were supposed to be in Japan to redeem the country and make it atone for past sins, not to enjoy themselves. The louche nightclub scene of 'burlesque' that characterised nocturnal Tokyo in the Occupation years, documented by Japanese photographers such as Tadahiko Hayashi, was off limits. The DPR's Douglas Lee captured a troupe of scantily clad performers at the Ebisu camp in Tokyo, but pictures of the pervasive sexuality of life in and around the camps were routinely suppressed.[43] Meanwhile, photographs of Japanese female nudity, often taken privately at striptease parties organised for the troops, circulated surreptitiously among the servicemen.

Domestic fears that the Australians were in grave moral danger in Japan seem to be anticipated by Neil Town in the *Australasian*, for he remarked, defensively and ungraciously:

> None of the Australians seemed to be interested in the girls—and Japanese girls in the mass, it must be admitted, do not have any particular attraction or charm [being] small, chunky, bow-legged, flat-faced, and with protruding teeth.[44]

Alan Queale was only marginally more chivalrous. Some of the 'Jap women', he noted in his 'Japan Diary', published by the Australian War Memorial in 1947, 'are tolerably good-looking' and are 'picturesque creatures' with their kimonos and pretty paper umbrellas; 'however, their wide moon-like faces often give one the impression that their heads are too large for their bodies'.[45]

To the contrary, the prolific photographs of Japanese women that adorn the often self-published memoirs of BCOF servicemen, albeit safely appearing years after the event, suggest that Japanese women *did* hold great appeal. A favoured photographic subject is the bare-breasted *ama*, the famous pearl divers employed at the Mikimoto establishment at Ise near

---

43 Lee, LEEJ0427.
44 Town and Johnston, 'Australia Is There', 25.
45 Queale, 'Japan Diary', 189.

Nagoya, a tourist magnet for the Australians in Japan. These risqué images could always be justified for their anthropological interest, a little like the photographs of naked native women that once proliferated in the pages of the *National Geographic*.[46] Half a century after the Occupation, the BCOF veteran John Collins looked back at the experience in language free from humbug: 'We were young and fit and horny and far from home'.[47]

The subtext of Australian putdowns of the appearance of Japanese women is that the men were chastely keeping themselves pure for the lady folk back home in Australia. Reflecting its conservative female readership, the *Australian's Women Weekly* discreetly avoided any sign of fraternisation with Japanese women in its photographic feature on the Occupation, published in May 1946. Rather, the lead photograph showed an Australian soldier dispensing chocolate to a 'swarm' of Japanese infants. In a long feature article entitled 'There's Plenty of Work for Our Boys in Japan', the *Weekly*'s special correspondent in Japan, Dorothy Drain, reassured readers that 'your soldier' is not having a good time in Japan. 'Don't be led astray by the photos they send home', she advised, for 'he is doing a job and is not enjoying the post-war tourist season'.[48] Acknowledging sexual relations between occupier and occupied was out of bounds. Any physical contact was incidental and strictly reserved to the performance of menial tasks. The *Weekly*'s staff photographer Bill Brindle's picture of a kimono-clad house girl tying the shoe laces of a senior Australian air force officer, which illustrated another of Drain's features on Japan, conveyed the decorum of the relationship.[49]

The sanitised version of impeccable Australian male behaviour provided by the *Women's Weekly* was confounded by stories of their scandalous off-duty activities that started circulating in the daily press, feeding suspicions that the men of BCOF were debauched malingerers on a paid holiday, and entrenching the impression that the troops were debasing the heroic standards set by Australian soldiers in battle. Certainly liaisons between troops and local women were common, even prolific, and prostitution of varying kinds and degrees flourished. Postwar Japan was a severely dislocated society. Male breadwinners were in short

---

46 See, for example, Philip M. Green, *Memories of Occupied Japan* (Blackheath: Phillip Maxwell Green, 1987), 128.
47 J.G. Collins, *The War of the Veterans* (Toowoomba: J.G. Collins, 2001), 33.
48 See *Australian Women's Weekly*, 11 May 1946, 18, 19.
49 Dorothy Drain, 'Air Force Officers Live in Jap Viscount's House', *Australian Women's Weekly*, 8 May 1946, 17.

supply and many Japanese women, including war widows, had hungry children and elderly relatives to support and were often in dire need. Having been complicit in the provision of what were euphemistically called 'Recreation and Amusement Stations' for foreign troops at the beginning of the Occupation, MacArthur's administration outlawed all forms of public prostitution in March 1946. However, it continued to flourish unofficially. In Tokyo, the *panpan*, the Western-styled nocturnal streetwalker catering to the prowling Allied soldier, became a symbol of the Occupation. In Hiroshima Prefecture, prostitution had thrived from the time the Americans first arrived in late 1945; when the Australians came early the following year they were greeted by women waiting at the Kure docks. Inhibitions were shed and scruples were discarded. In isolated cases, the occupiers' cameras were put to highly illicit use. One of the BCOF wives recalls a colleague of her husband's proudly displaying his homemade collection of pornography in the officer's mess one evening. Included among the usual images of festivals and the like were nude photographs of his wife, his 18-year-old daughter and his Japanese house girl.[50]

The unsavoury outcome of the sexual relations taking place between Australian men and Japanese women was documented by the MHS, a unit dedicated to the primacy of 'evidentiary' and objective still and moving images.[51] Alan Queale's photograph of five Japanese women employed by one of the Australian infantry battalions camped at Hiro near Kure betrays an unedifying story (see Figure 4.9). It was taken in September 1946, during an official crackdown on the spread of venereal disease in the BCOF community that led to the victimisation of Japanese women, including those who either worked with or in any way associated with Australian servicemen, such as domestic staff in BCOF housing. In what one disgusted Australian officer called 'a panic', 'Anti-VD Officers' rounded up local women found to be suffering from venereal disease.[52] Four such diagnosed women stand shamefaced before the official photographer, along with one who turns away from the camera, grinning perhaps through sheer embarrassment (Figure 4.9).

---

50   See Jennie Woods, *Which Way Will the Wind Blow?* (North Sydney: Jennie Woods, 1994), 64.
51   See Lakin, *Contact*, 113, on the MHS's emphasis on documentary veracity.
52   Major A.W. John, *Duty Defined, Duty Done: A Memoir* (Cheltenham: The Gen Publishers, 2004), 211. In her Occupation memoir, Jennie Woods recalled her Japanese house girls being systematically harassed and one removed from her service. See Woods, *Which Way Will the Wind Blow?*, 67. The round-ups of Japanese women for VD screening were not confined to BCOF; the Americans also employed the practice, especially in Tokyo in 1946.

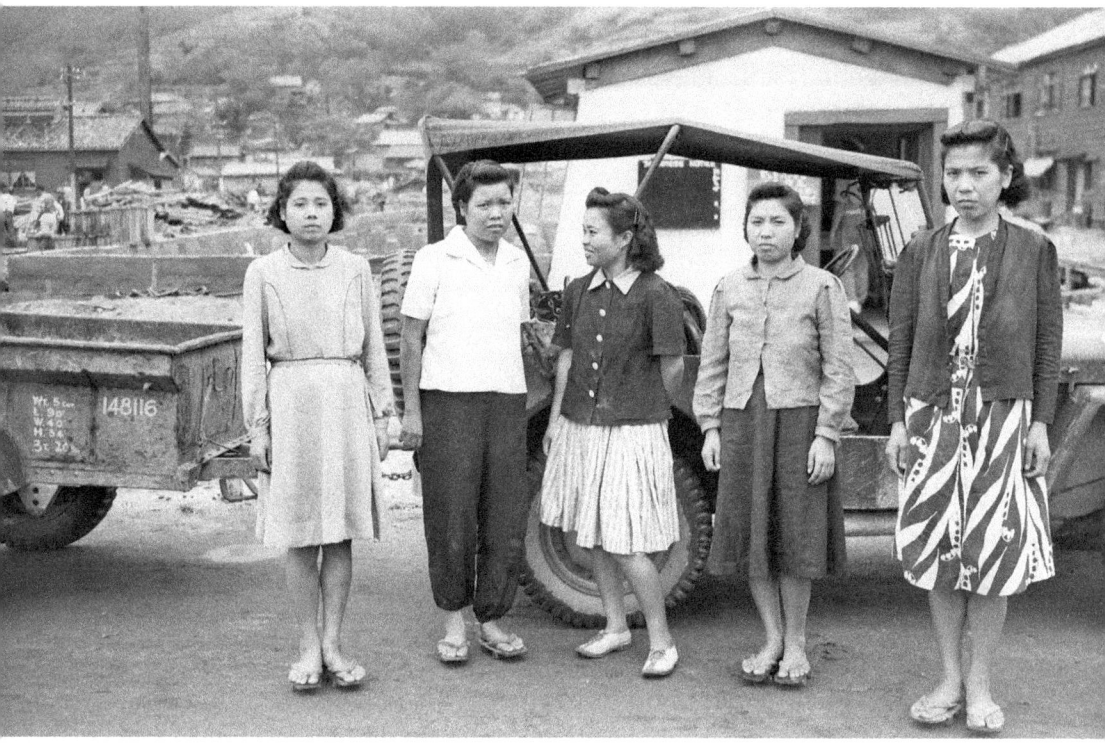

Figure 4.9. Alan Queale, *Venereal Disease Cases Discovered during a Medical Examination of Japanese Female Employees of BCOF*, Hiro, 26 September 1946.
Source: AWM 132118.

This ignominious episode was typical of BCOF's inability to deal constructively with the issue of sexual relationships. It refused to countenance official brothels to regulate the business and monitor the sexual health of Japanese women and, hence, that of its own men. Scapegoated, Japanese women did not matter; the good name of the diggers overrode everything. However, that too was under threat, as allegations about vaulting rates of venereal disease in the Australian contingent took effect, and the force came under fire from the federal president of the Legion of Ex-Servicemen, who described the Australians in Japan as 'morally rotting'.[53] Having noted the potential pleasures of the country to young men in February 1946, Massey Stanley found himself in Japan a little over two years later as a member of an official investigatory

---

53   '"Moral Rot" among BCOF Men', *Daily Telegraph*, 13 January 1948. Prue Torney, '"Renegades to Their Country": The Australian Press and the Allied Occupation of Japan 1946–1950', *War & Society* 25, no. 1 (May 2006) provides an excellent account of the press controversies surrounding BCOF.

team sent by the army minister that was dubbed the 'Sin Busters'. Press outrage at Australian hedonism in Japan was a touch hypocritical. On assignment in Japan in 1950, the *Age* photographer Ron Lovitt—later famous for capturing the climactic moment of the 'tied' cricket test in Brisbane in 1960 between Australia and the West Indies—captured some unnamed pressmen on a night out, evidently relishing the attention of 'geisha girls' (see Figure 4.10). Occupied Japan was a moveable feast, in more ways than one.

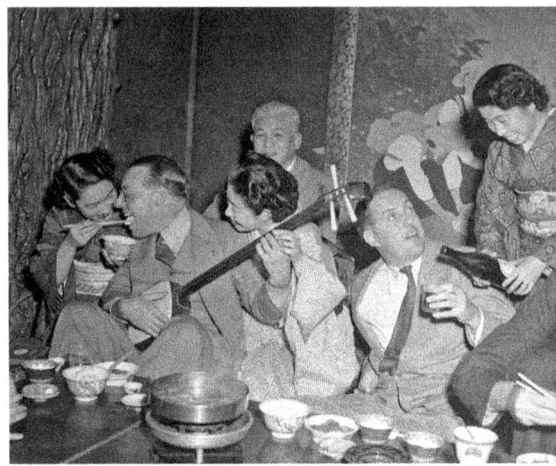

Figure 4.10. Ron Lovitt, *Pressmen Being Entertained*, Japan, date unknown.
Source: Courtesy of Fairfax Syndication.

In any event, neither the barrage of criticism from home nor the threatened loss of their precious beer ration stopped the Australians' liaisons with Japanese women. In one of the Occupation's most uplifting developments, these relationships sometimes blossomed into marriage—over 600 of them—in Japan or back home in Australia. At least two Australian military photographers, the MHS's Claude Holzheimer and the battalion photographer Ian Robertson, wed Japanese women. For Japanese men, these foreign relationships were a humiliating reminder of the completeness of the national defeat in the war.

To the official BCOF photographers, the 'Japs' (the sneering denomination was mostly confined to the males) were automatically associated with the horrors of the recent war. Accordingly, the photographers frequently produced images of Japanese men as humbled, demeaned and emasculated—they were pictured working in a BCOF typing pool, doing BCOF's bidding as cooks or servants, or peddling tourist paraphernalia to BCOF tourists, as in the image of the digger in Ginza. One image, also taken in downtown Tokyo, shows a Japanese man shining BCOF boots.[54] Some of the photographic putdowns are rather

---

54 See AWM 147661; AWM BROJ0288; AWM HOBJ5642; AWM SWEJ0029.

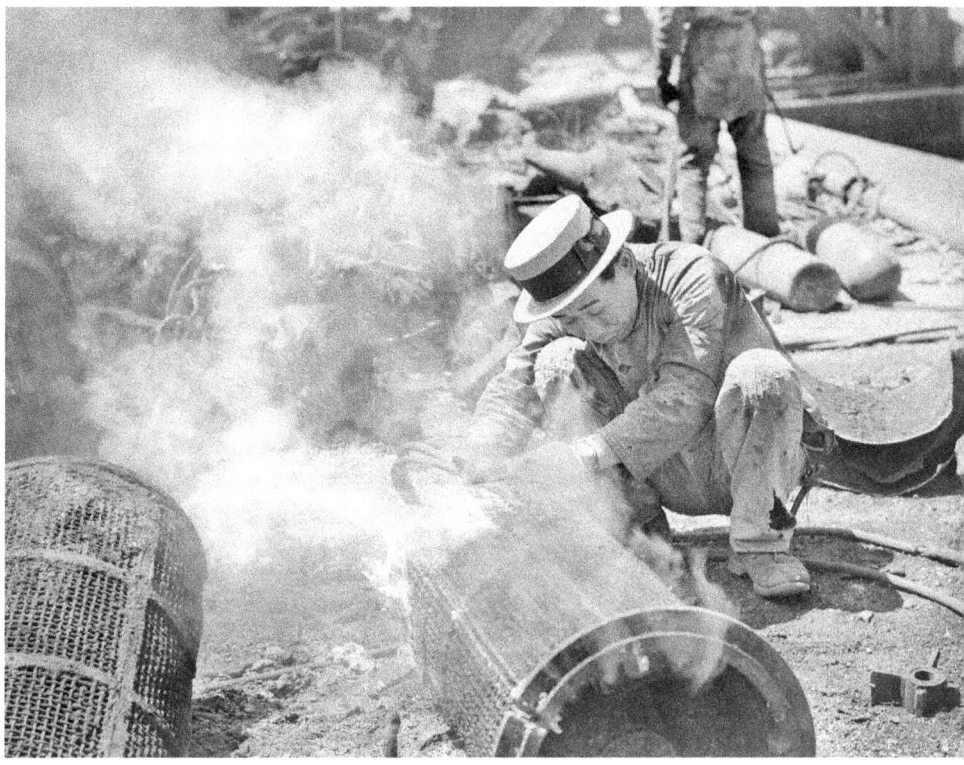

Figure 4.11. Allan Cuthbert, *Japanese Shipyards Labourer*, Kure, 1948.
Source: AWM 145572.

more subtle. In one of Allan Cuthbert's photographs (see Figure 4.11), a Japanese labourer works with an oxyacetylene torch in the shipbreaking yards. His clothes are virtually rags except for the straw boater—suitably nautical for a shipyard scene, perhaps, but incongruously jaunty and ridiculous in the gritty context. Military defeat and occupation had effected a transformation in fearsome Japanese male stereotypes. The fanatical Japanese warrior had become something other altogether—obedient and hardworking, but faintly vaudevillian.

The vigorous sexual life of the Australian Occupation also created another challenge for the official cohort of photographers, one that was assiduously shirked. They habitually photographed newborn BCOF babies with their mothers (it was a fertile force), but Australian children born to Japanese women were a consensual taboo, on both Australian and Japanese sides. In 1948, press reports of children of Australian paternity in a Hiroshima orphanage caused a stir, but the extent of this legacy remained largely unpublicised for decades until the recent investigative work of Walter Hamilton.[55] You will not find photographs of the more than 100 Australian–Japanese children in the official Occupation oeuvre. BCOF's hypocritical response to sexual interactions with Japanese women marred one of its major achievements in Occupied Japan, its role in overseeing Japan's first postwar election in April 1946, in which the nation's women were able to vote for the first time. This historic occasion was enthusiastically supported by the Australian Government, and was a source of satisfaction to many of the men of BCOF itself. Australian observer teams visited thousands of polling pools on election day and the poll was a resounding success. Some 66 per cent of eligible female voters turned out, 14 million of them, and 39 women were elected to the Japanese Diet. Ironically and indicatively, one of these newly elected female members of parliament was a former prostitute.[56]

An Airbrushed Japan

Despite its ostensible power, BCOF was acutely aware of its vulnerability in Japan. The Australian military leadership never stopped distrusting the Japanese. As late as December 1946, after six months in the job, BCOF Commander Robertson was unwilling to be put into social or even diplomatic situations in which he would be forced by protocol to shake hands with a Japanese, even refusing to attend a Tokyo welcome for the visiting Australian Roman Catholic cardinal, Normon Gilroy, because one of the hosts was the Japanese archbishop of Tokyo.[57] Like timid travellers, the Australians in Japan feared they were at the locals' mercy. Gullivers in the land of Lilliput, the Australians suspected that an intimidating military presence was no guarantee of mastery, and that the dextrous, determined Japanese still pulled the strings on their own turf.

---

55   See 'Hiroshima Orphans', *Sydney Morning Herald*, 26 April 1948; Walter Hamilton, *Children of the Occupation: Japan's Untold Story* (Sydney: NewSouth Publishing, 2012). Hamilton wrote of the social tragedy of the mixed-race children, disowned by Australia and discriminated against (as were their mothers) in Japan.
56   George Davies, *The Occupation of Japan* (St Lucia, Brisbane: University of Queensland Press, 2001), 185–86. See also Takemae, *Allied Occupied of Japan*, 265.
57   See Ball anecdote in Alan Rix, ed., *Intermittent Diplomat: The Japan and Batavia Diaries of W. Macmahon Ball* (Carlton: Melbourne University Press, 1988), 150.

This anxiety is reflected in the official photographs. Compensating for the relative lack of active soldiering, and sensitive about its subsidiary role in an Occupation largely dominated by the Americans, BCOF strove to keep up appearances with a penchant for ceremonial marchpasts. The MHS was there to capture every salute and every formality when visiting dignitaries required the Australians to display their skill at drill.[58] Guard duties in symbolic locations, notably outside the imperial palace in Tokyo, were a favoured photographic subject. The impression is that of a force determined to keep the emperor *within*, rather than to deter intruders. Australians were less forgiving of Hirohito than their American counterparts, believing he should have been tried as a war criminal along with General Tojo at the Tokyo war crimes trials that began in April 1946, under the stern judicial eye of the Queenslander Sir William Webb.

The Americans had retained Hirohito as a crucial plank in their program to stabilise Japan and have his subjects accept the process of reform.[59] As early as February 1946, *Life* magazine published a photographic essay entitled 'Sunday at Hirohito's', showing a reassuringly normal family man with an improbable interest in American culture—one photograph shows him purportedly reading 'the funnies' from the US military newspaper the *Stars and Stripes* to his son, the Crown Prince.[60] However, turning the 'living god' into a sympathetic human being had the disconcerting effect of boosting Hirohito's public appeal. His tour of Kure and Hiroshima in December 1947—his first visit since the cataclysm of August 1945—was a source of official anxiety in the upper echelons of the Australian Mission in Japan.[61] The tour occasioned a welter of photographic activity. A report compiled by the Japan expert A.B. Jamieson for the Australian Mission quoted the worrying remark from a Hiroshima city official, made to Allied pressmen covering Hirohito's tour of the city: 'The Emperor is the source of our atomic energy for reconstruction, as powerful as the American atomic energy

---

58   Photographs of 'spectacular' parades dominate the final, commemorative edition of the Osaka-based broadsheet *BCON*. See *BCON*, 6 April 1950, 'Special Last Supplement'.
59   See Morris Low, *Japan on Display: Photography and the Emperor* (Abingdon: Routledge, 2006), 112.
60   *Life*, 4 February 1946, 75–79.
61   See Patrick Shaw, Head of the Australian Mission in Japan, 'The Emperor's Visit to Hiroshima', despatch no.45/1947, Department of External Affairs, Australian Archives Canberra, CRS A 1838, item 477/511, 1.

PACIFIC EXPOSURES

is for destruction'.⁶² Harry Freeman's photograph of Hirohito's visit to Osaka the previous year (see Figure 4.12) reflects Australian fears that the emperor was a potent source of national devotion to a public unused to his visibility and accessibility. As American and Japanese police strain to hold the adoring masses back, Hirohito doffs his hat to a common countryman in the crowd doing the same, an act of hitherto unknown humility and mutual respect. Compared with the static staidness, verging on sterility, of much of the MHS's work, this image radiates energy and movement, capturing something new, dangerous and volatile in Japanese public life.

The official photographers liked to portray the Australians in situations of mastery, often in the pose of taking in Japanese landscape as they went about their military tasks. In Allan Cuthbert's photograph (see Figure 4.13), a group of diggers on patrol view the countryside near Fukuyama in Hiroshima Prefecture in the late summer of 1946 while in search of sequestered stores and weapons. The Australians occupy the space as well as look down on it, surveying a subordinate and depopulated landscape that invites inspection, appreciation and, ultimately, appropriation. Cuthbert provides a reassuring picture of Occupied Japan, eliciting a calm control that suggests all is well—the Australians are in cool command of all they survey. The picture taps into a representational tradition of spectatorship dating back to the halcyon days of the British Empire, what James R. Ryan has called an 'imperial way of seeing'. Along with topographical survey and cartography, photography was a vital instrument of visual colonisation in the political and military project of British imperial power. The 'very idea of Empire', Ryan wrote, 'depended in part on an idea of landscape, as both controlled space and the means of representing such control'.⁶³ Yet, if Cuthbert's photograph reproduces this colonialist aesthetic, it also belies the sense of a force never fully confident of its place both in Japan, and within the American-dominated Occupation itself.

---

62 'Emperor's Visit to Hiroshima', 9 cited in Low, *Japan on Display*, 114.
63 James R. Ryan, *Picturing Empire: Photography and the Visualization of the British Empire* (London: Reaktion Books, 1997), 46, 72.

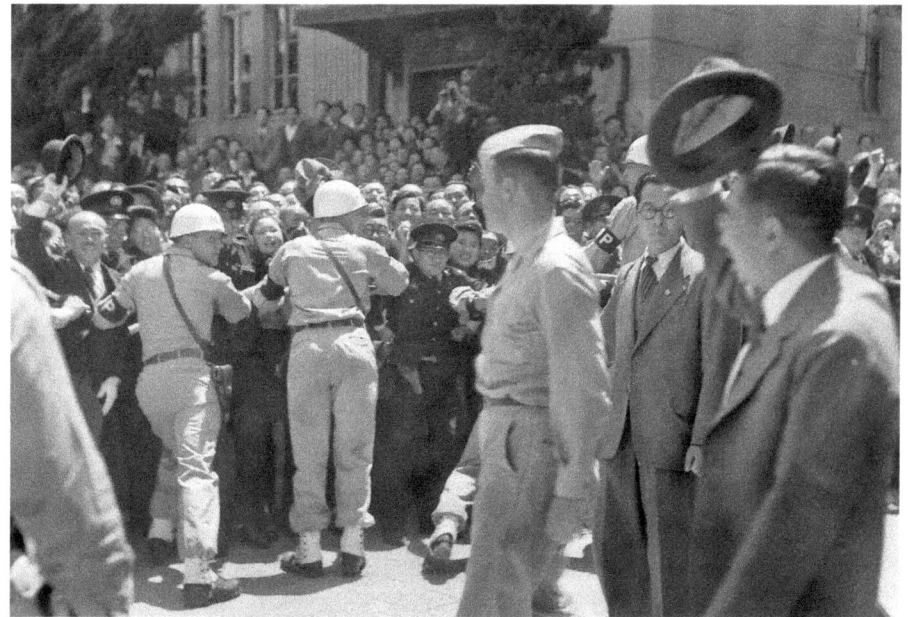

Figure 4.12. William Harry Freeman, *Emperor Hirohito on Tour*, Osaka, 1947.
Source: AWM 133228.

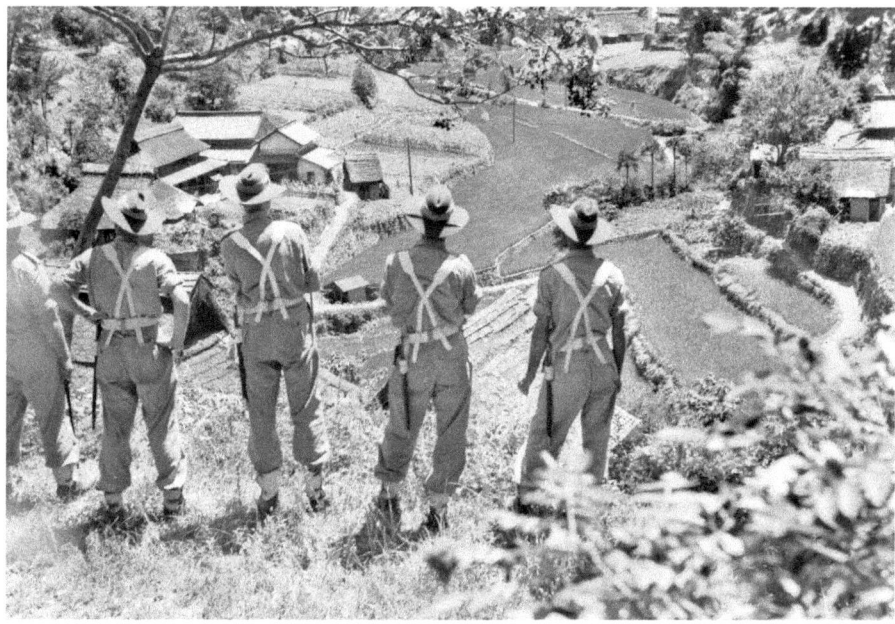

Figure 4.13. Allan Cuthbert, *Soldiers of BCOF 65th Battalion, on Patrol*, Fukuyama Prefecture, 10 September 1946.
Source: AWM 132639.

Significantly, Cuthbert's image of a rural idyll purges Japan of signs of the war and its difficult social aftermath. Australian photographers tended to turn a blind eye to the manifest social problems of postwar Japan, which were especially evident in its cities. Selective vision also improved the appearance of a Japan pockmarked with eyesores, caused by the Allied bombing and by a country improvising and rebuilding at breakneck speed. While charged with the task of making the Australian Occupation look good, some of the less flagrantly propagandistic work of DPR photographers like Hobson and Harold Dunkley reveal a strong attraction to aspects of Japanese culture and landscape. Hobson composed a series of studies of Buddhist statues, while Dunkley was drawn to photographing domestic architecture and gardens.[64] However, the social disturbances evident in the cities, including strikes and mass demonstrations of support for communism, are largely ignored in favour of a rustic and essentially docile Japan.[65]

A representative picture is Phillip Hobson's photograph of the quiet communion of a Japanese girl and her grandmother at work in a tranquil vegetable garden somewhere in rural Japan in November 1949 (see Figure 4.14). The image is an example of what John Urry and Jonas Larsen call professional photographic 'gardening', in which the appearance of idealised tourist sites are kept intact by the 'airbrushing away' of unsettling and unsightly evidence of modernity.[66] Overtly a celebration of the decorous formality of Japanese life, it is an implicitly political picture of a Japan in need of benign nurture. At least Hobson's image is a representational advance on the wartime stereotype of the fanatical Japanese warrior. We see a photographer struggling to balance the didactic requirements of effective public relations with a visual sensibility responding to the (conspicuously feminised) cultural spectacle before him.

---

64 See for example AWM HOBJ0467; AWM DUKJ3276.
65 In a photomontage depicting the changes in Occupied Japan during 1946, and 'the new way of life under democracy', the Christmas and New Year Souvenir edition of the service newspaper *BCON* included an unattributed photograph of demonstrating strikers in Tokyo. In fact, the Australian Government strongly advocated workplace reform in Japan, including supporting the organisation of trade unions. Christine de Matos, *Encouraging Democracy in a Cold War Climate* (Canberra: Australia-Japan Research Centre, 2001) provides a detailed account of constructive Australian political policies relating to postwar Japan. These often conflicted with the American Cold War mentality, especially as the Occupation progressed and the US reprioritised Japan as a regional bulwark against communism.
66 See John Urry and Jonas Larsen, *The Tourist Gaze 3.0* (London: Sage, 2012), 174–75, 169.

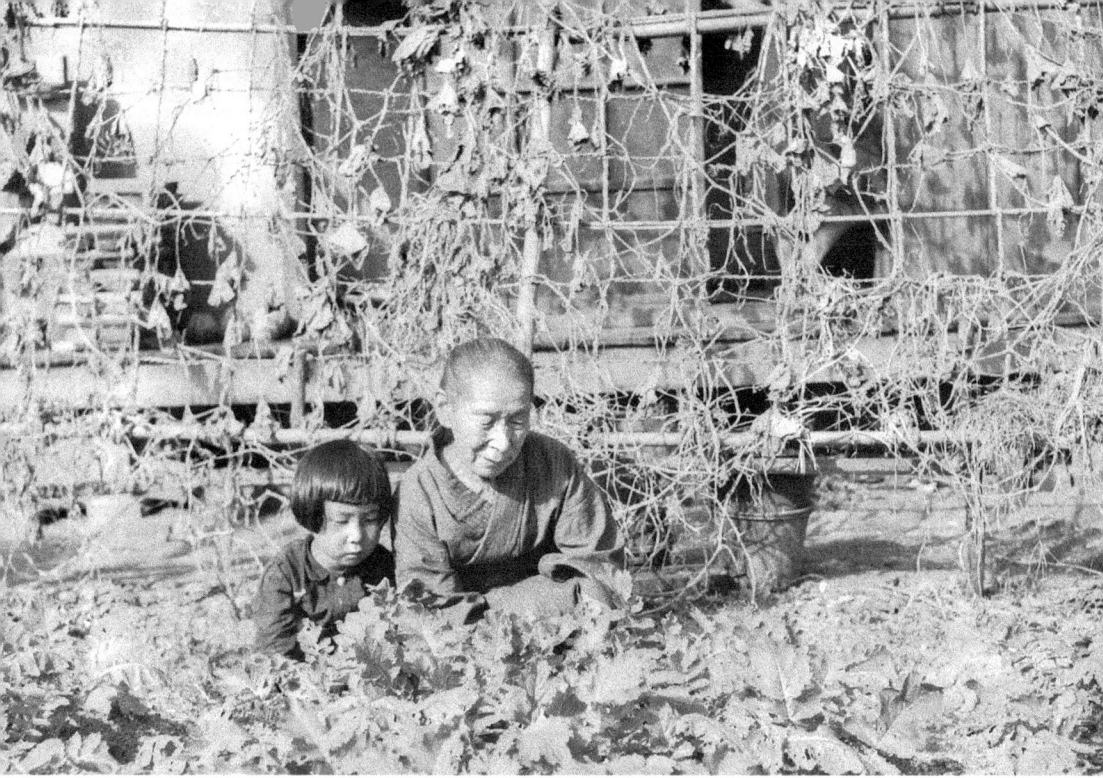

Figure 4.14. Phillip Hobson, *Grandmother Gardening with Granddaughter*, Kure area, c. Nov 1949.
Source: AWM HOBJ0199.

Individual photographic portraits of the Japanese indicate a preference for traditional national types mostly encountered in the waterways, paddies and mountain valleys outside the cities. When he was not photographing BCOF routines and activities, Alan Queale sought the people and places of a Japan that was removed in every sense from the war. His private albums are dominated by bucolic Japan—by images of rural women of all ages from matriarchs to *musume*, and plain but evocative portraits of artisans and workers, such as his picture of a Hiroshima oysterman (see Figure 4.15). Modernity is strictly the privilege of the foreigners. Hobson's photograph of a BCOF despatch rider on a motorcycle swiftly passing a Japanese tradesman labouring with a bullock cart provides a stark example of what is an essentially imperialising photographic discourse.[67]

---

67   Hobson was in full public relations mode, and the photograph was carefully staged (two shots from different angles were taken) (AWM HOBJ0067; AWM HOBJ0072).

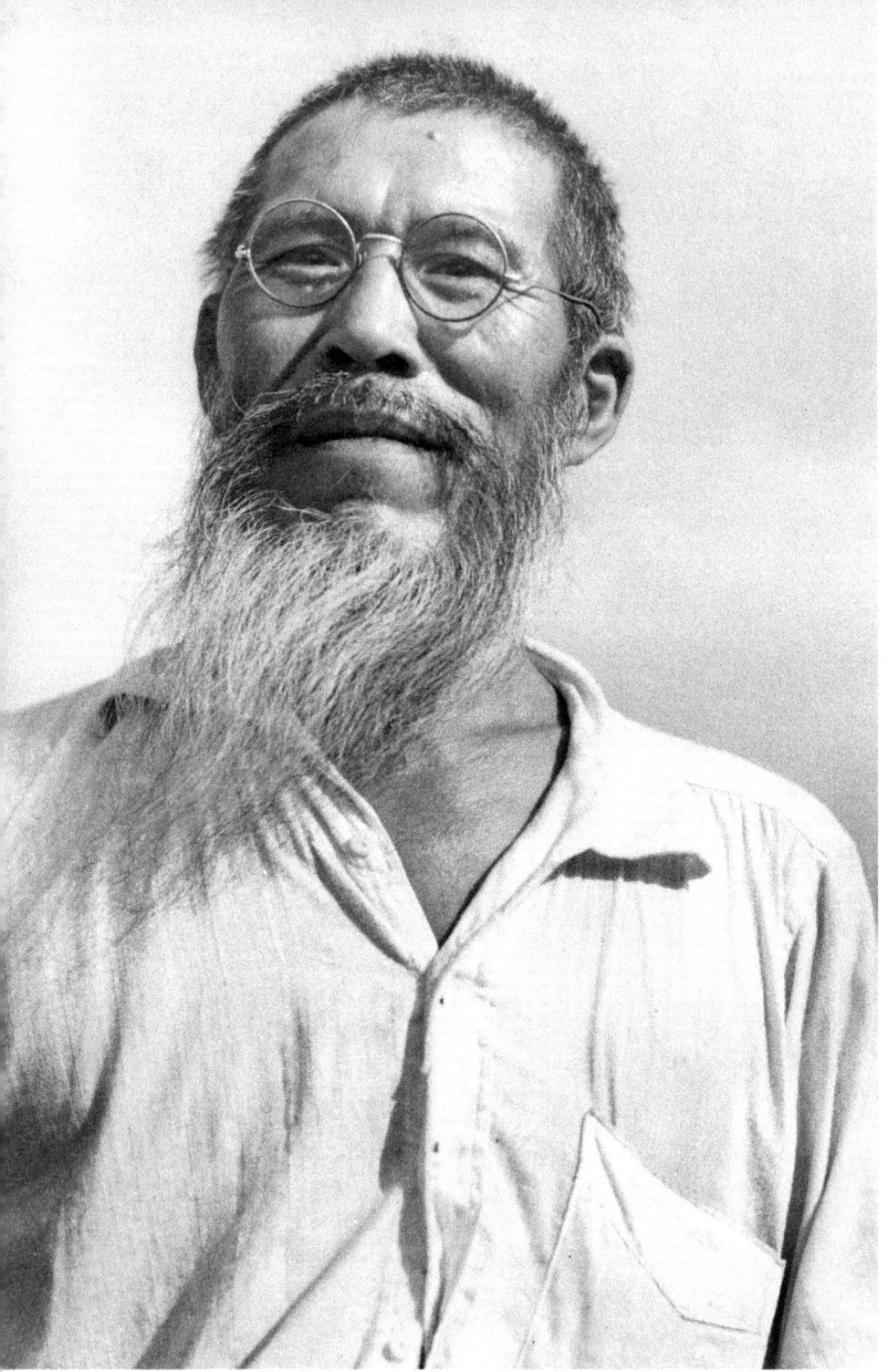

Figure 4.15. Alan Queale, *Oysterman*, Kaitaichi, Hiroshima Prefecture, c. 1946–48.
Source: AWM 12000.006.001.

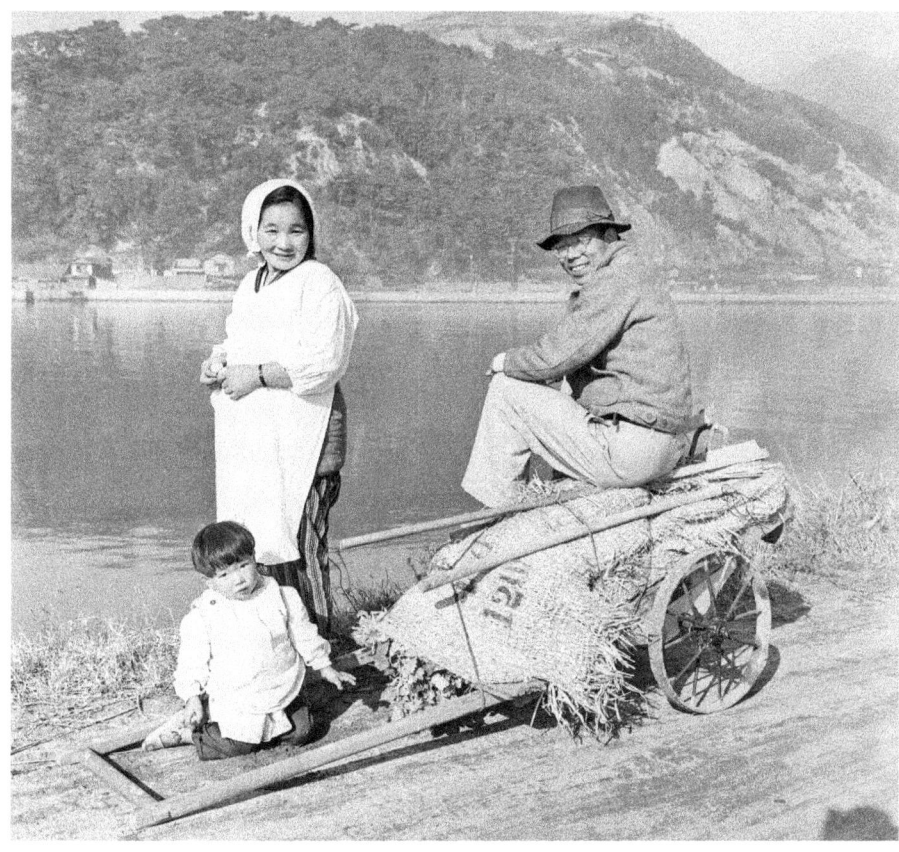

Figure 4.16. Claude Holzheimer, *Japanese Farming Family*, Hiroshima Prefecture, c. 1953.
Source: AWM 148750.

Reminiscent of Victorian-era anthropological images of vanishing peoples, the official photographs provide a human catalogue of a beguilingly backward Japan being preserved by an appreciative Occupier. Somewhere in Hiroshima Prefecture in the early 1950s, a farming family obligingly smiles for Claude Holzheimer's camera (see Figure 4.16). The Australian Government supported the difficult process of agrarian reform in postwar Japan, involving the prohibition of absentee ownership and the transfer of agricultural land to former tenant farmers.[68] Perhaps the photograph is a visual register of this official support. Certainly, the vivid individuality of father, mother and child shines through. Yet it is an image in which the processes of history are absent—the family is frozen in time. It is almost as if the war, and the atomic destruction of Hiroshima and Nagasaki, had never happened.

68 See Davies, *The Occupation of Japan*, 296.

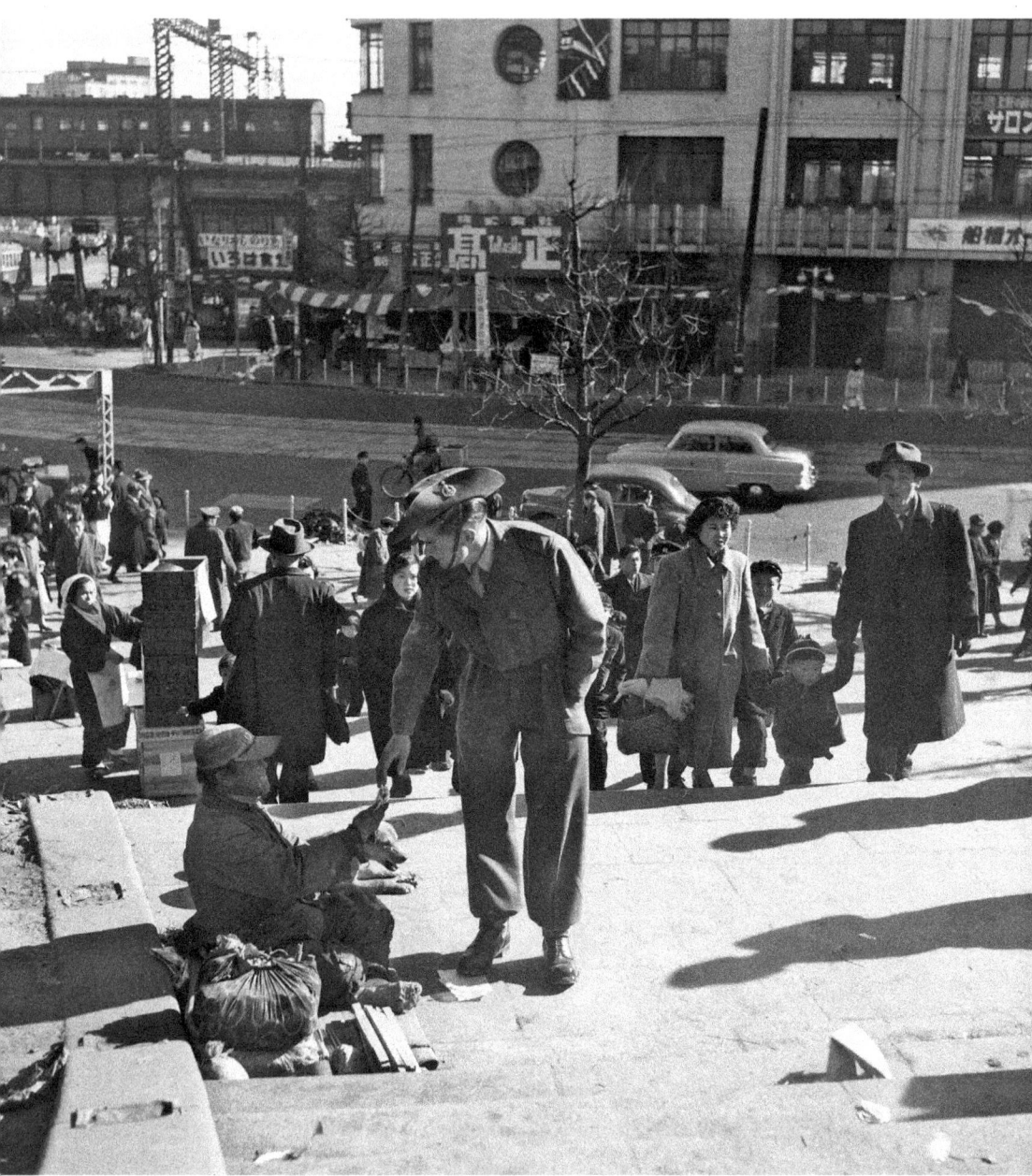

Figure 4.17. Phillip Hobson, *Australian Soldier Offering Money to Beggar*, Tokyo, 11 January 1955.

Source: AWM HOBJ5643.

The rural emphasis of Australian Occupation photography is strikingly at odds with Japanese photography of the edgy postwar era. Realist Japanese photographers such as Ken Domon and Tadahiko Hayashi identified urban images of social dislocation and degradation. Streetwalkers, ex-military down-and-outers, and vagrants were identified as the appropriate visual material for a shattered country contending with the cultural and psychological pressure of the Occupation itself and the upheaval created by the war. Shocking images such as Hayashi's 1946 picture of a filthy young street waif, perhaps 10 years of age, smoking in the proletarian Ueno station district of downtown Tokyo, are virtually absent from the photographic archive of the Australian Occupation.[69] When Phillip Hobson made a rare, belated visit to a similar milieu, he bleached the grime and squalor with crisp winter sunlight, and populated it with a well-dressed and well-fed Japanese family on an outing and an Australian soldier providing charity in the form of a 10 yen note to a cheerfully grateful beggar (see Figure 4.17). Japanese postwar social distress becomes a validation of the Occupation, and testimony to the radiant beneficence of BCOF itself.

'No Loitering'

One final image, taken by the prolific Hobson, provides an illuminating footnote to the story of Australian official photography of the Occupation. The longest serving member of the Australian photographic cohort in Japan, Hobson knew the country well; he based himself there from 1950 while making sporadic visits to Korea to cover the war, during which time he took many fine pictures of Australians in action. He learned the Japanese language and set up a photographic laboratory in Tokyo, staffed by Japanese, to facilitate the processing and distribution of his pictures to Australian and overseas newspapers. As we have seen, Hobson was highly receptive to the visual seductions of Japan and several of his pictures express a strong liking for the country.

---

69 Thomas, 'Power Made Visible', esp. 373–79. The Hayashi photograph of the smoking street waif in Ueno appears in Tadahiko Hayashi, *Kastori no jidai* (Tokyo: Pie Bukkusu, 2007), 37. *BCON* reproduced two unattributed photographs of malnourished orphans in Osaka, in a news story on the issue of homeless children (*BCON*, 12 February 1947, 5).

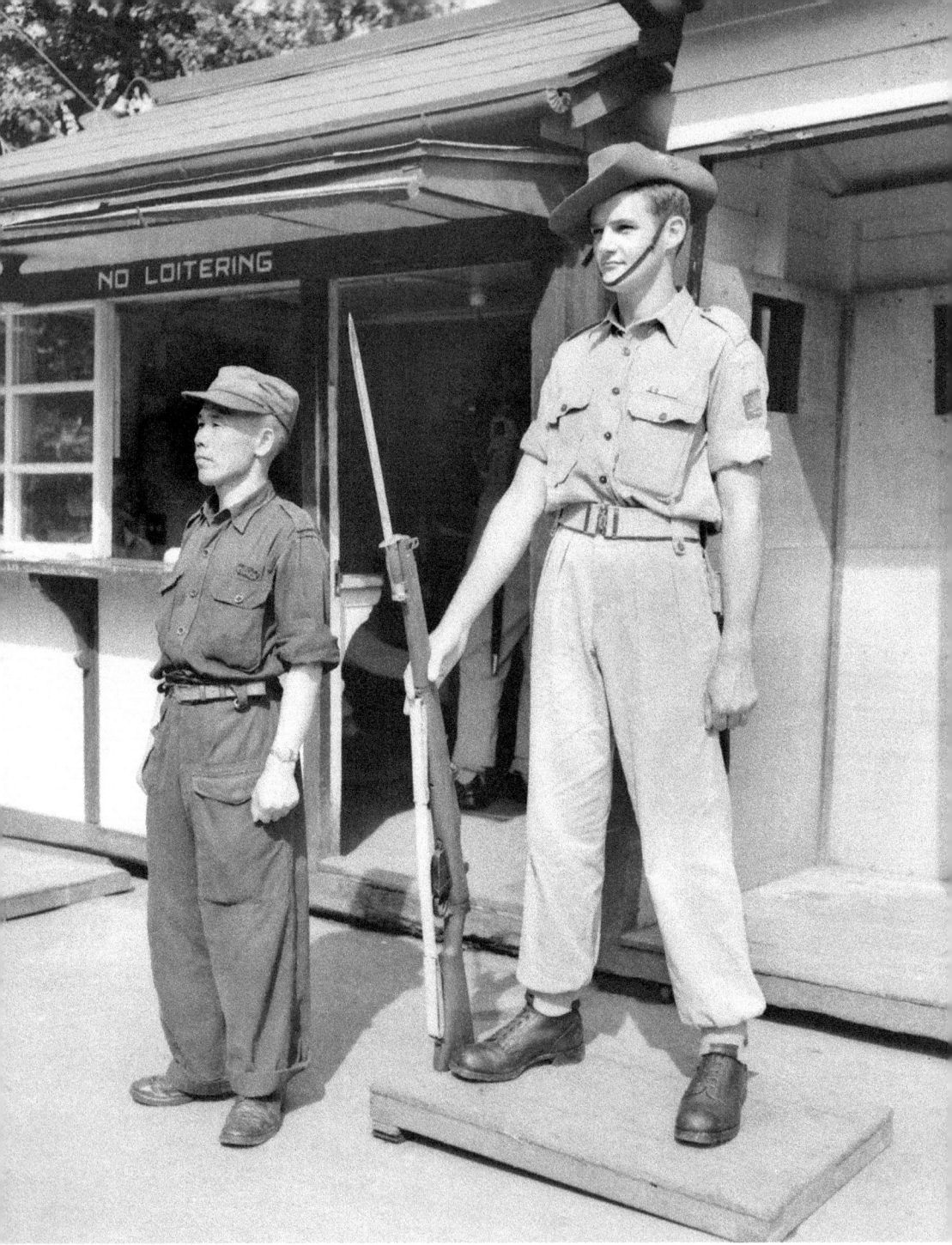

Figure 4.18. Phillip Hobson, *Australian Soldier and Japanese Stand Guard at Ebisu Camp*, Tokyo, 8 August 1954.
Source: AWM HOBJ5286.

However, in August 1954, the year before he left Japan for good, Hobson took a photograph (see Figure 4.18) of an Australian soldier named 'Dasher' Dean standing guard at the Ebisu barracks in Tokyo. Beside the lanky Australian and rigidly standing to attention is his fellow guard, a small-statured Japanese. The scene disconcertingly resembles that first historic meeting of Hirohito with the towering MacArthur. The Occupation was well over by 1954. BCOF had officially ceased to exist two years earlier when the Peace Treaty with Japan came into effect, although Australia maintained a tiny military presence in Japan until the mid-1950s—Ebisu had served as rest camp for Commonwealth forces fighting in Korea. Rapprochement between bitter enemies was underway, with diplomatic links being forged and trade deals soon to be signed. The two antagonists were now standing side by side. However, Hobson's photograph suggests they were not yet on an equal footing— one thinks it unnecessary to have Dasher Dean accentuate his height advantage by standing on a raised platform. Above the Japanese a sign reads 'NO LOITERING'.

Such are the humiliating legacies of military occupation; perhaps Hobson thought it an amusing visual joke. Yet it was the occupied people who had the last laugh, for Japan itself was hardly 'loitering'. It was on the move, busily engaged in a process of national regeneration and well on the way to becoming the powerhouse of the 1960s and beyond, leaving Australia, and virtually the rest of world, lagging in its wake. It took Australians some years to appreciate the implications of the Japanese proverb *makeru ga kachi* ('losing is winning').[70] Well intentioned but complacent, the BCOF photographers of the Allied project to remake Japan had produced a representational absurdity—a window into the country's past, rather than an anticipation of its future. The melding of travel and military imagery had not so much captured Japan as revealed the shallowness at the heart of the Orientalist ideology of the Occupation. In the end, Japan rebuilt and adapted while staying true to itself.

---

70 See 'The Trade War: Winner: Japan, Loser: Australia', *Bulletin*, 28 June 1983, cover.

5

THROUGH NON-MILITARY EYES:
DEVELOPING THE POSTWAR BILATERAL RELATIONSHIP

Somewhere in the vast ruin of post-nuclear Hiroshima, two middle-aged Japanese men walk towards a stationary camera (see Figure 5.1). They look purposeful and strangely cheerful. As two Australian diggers slouch back into the colossal bombsite and towards the vanishing point beneath a cluster of stripped trees, the conspicuously civilian, Western-attired Japanese duo stride out of it, moving away from the militarism that led to such wholesale destruction and into a future that would be independently determined by men such as them. The photograph is carefully conceived, staged to capture a significant point of departure in postwar Japanese history—a people leaving war and military occupation behind and embarking on the task of rebuilding and remaking the nation.

Significantly, this richly allegorical image was not taken by one of the professional photographers affiliated to the military and official civilian agencies. Rather, it is the work of an amateur, Hungarian-born Stephen Kelen, who served with British Commonwealth Occupation Force (BCOF) Intelligence before joining the military newspaper *British Commonwealth Occupation News* (*BCON*). Kelen was an enthusiastic and accomplished photographer. Several of the images that illustrate his memoir, *I Remember Hiroshima*, have become iconic pictures of the stricken city in the early stages of its reconstruction. His photographs of orphans and of an outdoor schoolroom that had sprung up in the rubble are among the best known pictures of atomic Hiroshima, featuring in

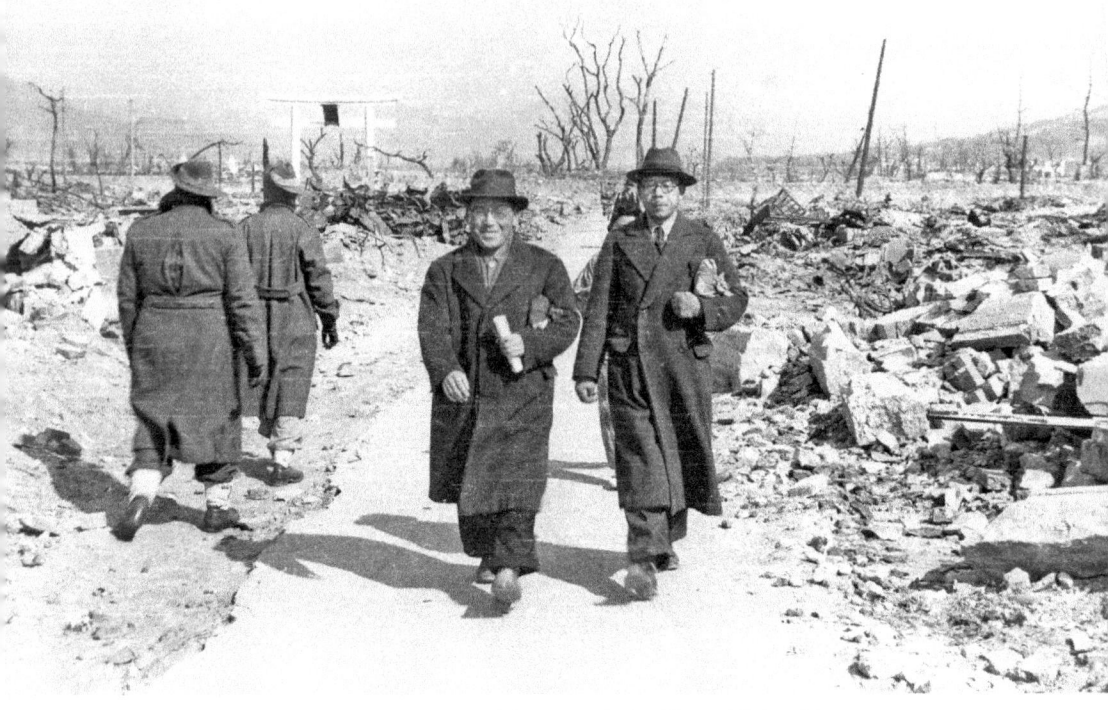

Figure 5.1. Stephen Kelen, *Hiroshima*, c. 1946–48, published in *I Remember Hiroshima* (Sydney: Hale & Iremonger, 1983), 18.
Source: Courtesy of S.K. Kelen and Hiroshima Municipal Archives.

online educational material published by the municipal authorities such as the Hiroshima Peace Memorial Museum, to teach the history of the bombing and to spread the anti-nuclear gospel.[1]

Their documentary value aside, Kelen's pictures suggest a shift in Australian apprehension of its recent enemy and the identification and recognition of the emerging new (or remodelled) Japan. The camera was a crucial instrument of rapprochement in the postwar period, as Australians began to look at Japan with what BCOF serviceman Halton Stewart called 'non-military eyes'.[2] This is particularly true of the unofficial pictures taken independently by the legion of amateur photographers in the occupying force that compose an alternative visual narrative of postwar Japan. Freed of the obligation to produce a sanitised view of a Japan dependent on the beneficent presence of the Occupier, they were

---

1   See 'Children in Post-War Hiroshima', Hiroshima Peace Memorial Museum, accessed 11 January 2018, www.pcf.city.hiroshima.jp/kids/KPSH_E/hiroshima_e/sadako_e/subcontents_e/12kidssengo_1_e.html.
2   Halton Stewart quoted in Robin Gerster, *Travels in Atomic Sunshine: Australia and the Occupation of Japan* (Melbourne: Scribe, 2008), 235.

receptive to the signs of a people regrouping from mass devastation and mutating into a forward-looking nation while remaining true to their ancient traditions.

To the Australians, the Occupation was both conquest and cultural reconnaissance, the first time in history that large numbers of them were able to explore an Oriental culture and landscape; it was the precursor of the mass Asian travel of Australians today. As travellers and as photographers, the Australians of the Occupation pioneered an era of engagement with the region generally, signified in the years to come by reoriented travel itineraries and the belated Australian embrace of Eastern cultures. Camera enthusiasts in the touring BCOF community such as Kelen, Frederick Frueh and Neville Govett ignored the visual clichés of picturesque Japan that existed before the war and rejected the negative stereotypes generated by the war itself. The unofficial Occupation photography testifies to the unfashionably positive view of tourist image-making articulated by Jonas Larsen, who posited that tourist photographers are not passive reproducers of a received imagery of 'the exotic' but producers of new geographies with potentially creative, personal visions of the world.[3]

A somewhat more ambiguous picture of Japan emerged in the public photography produced in the post-Occupation period, during the fraught process of political reconciliation with the former enemy. From the 1950s until well into the 1970s, successive Australian governments remained sensitive to lingering memories of Japanese military turpitude, and the image of Japan remained largely filtered through the lens of war. At the same time, they encouraged cultural and economic links to flourish and ensured that they be conveyed attractively, through official channels, to the people. Photographers working for the Australian News and Information Bureau (ANIB) were particularly active in the period, taking promotional images of cultural as well as diplomatic and political engagement that collectively signposted the path to a strong bilateral relationship that remains in place today. The reviled Japanese adversary of wartime propaganda was humanised as a friend and ally, and Japan itself reframed into a dynamic, embryonically modern society whose bright future Australia could share.

---

3   Jonas Larsen, 'Geographies of Tourist Photography', in *Geographies of Communication: The Spatial Turn in Media Studies*, ed. J. Falkheimer and A. Jansson (Goteborg: Nordicom, 2006), 250–51.

That so many of these official pictures are so blatantly intended to transmit a message of bilateral amity betrays the artificial element to the developing Australia–Japan relationship. As Alan Rix implied by the pointed title of his study of the politics of postwar trade with Japan, *Coming to Terms* (1986), Australia's compulsion to get on with its recent antagonist was essentially a mercenary enterprise, for commerce with economically regenerating Japan provided massive business opportunities.[4] The trade and commerce agreement of 1957, deepened and extended by the Basic Treaty of Friendship and Cooperation signed in Tokyo in 1976, provided the diplomatic context for a set of photographic images designed to dignify and formalise a partnership that once seemed inconceivable.

Yet, 'coming to terms' was also about expressing genuine fellow feeling. As cultural contact between the two countries accelerated during this period, facilitated by fairs and exhibitions and by burgeoning trans-Pacific travel, photography became a powerful interpretive medium, a tool of cultural translation that created sympathetic responses to a country that both beguiled and bewildered.

New Ways of Seeing Japan: The Amateur Photographers of BCOF

Australian servicemen in Occupied Japan sometimes used the language of visual perception and representation to explain the effect the personal encounter with the country had on them and how it had transformed their view of the country. Halton Stewart's remark that he began to see the Japanese through 'non-military eyes' was echoed by BCOF medico Murray Elliott, who recalled being exposed to a 'new and great culture' that provided him with 'a new perception of the world'. Japan, he declared, transformed his 'way of seeing'.[5] The principal focus for this perceptual change was the ordinary people of Japan encountered by the Australians, and their favoured means of registering it was the camera.

---

4   Alan Rix, *Coming to Terms: The Politics of Australia's Trade with Japan 1945–1957* (Sydney: Angus & Robertson, 1986).
5   Murray Elliott, *Occupational Hazards: A Doctor in Japan and Elsewhere* (Brisbane: Griffith University, 1995), 80, 91, 93.

Often fatherless or orphaned, the children of Japan attracted an especially sympathetic lens. The soldiers found them irresistible and they were instrumental in softening attitudes to the Japanese. The children could not be lumbered with the misdemeanours of their elders. In *Ashes of Hiroshima* (1950), Frank Clune blamed the destruction wrought by the atomic bomb on the Japanese themselves, for being 'too stupid and ignorant to build solidly'. Yet, even Clune had his enmity qualified by the sight of Japanese children. 'No man could see the ashes of Hiroshima and fail to feel qualms', he wrote. Driving along the perilously narrow coastal road back to Kure, he saw Japanese kids playing in the water: 'They at any rate had no war-guilt', he remarked, 'we couldn't honestly say it served them right'.[6]

The disarming effect of Japanese children is best illustrated by Albert Tucker, better known as a modernist painter, who spent three months on secondment to BCOF in 1947. Tucker was essentially an amateur photographer, though he became more attracted to the medium later in his career. Apparently he did not even own a camera in Japan, using a borrowed Leica to take several hundred photographs, including a couple of covert shots at the war crimes trials in Tokyo. Years later, Tucker reflected that the immensity of Hiroshima's destruction defeated him as an artist; just as many writers bemoaned the event's unprecedented indescribability, he considered it unpaintable. Nonetheless, the secondment produced 'Hiroshima 1947', a scene of desolation solely populated by a homeless child standing near a blasted tree whose bare branches form the unmistakable shape of a swastika.[7] Somewhere near bomb-ravaged Osaka, Tucker selected a more straightforward means of capturing the face of postwar Japan (see Figure 5.2). In her collection of his photographs, *The Eye of the Beholder*, Janine Burke remarked how the camera liberated the artist, 'creating a fresh, intimate visual sense not found in his bleak, socially critical and sexually anxious paintings of the war years'. Burke noted that his close-ups are emotional and physical, evidence of photography's way of 'saying what is in the heart rather than the mind'.[8] Tucker's photograph of three boys seems to ask, 'how could anyone maintain their hatred of the Japanese?'

---

6   Clune, *Ashes of Hiroshima: A Post-War Trip to Japan and China* (Sydney: Angus & Robertson, 1950), 89–90, 93, 108.
7   Albert Tucker on Hiroshima, interview with Robin Hughes, ABC Radio National program 'Verbatim', 14 February 1994, www.australianbiography.gov.au/sujects/tucker/intertext3.html; 'Hiroshima 1947', Australian War Memorial (AWM) 29483.
8   Janine Burke, *The Eye of the Beholder: Albert Tucker's Photographs* (Melbourne: Museum of Modern Art at Heide, 1998), 18–19, see also 20. *Three Boys* is reproduced on 68.

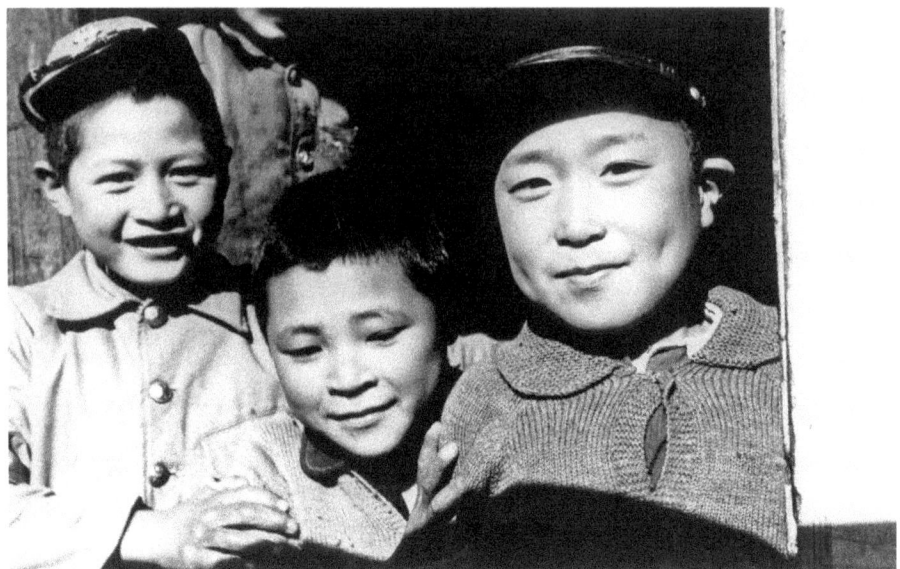

Figure 5.2. Albert Tucker, *Three Boys Near Osaka*, 1947.
Source: Albert Tucker Collection, State Library of Victoria H2010.72/1.

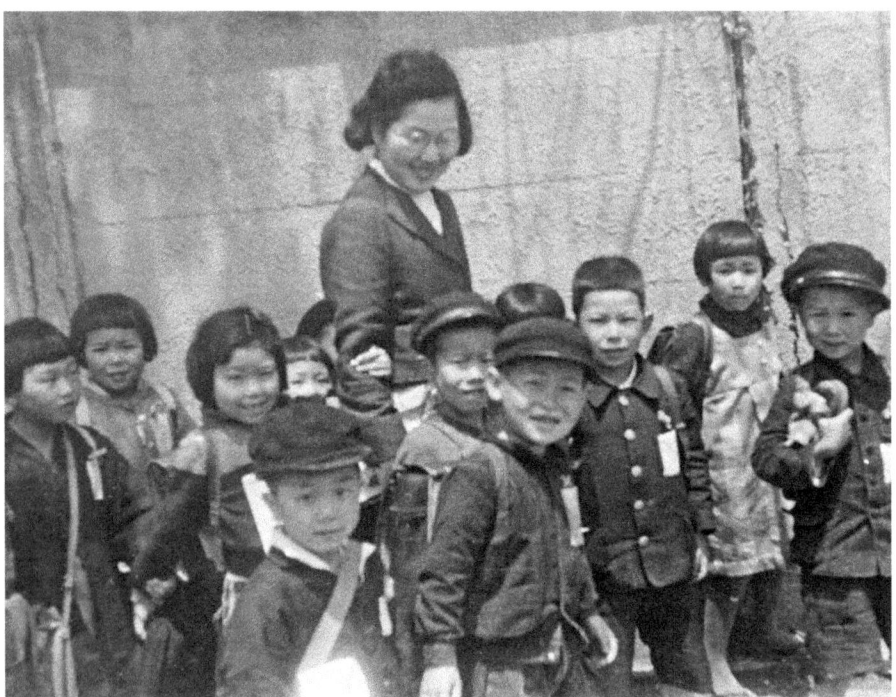

Figure 5.3. Herbert Cole ('Nugget') Coombs, *Children in a Tokyo Street*, May 1946.
Source: National Archives of Australia (NAA) M2153 5/12.

5. THROUGH NON-MILITARY EYES

On a visit to Japan in May 1946 accompanying Prime Minister Ben Chifley, leading bureaucrat H.C. 'Nugget' Coombs was also drawn to photograph the children. Away from the round of diplomatic business, he found many subjects that appealed to him, including the customary shots of Hiroshima's destruction. His apparently spontaneous photograph of a group of spirited young school children in a Tokyo street indicates the postwar Australian take on Japan (see Figure 5.3). Responsible for overseeing the national transition to a peacetime economy as the director-general of Australia's Department of Post-War Reconstruction, Coombs was alert to the potential of Japan's raw human material and its capacity for renewal.

Of course, there were strategic and altruistic dimensions to the Australian participation in the Occupation project, and Japan's children were useful in transmitting the message of Japanese acquiescence in the role being created for it as a reliable ally in the Asia-Pacific. Published in a photo spread in *Pix* in March 1946, Neil Town's image of two Australian soldiers traipsing through Kure with a crowd of adoring Japanese schoolgirls is afforded a revealing caption. That the Australians had 'made friends' with the children, the caption states, 'might even be good for the future generation of Japan'.[9] The short propaganda film *Watch Over Japan* (1947), directed by Geoffrey Collings for the Australian National Film Board, takes up this theme. The narrator intones that the men of BCOF saw the children as 'the real rays of the Japanese rising sun'; guided by the Allies, they would shape a democratic Japan, 'so that one day, perhaps, she will walk hand-in-hand with the peace-loving nations of the world'. The final scene shows a long line of diggers walking hand-in-hand with children through a sunlit village street.[10] No longer symbols of ancient and innocent Japan—'the child of the world's old age'—children had become symbols of its future.

The common soldier-photographer was willing to make the children themselves the subject of the pictures, unadulterated by the forced presence of the Occupier. Taking to the streets of Hiroshima with his Kodak 'Box Brownie', Neville Govett, a sergeant in a transport company, made effective use of the winter sunshine in a photograph of a boy selling black market cigarettes (see Figure 5.4). The boy confidently poses for the camera, to the evident amusement of his friends. Hiroshima was full

---

9   'Australia Is There—with our Occupation Force in Japan', *Pix*, 9 March 1946, 33.
10 Geoffrey Collings, cinematographer, *Watch Over Japan*, AWM FO1309.

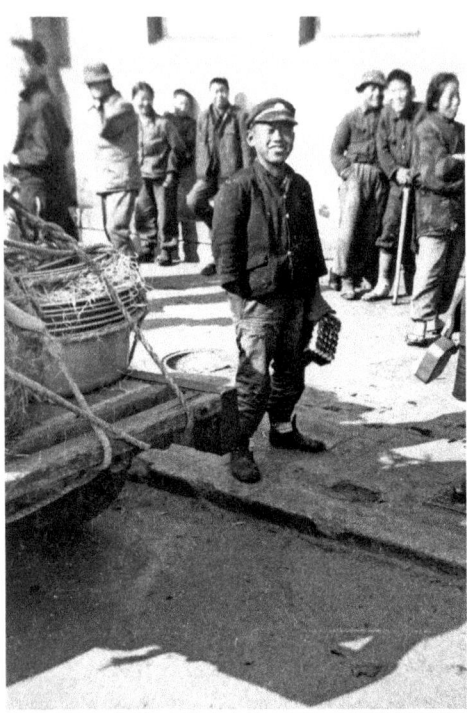 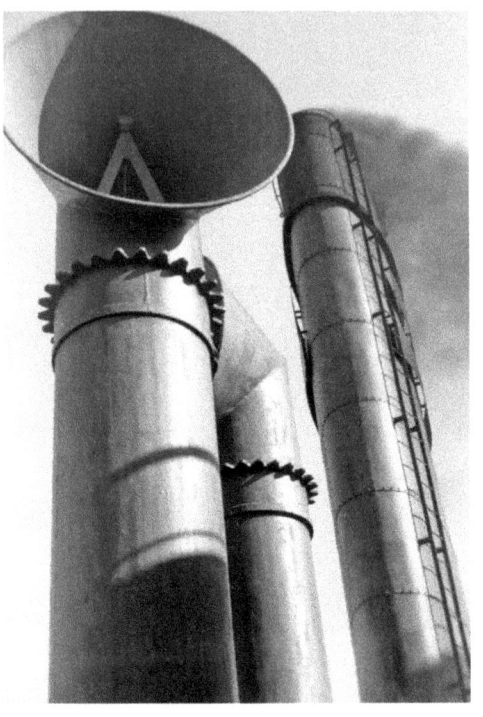

Figure 5.4. Neville Govett, *Street Scene*, Hiroshima, c. 1947–49.
Source: Mitchell Library, State Library of New South Wales MLMSS 8755 Box 3.

Figure 5.5. Neville Govett, *Smokestack and Ventilator on the Hokkaido Ferry*, c. 1947–49.
Source: Mitchell Library, State Library of New South Wales PXE 1498 Box 1.

of uprooted youngsters living rough, supporting themselves as best they could. Many had lost their fathers to the late war, or one or both parents in the atomic bombing. The survival instinct was strong, if not always especially edifying.

The vernacular photography produced by amateurs such as Govett was receptive to the new Japan emerging from the war and rather less reliant on anachronistic visual clichés than the work of the professionals. Govett was an active member of the BCOF Tourist Club (out of which emerged a Camera Club), enjoying group tours to various locations throughout the Japanese archipelago. Compiled by Govett himself, *The Story of the B.C.O.F. Tourist Club* (1950) records the full itinerary of some 200 outings, well over 20 of which were to Hiroshima and environs. The book is copiously illustrated with photographs of the club's activities, but only one of Hiroshima—a run-of-the-mill shot of the A-Bomb Dome. The club may have thought it in questionable taste to highlight a voyeuristic interest in a site of mass death. Several of the photographs are the work of the MHS photographer Claude

Holzheimer—clichéd pictures of castles, mountain views, tea ceremonies and the like. This was a wasted opportunity to showcase amateur work, for Govett's own pictures possess an immediacy lacking in much of the official photography and a willingness to take on unusual subject matter. Taken aboard a ferry plying the northern waters between Honshu and Hokkaido, his *Smokestack and Ventilator* (see Figure 5.5) is a heroically monumental industrial image that conveys a Japan freed from an inhibiting set of images originating from an earlier century. The oblique camera angle and dramatic contrasts of light and shade reveal a modernist photographer's eye for form that shames much of the professional work in Japan.

Like Govett, Royal Australian Air Force pilot Frederick Frueh was an ambitious photographer, alert for signs of modernising Japan. Frueh took several stylish images in the vicinity of the air base at Iwakuni to the west of Hiroshima. Iwakuni is the home of the 'brocade bridge', *Kintaikyo*, a structure built originally in the late seventeenth century. An elegant emblem of the traditional Japanese aesthetic drawn by the legendary Edo-era artist Hiroshige and a common feature of tourist paraphernalia, the bridge was ritually photographed during the Occupation as a signifier of the 'Real Japan'. Yet Frueh's photographer's eye lingered elsewhere. In *On the Road to the Railway Station*, a photograph taken in 1946, he composed a scene both highly romantic and suggestive of a Japan leaving its past behind (see Figure 5.6). The picture is a skilfully arranged blend of opposites—of horizontals and verticals, light and shade, human interaction and industrial impersonality, and of a rural Japan transforming itself into a modern powerhouse (suggested by the chimneys belching smoke emanating from underground factories). To Hal Porter, articulating the view of the elegiac school of writers and artists who bemoan the passing into history of picturesque Old Japan, postwar 'progress' was a 'pestilence', a desecration of the country's voluptuous natural landscape and a corruption of its traditional culture.[11] Frueh saw the country differently, visualising the harmonious coexistence of male and female; past, present and future; agrarian and industrial; old and new.

---

11   Porter, *The Actors: An Image of the New Japan* (Sydney: Angus Robertson), 45. Works such as Donald Richie's *The Inland Sea* (1971) and Alex Kerr's *Lost Japan* (1996) are among the best-known accounts of Japan's self-inflicted damage since the war.

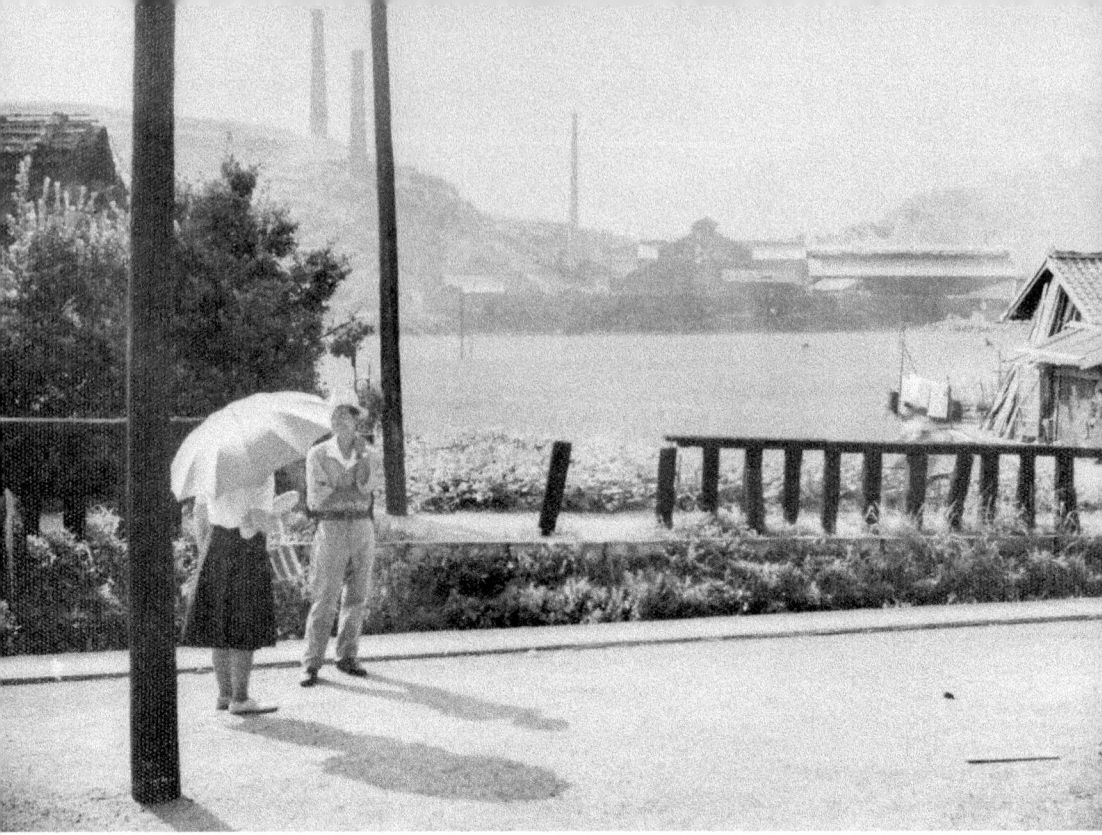

Figure 5.6. Frederick Frueh, *On the Road to the Railway Station*, Iwakuni, c. 1946.

Source: Australian War Memorial (AWM) P08640.007.

For many Australians, of course, the camera was simply a means of taking 'holiday snaps', pictures of the fleeting pleasures of people having the time of their lives. Like most tourist-photographers, they were drawn to the 'unspoiled' Japan that had either escaped the bombing or showed no evidence of postwar suffering. In *The Story of the B.C.O.F. Tourist Club*, Govett wrote that 'cameras clicked merrily' at the 'glorious sight' of cherry blossom at the famous viewing site at Mt Yoshino in Nara Prefecture.[12] Further, some of the private images expose tourism's propensity to encourage exhibitionism. In *Memories of Occupied Japan*, Royal Australian Air Force Flight Lieutenant Philip M. Green included a photograph of himself receiving a shoeshine in the city of Takarazuka from two small Japanese boys, for the price (we are told) of one cigarette per shoe. Such indulgences invoke Sontag's diatribe against the photographer as a 'supertourist' who uses the camera as 'a kind

---

12   Neville Govett, *The Story of the B.C.O.F. Tourist Club* (Hiroshima: Hiroshima Publishing Co., 1950), 25.

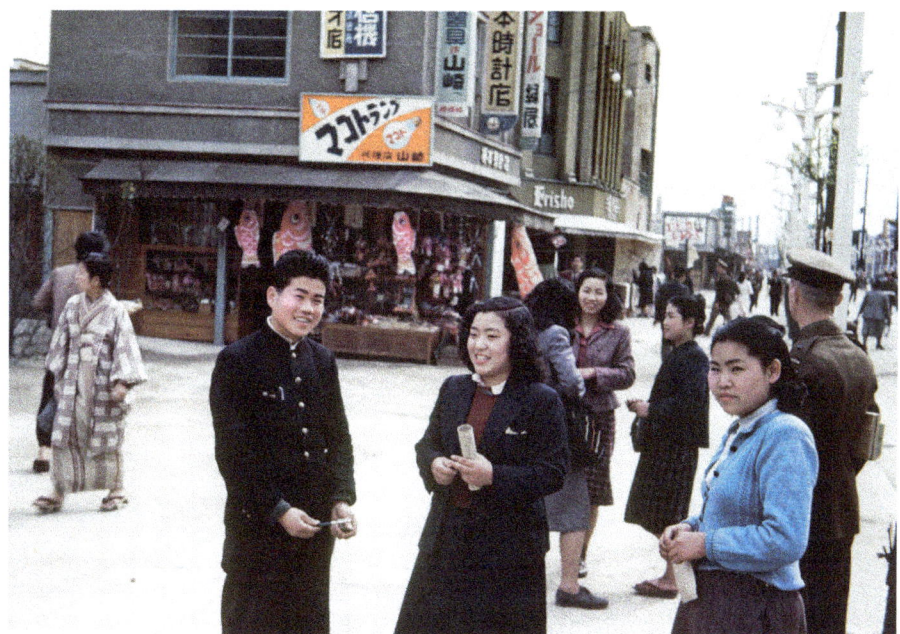

Figure 5.7. Brian and Cecilia McMullan, *Street Scene*, Kure, c. 1947–52.
Source: AWM P05195.017.

of passport that annihilates moral boundaries and social inhibitions, freeing the photographer from any responsibility toward the people photographed'.[13]

Yet, if the amateur photography revealed a degree of heedless hedonism, much of it also sought to connect with Japan itself, and even perhaps define the country it was in the process of becoming. The extensive collection of photographs taken by Brian McMullan, the pre-teenage son of an Australian officer, and his mother Cecilia, is a case in point. Brian and Cecilia used a 'Mycro I', a huge commercial success in 1947 and 1948, on family vacations throughout the length and breadth of Japan.[14] They captured a Japan in transition, one that was both vanishing and in the making. One of their most seemingly innocuous photographs, of a humdrum commercial area of Kure, is among the most eloquent (see Figure 5.7). A group of young Japanese, most likely senior high

---

13   Philip M. Green, *Memories of Occupied Japan* (Blackheath: Philip Maxwell Green 1987), 119; Susan Sontag, *On Photography* (1977; repr., New York: Anchor books Doubleday, 1990), 42–43.
14   The latest model of a nimble little 'subminiature' 14 mm camera first developed in Tokyo in 1939, the Mycro I was the chosen medium of the first ever photographic contest in postwar Japan. See camerapedia.wikia.com/wiki/Mycro (accessed 14 June 2016). For the Australian War Memorial record of the McMullin camera, see AWM REL35672. The McMullins were also proud owners of a Japanese-made cigarette lighter in the shape of a miniature camera set on a tripod (AWM REL35673).

school students, chat unselfconsciously as an anonymous BCOF officer looks away and a traditionally dressed woman clops out of the picture in her wooden *geta*. The well-stocked shops in the background indicate activity. Old Japan, and the recent past of war and occupation, was disappearing from view. Japan was open for business.

Photography and Reconciliation: 1952–57

The Occupation of Japan officially ended in 1952, though the Australian military presence in Japan was temporarily reinvigorated by the fighting in nearby Korea. With the Korean ceasefire in 1953, it began a terminal decline. By November 1956, the last remnants of the force departed Japan. The number of Australians in the country dwindled to virtually nothing. In 1958, a mere 248 Australians were registered as residing in Japan, only 17 of whom lived in the Chugoku region in western Honshu that was once the centre of BCOF activity.[15]

Back in Australia, the Japanese had not been forgiven for the misdemeanours committed by their military, especially the heinous mistreatment of its prisoners in sites of suffering such as the Burma Railway, and resentment still burned. A Gallup Poll of responses to the Peace Treaty taken in August 1951—five years after the war's end—showed a remarkable 62.5 per cent disapproval and 21.4 per cent in favour.[16] As late as 1956, the year of the Melbourne Olympic Games, most Australians 'still tasted bitterness' when they thought of Japan, observed the popular travel writer Colin Simpson.[17]

Australian ambivalence towards fostering a political and economic relationship with Japan was expressed in the public photography of the period—Australians still found it hard to 'see' the Japanese outside the frame of war. One of the most memorable images of the Melbourne Olympics, splashed across the front pages of local newspapers the day after the event, was the press photographer Bruce Howard's picture of the embrace of Australia's 'golden boy', the swimmer Murray Rose, and his Japanese rival Tsuyoshi Yamanaka after the 400 m freestyle final (see Figure 5.8). Influenced by the coincidence that the event fell on

---

15 Figures provided in *Australian Society Review* (April–September 1958), 3.
16 Australian Public Opinion Polls, *Morgan Gallup Poll*, nos. 788–90 (August–September 1951).
17 See Colin Simpson, *The Country Upstairs* (Sydney: Angus and Robertson, 1956), 5–6.

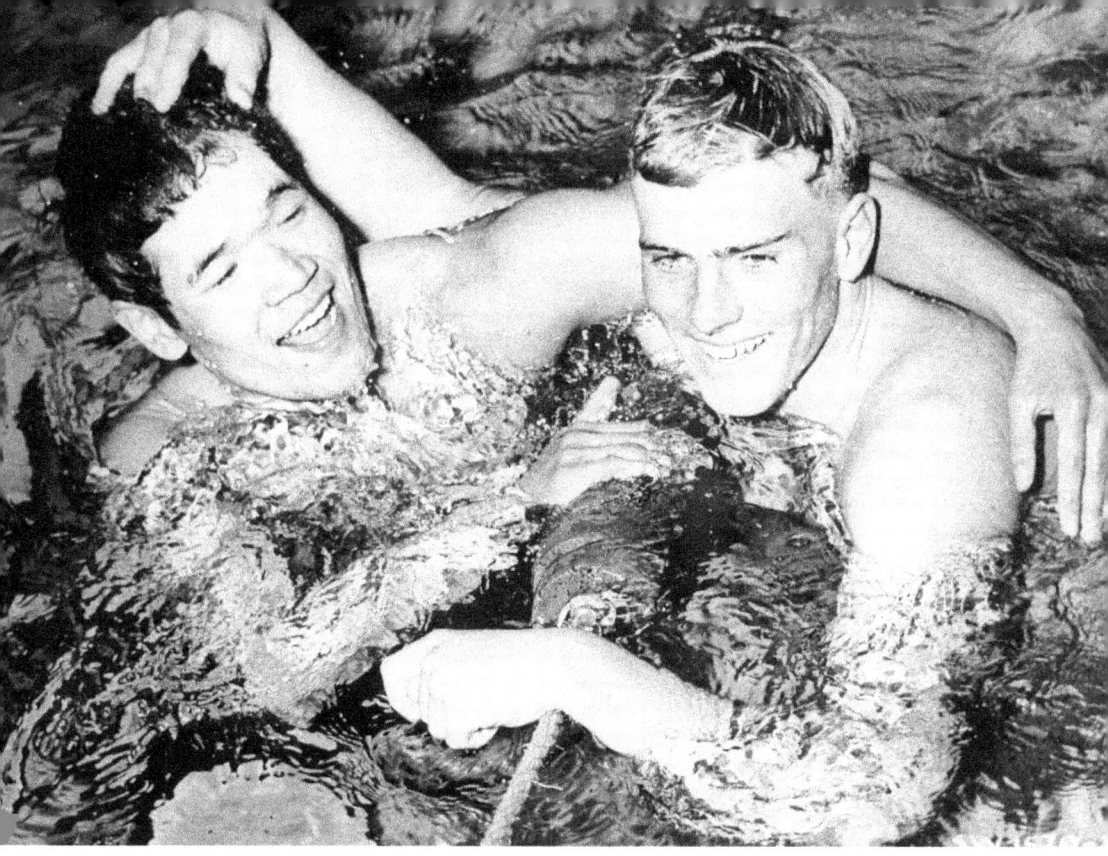

Figure 5.8. Bruce Howard, *Murray Rose with his Japanese Rival Tsuyoshi Yamanaka after the 400m Freestyle Final at the 1956 Olympic Games*, Melbourne, 4 December 1956.
Source: Courtesy of News Ltd.

the fifteenth anniversary of Pearl Harbour, *Pix* used the photograph to illustrate its story of the Rose/Yamanaka clash later in the games, the 1,500 m final won more narrowly by the Australian, reported to have heroically staved off a final thrust from 'the do-or-die Japanese'.[18] The Birmingham-born Rose had migrated with his British parents to Australia as a baby. Aged three or four, he had appeared in a wartime savings propaganda poster for the war effort, playing with a toy boat by the seaside and plaintively posing the question: 'Will the Japs come here in their big ships, Daddy?' A little over a decade later, there he was in the water pitted against a Japanese. Interviewed in 2011, Rose remembered the race as 'symbolic of two kids that'd grown up on opposite sides of the war', who had 'come together in the friendship of the Olympic

18   The photograph featured prominently on front pages the day after the event. See for example *Sydney Morning Herald*, 5 December 1956, 1; 'A Rose in Full Bloom', *Pix*, 22 December 1956, 18. Other publications also referenced the war in their account of the 1,500 m final, see 'Rose Beats Japanese in Fighting Final Lap', *Sydney Morning Herald*, 8 December 1956, 12.

arena'.[19] Appearing in Australian newspapers and reproduced in souvenir publications as representative of the 'Friendly Games', the photograph radiates male bonding, if gratifyingly once again showing an Australian proving superior to his Japanese counterpart.

Similarly, the developing commercial competitiveness of the nations was considered war by another means, but this time with an industrially revivified Japan emerging the victor. Dependably populist and increasingly sensationalist, *Pix* fanned this anxiety in 1957 with 'Japs Fight Again—For Trade', a photo essay documenting the intimidating pace of Japan's recovery.[20] Disquiet about Australia being swamped with Japanese goods fed anxiety that Japan might rediscover its martial propensities. It also inflamed longstanding national fears about Asian invasion, both literally and via migration. Not only was Japan rebuilding, it was also repopulating. As early as June 1950, *Pix* had highlighted its postwar baby boom, with its population growing by an alarming 5,000 babies per day. Recalling older anxieties about Japan's ready production of boy soldiers during the Russo-Japanese War, *Pix* posed the question, 'is the swiftly expanding nation to be ally or dangerous problem child?'. The feature is illustrated by juxtaposed photographs of a massed crowd in a Tokyo park and a mother with two young infants (as evidence of local disregard for birth control) and a helpful timeline showing Japanese military expansion from the late nineteenth century.[21]

Yet, the photographic image could be turned to Japan's advantage, helping soften attitudes and allay fears that the war had never really ended. The integration of several hundred Japanese war brides into Australian society in the early 1950s was a deeply symbolic event, the first significant breach in the fortress of 'White Australia'. Photographs of the brides' arrival and entry into Australian suburban communities appeared regularly in newspapers in the first years of the decade, notably featuring in the *Australian Women's Weekly*. In July 1952, the *Weekly* marked the imminent arrival of the first Japanese wife to arrive, 22-year-old Cherry Parker, with a feature on the 'warm welcome' she could

---

19 Rose and wartime propaganda poster, *Australian Women's Weekly*, 17 April 1957, 7; Rose 2011 interview reproduced in 'A Feeling For the Water—Transcript', *Australian Story* (ABC), www.abc.net.au/austory/a-feeling-for-the-water---part-one/9169846.
20 'Japs Fight Again—For Trade', *Pix*, 26 October 1957, 7–8.
21 'Jap Problem Grows by 5000 Babies a Day', *Pix*, 24 June 1950, 5–7.

expect to receive. The story was illustrated by a picture of the photogenic family—Cherry, her husband Gordon and two small daughters with the reassuringly familiar names of Margaret and Kathleen.[22]

The inconsistent imagery of Japan-as-threat and Japan-as-partner that circulated during the Cold War period reflected the unease that many people felt, as a recently hated nation moved into Australia's defence orbit as a client state of the US in the global fight against communism. Other forms of visual culture continued to reflect and exacerbate conflicting Australian attitudes towards Japan. In 1958, the national tour of the 'Hiroshima Panels', a collection of large canvases depicting the diabolical concoction of blast, fire and radiation inflicted on the Japanese city, deeply impressed Australian crowds and increased sympathy for the suffering of scores of thousands.[23] This was a time of heightened nuclear alarm. Nevil Shute's novel of nuclear apocalypse, *On the Beach*, set in and around Melbourne, was published in 1957. At the same time, the popular Hollywood epic *The Bridge on the River Kwai* (1957) reminded a mass audience of the horrors perpetrated by the Japanese on the Burma Railway. In July 1958, *Pix* mocked a group of newly released convicted war criminals photographed holding a reunion in Tokyo's Sugamo Prison. The written text reminded readers that this was the very place in which Prime Minister Kishi, with whom the Australian Government had just negotiated the Australia–Japanese Commerce Agreement, had been imprisoned as a member of Tojo's War Cabinet after Japan's surrender.[24]

---

22 See Mary Coles, 'Warm Welcome Arranged for Japanese Wife', *Australian Women's Weekly*, 9 July 1953, 23. The uplifting story of Gordon Parker and his fight to bring his family home contrasted with one of the Occupation's most unedifying legacies, the hundreds of mixed-race children abandoned by their Australian fathers and scorned by Japan. Long ignored, their plight came to light around the time of the signing of the trade agreement. This was 'a story of shame', announced by *Pix* in an August 1957 article illustrated with several photographs of children with unmistakably Western features. One is said to look 'almost like any Australian schoolboy with freckled skin and brown eyes'. See 'A Story of Shame', *Pix*, 6 August 1957, 6–10.
23 See 'The Hiroshima Panels: Showings Draw Hushed Crowds', *Australian Woman's Weekly*, 9 July 1958, 7.
24 'Jap Criminals Stage Party', *Pix*, 26 July 1958, 5.

Both the intimate and public role of photography in the negotiation of the Commerce Agreement attests to the definitive part played by the camera in defining Australia–Japan bilateralism. The most overt agent of reconciliation was the prime minister of Australia in the 1950s, Robert Menzies. For several years, Menzies had sought to persuade Australians to quell their anger and to adopt a 'grown-up' attitude to Japan. 'The war is over', he remarked in a broadcast in March 1954. The communists posed a greater threat to peace and prosperity than the prospect of a rejuvenated Japan.[25]

Menzies was a camera enthusiast who would habitually take his equipment with him on his overseas tours. Phillip Hobson photographed him indulging his passion for 16 mm home movie making on an official visit to Kure, Hiroshima and surrounds in August 1950. Over the prime minister's shoulder, a leather camera case is adorned with the initials 'R.G.M.'. It is a graphic illustration of political possession—the Australian leader taking private images of a beaten and humbled nation.[26] He had his Kodak with him when he revisited Japan in April 1957, unashamedly and possibly indecorously filming his hosts during the rituals of diplomacy. When he was not taking his own pictures, Menzies was the epitome of diplomatic courtesy, photographed trying his hand at chopsticks and stoically sampling sushi. In pictures widely circulated in newspapers, he even had his photograph taken with the formerly despised Hirohito, who the Australians had a decade earlier wanted to be held to account as a war criminal.[27] Three months after Menzies's trip, the Australia–Japan Commerce Agreement was signed, guaranteeing most favoured nation treatment on tariffs and non-discrimination in trade. The agreement was to become a key factor in Australia's economic growth in the 1950s and throughout the 1960s. Sixty years later, it was still being lauded for its historic importance by Australian and Japanese prime ministers.[28]

---

25 'Menzies Pleads: "Hate the Japs No Longer"', *Argus*, 18 March 1954, 1.
26 For Phillip Hobson's photograph of Menzies in Kure, see AWM HOBJ1190.
27 See 'P.M. Calls on Emperor', *Sun*, 15 April 1957, 9; 'Prime Ministers Meet in Tokio', *Sun*, 13 April 1957, 13.
28 Signing a new trade partnership in Canberra in July 2014, the Japanese Prime Minister Shinzo Abe and his Australian counterpart Tony Abbott lauded the signal economic significance of the 1957 commerce agreement and the more general relationship it seemed to indicate. The previous year, Abbott declared Japan Australia's 'closest friend in Asia'. See 'Putting Meat on the Bones of a 1957 Agreement', *Australian*, 21 July 2014, 10; 'Tony Abbott Says Japan is Australia's "Closest Friend in Asia"', *Australian*, 9 October 2013, 1.

Undertaken with tight security in response to negative publicity, the reciprocal visit to Australia in December 1957 of Japan's Prime Minister Nobusuke Kishi was intensively photographed. At a wreath-laying ceremony at the Australian War Memorial, a local businessman (and ex-serviceman) audibly shouted to the attendant group of press photographers to 'shut those cameras up', calling it 'an infamous day for Australia'.[29] That May, *Pix* headlined an article about the forthcoming trip 'Should Jap P.M. Visit Australia?', illustrating it with the barbed use of well-known photographs from the recent military past, including George Silk's famous photograph of a blinded digger in New Guinea being led by a loyal Papuan helper, as a vivid reminder of Australia's wartime travails.[30]

Kishi's brief sojourn in Australia, however, was a diplomatic triumph. At a luncheon held in his honour at Parliament House in Canberra, Japan's prime minister offered a formal apology of 'heartfelt sorrow' for what had occurred during the war. Menzies responded with portentous remarks about Australia and Japan's mutual 'destiny in the Pacific'.[31] Yet the trip's significance was more sharply articulated by a photograph than by fine words. On his initial arrival in Australia, at Melbourne's Essendon Airport, Kishi was greeted by Japanese women and children in traditional dress, and by Prime Minister Menzies, his hand extended in friendship with a swarm of photographers at the ready (see Figure 5.9). Menzies's injunction, 'We Must Be Friends', had featured on the front page of the Melbourne *Sun* on the morning of Kishi's arrival and, by the afternoon, a photograph of the historic handshake dominated the evening newspaper the *Herald*.[32] The leaders of the two countries were photographed enacting a definitive political version of burying the hatchet.

One cannot underestimate the image's significance. Fifty years on, in the context of the signing of the Japan–Australia Joint Declaration on Security Cooperation in 2007, it was recycled in a photomontage to signify the political partnership of Japan's Prime Minister Shinzo Abe—Kishi's grandson—with his Australian counterpart John Howard.[33]

---

29 'Ex-Serviceman Protests at War Memorial', *Canberra Times*, 5 December 1957, 1.
30 'Should Jap P.M. Visit Australia?', *Pix*, 4 May 1957, 4.
31 'Kishi Offers Apology for Japanese War', *Canberra Times*, 5 December 1957, 1.
32 'Menzies: We Must be Friends', *Sun*, 29 November 1957, 1; 'Handshake at Airport', *Herald*, 29 November 1957, 1.
33 Michele Mossop photograph, *Australian Financial Review*, 6 July 2007.

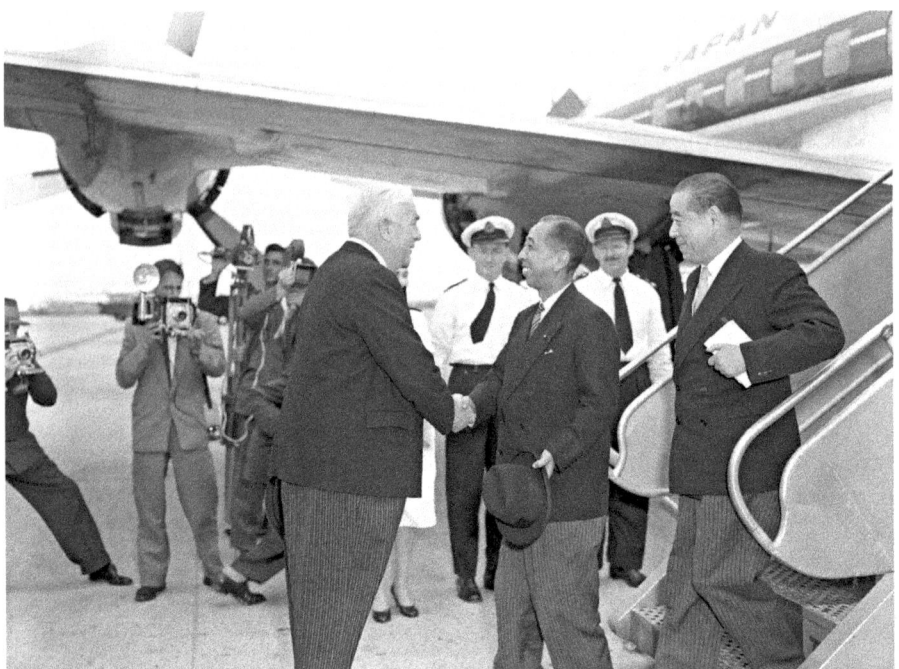

Figure 5.9. Photographer unknown, *Prime Minister Menzies Greets Japanese Prime Minster Kishi at Essendon Airport*, Melbourne, 2 December 1957.
Source: NAA A1671 JPM1/10.

Kishi's trip heralded a succession of official visits by Japanese prime ministers into the 1960s and 1970s. Kishi had flown into Australia with Japan Air; his smiling successors were usually pictured emerging down the stairs of a Qantas jet. Diplomacy evidently extended to the choice of airline carrier.[34]

Back in Tokyo, a few months before the public demonstration of bilateralism at the airport in Melbourne, an illustrated story in *Pix* revealed the link between photography and rapprochement in defining the postwar Australia–Japan relationship. It featured E.R. Walker, Australia's first postwar ambassador to Japan and an avid photographer. Entitled 'Ambassador's Album', the story described Walker's passion for the medium and his desire to use it positively to take his impressions of Japan.[35] A selection of his images reveals some attractive pictures of a small girl dressed in her best kimono on her way to a festival, and a pleasing photograph of the embassy garden under snow. Only

---

34   For examples see visit to Australia by Prime Minister Ikeda, 1963, NAA A1673 11836719; visit to Australia by Prime Minister Sato, 1967, NAA, A1200 11837972.
35   'Ambassador's Album', *Pix*, 12 January 1957, 42–43. See also Colin Simpson, 'Diplomat's Tokyo Garden', *Australian Women's Weekly*, 7 March 1956, 23.

a photograph of a girl burning incense at the tomb of the 47 Ronin, the legendary samurai who committed *harikari* to avenge their lord and master, was a reminder of the uncompromising martial nation that had so recently threatened to bring Australia to its knees—a newly pacific nation now Australia's best friend and partner in the Asia-Pacific.

Photography and Reconciliation: 1957–76

Photography continued to act as a mediator of the formalised relationship with 'new' Japan in the late 1950s into the 1960s, though in varied and occasionally contradictory ways. Japan had emerged as a modern industrial juggernaut, but it was packaged for potential Australian consumption in decidedly traditional terms. 'Australia's Overseas Airline', Qantas, began advertising its services to Tokyo in the mid-1950s. A Qantas shop window display in central Melbourne around 1955 that aroused the interest of the British Australian photographer Sarah Chinnery contained an image of a kimonoed woman and cherry blossom, used as a predictable lure. In 1957, an illustrated advertisement in the *Australian Women's Weekly*—later used to inaugurate the popular 'Cherry Blossom' cruises to Japan—revealed a Qantas jet flying perilously close to Mt Fuji.[36]

A photographic competition sponsored by the Japanese camera manufacturer Yashica and run by *Pix* throughout 1961 offered a 'millionaire's holiday' for two to the country, flying Qantas.[37] Yet, while the growth of commercial air travel promised to bring the two countries into closer contact, the vast majority of air travel to Japan during this period was for business and trade purposes, rather than leisure. Moreover, the numbers remained relatively small. In 1957, the year of the Commerce Agreement, the total number of Australian 'short-term' travellers to Japan was a meagre 1,153. This increased to some 6,371 in 1964.[38] Air travel

---

36   Sarah Chinnery, Photographic Collection of New Guinea, England and Australia, National Library of Australia PIC/11131/1692; Qantas advertisement, 'Fly Qantas to the Orient…', *Australian Women's Weekly*, 9 October 1957, 6.
37   See *Pix*, 21 October 1961, 32.
38   For tourism statistics see S.R. Carver, *Demography Bulletin*, no. 75 (1957); Richard White, 'The Retreat from Adventure; Popular Travel Writing in the 1950s', *Australian Historical Studies* 28, no. 109 (1997): 101–02. See also Jonathan Bollen, 'Here and There—Travel, Television and Touring Revues: Internationalism as Entertainment in the 1950s and 1960s', *Popular Entertainment Studies* 4, no. 1 (2013): 69, fn 34, 78. On business travel to Asia, see Agnieska Sobocinska, *Visiting the Neighbours: Australians in Asia* (Sydney: NewSouth Publishing, 2014), 45–46.

was still a privilege available to the few, rather than the many; the age of mass recreational tourism to Asia was some years off. Armchair travellers were catered to by best-sellers such as Colin Simpson's *The Country Upstairs* (1956), which went through numerous reprintings and editions, from the time of its original publication in 1956 right through the 1960s. *The Country Upstairs* was prodigiously illustrated by photographs, mostly stereotypical images of traditional Japan supplied by the Japan National Tourist Organisation.

The domestic appetite for Japan was largely expressed through the desirability of imported Japanese products, as a rapidly suburbanising Australia enjoyed a period of sustained prosperity. Belying the imagery of picturesque timelessness promoted by tourism, the ubiquitous 'Made in Japan' label, applied to everything from cameras to cars, signified modernity not tradition, the future not the past. A Japanese Trade Fair held in Sydney in January 1959 was heralded by fireworks over Sydney Harbour, reportedly attracting the biggest night-time crowd seen in the city since the 1954 royal tour. Advertising for the event had spruiked the 'industrial renaissance' of a 'time-locked feudal' Japan, along with its new status as 'a dynamic democratic ally', as being 'a miracle of our time'.[39] Not that the focus was entirely consumerist; along with the displays of Japan's technical acumen, the fair also featured film and fashion. The new trade agreement was synonymous with 'closer understanding and goodwill between the two countries', according to the representative of the Japan Export Trade Promotion Agency at an International Trade Fair held in Melbourne in 1959.[40] Among the Japanese exhibitors was the 'Tokyo Toys and Wholesalers Association'. The prospect of mass importation of toys from the Japanese 'invaders' had created controversy in the early 1950s—a news item in the Sydney *Sunday Herald* stated that it created 'almost as big a stir in toyland as the Japanese submarines caused in Sydney harbour'.[41] However, by the end of the decade, the transnational brand 'Japan' had become part of the Australian landscape.

---

39   Japan Trade Fair advertisement, *Daily Telegraph*, 23 January 1959, 17. See 'Huge City Traffic Tangle in Scramble to View Fireworks', *Sydney Morning Herald*, 24 January 1959, 1.
40   Japan Foreword by Michisuke Sugi, *Melbourne 1959, International Trade Fair Catalogue* (Melbourne: Melbourne Chamber of Commerce, 1959), 5.
41   'There Is War in Toyland (But No Real Invasion Yet)', *Sunday Herald*, 2 September 1951, 12. See also 'Japs "Ready to Dump"', *Argus*, 31 August 1951, 5.

By 1961, *Pix*, once prone to highlighting the pitfalls of closer national ties with the old enemy, had started producing positive photo essays about Japan. A story on successful Australian–Japanese marriages included glowing male tributes to 'wonderful' Japanese wives. A follow-up story claimed that Japanese men in their turn make 'wonderful husbands', from a Melbourne woman who met her spouse in Tokyo while working for Radio Australia.[42] This was a story unimaginable a few short years before. The small but growing community of Australians living and working in Japan also attracted attention. Published in *Pix* in 1960, 'An Aussie Tot in Tokyo' described the challenges Australian business families faced in raising children in Japan. The article concluded that, surprisingly, the teeming metropolis is 'a good place for rearing children'; a photograph of an Australian three year old playing happily in a multiracial Tokyo kindergarten illustrates the article.[43]

Nonetheless, while Japanese cultural phenomena such as its interior design (though not yet its cuisine) were gaining greater cultural currency in the Australia of the 1960s, the country itself remained *terra incognita*. Most Australian artists and writers still headed straight for London and the cultural capitals of Europe. Tourist photography taken during this period by the small cadre of Australian travellers that ventured to Japan reveals a nation on the move but perplexingly stuck in its ways. An album of photographs taken by Ellen Brophy, the wife of a BCOF serviceman who returned to Japan with him as a tourist in the late 1950s, contains a portrait of a disparate group of women in an unnamed location. The image, which reveals a tension between the tenaciously traditional and the utterly modern, is as confounding as it is fascinating (see Figure 5.10). The handwritten caption alongside the photograph reads: 'Have you ever seen anything like it?' Presumably, the photographer is alluding to the exposed breast of the older woman to the right of the picture. Equally, the caption may refer to all three. Were Japanese females not supposed to be decorous, passive and almost obsessive in their efforts to conform to good taste? This collective of postwar Japanese women look defiant and dismissive; certainly they do not feel the obligation to fake a compliant smile for the foreigner's camera.

---

42   'Japanese? They Make Wonderful Wives', *Pix*, 19 August 1961, 242–48; 'Australian Girl Tells: "Why I Chose a Japanese Husband"', *Pix*, 21 October 1961, 62–63.
43   'An Aussie Tot in Tokyo', *Pix*, 2 April 1960, 18–21.

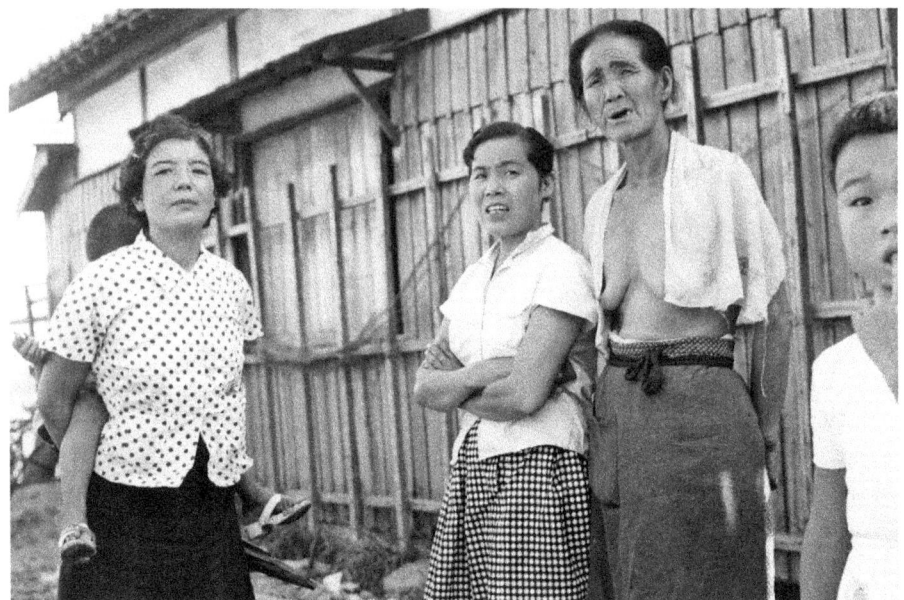

Figure 5.10. Ellen Brophy, *'Memories of Japan'* (Album), Kobe-Osaka, 1957–60.
Source: State Library of Victoria. Accession no. H2014.1002/125.

One trailblazing traveller photographer was the sculptor and printmaker Bill Clements, who lived in Kyoto for nearly three years from 1964 at around the same time as the noted Australian poet Harold Stewart. Japan was changing, and so was the venerable city of Kyoto itself. The repository of many of the nation's most prized structures and precious gardens, Kyoto had narrowly been spared the ravages of the wartime bombing, but it was 'a city in transition', Clements observed in a photo essay published in the *Kyoto Journal* in 2011.[44] Old Kyoto was embracing the modern world. As elsewhere in urban Japan, there was an explosion of interest in photography; camera stores, Clements noted, seemed to be on almost every corner.[45] Bill and his wife Barbara took to the streets with a Minolta SR7, taking hundreds of photographs that they hoped would one day become a book 'that might help open eyes, shape reconciliation'. The book, sadly, has not as yet materialised.[46]

The year of the Clements' arrival in Kyoto—1964—was big one for Japan. That October, the Tokyo Olympic Games demonstrated to the world its evolution into a confident contemporary nation. The choice of

---

44 Bill Clements, 'An Old Brown Overcoat: Kyoto in the Mid-Sixties', *Kyoto Journal* 76 (Summer 2011): 11.
45 Ibid., 12; Bill Clements interview with Melissa Miles, San Isidore, NSW, 30 June 2016.
46 Clements, 'An Old Brown Overcoat', 16.

a student born in Hiroshima on the very day of its nuclear destruction to light the Olympic flame highlighted Japan's civic reconstruction from the smouldering wreck of August 1945. The spectacle of the Olympics illustrated not merely Japan's ability to stage a huge international event but also revealed its cutting-edge modernity.[47] Tokyo was transformed by new expressways, hotels and sports facilities built for the games. The bullet train to Osaka was completed just days before the games opened. The fastest train in the word, the *shinkansen* changed travel within Japan and became a symbol of Japan's breathtaking renovation. 'A Pictorial Introduction' to the enlarged and revised edition of Simpson's *The Country Upstairs*, published in 1965, contains a two-page photograph of a bullet train hurtling past Mt Fuji—in what has since become an instantly recognisable image of Japan's mesmerising blend of serene timelessness and helter-skelter activity. In Australia, the Tokyo Olympics was marred by the arrest of its star swimmer, Dawn Fraser, for attempting to purloin an Olympic flag from the moated area outside the imperial palace. The competition was over, it was 2.30 am and Fraser, along with other Australians, had been partying at the Imperial Hotel across from the palace. Yet, even in this awkward moment, magnanimous new Japan was triumphantly revealed. When the Japanese police realised they had taken an Olympic champion into custody, Fraser was promptly released, and the next morning they made a *presento* to her of the flag along with a box of flowers.[48]

Six years after the Olympics, another state-sponsored event, Expo '70 in Osaka, provided further compelling evidence that Japan had left militarism behind for a more constructive future, while the mass nationalism it produced offered a disquieting reminder of the war years.[49] Sandra Wilson described the exposition site as a 'very effective advertising medium for the achievements of Japanese industry', a fantasia of pavilions containing futuristic homes and robots, moving walkways, electric cars and a state-of-the-art computer system—and, troublingly, the enthusiastic embrace of nuclearism.[50] Up to half of the Japanese population saw the expo;

---

47   See Sandra Wilson, 'Exhibiting a New Japan: The Tokyo Olympics of 1964 and Expo '70 in Osaka', *Historical Research* 85, no. 227 (February 2012). See esp. 159–60, 163, 167, 173–74.
48   The Australian sporting authorities took a less charitable view of Fraser's nocturnal escapade, banning her from competition for 10 years.
49   See Wilson, 'Exhibiting a New Japan', 163.
50   In the context of a growing dependence on nuclear energy, the Japan Pavilion displayed two 'Atomic Towers', along with the legend, 'Atomic power, if rightly used, will give us splendid power. It can enrich our lives and give us high hopes' (Wilson, 'Exhibiting a New Japan', 165).

visitors totalled a staggering 64 million.[51] A monorail was constructed to transport thousands of people by the hour to the site. The Berlin-born, Melbourne-based modernist photographer Mark Strizic, known for his pictures of architectural and industrial subjects, was in Osaka to photograph the event. Strizic captured both Japanese technological elan and the Australian attempt, in the dramatic design of its own pavilion, to illustrate to the Japanese audience that it too was no industrial backwater. He photographed the monorail from inside the pavilion as it snaked its way around the vast exposition complex (see Figure 5.11). In another photograph (see Figure 5.12), Strizic presents an exterior view of a tree sculpture of skeletal ghost gums—archetypally outback Australia—positioned in stark juxtaposition to a detail of the bold futuristic sweep of the Australian pavilion, fashioned from Australian steel.

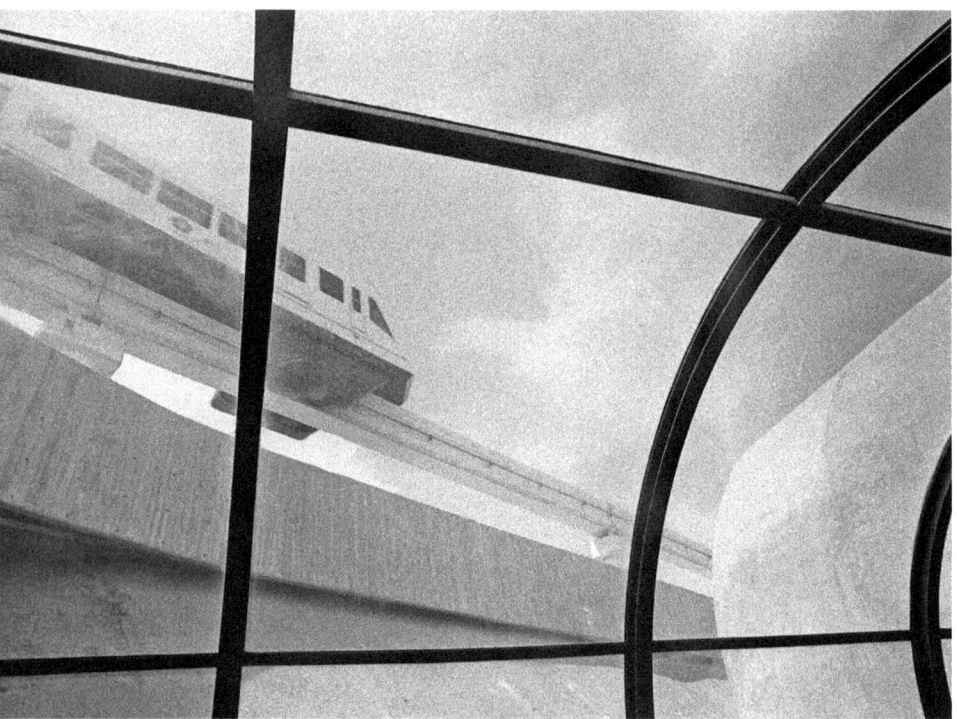

Figure 5.11. Mark Strizic, *Monorail Viewed from Inside the Australian Pavilion, Expo '70*, Osaka, 1970.
Source: Pictures Collection, State Library of Victoria. Accession no. H2011.55/1342b.

---

51   Ibid., 174.

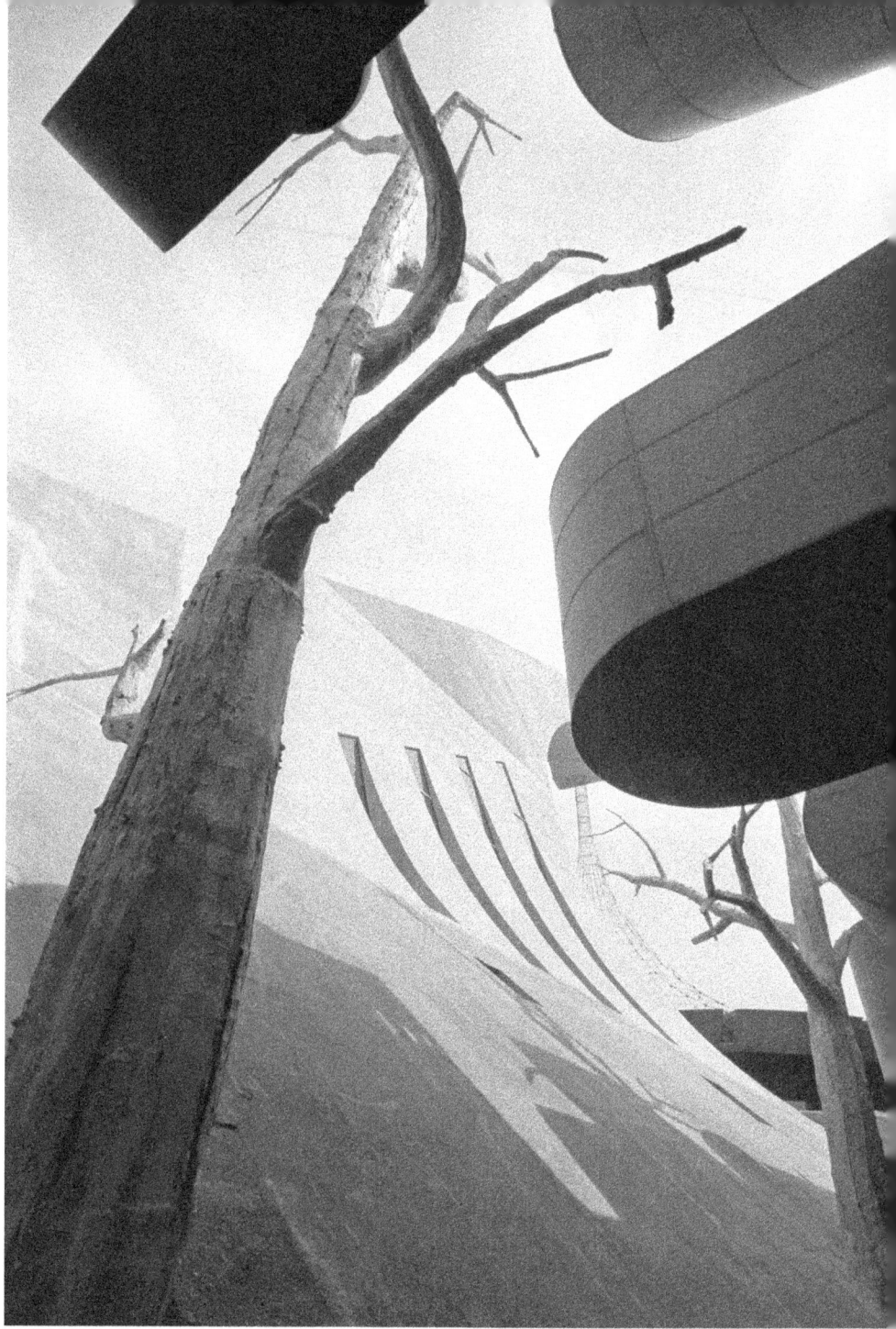

Figure 5.12. Mark Strizic, *Exterior of the Australian Pavilion, Expo '70*, Osaka, 1970.

Source: Pictures Collection, State Library of Victoria. Accession no. H2011.55/1296c.

Japan had already become Australia's main trading partner well before the end of the decade, and an important linchpin in its growing national engagement with the Asian region more generally. Thus, as Carolyn Barnes and Simon Jackson observed, Expo '70 was seen by the Australian Government as 'an important exercise in cultural diplomacy'. The 'ambitious engineering' of the pavilion itself and its exhibits (in spaces curated by Robin Boyd) were calculated to impress.[52] Designed by James Maccormick, the pavilion featured a monstrous arched cantilever holding in its jaws cables that supported a huge, lotus-like shallow-domed roof above the main exhibition hall. Maccormick claimed that the cantilever was inspired by the *Great Wave Off Kanagawa*, the famous print by the legendary nineteenth-century *ukiyo-e* artist Hokusai. More sceptical observers might have opined that it resembled a mock dinosaur in some suburban children's theme park.

Despite the growing familiarity of Japan, the number of short-term Australian travellers to Japan remained relatively low. The year after the Osaka Expo, 1971, just under 10,000 made the journey. Through its Community Relations Section, Qantas Airways did its best to inspire interest in the country by producing a series of teaching kits for distribution in both state and independent schools. Its *Family Japan* (1971) series of publications focused on purportedly representative families in Tokyo and the provinces, heavily illustrated by photographs mainly sourced from Japanese agencies, including the Japan National Tourist Organisation. *The Two Families from Tokyo* issue strongly emphasised the attractive modernity of suburban life in the capital. *Two Rural Families* suggested the passing of traditional ways of life, as land prices rise and urbanisation continued its sweep across the landscape.[53]

Conversely, Japanese travel to Australia was on the rise, increasing exponentially throughout the 1970s and 1980s. By 1988, Japanese tourism to Australia outstripped Australian travel to Japan twelvefold.[54] Japanese

---

52 Carolyn Barnes and Simon Jackson, 'Creature of Circumstance: Australia's Pavilion at Expo '70 and Changing International Relations', in *Panorama to Paradise: Proceedings of the XXIVth International Conference of the Society of Architectural Historians, Australia and New Zealand, Adelaide, 21–24 September 2007* (Adelaide: Society of Architectural Historians), 1–2.
53 Ted Myers, Qantas culture series no 5, *Family Japan: Two Families from Tokyo* (Sydney: Qantas Airways and the Asian Studies Coordinating Committee, 1974); *Family Japan: Two Rural Families* (Sydney: Qantas Airways and the Asian Studies Coordinating Committee, 1974).
54 See Ian Castles, *Year Book Australia*, no. 73 1990 (Canberra: Australian Bureau of Statistics, 1990), 381. In 1988, the number of Australian tourists to Japan was 31,000; that same year, Australia attracted 352,300 Japanese.

tourists came armed with their cameras, creating a national stereotype that has continued to the present day. By 2015, Tourism Australia had come upon the idea of creating a smartphone app, aimed specifically at young Japanese, which allows tourists to take 'selfie' photographs with iconic backdrops to inspire actual travel to the country.[55]

The camera was used more conventionally by some Japanese when they started gravitating to Australia in the early 1960s. A singular moment in the history of postwar Australia–Japan reconciliation—comprehensively if prosaically covered by the camera—came with the arrival of the Fujita Salvage Company in Darwin in 1959. This was to prove a story of 'salvage' in more ways than one. The city's harbour was still choked by the wrecks of ships destroyed by the Japanese aerial bombings in 1942 and needed to be cleared. After a worldwide search, the contract was awarded to a Japanese company, an irony not lost on the local people. Sensitive to a possible public backlash, the Australian Government stipulated that no former Japanese soldiers could be involved in what was a massive project. Yet, the company team of 120 Japanese workers, brave men diving in deep and dangerous waters, earned the respect of the Darwin community during their two-year stay. Housed aboard the first of the salvaged ships, the *British Motorist*, they interacted with the locals in various forms of social exchange, caught by the (anonymous) company photographer. In one photograph (see Figure 5.13), taken in 1961, Australian visitors to the Japanese quarters (for what appears to be a Japanese meal) make a toast for the camera in a convivial domestic scene unimaginable a decade earlier.[56]

Further Japanese arrivals to Australian shores during the 1960s provided more profound opportunities to produce definitive images of postwar reconciliation, especially for the cluster of official photographers attached to the ANIB. In 1964, the formal establishment of the Cowra War Cemetery, containing the remains of Japanese prisoners of war killed in the wartime 'breakout', occasioned the visit of still-grieving relatives, whose arrival in Australia was photographed by Bill Brindle for the

---

55 Damien Larkins, 'Selfies "on Steroids" Set to Lure Japanese Tourist to Australia', *ABC Gold Coast News*, 3 September 2015.
56 The spirit of amity was further fostered by the company owner, Ryogo Fujita, a pacifist, who crafted 77 bronze crosses from the metal of one of the sunken vessels and donated them to Darwin's Uniting Church, destroyed during the air raids, now being rebuilt with the aid of its sister church in Kyoto. The extensive photographic collection of the salvage operation went on public display as 'Mr Fujita's Photo Album' at Darwin's Northern Territory Library from November 2016 to February 2017.

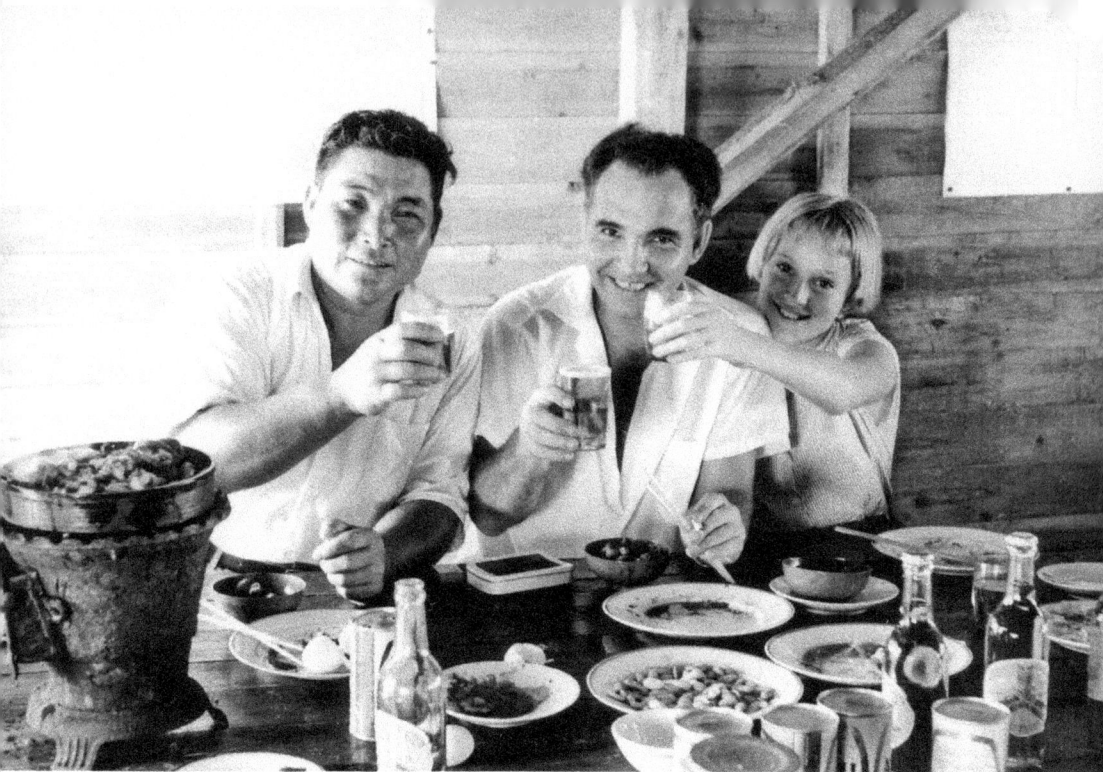

Figure 5.13. Photographer unknown, *Visitors and Crew Make a Toast*, Darwin Harbour 1961.
Source: Senichiro Fujita Collection, Northern Territory Library PH0874/0126.

ANIB.[57] However, by far the most moving Japanese familial pilgrimage, widely covered by the press and television as well as the ANIB, was that, in 1968, of Matsue Matsuo, the aged mother of the submariner Lieutenant Keiu Matsuo, who was killed in the midget submarine raid in Sydney Harbour in 1942. In Canberra, Mrs Matsuo met with the Australian Prime Minister John Gorton and made an emotional visit to the Australian War Memorial to formally receive her son's bloodstained body belt, until then kept on public display.[58] Paid for by funds raised by public subscription in Japan, Mrs Matsuo's sentimental journey created immense public interest in Australia and in her home country.

The most affecting moment of the trip came when, accompanied by her daughter, Mrs Matsuo was taken by launch to Taylor's Bay in Sydney Harbour, where her son's vessel had been destroyed. Supported by two Australian sailors, the frail, traditionally attired mother stood shakily on the launch's rear deck and read a poem expressing her yearning for her dead son, before casting flowers and pouring *sake* from his home town

---

57 See NAA A1501 A5755/1; A5755/2.
58 See photograph, AWM 135591.

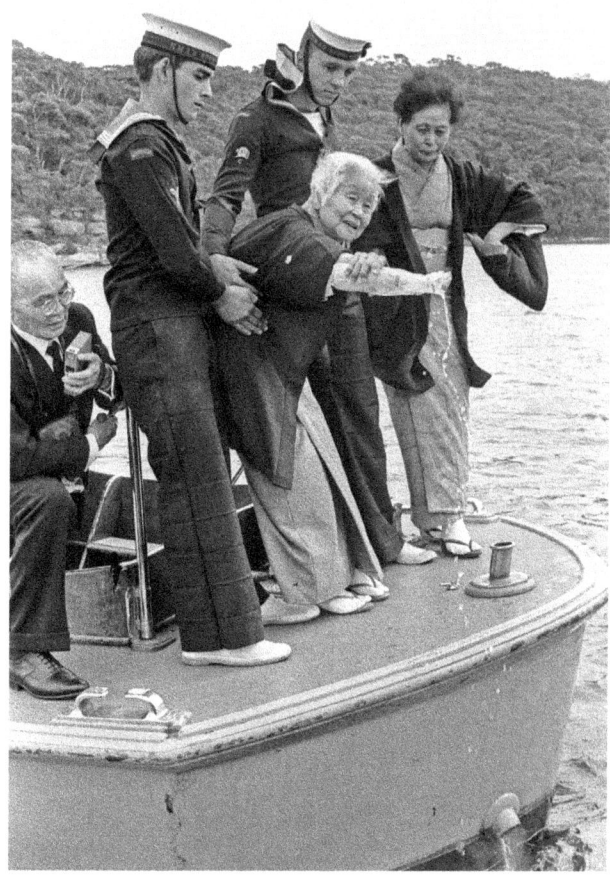

Figure 5.14. George Lipman, *Matsue Matsuo Pays Her Respects to Her Son Lieutenant Keiu Matsuo*, Sydney Harbour, 29 April 1968.
Source: Courtesy of Fairfax Syndication.

into the sea. The *Sydney Morning Herald's* George Lipman was there to capture an extraordinary moment in modern Australian and Japanese history, one that illustrates the camera's ability to distil the abstract forces of history into snapshots of shared human emotion (see Figure 5.14). The visit and the emotive visual imagery with which it was rendered made undeniably good public relations material at the time, and has continued to provide a useful historical touchtone for political rhetoric celebrating bilateralism—in a speech to the Australian parliament in July 2014 celebrating the two countries' 'special relationship', the Japanese Prime Minister Shinzo Abe confessed that the episode 'pulls at my heartstrings even now'.[59] For her part, the frail 83 year old was put to work on her visit,

---

59 Abe speech, 8 July 2014, japan.kantei.go.jp/96_abe/statement/201407/0708article1.html.

laying a wreath for the Australian war dead at the cenotaph in Sydney's Martin Place and calling on Healesville Sanctuary outside Melbourne for the obligatory close encounter with Australian fauna.[60]

Staged encounters of visiting Japanese with iconic Australiana were the stock-in-trade for the ANIB photographic cohort. An incarnation of the wartime Department of Information, the ANIB was set up in 1947 to promote Australia abroad, with one eye on encouraging migration.[61] Stimulating Japanese investment (and not migration) was the name of the game in the 1960s. Nevertheless, photographers working for the ANIB doggedly documented the developing cultural links between the two nations, usually by placing the Japanese in 'typical' Australian environments. In 1965, the onetime Sydney *Daily Telegraph* photographer Keith Byron—fresh from a stint in the US photographing presidents and Hollywood celebrities for United Press International and other agencies—captured members of a Japanese Youth Goodwill Mission observing a sheep-shearing demonstration at Werribee near Melbourne.[62] Visits by Japanese business delegations, local government figures forging 'sister city' links and members of the royal family were also comprehensively photographed by the ANIB. Some of its images reveal the tourists themselves photographing fellow Japanese, often in the act of tentatively attempting to cuddle a koala or a kangaroo.[63]

Photographing the mundane niceties of cultural exchange between Australia and Japan evidently presented a representational challenge to the ANIB cohort, some of whom, such as the noted war photographer Cliff Bottomley, had experienced rather more bracing professional conditions. Badly wounded in New Guinea in 1942–43, Bottomley took some dramatic pictures of the Papuan campaign after having been present at Singapore in the lead-up to its fall in February 1942; his photograph of local women wailing beside the corpse of a child killed in a Japanese air raid is one of the most upsetting images of the Pacific

---

60   Mrs Matsuo seems to have enjoyed the visit to Healesville. See 'It Is Paradise, Says Mother', *Canberra Times*, 6 May 1968, 14.
61   In 1973, the bureau was renamed the Australian Information Service. One of its later titles (from 1986) was *Promotion Australia*.
62   Byron image, NAA A1501 A5553/2. For a resume of Byron's career, see 'Press Photography in Australia: Keith Byron 1930–2002', accessed 5 January 2018, ppia.esrc.info/website/kbyron.html.
63   See, for example, the image of members of a 1963 Goodwill mission with kangaroo, NAA A1501 A4719/1; 1963 image of the mayor of Takada, in Australia to sign a 'sister city' agreement with Lismore NSW, NAA A1501 A4568/1; members of Japan's 'Floating University' taking photographs of a woman holding a koala (1965), NAA A1510 A5894/8; the 1965 visit to Canberra of Princess Misako, NAA A1501 A6063/8.

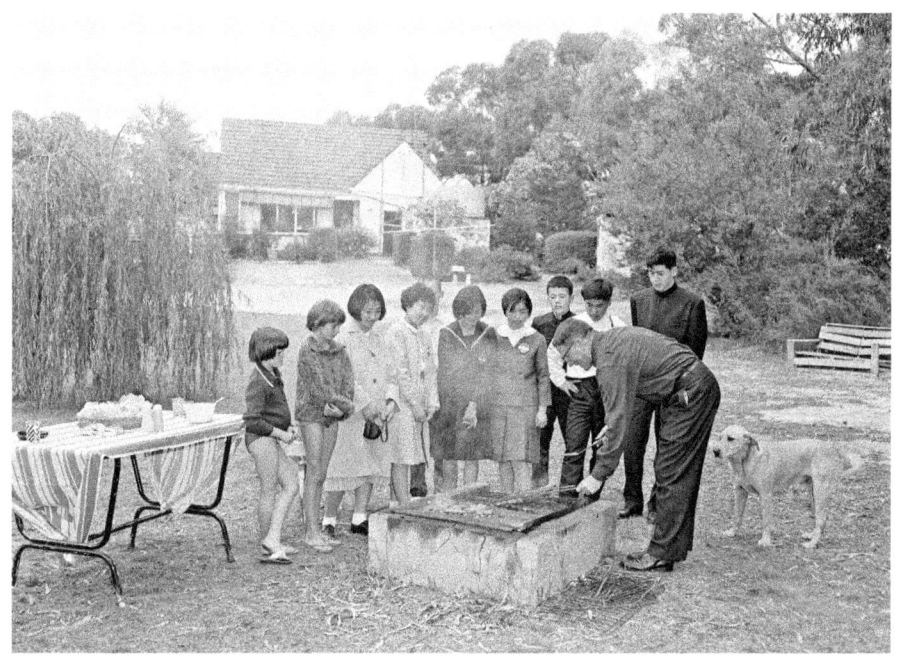

Figure 5.15. Cliff Bottomley, *Visiting Japanese Schoolchildren at an Australian Family Barbecue*, near Melbourne, 1963.
Source: NAA A1501 A4288/5.

War. Later, in 1944, he captured General MacArthur triumphantly returning to the Philippines, striding ashore what had been Japanese-held territory, like some latter-day Poseidon.[64] Back home in Australia, Bottomley did occasional work for the ANIB. In 1963, he went to the outer suburbs of Melbourne to picture a party of Japanese school children attending a barbecue hosted by a local family. The students had won a trip to Australia in a competition co-sponsored by the Mainichi Broadcasting Company, the Australian Broadcasting Commission and Qantas Airways. Their task had been to either paint or write an essay on what they thought Australia was like. The competition was reciprocal; Australian students were asked to do the same of Japan, with a visit also the prize for them. Bottomley's image of the barbecue conveys the stilted nature of these official or quasi-official gestures and merely serves to accentuate the essential differences in the two cultures (see Figure 5.15). The two Australian children are dressed disarmingly casually, compared with the more formal and conventional attire of the Japanese. Even the family dog seems constrained by the formality of the occasion, though perhaps it was transfixed by the sight and smell of the meat on the grill.

---

64   See Shaune Lakin, *Contact: Photographs from the Australian War Memorial Collection* (Canberra: Australian War Memorial, 2006), 133, 141, 163.

The Whitlams Go to Tokyo

Like the humble domestic encounters dutifully photographed by the ANIB, the imagery of Australia–Japan political diplomacy during this period inadvertently captured a continuing unease in the bilateral relationship, one which perhaps went beyond the intrinsically artificial nature of such high-end tête-à-têtes. In October 1973, two years after his historic trip to Peking as opposition leader to meet with Chinese Premier Chou En-lai, Australian Prime Minister Gough Whitlam visited Japan. He was en route to China to confer again with Chou en-lai, call on Chairman Mao and give (as he put it) further expression to Australia's 'new international outlook'.[65] Post-Vietnam, Australia was re-engaging with Asia. The Japan visit was no mere sideshow to China. Accompanied by the largest ministerial delegation ever to leave Australian shores, and his wife Margaret, Whitlam had important business to conduct. It was, observed the commentator Max Suich at the time, the 'most crucial encounter between Japanese and Australians in the last 20 years'.[66]

Australian and Japanese officials had long been negotiating to diversify and extend the trade and economic partnership formalised by the 1957 Commerce Agreement. On the Japanese side, there was the desire for a broader, deeper relationship. Australia, for its part, had traditionally resisted treaties with other nations.[67] Upon the successful conclusion of the discussions in Tokyo, Whitlam and the Japanese Foreign Minister Ohira appeared together at a press conference at which the former talked of the 'reluctance' and the 'negative attitude' of Australian administrations towards the longstanding Japanese proposal for a broad-ranging treaty between the two countries. His government was determined to redress this negativity with what was to be known as the Nippon–Australian Relations Agreement (NARA). At the press conference, Whitlam casually mentioned that Japan's Prime Minister Tanaka had suggested the treaty might be named the Treaty of Nara, after the ancient capital and cultural centre, which Whitlam had toured a couple of days earlier. In fact, the suggestion had come from Whitlam himself, possibly via his

---

65 Whitlam quoted in Fred Brenchley, 'Whitlam in Tokyo and Peking Mixes Business with Symbolism', *National Times*, 5–10 November 1973, 7.
66 Max Suich, 'PM Woos Japan in Crucial Tokyo Encounter', *National Times*, 29 October – 3 November 1973, 31.
67 See Moreen Dee, *Friendship and Co-operation: The 1976 Basic Treaty Between Australia and Japan* (Canberra: Commonwealth of Australia, 2006), 2.

press secretary Graham Freudenberg. No doubt Whitlam was attracted to the historical resonance of the nomenclature, but the suggestion was greeted coolly by the Japanese, in part because the title contained what was diplomatically called 'an unfortunate pun'—for 'onara' is the Japanese word for 'fart'.[68]

In Tokyo, Whitlam had hoped that the NARA treaty might be signed in Australia the following year, on the occasion of Prime Minister Tanaka's reciprocal visit. However, the negotiations became protracted and Whitlam, dismissed from office on 11 November 1975, never saw the process through to fruition. Renamed as the less offensive 'Basic Treaty of Friendship and Cooperation'—the first (and still the only) official treaty of friendship and amity between Australia and any other country—it was signed by Whitlam's successor, Malcolm Fraser, in Tokyo in June 1976. It was an occasion, Fraser noted, 'born of goodwill and mutual interests'.[69]

As is *de rigeuer* with state visits, the Whitlams' trip to Japan was assiduously captured by a bevy of official and press photographers, from the welcoming handshake from Prime Minister Tanaka at the airport to scenes of both Whitlam and his wife interacting with the local people. At Nara, the immensely tall Australian was pictured standing like a skyscraper over a cluster of Japanese children.[70] The formal portrait of the Whitlams' audience with Empress Hirohito and Empress Nagako at the Imperial Palace, broadly circulated in the Australian press, suggests the inevitable awkwardness of such formal occasions (see Figure 5.16). Gloved and frocked to the hilt, Margaret Whitlam looks glumly away from the camera while the emperor looks in the opposite direction. Meanwhile, the tiny empress appears to be faintly amused, and Whitlam, fists clenched, looks tense and uncharacteristically uncertain. Seemingly without irony, the picture was captioned in the Melbourne *Sun* as a 'Happy Visit to Japan'.[71]

---

68   Ibid., 12, 52 (fn 66). See also Deborah Cameron, 'Ill Wind Blows around Nara Treaty', *Sydney Morning Herald*, 15 June 2006, www.smh.com.au/news/world/ill-wind-blows-around-nara-treaty/2006/06/14/1149964584749.html.
69   Malcolm Fraser quoted in Dee, *Friendship and Co-operation*, 40.
70   'PM Takes a Hand in Old Japan', *Sun*, 29 October 1973, 1. Handshake photograph in *National Times*, 29 October – 3 November 1973, 31.
71   'A Formal Portrait on a Happy Visit to Japan', *Sun*, 27 October 1973, 2.

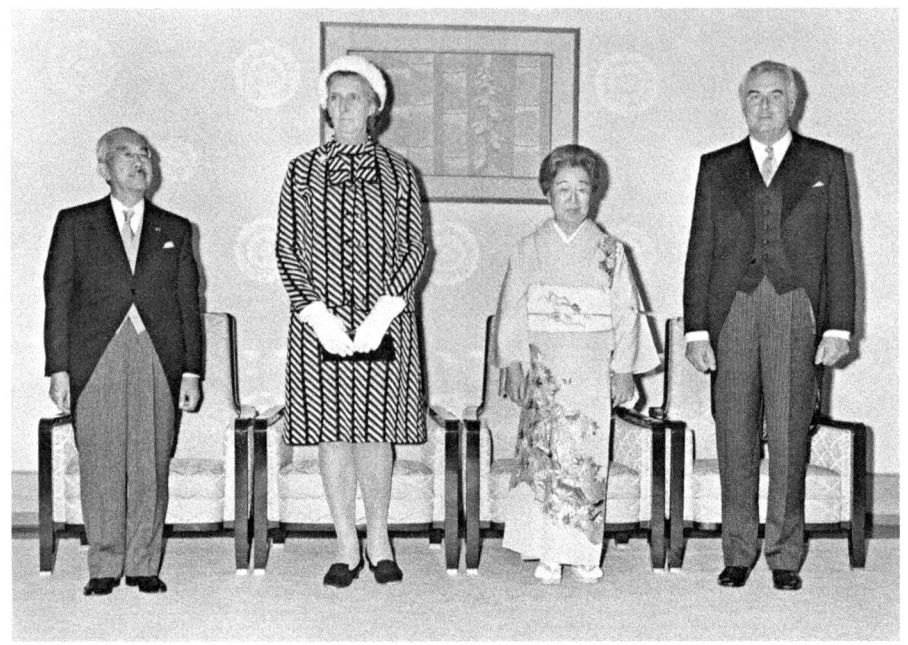

Figure 5.16. Photographer unknown, *Gough and Margaret Whitlam with the Emperor and Empress of Japan*, Tokyo, 26 October 1963.
Source: NAA A6180 15/11/73/39.

The Whitlams must have understood that physical stature did not equate with strength, and that the Japanese remained masters of their own territory. One cannot help comparing the scene with the photograph of MacArthur towering above Hirohito at the American Embassy in 1945, in which there is no doubt about who is most at home and self-confidently in charge. Of course, the contexts are starkly different; MacArthur was the triumphant conqueror and Gough Whitlam merely a slightly awestruck visitor. Yet this awkwardly staged display of bilateral camaraderie with the once-despised emperor illustrates the sensitivities still surrounding the Australia–Japan relationship in the early 1970s.[72] Certainly, as the Melbourne *Herald* editorialised, the Tokyo agreement of October 1973 clinched 'a welcome Pacific partnership' that had opened 'an historic new chapter' in bilateral relations.[73] Nonetheless, some Australians still harboured conflicted feelings about the Japanese, and perhaps a niggling sense of inferiority.

---

72   First performed at Melbourne's Pram Factory theatre a few months after Whitlam's visit, in early 1974, John Romeril's *The Floating World* placed these sensitivities on full dramatic display. The play enacted the crack-up of an Australian war veteran on a *Women's Weekly* 'Cherry Blossom' cruise to Japan, tapping into contemporary disquiet about Japan's new economic dominance while satirising the war-derived hatred that lingered in sections of Australian society.

73   'A Welcome Pacific Partnership', *Herald*, 31 October 1973, 4.

6

CROSS-CULTURAL (MIS)UNDERSTANDINGS:
INDEPENDENT PHOTOGRAPHY SINCE THE 1980s

It may seem paradoxical that, as the bilateral relationship has continued to mature since the 1970s, several contemporary Australian photographers have sought to focus on ambiguity and hidden tensions when picturing Japan. The deepening of relations—formalised in a series of new agreements on investment, industry, trade and defence[1]—has coincided with growing official interest in the value of cultural diplomacy and recognition of the role of culture in promoting mutual understanding. The staged pictures of cultural exchange produced by the Australian News and Information Bureau in the 1960s revealed that interest-driven governmental photographic practices regularly trade in national clichés. Such a trade continues in the present, recycling the very outmoded stereotypes that governments seek to modernise. The independent photographers who are the focus of this chapter, by contrast, reject such representational complacencies to pursue more adventurous modes of image-making.

Unafraid to address complex and often challenging issues, their practices may nonetheless be seen as the product of an increasingly relaxed relationship between the two nations. The diversity of this work also

---

1   These include a Joint Declaration on Security Cooperation (2007), an Information Security Agreement (2013) on the sharing of classified information, the Japan Australia Economic Partnership Agreement (2015) and an Acquisition and Cross Servicing Agreement (2017) on defence logistics cooperation.

speaks to the many channels through which today's photographers can engage with Japan, including cheap and frequent travel; opportunities to live and work in Japan for extended periods; ever-widening access to Japanese literature, art, popular culture, news, photobooks and fashion; and online media and social networking that provide the means to build and maintain friendships and professional connections from afar. These contemporary travelling photographers use their cameras not so much to 'explain' Japan or make the strange familiar as they do to raise questions and challenge assumptions. By seeking out the unsettling and the uncertain, interrogating them and making them sites for creativity, they highlight how moments of confusion and misunderstanding can be fertile ground in the photography of cross-cultural encounter.

The Art of Cultural Diplomacy

It was not until the 1970s that cultural diplomacy was formalised as a key component of Australian–Japanese relations. Cultural diplomacy is typically understood as a form of 'soft power' that helps to further national interests by encouraging other states to be receptive to one's own national values.[2] Prime ministers Kishi and Menzies discussed the expansion of cultural connections in the form of travelling art exhibitions and the exchange of students and scholars during the Australian leader's visit to Japan in April 1957.[3] Japan's desire to gain acceptance internationally in the postwar order—beyond being a diplomatic or trading partner— meant that cultural diplomacy was to play an increasingly important role in its foreign policy in the following decades. Created with a five billion yen endowment (later increased to 50 billion), the Japan Foundation was established in 1972 as an international cultural agency that complemented Foreign Minister Takeo Fukuda's policy focus on fostering 'mutual understanding'.[4] One of the main aims for the Japan

---

2   Jessica C.E. Gienow-Hecht, 'What Are We Searching For? Culture, Diplomacy, Agents and the State', in *Searching for a Cultural Diplomacy*, ed. Jessica C.E. Gienow-Hecht and Mark C. Donfried (New York: Berghann, 2010); J.M. Mitchell, *International Cultural Relations* (London: Allen and Unwin, 1986), 5–6; Joseph Nye, 'Soft Power and American Foreign Policy', *Political Science Quarterly* 119, no. 2 (June 2004).
3   Alan Rix, *The Australia-Japan Political Alignment 1952 to the Present* (London: Routledge, 1999), 31, 104.
4   Maki Aoki-Okabe, Yoko Kawamura and Toichi Makita, 'Germany in Europe, Japan and Asia: National Commitments to Cultural Relations within Regional Frameworks', in *Searching for a Cultural Diplomacy*, ed. Jessica C.E. Gienow-Hecht and Mark C. Donfried (New York: Berghann, 2010), 222–23.

Foundation was to promote Japan as a peaceful and economically advanced nation in other countries.[5] Rising anxiety in the Asia-Pacific over Japan's perceived economic strength and local dependence on Japanese trade,[6] investment and development assistance was countered with the opening of Japan Foundation offices in most South-East Asian countries during the 1970s and 1980s. Its Australian office was opened in Sydney in 1978.

Australia likewise sought to ensure a healthy bilateral relationship through cultural diplomacy initiatives in the 1970s. An Act of parliament established the bilateral body the Australia-Japan Foundation in 1976. One of its main functions was to 'encourage a closer relationship between the peoples of Australia and Japan, and to further the knowledge and understanding of each other'.[7] It was hoped that, by fostering people-to-people relations at the non-government level, the foundation would help to maintain friendly relations and confront negative, limiting or deep-seated stereotypes that could undermine successful diplomatic relations.[8] In place of lingering perceptions of Australia as a large country with a small population, blessed by natural resources and populated by picturesque flora and fauna, the Australian Government actively promoted the image of a stable, multicultural and technologically advanced society distinguished by its artistic and intellectual excellence.

Cultural diplomacy initiatives are traditionally distinguished from cultural relations, which tend to be driven by non-state actors whose international activities are the result of trade, travel, personal relationships, migration, entertainment, communication and cultural exchanges.[9] However, this distinction is not always clear cut. Governments often pursue their aims by sponsoring or exhibiting the work of independent practitioners, provided that the initiatives reflect the state's agenda. One example of this crossover is the exhibition *Continuum '83*, the first major exhibition of Australian contemporary art in Japan held in 1983. *Continuum '83* was initiated by a group of Australian artists who

---

5   Kazuo Ogoura, 'From Ikebana to Manga and Beyond', *Global Asia* 7, no. 3 (2012): 25.
6   David Goldsworthy and Peter Edwards, *Facing North Volume 2: 1970s to 2000* (Carlton: Melbourne University Press, 2001), 133.
7   Australia Japan Foundation, *Annual Report 2002–03*, Canberra: Australian Government, 3, dfat. gov.au/people-to-people/foundations-councils-institutes/australia-japan-foundation/Documents/ajf-annual-report-2002-03.pdf.
8   Mitchell, *International Cultural Relations*, 17–18.
9   Ibid., 5; Richard Arndt, *The First Resort of Kings: American Cultural Diplomacy in the Twentieth Century* (Washington: Potomac, 2005), xviii.

lived and worked in Japan in the late 1970s and early 1980s, including performance artist Stelarc, the sculptor John Davis, the sculptor and video artist Peter Callas and jeweller and sculptor Maryrose Sinn. Produced with the help of Emiko Namikawa, director of the Lunami Gallery in Tokyo, and several gallerists and curators in Melbourne, *Continuum '83* involved 15 rental galleries in Ginza and 18 major artists including installation artists, performance artists, sculptors and photographers. These exhibitions were supplemented by programs of video art, film, sound, posters, artists' books and performance art, bringing the total number of artist participants to over 70.

Rather than producing new work in direct response to Japan or Australian–Japanese relations, organisers selected existing artworks that complemented the central curatorial theme of 'Land, Earth, Environment and Australia's Polycultural Society'. This theme tapped into long-held Japanese impressions of Australia as a vast, underpopulated outback, while the emphasis on sculpture, installation, performance and photography reflected Japanese interests in contemporary art. The photography component included Sue Ford's portraits *Time Series*, Virginia Coventry's conceptual landscape work *Whyalla-Not a Document*, John Williams' *Living Room Portraits* and Douglas Holleley's *A Portfolio of Colour Photographs Made on the Last Day of Luna Park*. It was hoped that, by focusing on common creative ground and building on existing impressions of Australia, the event would provide a means of pursing the larger aim of encouraging dialogue between Australian and Japanese artists and galleries based on 'mutual interests'.[10]

Although *Continuum '83* was an initiative of independent artists rather than governments, its discourse of mutual understanding and interest lent itself well to the concerns of cultural diplomacy. *Continuum '83* received funding from the Japan Foundation, Australia-Japan Foundation, Australian Embassy in Tokyo and Australia Council Visual Arts Board, in addition to support from many corporate sponsors from both countries. Ken Scarlett, the director of Gryphon Gallery who was instrumental in organising *Continuum '83*, adopted the official discourse of 'friendship' and 'mutual understanding' in the bilingual catalogue:

---

10 Peter Callas, 'Editorial', Special issue on contemporary Japanese art, *Art Network*, Spring 1984, 23.

Forty years ago we were enemies at war—but no nation suffered more than Japan at Hiroshima and Nagasaki. Now trade and tourism are helping to destroy the memories of those tragic years. But friendship based on trade may last only as long as the trade is profitable.

Continuum '83, Scarlett proclaimed, is:

'A further step, a significant advance in understanding. Japanese and Australian artists and gallery directors are working together to make their respective cultures known outside their own countries … Not just Australian coal to Japan and Japanese cars to Australia but a two-way trade in people and ideas!'[11]

This two-way trade was pursued further two years later with *Continuum '85*, which presented Japanese contemporary art to Australians.

The ideal of mutual understanding recurs in discourses surrounding more recent touring exhibitions, including *Sun Gazing: The Australia-Japan Art Exhibition Touring Program, 2002–04* supported by Asialink and the Australia-Japan Foundation; *Rapt!: 20 Contemporary Artists from Japan* (2006) held in the Australia–Japan Year of Exchange; and *Imminent Landscape* (2012) exhibited at the Japan Foundation Gallery in Sydney.[12] The artistic director and exhibitor in *Imminent Landscape*, Utako Shindo, commented in the bilingual catalogue that the aim of the initiative was 'to create active dialogues for not just the artists but also the broader art communities in both Japan and Australia'.[13]

However, in selecting cultural forms for export that are expected to be meaningful to a foreign audience, there is often a temptation to draw on imagery that already has currency and neglect the more complex relationships that nations share. *Continuum '83* highlights how, in aiming to foster mutual understanding, initiatives may end up exporting imagery that reinforces, rather than challenges, stereotyped impressions. In her critique of this event for *Art Network*, Lyndal Jones noted: 'It is apparent that there was an attempt at providing a bridge of understanding; the ease

---

11   Ken Scarlett, 'Australia, Japan and "Continuum '83"', in *Continuum '83: The 1st Exhibition of Australian Contemporary Art in Japan* (Tokyo: Japan-Australia Cultural & Art Exchange Committee, 1983), unpaginated.
12   Alison Carroll, *Sun Gazing: The Australia-Japan Art Exhibitions Touring Program, 2002–04* (Carlton: Asialink, 2004); Reuben Keehan, 'Hello Tokyo! Good to See You Again', *Artlink* 28, no. 4 (2008): 55–56.
13   Utako Shindo, *Imminent Landscape* (Sydney: Japan Foundation, 2010), unpaginated.

of familiarity rather than the shock of foreignness'.[14] This emphasis on the 'ease of familiarity' meant that, at least to some Japanese critics, *Continuum '83* confirmed long-held conceptions of Australia as a 'fenceless zoo' set apart from heavily urbanised, densely populated Japan.[15] Writing in response to *Continuum '83*, Toshio Matsuura argued that Australian and Japanese artists were concerned with fundamentally different approaches to nature, underpinned by Australia's youth—and implicit lack of development—in comparison to Japan's ancient cultural traditions. Australian art has not yet come to terms with its environment, argued Matsuura, as evinced in artworks that provide 'literal translations of nature'. The critic contrasted this lack of maturity with the deeper engagement with nature developed over centuries of Japanese fine art practice.[16]

The hugely popular feature film *Crocodile Dundee* (1986)—widely screened in Japan—nourished such impressions, as did Australian tourism promotion in the 1980s, whose reductive emphasis on wildlife and outback imagery simplified and commodified Australia. In a speech about public diplomacy to the Australia-Asia Association in Melbourne in 1990, then–Minister for Foreign Affairs and Trade Gareth Evans stressed the importance of challenging such narrow views of Australia as 'a land of open spaces, exotic flora and fauna, an exporter of commodities – and a good place to relax'. 'At a time of great change in the structure of international relations', he argued 'it is more important than ever that relations among nations be based on an accurate understanding of each other's society and culture'.[17] Yet, the image of the unpeopled outback continues to be invoked in cultural diplomacy initiatives as a dominant signifier of Australia. The Culture Centre of the Australian Embassy in Tokyo, for example, has promoted the work of Japanese photographer Aihara Masaaki, who has been photographing the Australian landscape for over 20 years. Aihara's colour photographs typically present a landscape that is undeveloped and devoid of signs of human inhabitation. Emphasis is on the rich colours of the earth, the enormous skies and apparently boundless expanses of land. As well as featuring this work on its website,

---

14   Lyndal Jones, 'The Continuum Symposium on Australian Art', special issue on contemporary Japanese art, *Art Network*, Spring 1984, 49.
15   These ideas can be tracked to the Meiji period. See Alison Broinowski, 'About Face: Asian Representation of Australia' (PhD diss., The Australian National University, Canberra, 2001), 8.
16   Toshio Matsurra, 'Notes of a Traveller: Continuum '83 Reviewed', *Bijutsu Techo* 35, no. 517 (1983): 174–79.
17   Gareth Evans, 'Australia and Asia: The Role of Public Diplomacy', Address by the Minister for Foreign Affairs and Trade, Senator Gareth Evans, to the Australia-Asia Association, Melbourne, 15 March 1990, www.gevans.org/speeches/old/1990/150390_fm_australiaandasia.pdf.

the Australian Embassy in Tokyo hosted exhibitions of Aihara's work in 1998 and 2000 and has acquired some of his photographs for its official collection. While the embassy's support of a local photographer is laudable, its choice of this particular work does little to challenge the impression that the Australian Government has long sought to change.

Landscape was again featured prominently in the Australian Government's publicity for the 'Australia Now' initiative, delivered in Japan in 2018 as part of its public diplomacy 'Focus Country Program'. The website of the Australian Embassy in Tokyo described the aims of the program in terms of overcoming stereotypes: 'strengthening and deepening bilateral ties and building understanding beyond our landscape and lifestyle. Most of all Australia Now is about building relationships for the future'. The diverse program involved performances, cultural and sporting events, and offered opportunities for partnership building in business. However, despite the goal of building understanding 'beyond our landscape and lifestyle', the online event promotion was illustrated, predictably, with photographs of the unpopulated outback.[18]

The Shock of Foreignness

Unmotivated by the economic and political benefits of soft power, the contemporary photographers discussed in the remainder of this chapter relish the creative potential of more complex histories and experiences when forging alternative, informal cross-cultural photographic relations. While *Continuum '83* aimed to eschew 'the shock of foreignness' to promote mutual understanding, Melbourne photographer Christopher Köller embraced it. Fulfilling a long-held ambition to spend time in Japan, Köller lived in Kyoto for 19 months between August 1982 and January 1984, supporting himself by teaching English. Japan's economic growth in the 1970s meant that more Japanese citizens had the means and opportunity to travel overseas, and more came into contact with foreigners as part of their business activities. As interest in learning English increased, so did opportunities for Australians to teach in Japan. Teaching provided a certain amount of flexibility for Köller, allowing him to spend his free days studying bonsai and photographing. His experience at the bonsai nursery was a reminder of the limits of intercultural connection and understanding: 'They never called me by

---

18 'Australia Now', accessed 3 January 2018, japan.embassy.gov.au/tkyo/australianow2018.html.

my real name the entire time. They just banged on the table with a big stick and pointed at me to do things. It was hysterical'.[19] However, Köller's work is also the product of many happy, productive and enduring relationships with new friends.

Köller began working on his series *Zen Zen Chigau* (1984) four months into his stay. The title translates roughly as 'something out of the ordinary' and is indicative of Köller's choice of subjects. Rejecting a photojournalistic approach and a reliance on the visual clichés of temples and geisha, Köller's 23 black and white photographs are staged to reflect his own responses as an outsider to strange occurrences and stories encountered in Japan.[20] 'These photographs are about my Western preoccupation with and attempts to understand an alien culture and thinking', said Köller. 'Their purpose in my mind is not to document "objective" thinking'.[21] The photographs also reflect the ever-diversifying ways that contemporary Australians could access and consume Japanese culture in the 1980s. The images are variously inspired by newspaper articles, Japanese literature, Zen Buddhist philosophy, television programs, film, traditional theatre, popular music and Köller's own observations as a traveller and temporary resident in Japan. He recalled: 'I read a lot of Japanese novels by Kōbō Abe and by Jun'ichirō Tanizaki and also by Yukio Mishima and I would get ideas from there'.[22] Being without a studio pushed Köller to be creative in his staging of these ideas. The cast was selected from his circle of friends and students, and sets were improvised in spaces that he could find. Köller's sketchbooks and notes reveal how carefully he considered his tableaux, noting details like the expression on the models' faces and the direction of their gazes, as well as composition, costume and lighting.

There is an evocative tension in the finished photographs, in which stories are implied but never fully explained. Inspired by the words of English painter Francis Bacon—who aimed to 'give the sensation [of a story] without the boredom of its conveyance'[23]—Köller carefully stripped back elements of the story to leave something for the viewer to invest in the work. This process is evident in his photograph inspired by the horrific

---

19   'Interview with Christopher Koller, A Dialogue', *Fierce Latitudes*, accessed 20 January 2018, www.fiercelatitudes.com/new-page/.
20   Christopher Köller, interview with Melissa Miles, 6 February 2018.
21   Christopher Köller, 'Statement' on *Zen Zen Chigau* (1984) from the artist's personal archives.
22   'Interview with Christopher Koller, A Dialogue', *Fierce Latitudes*, accessed 20 January 2018, www.fiercelatitudes.com/new-page/.
23   David Sylvester, *Interviews with Francis Bacon* (London: Thames and Hudson, 1975), 65.

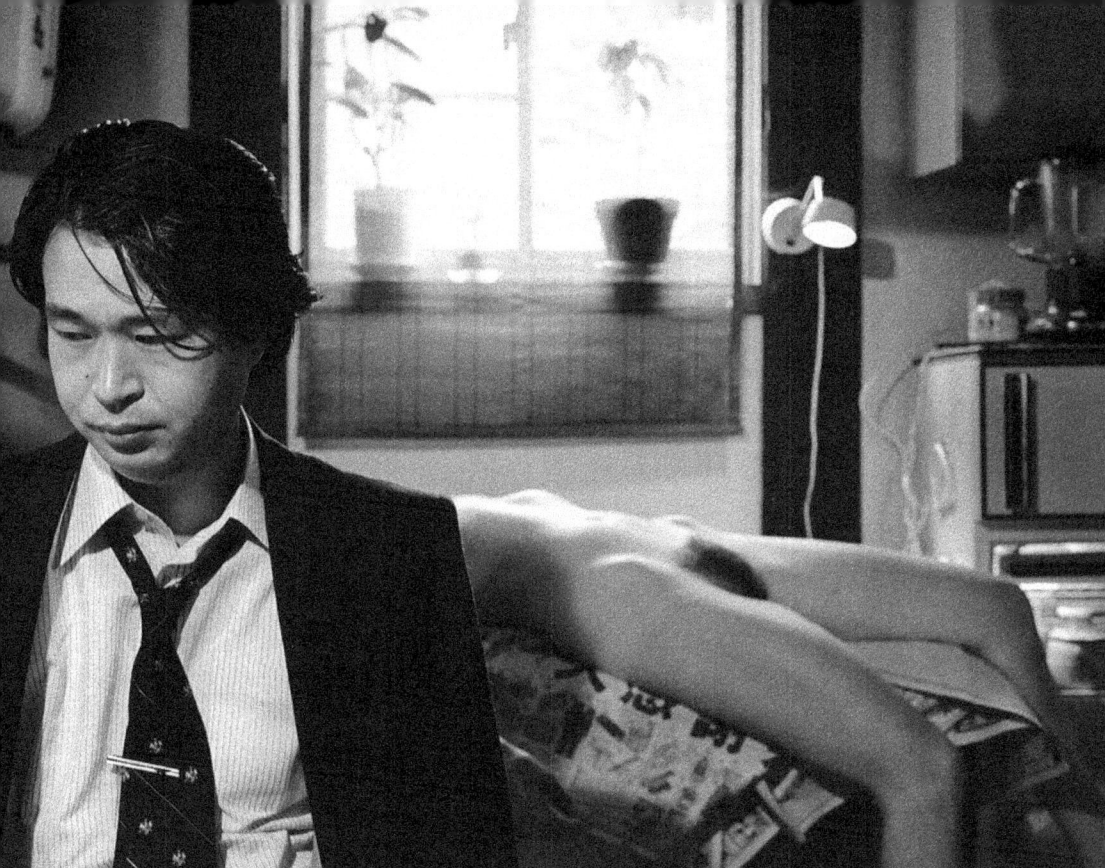

Figure 6.1. Christopher Köller, *Untitled* from the series *Zen Zen Chigau*, 1984.
Source: Courtesy of the artist.

crimes of Issei Sagawa, sensationalised in press coverage while Köller was in Japan (see Figure 6.1). Sagawa was living in Paris studying literature at the Sorbonne in 1981 when he murdered his classmate, a Dutchwoman called Renée Hartevlt, raped her corpse and, over two days, cannibalised her. When Sagawa was arrested he was carrying a suitcase containing her body parts; he had been attempting to dispose of them in a public park. The police discovered other body parts in Sagawa's refrigerator at home. After reading about this case of cannibalism, Köller became conscious of the recurrence of this sexual fetish in Japanese literature. A passage from Kōbō Abe's *Box Man: A Novel* was copied into Köller's notebook:

> First I shall woo the girl boldly, and if I am refused (and refused I shall be), I shall kill her over a period of days. I shall enjoy eating her corpse. This is not a figure of speech; I shall literally put her in my mouth, chew

on her, relish her on my tongue … She is submissive, and even when she turns into meat, her smile will be unquenchable and she will have a taste somewhere between veal and wild fowl and will be utterly delectable.[24]

Recreated with the help of one of Köller's students and a friend who worked as a nude model, his photograph does not sensationalise Sagawa's crime. There is no blood or gore; the violence is implied by the nude woman seen only from the waist down lying on a table covered in newspapers, the open fridge door and the dishevelled male figure positioned to the side of the foreground to create compositional tension. Sagawa's story grew stranger after Köller made this work. After his return to Japan and subsequent release from a psychiatric hospital in 1986, Sagawa made a living writing restaurant reviews and books, appearing in an exploitation film and public speaking, and was the focus of the 2007 documentary *The Cannibal that Walked Free*.

Another of Köller's photographs refers to a news article, this time about a suicide pact between three junior high schoolgirls who jumped off the roof of a high-rise building in Yokohama (see Figure 6.2). The girls reportedly appeared cheerful to their families, who could not fathom what led them to take their own lives. Japan's seeming obsession with self-destruction—from the ceremonial disembowelling known as *harakiri* or *seppuku* to the kamikaze 'suicide gods' that terrorised Allied navies in WWII—has long fascinated Western observers.[25] Attitudes to Japanese schoolgirls are another source of fascination. Thanks to *manga*, Japanese porn and the Western media's reports on *joshi-kosei* cafes—where adult men pay a premium to share the company of schoolgirls—demure, innocent schoolgirls have become key symbols of fetishised Japanese femininity. Pointedly, however, Köller does not sexualise his schoolgirl models. Their dowdy uniforms suggest they are utterly respectable and the brown paper he put down so that their uniforms would not be dirtied by lying on the concrete roof suggests his concern for his models. The girls' staged yet subtle expressions convey a range of possible emotions—the central figure's eyes are closed in introspection and she is without her shoes, one friend looks to her for guidance, while the other

---

24 Excerpt from Kōbō Abe, *Box Man: A Novel*, trans. E. Dale Saunders (New York: Knopf, 1974) in Christopher Köller's unpublished notebooks.
25 Albert Axell and Hideaki Kase, *Kamikaze: Japan's Suicide Gods* (Harlow: Longman, 2002); Ian Littlewood, *The Idea of Japan: Western Images, Western Myths* (Chicago: Ivan R. Dee, 1996), 36.

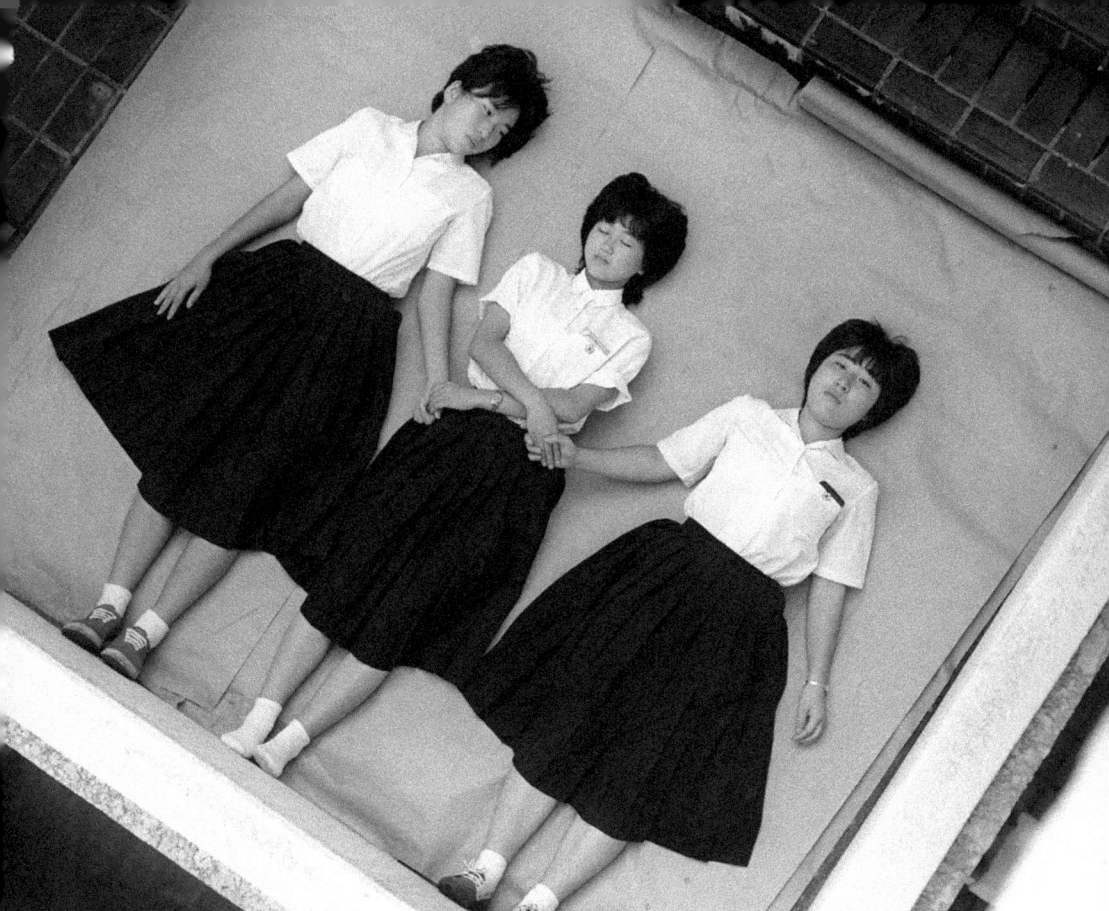

Figure 6.2. Christopher Köller, *Untitled* from the series *Zen Zen Chigau*, 1984.
Source: Courtesy of the artist.

appears anxious as she stares straight ahead. The vertiginous tilt of the composition creates the impression that the girls are about to fall, their hands linked to signify their pact.

Other photographs in Köller's series are much less confronting; they include portraits of his friends, his bonsai teacher and uniformed workers, as well as references to Japanese literature and theatre. Together, the photographs appealed greatly to contemporary Australian audiences. Köller recalled:

> My Japanese show was very successful. I made enough money to go back overseas and I just couldn't print them fast enough. Everybody loved the show, I got great reviews and it seemed like everybody wanted another Japanese show.[26]

---

26 'Interview with Christopher Koller, A Dialogue', *Fierce Latitudes*, accessed 20 January 2018, www.fiercelatitudes.com/new-page/.

Between 1984 and 1988, *Zen Zen Chigau* was exhibited in Melbourne, Adelaide, Sydney and London, and a selection was later exhibited in a group show in 2005.[27] Beatrice Faust's review of *Zen Zen Chigau* at Melbourne's Photographer's Gallery in 1984 suggests that the photographs tapped into popular impressions of enigmatic Japan:

> Owing little to current Japanese photography, they are still peculiarly Japanese, at once familiar and bizarre, open and shuttered, humanly emotional and dispassionately controlled, whimsical and earnest, trivial and important, elaborate and simple.[28]

Robert Rooney similarly spoke of the contradictions that characterise 'outsiders' views of this 'land of contrasts', its refined taste and its perceived capacity for extreme cruelty.[29]

The exhibition of Köller's work coincided with rising public anxieties about the threat posed by Japanese business and export activities to local interests. In this context, his photograph of a young, suited Japanese man who had killed and was about to devour a European woman perhaps resonated in ways that Köller did not intend. As the Japanese economy matured in the late 1980s and early 1990s, there was rising concern in the Asia-Pacific about Japan's rapidly growing power. Japan's share of total investment in Australia increased from 8.7 per cent in 1981 to 17.9 per cent in 1991, making it the second largest source of investment after the US. The rise in Japanese investment in Australian real estate skyrocketed from zero in 1980–81 to 49.2 per cent, or US$1,255 million, in 1991–92. The public perception of this investment was bound up with the increased visibility of Japanese visitors, including businessmen and ever-growing numbers of tourists. The total number of visitors from Japan increased nearly fourfold from 1984 to 1988, and tourist visitors increased fivefold (to 294,000) in 1988. Japanese visitor arrivals continued to increase substantially in the early 1990s, reaching 813,100 in 1996.[30]

---

27   For example in the group exhibition *Loaded* at Gallery 101 in 2005.
28   Beatrice Faust, 'From Japan, an Exhibition of Images to Haunt the Memory', *Age*, 10 December 1984, 14.
29   Robert Rooney, 'Powerful Images in a Land of Contrasts', *Australian*, 15–16 December 1984, Arts 12.
30   Rix, *The Australia-Japan Political Alignment 1952 to the Present*, 107.

Political leaders naturally embraced the palpable Japanese interest in Australia. Then-Treasurer Paul Keating declared during the visit of Prime Minister Takeshita in 1988 that:

> Our friendship is reflected in the very large numbers of Japanese families who are visiting our country as tourists, and enjoying our hospitality and the grandeur of our landscape. Let me say, Mr Prime Minister, that your fellow countrymen and women are very welcome guests to Australia.[31]

However, the mass media and general public were not always as supportive of the growing Japanese presence. Two particular Japanese investment initiatives were met with heated public debate—a plan to establish Japanese retirement settlements in Australia (the 'Silver Columbia' project) and the Japanese Government's proposal for a Multi-Function Polis. References in the press to the 'Japanese takeover', 'Japanvader' and 'the polite invasion', along with the catchcries 'Australia for Australians' and 'Wake up Australia', recurred in the late 1980s. 'Lest we forget' was a particularly pointed rebuke of excessive Australian enthusiasm for Japanese investment.[32] In the press, photographs helped to establish the link between the growing presence of Japanese tourists and Australia's historical fear of Asian invasion, which had seemed likely to be realised in 1942. In a special supplement to celebrate the fiftieth anniversary of the end of WWII in 1995, the *Sydney Morning Herald* included a large photograph of four smiling young Japanese tourists posing in front of the Sydney Harbour Bridge under the headline 'Engaging the Enemy'. While the article itself told the story of a positive relationship built after the war, the combination of photograph and headline linked the mass arrival of Japanese tourists to this wartime history.[33]

As Japan experienced a comparable backlash in other parts of Asia, Japanese cultural diplomacy became one of the 'three pillars' of its foreign policy, alongside official aid policies and contributions to international peacekeeping operations. Politically, Japan and Australia became strong regional allies during this period. Australia acted as kind of a mediator or 'cushion' when much of Asia remembered all too clearly Japan's wartime history of aggression and brutality. Prime Minister Hawke supported Japan's permanent membership on the United Nations Security Council and the participation of the Japanese defence force in United Nations

---

31 Quoted in ibid., 109.
32 Ibid., 108.
33 David Jenkins, 'Engaging the Enemy', *Sydney Morning Herald*, 15 August 1995, 10V.

peacekeeping missions in Cambodia and the Persian Gulf. Although Japanese troops in Cambodia were admitted on the condition that they remain unarmed, the nation's eagerness to send its troops to a foreign country on policing operations opened old wounds. Coupled with renewed disputes with China and South Korea over ownership of what Japan calls Takeshima and the Senkaku Islands, activists and government officials in both countries repeatedly criticised Japan for its perceived 'lack of contrition' for the brutalities committed during their periods of annexation and occupation earlier in the twentieth century.[34] Speaking to the *New Sunday Times*, Singapore's Senior Minister Lee Kuan Yew claimed in 1991: 'Allowing Japan to once again send its forces abroad is like giving a chocolate liqueur to an alcoholic. Once the Japanese get off the wagon, it will be hard to stop them'.[35]

Cooperation between Australia and Japan was critical in this regional context and central to the creation of the Asia-Pacific Economic Cooperation (APEC) in 1989 and the development of APEC leaders meetings in 1993–95. It was hoped that, by coming together, Australia and Japan could build regional cooperation.[36] This diplomatic relationship was not without its tensions. Japanese concern over Australia's protection of its manufacturing industry and Australia's grievances about Japan's agricultural protectionism were among the issues. There were also ongoing disagreements over Japanese whaling and Japan's refusal to acknowledge its abuse of comfort women during WWII. The Japanese Government's unwillingness to apologise for its wartime brutality, particularly regarding its mistreatment of prisoners of war, added another point of tension.

Given the importance of this bilateral relationship, Australia's dwindling investment in cultural diplomacy during the 1990s is surprising. Asialink was established in 1990 amid an apparent upward turn as a body dedicated to delivering high-level forums, international collaborations, leadership training, education, community health and cultural programs in Australia and Asia. Its art program helped Australian

---

34   Steven H. Green, 'The Soft Power of Cool: Economy, Culture and Foreign Policy in Japan', *Toyo Hogaku* 58, no. 3 (2015): 56.
35   Quoted in Lindsay Murdoch, 'Push for Power in Asia', *Age*, 30 December 1991, 7.
36   Rikki Kersten, 'Japan and Australia', in *Japanese Foreign Policy Today*, ed. Inoguchi Takashi and Purnendra Jain (Basingstoke: Palgrave, 2000), 292; Takashi Terada, 'The Australia-Japan Partnership in the Asia-Pacific: From Economic Diplomacy to Security Co-Operation?', *Contemporary Southeast Asia* 22, no. 1 (April 2000): 177, 186.

artists to work more effectively and easily in the Asian region.[37] In 1991, a new international arts policy was introduced with a commitment that, by 1992–93, 50 per cent of the international budget would be spent on Asian or Pacific-oriented projects under the title 'Asia-Pacific Connections'. However, this new policy impacted on a small percentage of the overall Australia Council budget and was criticised as a symbolic stunt for 'political self-protection'.[38] Several commentators have noted the subsequent, ever-dwindling governmental support for Asialink and Australian cultural programs in Asia.[39] Ien Ang, Yudhishthir Raj Isar and Phillip Mar argued that despite government attempts to develop a more integrated approach, cultural diplomacy activities tend to be modest, dispersed and have been subject to 'almost continual budget erosion over the past fifteen years, leading some commentators to speak about Australia's diplomatic deficit'.[40] In this climate, non-state cultural organisations and actors have become increasingly more important in filling the void. While there is a chance that photography projects that explore cross-cultural tensions—like Köller's—may be received in a manner that reinforces attitudes that run counter to the interests of governments, such projects are valuable because they acknowledge important issues of interpretation and dynamism in bilateral relations.

Photographic Connections and the Limits of Understanding

For Australian photographer Kristian Häggblom, photography offers a means of immersing himself in Japan and thinking deeply about its culture, spaces and people. Häggblom first travelled to Japan in 1999 after graduating from his photography studies in Melbourne. In contrast to Köller, Häggblom was not pursuing a long-term ambition to visit Japan and did not have many expectations about what he might find there. His reasons for choosing Japan were more pragmatic— employment opportunities and favourable visa requirements meant that it was a place where he could feasibly spend an extended period of

---

37   Alison Carroll, 'Art to Life: 20 Years in the Australia-Asian Arts Atmosphere', *Art Monthly Australia*, no. 235 (November 2010).
38   Robert J. Williams, 'Australia's International Cultural Relations: Some Domestic Dimensions', *Australian Journal of Political Science* 30, no. 1 (1995): 65–67.
39   Evans, 'Australia and Asia'; Carroll, 'Art to Life'.
40   Ien Ang, Yudhishthir Raj Isar and Phillip Mar, 'Cultural Diplomacy: Beyond the National Interest?', *International Journal of Cultural Policy* 21, no. 4 (2015): 376.

time.⁴¹ Häggblom ended up living in Japan for eight years, mainly in Tokyo, and married a Japanese woman. The income Häggblom earned working as an English teacher and his flexible working hours freed him to spend time walking through Tokyo, photographing as he went, in particular, exploring the photography galleries and second-hand camera stores in hyper-urban Shinjuku. During his walks, Hägbblom was also mindful of his own family history. His uncle Michael (Mick) Kelly's ship was sunk by the Japanese in WWII. During the subsequent Occupation, Kelly managed a port in Kobe and developed a great fondness for Japan. He returned regularly, including while Häggblom was living there. Although Kelly rarely spoke about his war experiences, his time in Japan was in Häggblom's mind as he walked the Tokyo streets and throughout the country.⁴²

In 2001, with fellow Australian Warren Fithie, Häggblom opened a gallery called Roomspace above one of the many bars in Shinjuku's famous Omoide Yokochō, known colloquially as 'Piss Alley'. Roomspace was a modest gallery, as its name suggests, that exhibited photographs, paintings and other experimental works for over a year. After returning to Australia, Häggblom also worked to introduce Australian audiences to less well-known Japanese photographers at his Wallflower Photomedia Gallery in regional Victoria, established in 2012 with Ross Lake through Arts Mildura.⁴³ Häggblom continues to return to Japan regularly to develop new bodies of photographic work and heighten the profile of Japanese photographers in Australia.

Häggblom's own photographs reflect his cerebral approach to photography in which ideas are explored over time through large interconnected bodies of work. Drawn to open areas where urban landscapes and nature meet, such as riverways and parks, he is interested in 'vernacular spaces' and how these are used in diverse, very personal or ritualised ways. Häggblom's series *O'Hanami* centres on the parks occupied en masse during the annual cherry blossom festival. He steadfastly avoids fetishising the delicate blossoms as symbols of the cycles of life and death or an essentially feminine Japan. Rather, he turns his camera towards the

---

41   Kristian Häggblom, interview with Melissa Miles, 17 January 2018.
42   Häggblom plans to investigate Kelly's wartime history further in the future.
43   Wallflower Gallery closed at the end of 2015. Häggblom still works under this title as a not-for-profit organisation to facilitate activities that include an exhibition at the Centre for Contemporary Photography, Melbourne, of contemporary Japanese photography. See www.tsukaproject.com/ (accessed 12 March 2018).

sometimes drunken *hanami*, or cherry blossom viewing parties, that take place in public parks across Tokyo. Shooting in large format, Häggblom's photographs are exceptionally detailed. One photograph (see Figure 6.3) focuses on young men dressed in eggplant and daikon costumes, relaxing on the outstretched blankets that mark out their much sought after place beneath the trees. A pair of legs and torso belonging to a man partially out of shot, and seemingly passed out, can be seen next to two young women slouched at a picnic table, looking right at Häggblom's camera, bleary-eyed from the day's celebration. Another photograph (see Figure 6.4) shows older men sitting on unfeasibly small picnic chairs around an equally tiny table on which food and drink has been served. Younger women sit by the river, with their pile of plastic bags gathered behind them. The hole in Häggblom's camera bellows creates light leaks in several photographs that pit the slightly awkward and messy reality of the festival against a romanticised ideal.

The product of countless hours spent walking off the track beaten by tourists in the areas between metropolitan train lines, Häggblom's substantial body of work *Nihon* (1999–ongoing) brings together large format photographs of open urban spaces and anonymous-looking buildings. The scenes are sometimes taken from slightly different angles or moments apart to afford subtle changes in light and texture. These large photographs act as structuring elements that map the terrain of Tokyo for the project, while other images explore more poignant uses of space, including those in rural areas. Some photographs in *Nihon* are carefully staged with the help of Japanese friends and students to recreate odd moments that Häggblom witnessed, such as a man chopping a whole watermelon by a river, or another young man posing nude by a waterway in front of his camera phone mounted on a tiny tripod. These images are punctuated with studies of small details observed in the streets from Häggblom's *Dossier #1* (2015–ongoing). Including strange photographs of a doorknob encased in paint, an abandoned suitcase and folding table stacked neatly by a footpath, and a second-storey doorway leading to a sudden, deadly drop into an alley, this large body of photographs can be edited and arranged to allude to different open-ended narratives.

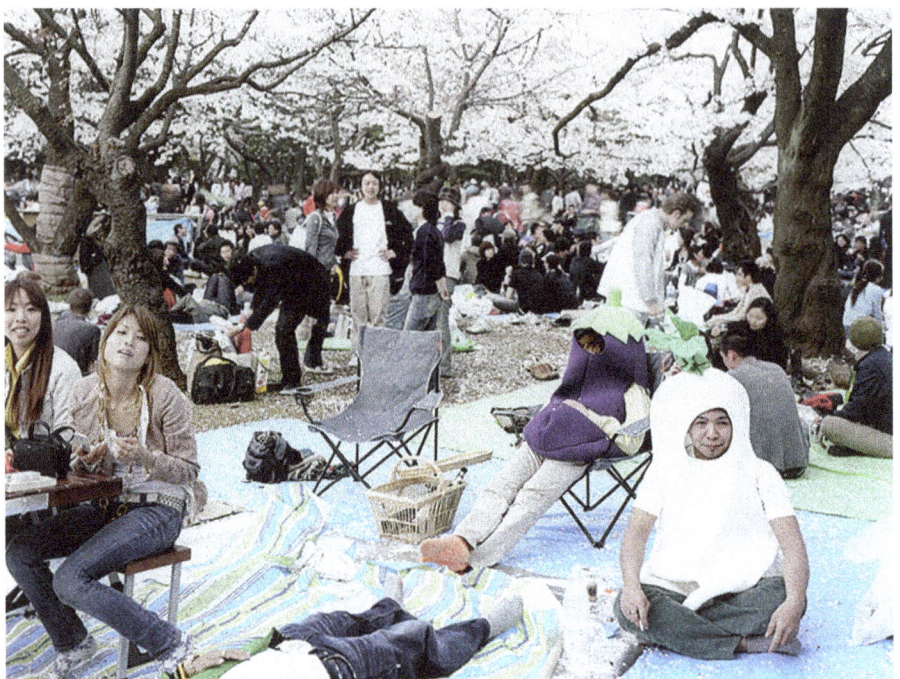

Figure 6.3. Kristian Häggblom, *Yoyogi #11*, 2006.
Source: Courtesy of the artist.

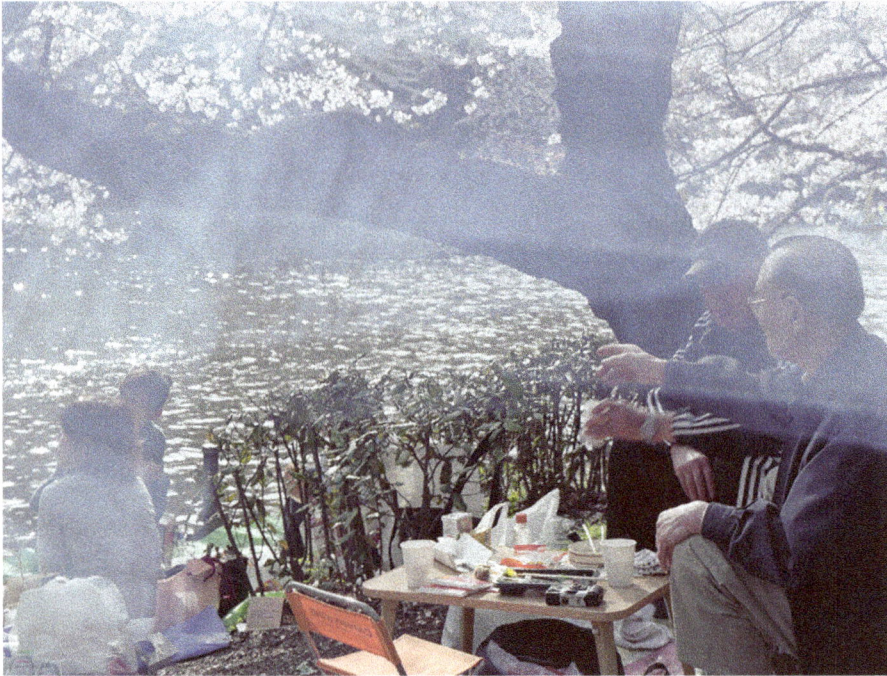

Figure 6.4. Kristian Häggblom, *Kichijoji #6*, 2006.
Source: Courtesy of the artist.

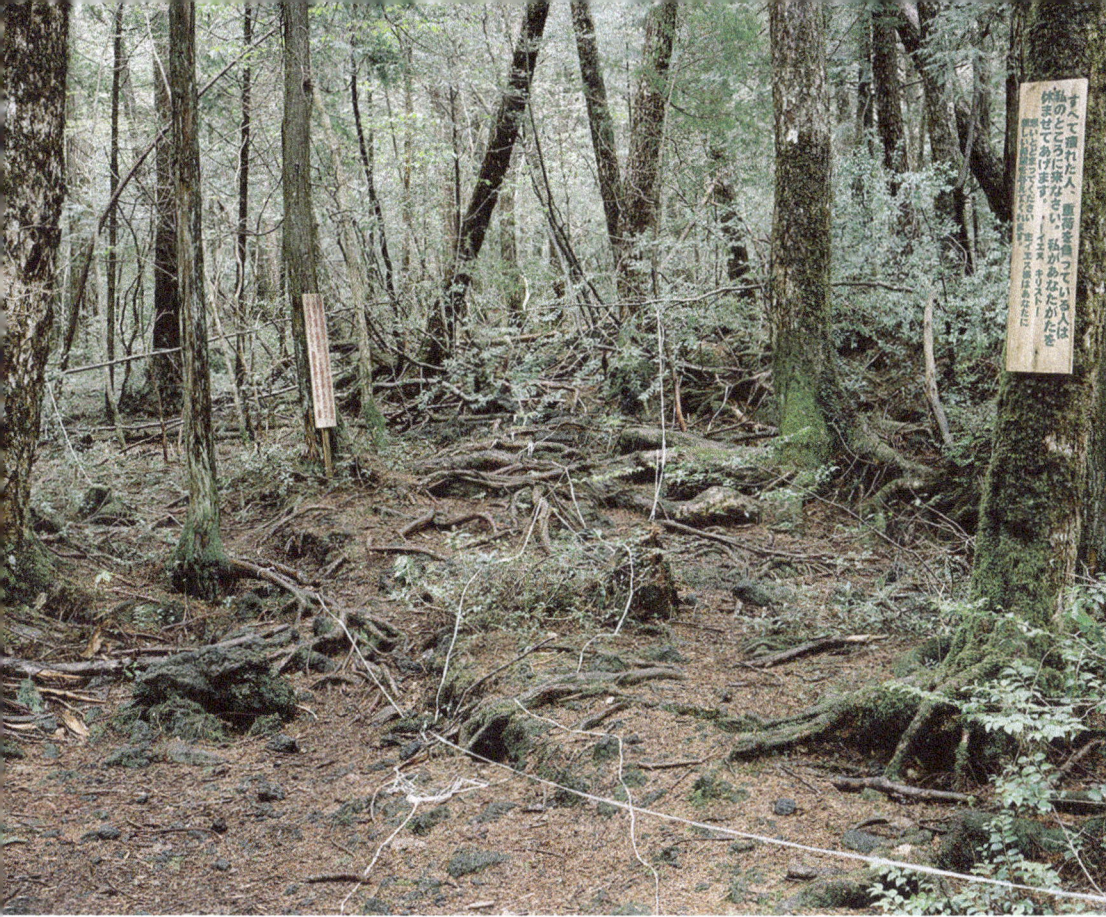

Figure 6.5. Kristian Häggblom, *Aokigahara Jukai, Bible Translations*, 2000.
Source: Courtesy of the artist.

Aokigahara Jukai (The Blue Sea of Foliage) is Häggblom's best known and most personal series. It is concerned with a stretch of forest situated at the base of Mt Fuji. Häggblom returned to this forest several times between 2000 and 2018. These photographs reflect his larger interest in the ritualised uses of open outdoor spaces and how the landscape has been shaped by those uses. Noted in tourist guides for its views of Mt Fuji and its lakes, the area is a popular hiking spot. In Häggblom's photographs, the forest is largely devoid of people but is littered with remnants of their visits. Whether due to the disorienting, undulating landscape or stories about the magnetic properties of iron deposits in the soil that purportedly confound compass readings, this area has a reputation as a site where people get lost. A confusing tangle of strings is visible in some of Häggblom's photographs (see Figure 6.5), left by visitors who trail the long lengths behind them as they enter the forest so they may follow the string to navigate their way out again.

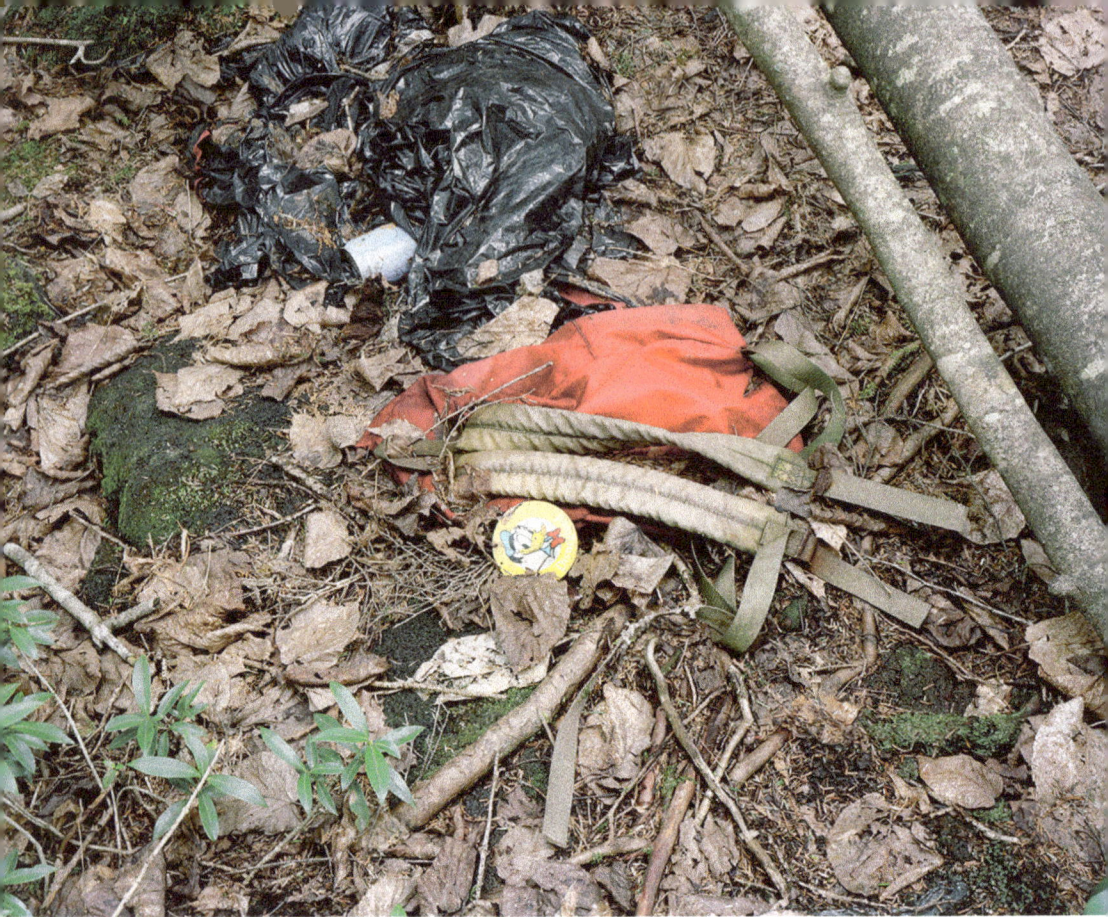

Figure 6.6. Kristian Häggblom, *Aokigahara Jukai, Donald Duck Badge*, 2000.
Source: Courtesy of the artist.

This is also a site where people willingly submit to the enveloping forest.[44] Signs pleading visitors not to end their lives and religious texts nailed to trees reveal the forest as an infamous suicide spot; indeed, it is described in Wataru Tsurumi's best-selling book, *The Complete Manual of Suicide*, as the perfect place to die.[45] Occasionally seen among the dead leaves on the forest floor are personal objects that people have left behind. A backpack, a Donald Duck badge and a plastic bag can be seen in one of Häggblom's photographs (see Figure 6.6), while others show a membership card, a shoe and the remains of a meal. There is a sense of intimacy in these objects, as we wonder why they were taken into the forest and by whom.

---

44 Kyla McFarlane, 'Kristian Häggblom', *Un Magazine* 7, 2006, 6.
45 Wataru Tsurumi, *Kanzen jisatsu manyuaru* (*The Complete Manual of Suicide*) (Tōkyō : Ōta Shuppan, 1993).

One photograph includes decomposing human remains, thus drawing attention to some challenging ethical questions. There is ongoing debate in Japan about whether it is the responsibility of the local council to recover and attempt to identify human remains that lie in the forest. The 'suicide forest' has also become a site for dark tourism. There have been no less than seven films made about the 'haunted forest', including independent films like Shan Serafin's *Forest of the Living Dead* (2010) and Gus Van Sant's *The Sea of Trees* (2015) starring Matthew McConaughey, Ken Watanabe and the Australian actress Naomi Watts. Sensationalised responses to *Aokigahara Jukai* reached a new low in 2017 when 22-year-old American YouTube star Logan Paul used one man's suicide as clickbait for his 15 million plus subscribers. In Paul's video, he and his friends laugh and joke near the body of a young man who hangs limp from a tree. The camera scans up and down his body, lingering on his blue hands and the wallet that still sits in his back pocket. 'This is the craziest moment in my life', proclaims Paul in an extraordinary moment of narcissism, before the video continues with a scene of him greeting fans in the carpark. The international outrage at Paul's post led him to apologise for his thoughtlessness. Yet, this and so many other references to the forest in popular culture underscores the way that suicide persists as a marker of the 'otherness' of Japan in contemporary Western cultures. Debt suicides supposedly speak to the Japanese sense of duty, while the suicides of depressed teenagers who had withdrawn from life are seen as signs of the pressures of conformity and family obligation.

Rather than subscribe to these clichés of quintessential 'Japaneseness', Häggblom's photographs quietly underscore the humanity of those affected by suicide. The photographer comments on the importance of addressing the enormity of suicide in Japan, where help lines are overstretched, investment in prevention programs is lacking, mental health care for those at risk is inadequate and some 25,000–30,000 Japanese succeed in taking their own lives each year. Häggblom stresses the need to talk about suicide in Japan and understand its causes and profound impacts. However, this is a fine balancing act in photography. In the critical reception of these photographs in Melbourne when they were exhibited in 2005, it was suggested that the photographs act as 'evidence' of something fundamentally Japanese:

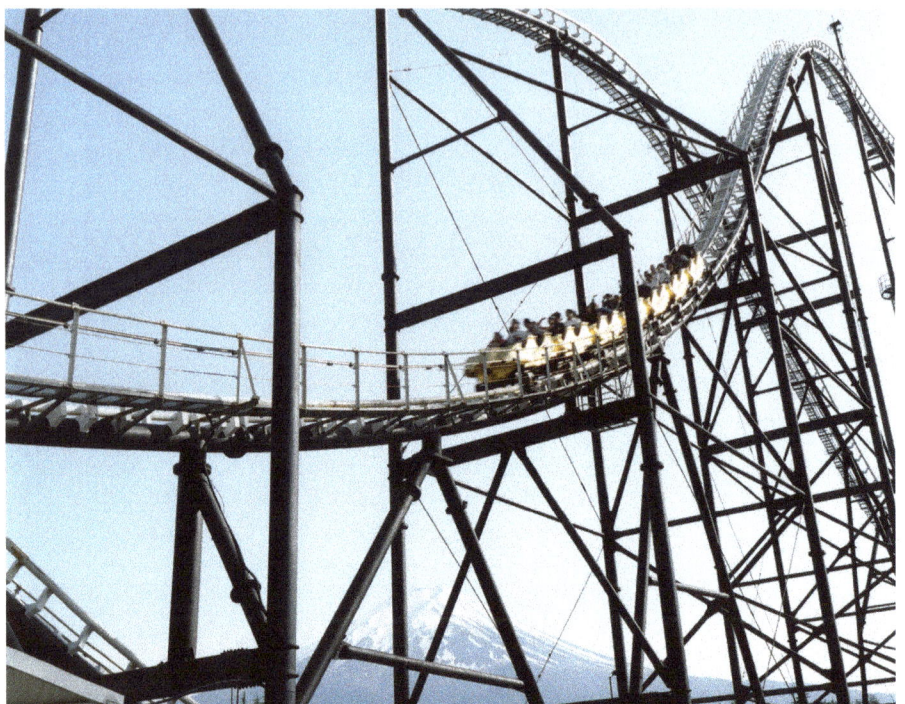

Figure 6.7. Matthew Sleeth, *12 Views of Mt Fuji #4 [Fujikyu Highland Park]*, 2004.
Source: Courtesy of Matthew Sleeth/Claire Oliver Gallery (New York).

In depicting evidence of these contradictory, yet co-existing engagements with Aokigahara Jukai, Häggblom alludes to the tangle of cultural, social and psychological forces that shape Japanese society beyond the forest but which are thrown into sharp relief in this small stretch of land.[46]

Other responses to this work have been far less sensitive. Häggblom made the decision to remove one of his photographs from his website because it had been taken without permission and used in an offensive online video. A risk is that the fetishisation of Japanese suicide by Western audiences will see this critical issue pushed off the international agenda altogether. Häggblom ultimately highlights the importance of being mindful of this Orientalist tendency and maintaining empathy and respectful conversation. Although it is highly unlikely that photographs about suicide will be embraced officially in aid of bilateral relations, Häggblom's work opens up a space for another, extremely important type of dialogue.

---

46   McFarlane, 'Kristian Häggblom', 6.

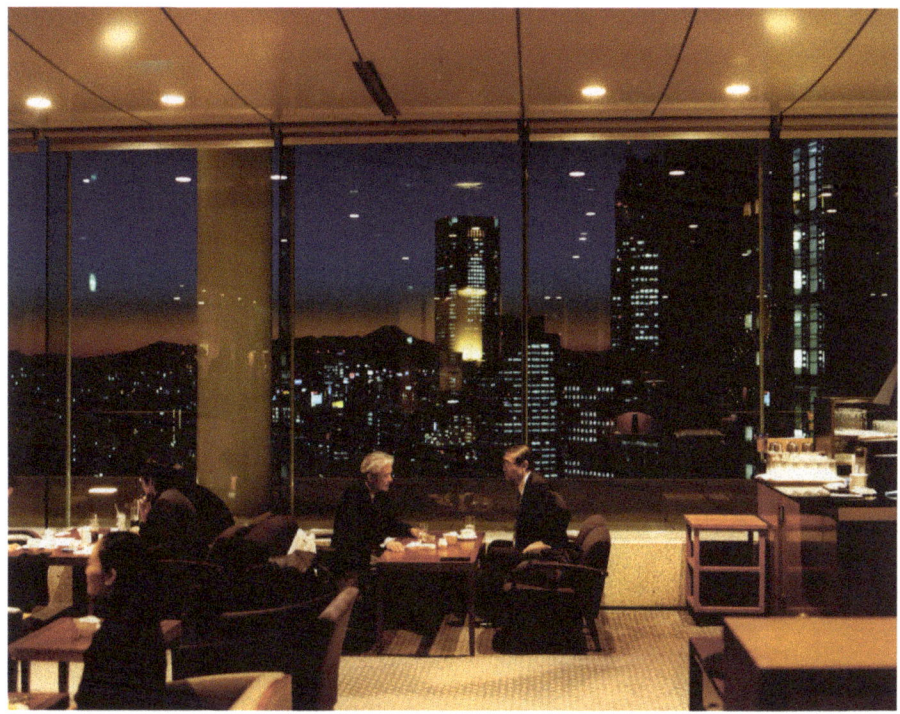

Figure 6.8. Matthew Sleeth, *12 Views of Mt Fuji #43 [Shinjuku Southern Tower Hotel]*, 2005.
Source: Courtesy of Matthew Sleeth/Claire Oliver Gallery (New York).

Like Häggblom, Matthew Sleeth returns to the same subjects to form large bodies of photographs that address a central idea. Whereas Häggblom's work is the product of many years living and working in Japan, Sleeth's photographs reflect the preoccupations and experiences of a repeat, short-term visitor. His more recent practice is concerned with sculpture, installation, performance and film, but photography was a major focus during Sleeth's early trips to Japan. Sleeth first visited Japan in 2002 while accompanying his partner, furniture designer Sally Thomas, who was participating in a group exhibition at the Australian Embassy in Tokyo. The city's glary neon, consumer culture and dense urban environment lent itself well to Sleeth's photography practice at that time. His approach built on the somewhat 'joyless' deadpan 1960s conceptual art photography—in which photographs were produced to convey a central idea—and infused it with the 'seductive visual language' of popular culture, fashion and cinema.[47] On that first brief visit in 2002, Sleeth produced *Feet* (2002), a series of colour photographs framed tightly on the feet and legs of train commuters. Together, the

---

47 Matthew Sleeth, interview with Melissa Miles, 18 January 2018.

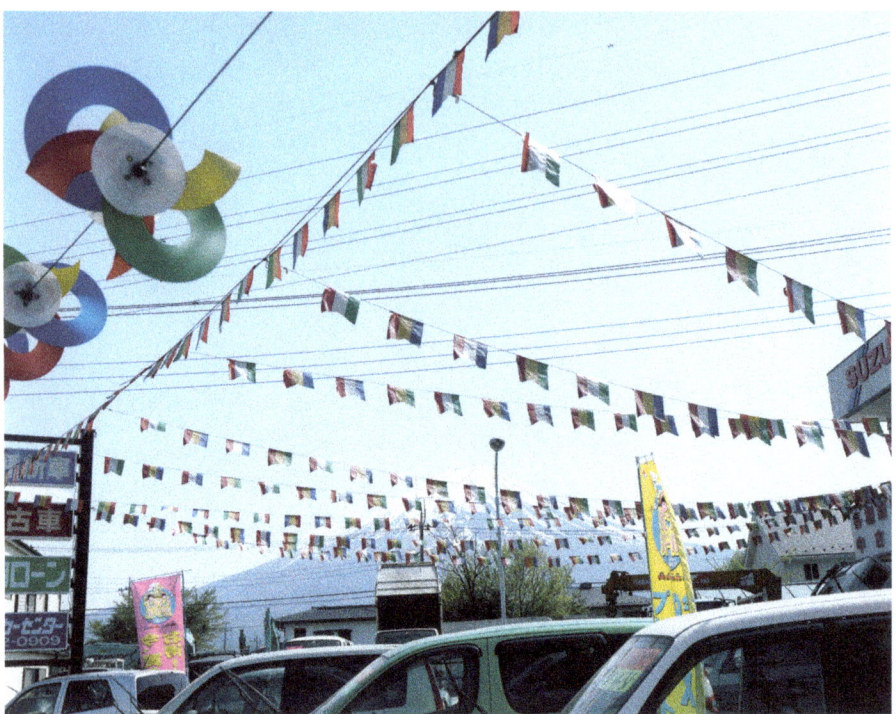

Figure 6.9. Matthew Sleeth, *12 Views of Mt Fuji #24 [Kawaguchiko]*, 2004.
Source: Courtesy of Matthew Sleeth/Claire Oliver Gallery (New York).

photographs of differently clad feet variously dangling, sitting neatly, 'manspreading' or pointing towards the train door in anticipation of a quick exit, draw attention to the subtle social habits that occupy our attention amid the confinement and boredom of an urban train trip. Sleeth returned to Tokyo several times following this initial visit. *Abandoned Umbrellas* (2004) responds to Japanese umbrella culture. It centres particularly (but not exclusively) on the cheap clear plastic umbrellas sold in convenience stores when rain unexpectedly pours down on the city and are discarded when the weather clears up. When gathered together, Sleeth's photographs of twisted, bent and broken umbrellas jutting out of overfull rubbish bins or lying in the rain-soaked gutter allude to the failure of mass-produced consumer goods and the excessive waste of consumer culture.

Sleeth returned yet again for an Australia Council residency over the Japanese winter of 2005–06. Among the several series he completed during this Tokyo residency was *Twelve Views of Mount Fuji* (2004–06) (see Figures 6.7–6.9). This series began during a trip in Spring 2004 and reflects Sleeth's desire to respond to Japan's art history and contemporary context, while carefully avoiding the tendency towards Orientalist

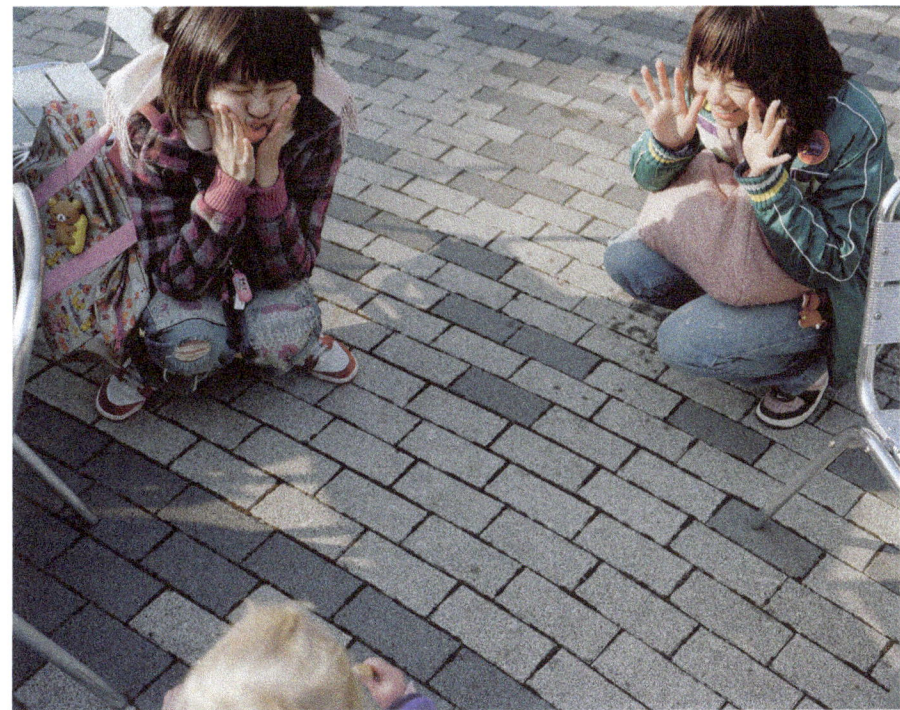

Figure 6.10. Matthew Sleeth, *Kawaii Baby #15 [Tokyo]*, 2006.
Source: Courtesy of Matthew Sleeth/Claire Oliver Gallery (New York).

travelogue that often looms large in Australian representations of Japan. This series is a homage to Katsushika Hokusai's woodblock prints *Thirty-six Views of Mount Fuji* (1830–34), which informed a popular tradition of visualising Japan. Hokusai's prints pictured the iconic volcanic mountain from different perspectives and in different landscapes and seasons, framing it with clouds and foreground elements like arched bridges, snowy fields and cranes. Rather than recreating Hokusai's images, Sleeth pictured the distant Fuji against foregrounds that could not have been envisaged by Hokusai, including a used car yard, a tangle of power lines, contemporary housing, a roller coaster and Tokyo's extraordinary contemporary illuminated skyline.

Kawaii Baby (2005–06) (see Figures 6.10 and 6.11) operates at a more personal level, while maintaining Sleeth's conceptual interest in documentary photography, seriality and consumer culture. These photographs capture the surprising encounters between Sleeth's baby daughter and members of the public in busy Tokyo. Sleeth and his wife were initially taken aback by the way that strangers would so readily approach the little blonde-haired blue-eyed girl exclaiming '*kawaii*' (cute), playing with her, adjusting her clothes and even feeding

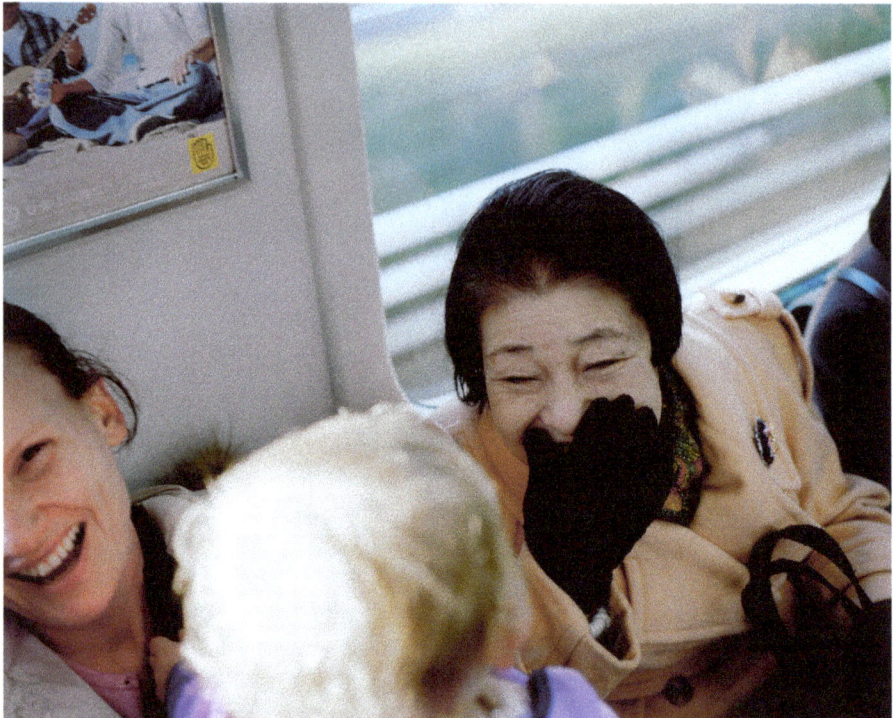

Figure 6.11. Matthew Sleeth, *Kawaii Baby #16 [Tokyo]*, 2006.
Source: Courtesy of Matthew Sleeth/Claire Oliver Gallery (New York).

her, sometimes without acknowledging her parents. While knowing that they meant well, Sleeth was confronted by the treatment of the infant as public property:

> Japan is a very child-friendly place, which is one of the reasons we moved there, but it was quite weird, and one of the reasons I started taking these photographs was to help me deal with it.[48]

Taken from above and behind the little girl's head—so her wispy blonde hair is just visible in the bottom of the shot—the photographs focus on the warm, joyous smiles and playful expressions on the faces of fellow train passengers, teenagers and office workers as they entertain the baby. Central to the appeal of these photographs is the warmth and sincerity of this interaction. In sharp contrast to the commercial use of photographs of children to transmit adult values and world views, of which Sleeth remains conscious, these people seem to utterly forget the adult world as they coo and giggle at the baby girl.[49]

---

48 Diana Smyth, 'Baby Face', *British Journal of Photography*, 19 December 2007, 17.
49 Matthew Sleeth, interview with Melissa Miles, 18 January 2018.

Sleeth brought together *Feet, Abandoned Umbrellas, 12 Views of Mt Fuji* and *Kawaii Baby*, along with other photographs made in Japan and elsewhere in the world, in his book *Ten Series/106 Photographs* (2007). This book is the first by an Australian photographer to be produced by the renowned American publisher Aperture in its 55-year history. In the critical response to Sleeth's book, much of the focus is on his process of creating visual typologies and the photographer himself—his 'obsessions' and travels—rather than what the photographs may say about Australian engagement with Japan.[50] However, when *12 Views of Mt Fuji* was included in the Queensland University of Technology Art Museum group exhibition *Zen to Kawaii: The Japanese Affect*, the reception was reframed. The Japanese art expert Gary Hickey was highly critical of how the exhibition represented impressions of Japan by Australians but failed to offer meaningful insight into Japanese culture:

> What is also apparent from the works in the *Zen to Kawaii* exhibition is that there has been little historical development in Australian understanding of Japanese culture since Japanese art travelled to the West in the late 19th century. This neglect has much to do with the dearth of any in-depth engagement with Japanese art by our educational and cultural institutions.[51]

This critical objection tends to reinforce the long tradition of presenting Japan as an enigma waiting to be unravelled by the expert. The value of Australian photographic engagements with Japan must not be limited to the expectation that they will 'explain' Japan to a foreign audience. Rather, these photographers' interest in confusion, misunderstanding and their place as outsiders may offer other valuable insights and perspectives.

To Sleeth, the pervasive sense of being at odds with Tokyo, of being unable to speak the language, read its street signs or understand the conversations of passers-by, allows him to gain a productive sense of presence in the moment.[52] This impression of contemplation amid the

---

50   Jo Roberts, 'Australian Photographer Captures Focus of Esteemed Arbiter', *Age*, 4 October 2007; Michael David Murphy, 'Ten Series/106 Photographs', *Foto8*, 14 November 2008, www.foto8.com/live/ten-series106-photographs/; Robert McFarlane, 'Images of Life's Ups and Downs', *Sydney Morning Herald*, 23 October 2007; Paddy Johnson, 'Matthew Sleeth', *Art and Australia* 45, no. 4 (2008): 646–47; Edward Colless, 'World Vision', *Australian Art Collector*, July–September 2007, 109–17.
51   Gary Hickey, 'Impressions of Japan', *Art Monthly Australia*, no. 236 (December 2010): 20.
52   Matthew Sleeth, interview with Melissa Miles, 18 January 2018.

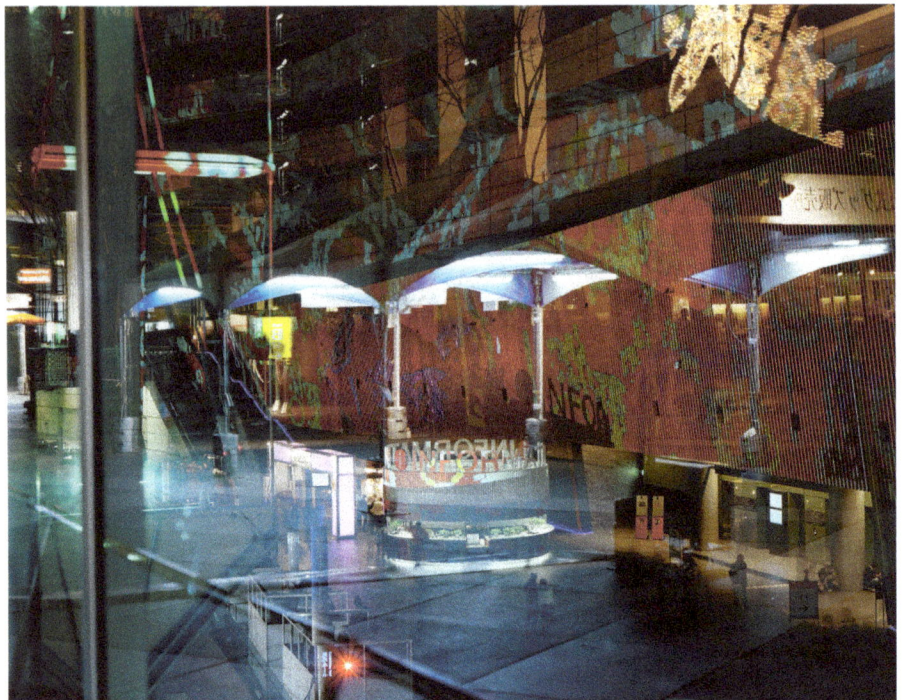

Figure 6.12. Matthew Sleeth, *Millenario Lights, Marunouchi [Tokyo]*, 2006.
Source: Courtesy of Matthew Sleeth/Claire Oliver Gallery (New York).

bright lights and white noise of the city is particularly evident in Sleeth's large-scale photographs in which he layers and heavily works over the images. Printed at 127 x 153 cm or 182 x 228 cm, the photographs are large, immersive and cinematic, and create a sense of artificiality that heightens the seductive appeal of Tokyo's bright lights. These works build on Sleeth's previous work with film and video and look forward to the more experimental video work to come. 'I'm interested in found narrative', says Sleeth, 'but photographed in a way where everything is so controlled that it looks staged'.[53] The spectacular winter light displays in a busy Tokyo square accentuates that sense of a staged backdrop in *Millenario Lights, Marunouchi* (2006) (see Figure 6.12). Turning away from the illuminated decorative arches and towards the lights and images reflected in the glass of nearby buildings, Sleeth creates the impression of a confusing, disorienting space that is nonetheless kept at a distance, as though being viewed on an enormous screen.

---

53   Colless, 'World Vision', 116.

The Western sense of Tokyo as a disorienting city goes back at least as far as Roland Barthes in *Empire of Signs* (1970), with his famous characterisation of a 'city with an empty centre'. The city is 'routinely described as chaotic', observed the architectural critic Peter Popham in 1985.[54] The idea of Tokyo as both anarchic and labyrinthine has gained traction over the decades. Significant was Toyo Ito's multimedia installation in the *Visions of Japan* exhibition at the Victoria and Albert Museum in 1991, which represented this 'simulated city' using a jarring mass of screens, sounds and images. Australian-based architecture historian Ari Seligmann argued that the 'chaos trope' has long positioned Tokyo as a territory for creative intervention, with varying implications. Chaos may be understood in light of Tokyo's uncoordinated conglomeration of architectural styles and developments; the saturation of images, signs, billboards and neon in urban space; and the sheer enormity of the city set against thoughtful details at street level, such as neatly clipped street trees. The structure-defying layout of the city, in which nameless streets meander in all directions and are interwoven with snaking overpasses and rail lines, adds to the confusion.[55] In Sleeth's views of illuminated Tokyo from a Shinjuku high-rise (see Figure 6.13),

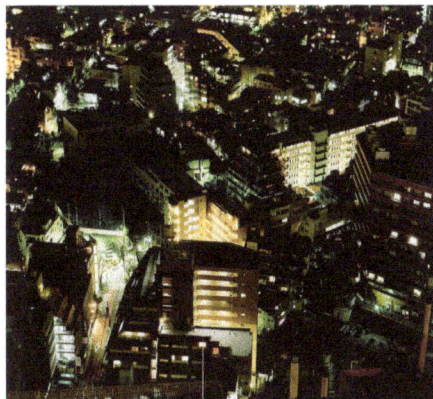
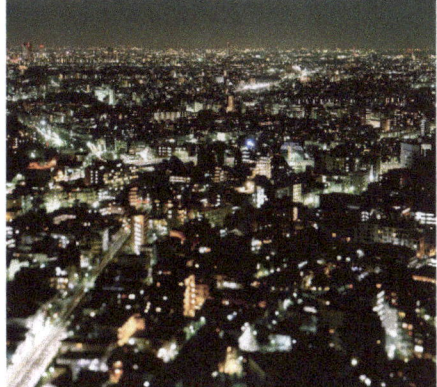

Figure 6.13. Matthew Sleeth, *North West from Shinjuku [Tokyo]*, 2005.
Source: Courtesy of Matthew Sleeth/Claire Oliver Gallery (New York).

54 Barthes and Popham quoted in Paul Waley, 'Re-Scripting the City: Tokyo from Ugly Duckling to Cool Cat', *Japan Forum* 18, no. 3, (November 2006): 368, 369.
55 Ari Seligmann, 'Tokyo Tropes, the Poetics of Chaos', in *Fabulation: Myth, Nature, Heritage: The Proceedings of the 29th Annual Conference of the Society of Architectural Historians Australia & New Zealand*, ed. Stuart King, Anuradha Chatterjee and Stephen Loo (Launceston, Tas.: Society of Architectural Historians of Australia & New Zealand, 2012).

structures seemingly jut up against one another without any organising principle. A comparable perspective was used in Sofia Coppola's film *Lost in Translation* (2003) to reflect the sense of alienation of the American protagonists. Some Japanese and foreign architects have sought to reveal the hidden logic that sits beneath this alienating disorder—a strategy that is part of the wider tradition of shedding light on 'inscrutable Tokyo'.[56] However, that hidden logic is not apparent in Sleeth's *Millenario Lights, Marunouchi* or *North West from Shinjuku [Tokyo]*. Nor was it sought. Glimpses of distinct spaces seem to collapse into one another, allowing the city to become a stimulating space for creativity.

'Cool Japan' in an Anxious Age

Although Sleeth was not motivated by the interests of Japanese cultural diplomacy, his work picks up on the concurrent interest in bright lights and pop culture as part of a distinctly Japanese brand of cultural 'cool'. The American journalist Douglas McGray famously observed in 2002 how a 'whiff of Japanese cool' had become a selling point around the world and proposed that cool had great potential as a form of soft power:

> There is an element of triviality and fad in popular behaviour, but it is also true that a country that stands astride popular channels of communication has more opportunities to get its messages across and to affect the preferences of others.[57]

Inspired by the success of the United Kingdom's 'Cool Britannia' campaign in the 1990s and the international explosion of South Korean K-pop music and communications technologies, Japan's Ministry of Foreign Affairs officially launched its 'pop-culture diplomacy' strategy in 2006. Two Cool Japan books were also published locally that year.[58] It was hoped that Cool Japan would provide a means of countering negative regional perceptions of Japan's international interventions, develop a new driving force for cultural exports and stimulate the local economy, which had been struggling since the rupture of the bubble

---

56   Ibid., 986. Peter Popham has alluded to the city's 'hidden sense of order'. Rather than chaotic, it is marked by 'a remarkably strong and simple structure', he argued. See Peter Popham, *Tokyo: The City at the End of the World* (Tokyo: Kodansha International, 1985), 93.
57   Douglas McGray, 'Japan's Gross National Cool', *Foreign Policy* 130 (May–June 2002): 583–84.
58   I. Nakamura and M. Onouchi, *Nippon No Poppupawaa (Japanese Popular Power)* (Tokyo: Nihon Keizai Shimbunsha, 2006); T. Sugiyama, *Kūru Japan. Sekai Ga Kaitagaru Nippon (Cool Japan. The Japan the World Wants to Buy)* (Tokyo: Shoutensha, 2006).

economy in the early 1990s. Everything from *manga* and *anime* to J-pop, games, cosplay and food were heralded as icons of Japanese cool. Among the government's many 'cool' initiatives was the appointment of three young female fashion leaders as '*Kawaii* Ambassadors' to travel the world promoting contemporary Japanese culture. The Ministry of Economy, Trade and Industry (METI) was reorganised with a view to supporting creative industries and the rebranding of Japan. The Creative Industries Promotion Office was established in June 2010 and the Cool Japan Advisory Council began work in November that year.

In the wake of the natural and technological calamity that befell northern Honshu on 11 March 2011, Cool Japan increasingly became 'both a defensive response against and an adaptation to globalization'.[59] Just two months after the triple disaster of earthquake, tsunami and nuclear meltdown, the Cool Japan Advisory Council issued recommendations for the advancement of national branding and creative industries in the 'Creating a New Japan' proposal.[60] The illustrated bilingual booklet *Roots of Japan*, produced as part of METI's November 2011 initiative, 'The Japan Mother Program', is indicative of the way that Cool Japan was refigured. The publication explains that 'Our "mother country" is in great need of protection, of recovery, and of nurturing the strength required to make a bold leap into the future'.[61] The disaster was a shocking reminder that:

> We Japanese seem to have forgotten some of the critical codes that made up our mother country, Japan. In the heat of pursuing success, wealth, and industrial development, we never paused to inquire into the fact that Japan was, at once, both singular 'Japan' and plural 'Japans'.[62]

The Japan Mother Program aimed to collect, record and distribute stories about the revival of the Japanese 'mother country' nationally and internationally in an effort to reinvent Japan's industry, culture and economy. *Roots of Japan* marked the start of this process by laying

---

59 Yoshitaka Mōri, 'The Pitfall Facing the Cool Japan Project: The Transnational Development of the Anime Industry under the Condition of Post-Fordism', *International Journal of Japanese Sociology*, no. 20 (2011): 40.
60 Katja Valaskivi, *Cool Nations: Media and the Social Imaginary of the Branded Country* (London and New York: Routledge, 2016), 17.
61 Seigow Matsuoka, *Roots of Japan(s): Unearthing the Cultural Matrix of Japan* (Tokyo: Ministry of Economy, Trade and Industry, 2011), 62.
62 Ibid., 62.

'a foundation for the re-creation of Japan's industries and cultures—through which we will attempt to create a connection between the country's origins and future'.[63]

The result was a paradox. Post-disaster, Cool Japan was an attempt to embrace globalisation and a desire to rebrand Japanese values as universal. However, it also constituted an inwardly focused 'Japanese only' nationalism—reiterating the 'closed' and supposedly unique qualities of Japanese national identity and seeking to export them as a form of global engagement.[64] This embrace of internationalisation by shoring up national identity finds visual form in the 2013 photography exhibition, *Cool Japan! Through Diplomats' Eyes*. Launched in 1998, the *Through Diplomats Eyes*' series of annual exhibitions presents photographs of Japan taken by international diplomats and their families. The exhibitions are promoted as a means of fostering 'cultural exchange'.[65] Each year, a different theme is selected that complements the Japanese Government's approach to cultural diplomacy. The 2013 theme 'Cool Japan!' was addressed by representatives of Albania, Australia, Egypt, France, Korea, Russia, Saudi Arabia, Sweden, Zimbabwe and the European Union, among others. Selected for the cover of the catalogue was the contribution by the Australian Embassy in Tokyo's first secretary, Ciaran Chestnutt, which was also judged the winner of the Prince Takamado Memorial Prize. The photograph (see Figure 6.14) features Chestnutt's young niece 'enthralled by a geisha' while walking back from Sensō-ji—Tokyo's oldest and most popular Buddhist temple, first built in the seventh century. The temple is located in Asakusa, a principal entertainment district in the Edo era that was badly damaged by the American firebombing of March 1945, but which has regained its status as an attraction for both foreigners and Japanese alike, as much for its modernity as its tradition. Looming over the area is the world's tallest tower, the Tokyo Skytree, which opened in 2012, standing well over 600 m tall on the city's earthquake-prone ground. Chestnutt's photograph captures this meeting of tradition and modernity. Shot from behind, the photograph focuses on the geisha's elaborate silk dress and

---

63   Ibid., 2.
64   Chris Burgess, 'National Identity and the Transition from Internationalization to Globalization: "Cool Japan" or "Closed Japan"', in *Languages and Identities in a Transitional Japan: From Internationalization to Globalization*, ed. Ikuko Nakane, Emi Otsuji and William S. Armour (London: Routledge, 2016), 25.
65   'Through Diplomats Eyes' website, accessed 7 February 2018, www.diplomatseyes.com/contents.html.

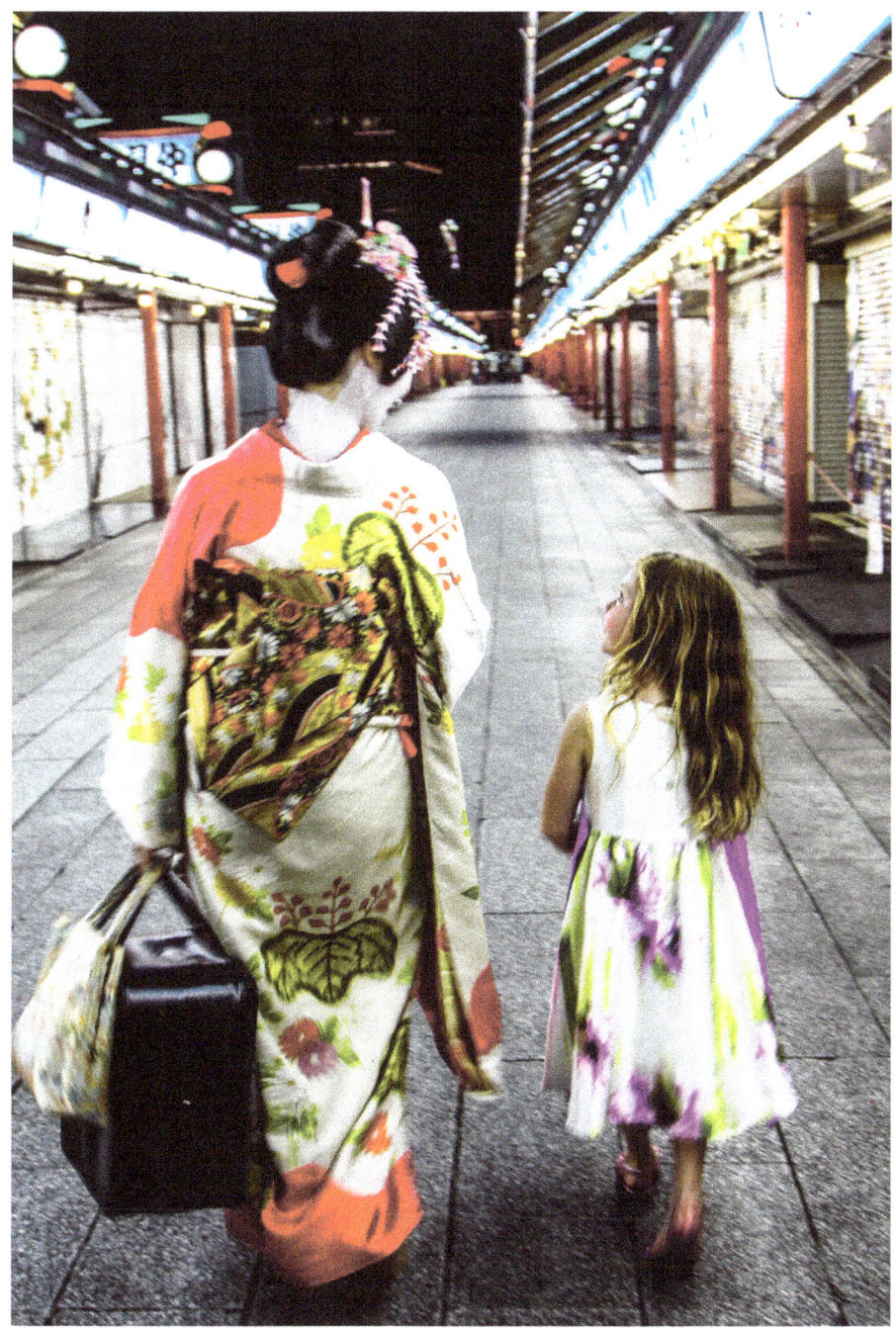

Figure 6.14. Ciaran Chestnutt, *My Niece, Enthralled by a Geisha, Strolling Back from Senso-ji*, 2013.
Source: Courtesy of Ciaran Chestnutt.

her decorated upswept hair, which contrast with the little girl's simple dress and free-flowing blonde locks. The pair seem to be in conversation, while the slight blur of their dresses create a sense of movement. The closed shutters of the souvenir shops on the empty, neon-lit Nakamise shopping street provide a dramatic stage for this encounter between ancient Japan, cool, contemporary Japan and the young international guest who soaks it all up. Thus, Chestnutt's photograph provides an evocative mirror in which Japan can enjoy a distilled version of its self-image reflected back onto itself.

Criticism of Cool Japan has been widespread. The Australian-based Japanese media and cultural studies scholar Koichi Iwabuchi is concerned that 'pop-culture diplomacy goes no further than a one-way projection and does not seriously engage with cross-border dialogue. The Japanese case also shows that pop-culture diplomacy hinders meaningful engagement with internal cultural diversity'.[66] Moreover, as a form of soft power, Cool Japan has had questionable success. Cool Japan may promote tourism and the consumption of Japanese media cultures, but there is no evidence that this translates into foreign policy benefits.[67] Steven Green looks at a BBC World Service Poll that measures global attitudes towards other nations. He points to China, where 31 per cent of people view Japan in mainly negative terms and only 58 per cent view it in mainly positive terms. A Pew Research Centre survey in 2013 produced even more stark results, with 90 per cent of Chinese having 'unfavourable' feelings towards Japan and just 4 per cent feeling 'favourable'.[68] These results suggest that it is relatively easy for people to separate their consumption of Japanese pop culture from perceptions of the country's historical military misdemeanours, and that Japanese popular culture does not necessarily make foreigners more amenable to Japan itself.

---

66   Koichi Iwabuchi, 'Pop-Culture Diplomacy in Japan: Soft Power, Nation Branding and the Question of "International Cultural Exchange"', *International Journal of Cultural Policy* 21, no. 4 (2015): 419.
67   Burgess, 'National Identity and the Transition from Internationalization to Globalization', 26; Yasushi Watanabe, *Bunka to Gaikō: Paburikku Dipuromashii No Jidai* (*Culture and Diplomacy: The Age of Public Diplomacy*) (Tokyo: Chukōshinso, 2011), 89; Christopher Graves, 'Cool Is Not Enough', in *Reimagining Japan: The Quest for a Future That Works*, ed. Clay Chandler, Heang Chhor and Brian Salsberg (San Francisco: VIZ Media, 2011), 413.
68   Green, 'The Soft Power of Cool', 64–65.

The neglect of the more challenging aspects of Japan's international history is a recurring theme in the critical commentary. Commenting on the use of the Sanrio character Hello Kitty as Japan's Ambassador of Tourism to Taiwan, China and Korea in 2008, Christine Yano argued that the export of *kawaii* and cool helped to paper over international disputes about territory and history:

> The positioning of Hello Kitty as one face of Japan represents the power of the would-be child, at once appealing, seemingly benign, and ever in need of care and nurturance. *Kawaii* diplomacy builds upon affect and nostalgia, rather than on critical thinking. And in doing so throws a soft pink blanket upon the razor-sharp edges of history.[69]

Australian journalist and Kwansei Gakuin University media studies teacher Sally McLaren expressed deep concern about the post-disaster manifestation of Cool Japan, noting that Japan is simultaneously 'sliding backwards into a nationalistic cocoon and preparing to switch the nuclear power stations back on. It's irradiated to an unknown degree, increasingly chauvinistic and, slowly but surely, re-militarising'.[70] To Burgess, Japan's reluctance to embrace globalisation and its inward focus risks ultimately limiting the influence it hopes to achieve through soft power diplomacy.[71]

Despite these concerns, the Australia–Japan bilateral relationship remains strong and Australians generally have favourable attitudes to Japan. A 2017 Lowy Institute Poll found that 86 per cent of Australians trust Japan 'to act responsibly in the world'. This result is second only to trust held in the United Kingdom (90 per cent) and was equal to Australians' trust in Germany.[72] Japan remains Australia's second largest foreign investor, and the trade and investment partnership has been further reinforced by the Japan–Australia Economic Partnership Agreement, which began operating in 2015. Yet, questions over the potential cultural impact of Japan's approach to cultural diplomacy remain. Iwabuchi argued that Cool Japan's homogenisation of culture and movement away from recognising true cultural diversity brings

---

69 Christine Yano, 'Hello Kitty and Japan's Kawaii Diplomacy', *East Asia Forum*, 10 October 2015, www.eastasiaforum.org/2015/10/10/hello-kitty-and-japans-kawaii-diplomacy/.
70 Sally McLaren, 'Made in Cool Japan: Delights and Disasters', *Griffith Review*, no. 49 (2015): 165.
71 Burgess, 'National Identity and the Transition from Internationalization to Globalization', 17–18.
72 '2017 Lowy Institute Poll', 21 June 2017, accessed 7 March 2018, www.lowyinstitute.org/publications/2017-lowy-institute-poll.

to mind Edward Said's observation that the constructions of cultures in dualistic, overly simplistic terms amounts to a form of symbolic violence.[73] If pop cultural diplomacy is to work, insisted Iwabuchi, it should advance transnational connections in a manner that promotes 'self-reflexive international conversation' around challenging historical issues and enhances 'intercultural understanding of cultural diversity'.[74]

Working beyond the remit of official Cool Japan programs, the work of independent Australian photographers in Japan indirectly helps to further these goals. Meg Hewitt's body of work *Tokyo is Yours* (2015–17) marks her response to a prevailing sense of disquiet in post-disaster Japan. The title comes from a graffiti tag that has appeared throughout Tokyo in recent years declaring in English 'Tokyo is Yours'. Reflecting the openness of Hewitt's work, this phrase has at least two possible interpretations—part gift to Tokyo's inhabitants, part confidant reclamation of the city after the disaster. *Tokyo is Yours* is the product of eight short-term trips to Japan between 2015 and 2017. Spending up to 12 hours a day walking through Tokyo, this Sydney-based photographer pictured small details that captured her attention and the people that she met. Like Sleeth and Häggblom, Hewitt speaks of the sense of freedom and creativity that can come from language barriers:

> I suppose being in a country like Japan—where I don't understand most of the language—leads me to question things on a more basic level. Humanity plays out in front of me, and I seek meaning separate from words. I like to pick up the *manga* at the corner store and flick through, interpreting the story from the pictures alone.[75]

Ironically, Hewitt's language limitations help her to explore the city freely, to take it in without distraction and to interpret what she sees as symbols, archetypes, metaphors and potential stories.[76] 'When making the work, I looked for fantasy, the absurd and metaphor in reality. Through the photographs, I explore the layers between things, as well as memories, human connection, fear and escapism.'[77]

---

73 Edward W. Said, *Orientalism* (1978; repr., New York: Vintage, 1994), 204.
74 Iwabuchi, 'Pop-Culture Diplomacy in Japan', 429–30.
75 Meg Hewitt, 'Tokyo Is Yours: Seeking Sense through Street Photography', *Lens Culture*, 2017, accessed 25 January 2018, www.lensculture.com/articles/meg-hewitt-tokyo-is-yours-seeking-sense-through-street-photography.
76 Meg Hewitt, interview with Melissa Miles, 24 January 2018; Meg Hewitt, 'Tokyo Is Yours'.
77 Meg Hewitt, 'Tokyo is Yours', *Lens Culture*, 2016, accessed 25 January 2018, www.lensculture.com/articles/meg-hewitt-tokyo-is-yours.

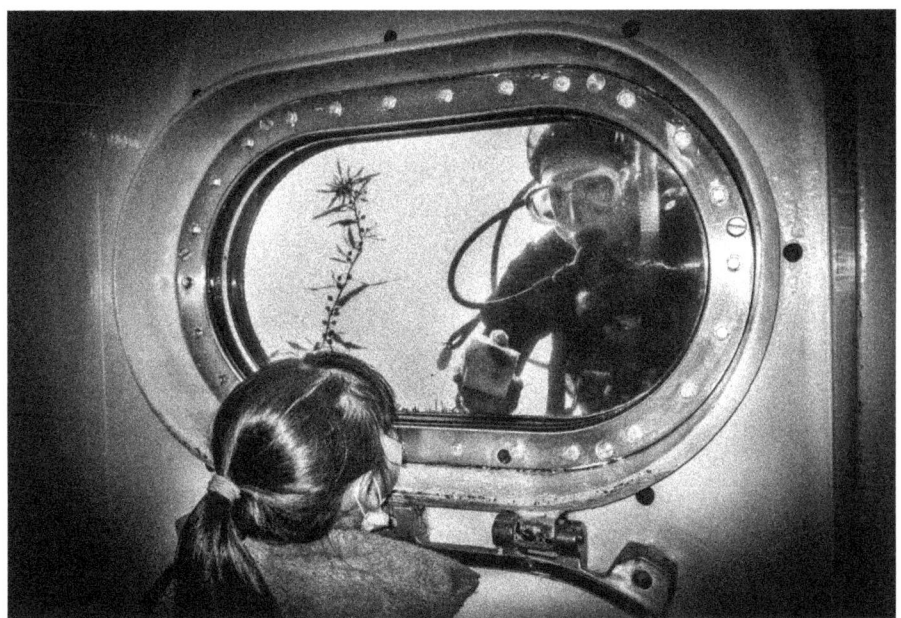

Figure 6.15. Meg Hewitt, *Underwater Observatory, Katsuura*, from *Tokyo is Yours*, 2016.
Source: Courtesy of the artist.

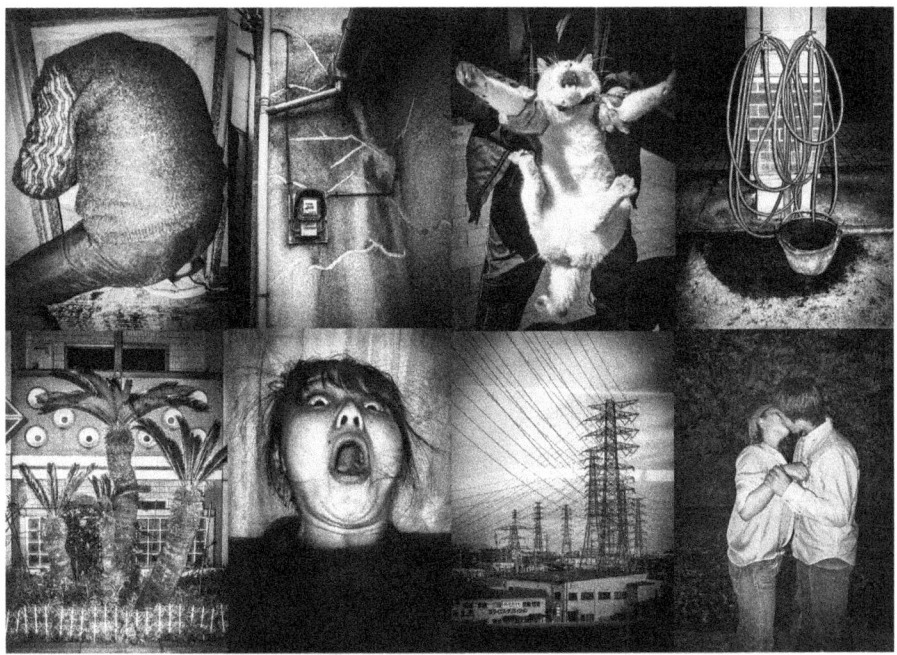

Figure 6.16. Meg Hewitt, *Tokyo is Yours*, 2015–17.
Source: Courtesy of the artist.

From the thousands of black and white photographs that Hewitt took, she selected 86 for publication in her photobook *Tokyo is Yours* (2017). One photograph focuses on a little girl looking up towards a scuba diver who cleans a window at the aging Katsuura Undersea Observatory (see Figure 6.15), while another shows a collection of worn concrete cranes found at the end of a street near an abandoned house. Many of the photographs are tightly framed so their original context is not apparent, allowing them to generate new meaning in relation to the other images. By often taking photographs at night with a flash, Hewitt uses light to isolate her subjects and absorb extraneous details into the black background. The resultant contrast creates a gritty, noir effect far removed from the highly polished and finished appearance of Sleeth's *Marunouchi* photograph. Paths, ladders, stairs and walkways leading to destinations unknown, animals caged in a zoo, a mass of electricity pylons and eerie suburban streets at night are interspersed with tranquil landscapes and images of young love (see Figure 6.16). Sequenced and layered in the pages of the book—to be read with the spine on the left by English-speaking audiences or from the opposite direction by Japanese audiences—these photographs cumulatively create a sense of spatial and psychological compression and an underlying desire for escape.

The meltdown at the deceptively distant Fukushima Daiichi nuclear power plant made Tokyo's vulnerability starkly apparent. Reflecting that Japan had come within a 'paper-thin margin' of a nuclear disaster, the former Prime Minister Naoto Kan remarked: 'From a very early stage I had a very high concern for Tokyo. I was forming ideas for a Tokyo evacuation plan in my head'.[78] Hewitt's book alludes to this narrowly averted catastrophe and the impossibility of escape. A photograph of a building in which a maze of cracks has been crudely patched acknowledges this sense of danger quite directly. By pairing this photograph with one of a bar owner squeezing through the impossibly small doorway of her establishment, Hewitt emphasises the psychological dimension of the desire for escape. Shot from behind, only the woman's back, shoulder and half of one leg and arm are visible, as though she is disappearing into another world. As well as heightening narrative intensity, the close physical proximity between Hewitt's lens and her subjects creates a sense of intimacy. At times, her connection with her

---

78   Andrew Gilligan, 'Fukushima: Tokyo Was on the Brink of Nuclear Catastrophe, Admits Former Prime Minister', *Telegraph*, 4 March 2016.

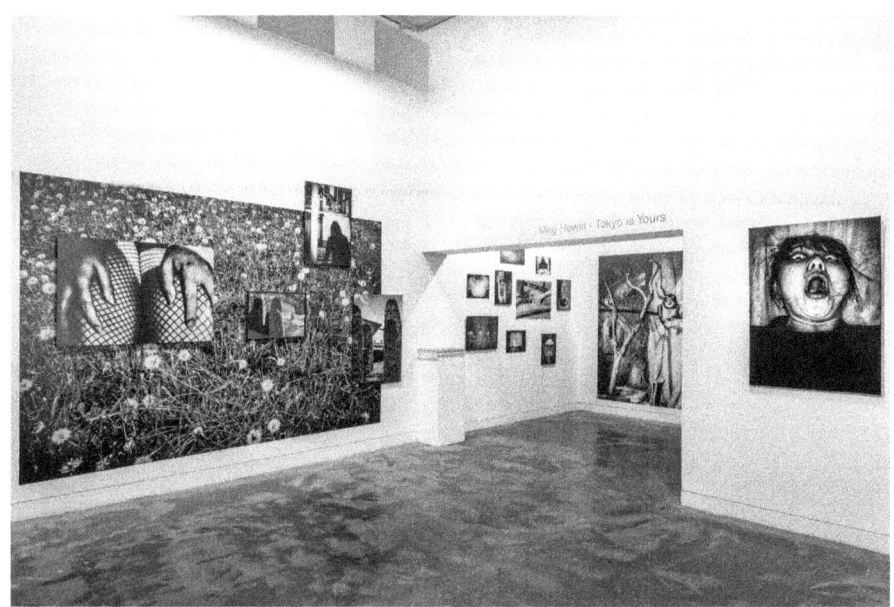

Figure 6.17. Meg Hewitt, *Tokyo is Yours*, installation view, Flinders Street Gallery, Surry Hills 2017.
Source: Courtesy of the artist.

subjects is clearly evident, as in the man who held up each of his eight cats to her camera, one after the other. It is also apparent in the care that she takes when shooting. This emphasis upon personal connection may be informed by Hewitt's admiration for the work of Masahisa Fukase, known for his deeply personal photographs of love and loss.[79] Whereas this Japanese photographer's focus was on his wife and family, Hewitt's abiding relationship is with Tokyo, its inhabitants and its post-2011 tensions.

When exhibiting these photographs, Hewitt prints them at different scales and installs them in a way that hints at other open-ended narratives—grouping, overlaying or displacing photographs to imply the interaction of different characters, objects, scenarios and places, and to suggest different atmospheres or feelings (see Figure 6.17).[80] These strategies have resonated with international audiences and in Australia. Hewitt exhibited these photographs as part of the fringe *Voies Off* program run in parallel to *Les Rencontres d'Arles* in France (2017), Sydney (2017), Canberra (2016) and regional Victoria at the Ballarat International Foto Biennale Fringe (2017), and her work has been covered in the *British*

---

79 Meg Hewitt, interview with Melissa Miles, 24 January 2018.
80 Ibid.

Journal of Photography.[81] Significantly, it has also generated interest in Japan. As well as being exhibited at Place M photography gallery in Tokyo, in 2018 it was shown in the Kodoji Photographer's Bar in the legendary Shinjuku precinct the Golden Gai, a hub for Japanese photographers like Daido Moriyama and Nobuyoshi Araki since the 1960s, and a site that rarely shows the work of non-Japanese. That Hewitt has attracted interest in Japan and at home is not coincidental. To be meaningful cross-culturally, photographs need to transcend the reductive binary of 'us' and 'them'. Hewitt's work is open, allusive and complex; she examines the emotions and desires that connect human beings and keenly observes the people and places in front of her.

Hewitt and the other independent photographers discussed here reject an export model of cultural relations; they do not attempt to project carefully crafted images of their own culture to foreigners in an effort to engender sympathy or favour. Nor do they aspire to enlighten audiences back home by presenting a supposedly 'accurate' view of the ever-elusive 'other'. These contemporary interpretations of one culture by another are compelling because they create a new representational language that draws attention to diverse perspectives and to new possibilities for forging cross-cultural connections.

---

81   Susanna D'Aliesio, 'Arles 2017: Tokyo Is Yours by Meg Hewitt', *British Journal of Photography*, 6 July 2017, www.bjp-online.com/2017/07/photobook-tokyo-is-yours-by-meg-hewitt/#closeContact FormCust00.n%20.

7

CONCLUSION:
REVISING 'US AND THEM'

'Life does not mean that same thing to them and us … What we feel is the difference, the gulf, the distance between us and them.'[1] This response to Japan's periodic but insistent criticism of the Immigration Restriction Act was printed in 1919 in Brisbane's evening newspaper the *Telegraph*. Some habits of mind die hard. Over the decades of Australia's evolving relationship with Japan since the Meiji period, it seems that photographers have often been intent on inscribing—and reinscribing—this entrenched sense of difference and distance. Yet, as this work has sought to reveal, the vast body of snapshots, lanternslides, art, news, military and governmental photographs through which Australian impressions of Japan have been imaged, conveys a diversity of perspectives, as well as conflicting and sometimes transgressive desires, anxieties and ambitions.

Now, in the first decades of the twenty-first century, the old simplistic dichotomy of 'us and them'—and the ideology that supports and perpetuates it—is both unproductive and redundant. Contemporary currents of the trans-Pacific photographic encounter lead to more fluid and sceptical modes of representation. In this context, it is worth noting the work of Mayu Kanamori, a Japanese photographer, poet and playwright long resident in Australia. Tokyo-born and Sydney-based, Kanamori's transnational photographic dialogue involves interrogating her own place in histories of the Japanese people in Australia and questioning persistent clichés. Kanamori has completed several projects on these subjects since she emigrated in 1981, including

---

1   'Japan's Protest against Race Prejudice', *Telegraph*, 24 March 1919, 6.

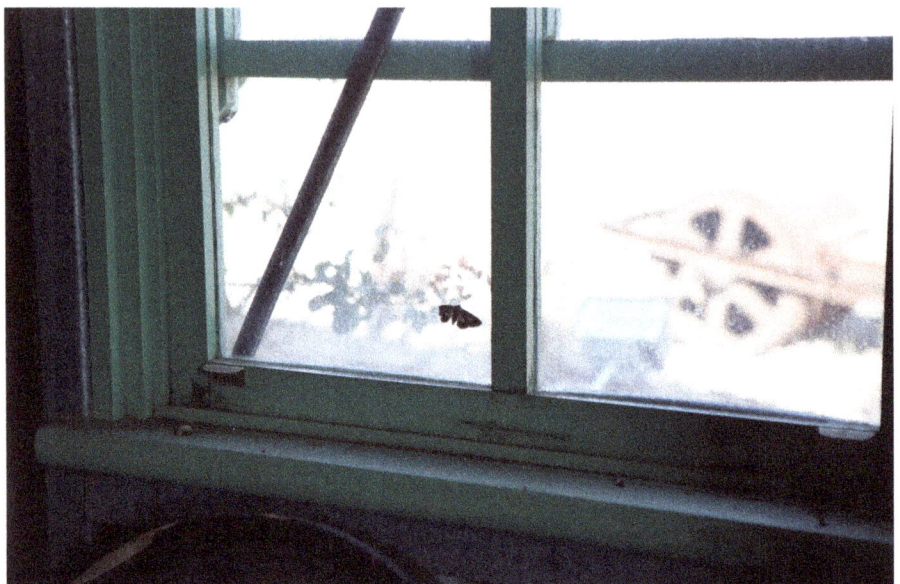

Figure 7.1. Mayu Kanamori, *Untitled* from *You've Mistaken Me for a Butterfly*, 2017–18. © Mayu Kanamori 2017.

Source: Courtesy of the artist.

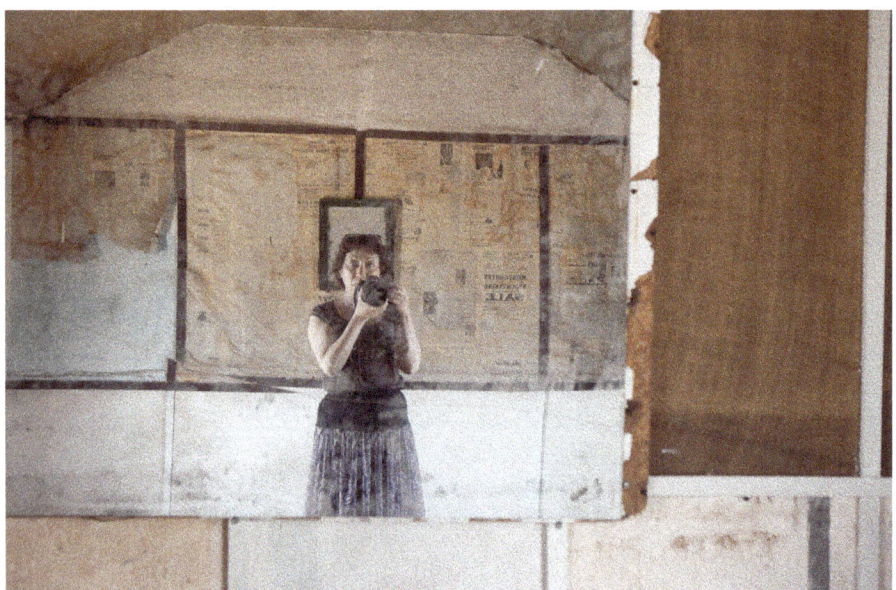

Figure 7.2. Mayu Kanamori, *Untitled* from *You've Mistaken Me for a Butterfly*, 2017–18. © Mayu Kanamori 2017.

Source: Courtesy of the artist.

her photojournalism in the mid-1990s and her play about a Broome photographer *Yasukichi Murakami—Through a Distant Lens* (2014). Photographs feature prominently in Kanamori's performance work *You've Mistaken Me for a Butterfly* (2017) (see Figures 7.1 and 7.2). As its title suggests, *You've Mistaken Me for a Butterfly* examines Western clichés of Japanese femininity, perhaps the most predominant of all the delimiting stereotypes that have saddled the country over the years.

Taken in the Goldfields-Esperance region of Western Australia, Kanamori's photographs are a long way from the images of eye-catching, butterfly-like geisha that have long captivated Anglo-Australians. There is a sense of melancholy in the dilapidated interiors, their browned peeling wallpaper and the red dirt paths marked with footprints of someone no longer present. A small brown moth flutters in one interior window—where it is likely to be mistaken by many viewers for a butterfly—while rusted industrial equipment stands idle outside. These photographs are fragments of a narrative that cannot quite be grasped. Kanamori places herself within this narrative as both its subject and author, photographing her reflection in a mirror in the old building with her camera held firmly in her hands.

The spoken word component of Kanamori's performance describes how she was led to the Western Australia goldfields by the story of a young woman named Okin.[2] In the 1890s, Okin lived in the town of Malcolm, 30 km north of a gold mine named Butterfly. There are no buildings left in Malcolm today, so Kanamori visualises her response to Okin's story elsewhere in the area. These goldfields became home to many Japanese in this period. Where camps and towns were established, prostitutes soon followed, working in brothels that frequently operated under the guise of laundries or boarding houses.[3] Frequently known as *karayuki-san* (literally 'those who go to China'), these travelling women were often poor and illiterate daughters of farmers and rural labourers. Many were tricked or kidnapped into prostitution and forced to work for extended periods to pay off the 'debts' incurred from their journey and board. Some *karayuki-san* saved their earnings, later using the funds to launch their own businesses, and several established lasting relationships with

---

2   Mayu Kanamori and Vera Mackie, 'You've Mistaken Me for a Butterfly', *Japanese Studies* 37, no. 3 (2017): 387–94.
3   It has been argued that most of the Japanese women counted in the 1901 Australian census worked as prostitutes. See Yuriko Nagata, 'Gendering Australia-Japan Relations: Prostitutes and the Japanese Diaspora in Australia', *Ritsumeikan Journal of Asia Pacific Studies* 11 (March 2003).

local businessmen. While the presence of these Japanese women in Australia has attracted the attention of several historians, very little is known about them as individuals with their own experiences, thoughts and perceptions.[4]

Kanamori first came across Okin in the archive of the eminent historian of Australian–Japanese relations, D.C.S. Sissons. Handwritten notes described Okin as the victim of a violent crime.[5] In July 1898, three men forced themselves into a house where Okin was staying. Two of them raped her while the third stood guard. A Japanese man named Enaba who lived with Okin tried unsuccessfully to help her, so he ran to fetch the local police constable who was able to apprehend, arrest and charge the men. At the subsequent trial, Okin's testimony that she was a laundress was challenged by the defence, who sought to establish that she was a prostitute and her home was a brothel. The accused asserted that they were paying customers of the brothel and that a dispute erupted about money. It was her word against theirs. Kanamori's performance quotes the crown solicitor's request to the jury in which he argued for Okin's right to justice:

> It is of great importance in all countries, especially in a country like this, where women were practically alone in outlying, far away parts, that the chastity of women be cherished and protected in the highest degree. No matter what their colour, race, creed or reputation.[6]

The jury could not agree initially, but the men were ultimately acquitted. Yet, Kanamori reminds us that fundamental questions remain unanswered about Okin. Was she a laundress or was she lying? Was Enaba her pimp or saviour?

These mysteries are amplified by the persistence of stereotypes surrounding Japanese women in foreign countries. Alison Broinowski has used the term the 'butterfly phenomenon' to describe the Orientalist rendering of Japanese women (and by extension Japan itself) as seductive

---

4   May Albertus Bain, *Full Fathom Five* (Perth: Artlook Books, 1982), 91; D.C.S. Sissons, 'Karayuki-San: Japanese Prostitutes in Australia, 1887–1916—II', *Historical Studies* 17, no. 69 (1977): 474–88; Nagata, 'Gendering Australia-Japan Relations'. For an early Japanese account of karayuki-san see Morisaki Kazue, *Karayuki-San* (Tōkyō: Asahi Shimbunsha, 1976).
5   Papers of D.C.S. Sissons, 1950–2006, National Library of Australia, MS 3092.
6   *Performance—Post Memory: You've Mistaken Me for a Butterfly (the Second Instalment)* (Crawley, Western Australia: Institute of Advanced Studies, University of Western Australia, 25 September 2017).

but fragile and subject to the demands of the West.[7] The term, of course, is derived from Puccini's opera *Madame Butterfly* (1904), which is about an impoverished 15-year-old Japanese girl who marries an American naval officer and eventually commits suicide after being abandoned by him and being forced to give up her child. The gender politics of *Madame Butterfly* and its geo-cultural overtones have been heavily critiqued in recent years. 'In Western eyes', Dorinne Kondo argued:

> Japanese women are meant to sacrifice, and Butterfly sacrifices her 'husband', her religion, her people, her son, and ultimately her very life … the predictable happens: West wins over East, Man over Woman, White over Asian.[8]

Kanamori is aware that this dualistic mode of critique is problematic because it reinforces the position of Japanese women as victims—'they' remain passive and silent while 'we' assert scholarly authority. The ways that such stereotypes affected the experiences of actual Japanese women remain obscured, as do the nuances and variability of representations of Japanese women over time. This history and its critique left Kanamori in a bind—how could she escape the enduring logic of 'us' and 'them'? In the end, Kanamori resisted narrating yet another story about the rescue of a vulnerable, victimised butterfly by the Australian policeman or, indeed, enacting a subsequent rescue of Okin from historical obscurity. Her open-ended narratives and photographs of empty buildings reflect her resistance to easy answers, while her use of the first person in the title *You've Mistaken Me for a Butterfly* implies the lingering legacy of the hegemony of foreign representations of the Japanese on her own experience and identity.

Central to Kanamori's work, and to this book more broadly, is the question, 'what do photographs do?' Photographs are understood not simply as representations of things that exist independently in the 'real' world. They are also material objects, a means of communication, a way of constructing meaning and disseminating ideas both locally and internationally. The photographs discussed in these pages highlight that, while much of the way that nations relate to one another happens at a distance among strangers, these international relationships also

---

7   Alison Broinowski, 'The Butterfly Phenomenon', *The Journal of the Asian Arts Society of Australia* 1, no. 3 (1992): 10.
8   Dorinne Kondo, *About Face: Performing Race in Fashion and Theatre* (New York and London: Routledge, 1997), 34–35.

affect familial and personal connections closer to home. Whether in government documents, commercial environments, family albums, or newspapers and galleries, photographs have been used to both boost official international relations and cement interpersonal bonds.

Moreover, these public and private photographic relationships often sit in conflict. In Australia, Japan has been variously positioned as an innocent child, potential invader, refined artist, despised enemy, beneficial trading partner and, finally (and albeit ambivalently), good friend and partner. Friendships and productive working relationships can flourish during periods of diplomatic dispute and political suspicion, just as clichés about racial difference may be used to express professional or personal admiration. As Kanamori suggests in her work, limiting critical analysis to cultural stereotypes risks reinforcing the racism that they articulate and perpetuate. This is especially important in today's Australia, where some are lamenting the impending loss of a national homogeneity that was always illusory. Australian–Japanese photographic relations highlight how national identities and histories are the products of encounters with foreign nations, individuals and cultures, rather than simply inwardly focused myths of imagined isolation and particularity. Understanding the significance of those encounters demands sensitivity to patterns of change and continuity in intercultural relations; it involves looking at and around the apparent similarities in images and their subjects—beyond that which can be read at a glance—to consider the changing role that photographs and photographic practices play in political, cultural and social life.

This interpretive task also recognises how the history of the Australia–Japan relationship, including but not limited to its visual traditions, continues to affect how intercultural relations are negotiated, formed and understood today. Although several contemporary artists who respond to this history are not interested in the popular clichés of picturesque Japan that have long pervaded photographic representations of the country, they do acknowledge how this history of representation shapes perception. Kanamori's self-reflexive approach considers the impact of this history on her own practice and sense of place in Australia, while Häggblom, Köller, Sleeth and Hewitt examine how stereotypes of Japanese difference have an impact on some very challenging issues such as suicide, natural disaster and globalising economies. These cross-cultural projects are driven by tension and complexity—by the desire to ask questions of the past and present rather than to propose neat resolutions. 'Us' and 'them' ultimately become impossible categories in this work, which also problematises the camera's power to seemingly separate the past from the present.

As the Australia–Japan relationship continues to evolve in both Asia-Pacific and global contexts, photographs and photographic practices will keep playing a significant role in the 'complex cultural flows and connections' that bind the two nations.[9] Maintaining a respectful, inclusive partnership involves balancing a range of perspectives and interests, and photography will remain a potent, if problematic, register of those interests. 'Picturing' Japan was always a selective and contingent endeavour; Japan itself has always in a sense remained out of view, close by but somewhere else. That Australians seem increasingly relaxed in this knowledge suggests a kind of ironic representational breakthrough. It reflects, further, a more assured view of the way they see the world itself and their own place in it.

---

9   Koichi Iwabuchi, 'Pop-Culture Diplomacy in Japan: Soft Power, Nation Branding and the Question of "International Cultural Exchange"', *International Journal of Cultural Policy* 21, no. 4 (2015): 430.

BIBLIOGRAPHY

Archival Sources

National Archives of Australia

A12508 32/128. Kagiyama, Sata. Personal Statement and Declaration by alien passengers entering Australia (Forms A42), Department of the Interior.

A981 JAP 55. Japan Espionage – General, Department of External Affairs.

C123 9904. Kagiyama, Sadako [Box 302], Security Service, NSW.

C320 J240. NSW Security Service file – Pre war Activities of Japanese and training of Interpreters, Security Service, NSW.

C320 J70. NSW Security Service file – Police Observation of Japanese Movements in the City [Box 11], Security Service, NSW.

C320 J78. NSW Security Service file – Japanese firms in Australia [Box 12], Security Service, NSW.

C320 J79. NSW Security Service file – Japanese Society of Sydney [Box 12], Security Service, NSW.

C320 J208. NSW Security Service file – Japanese Organisation in Sydney [Box14], Security Service, NSW.

CRS A 1838, 477/511. Patrick Shaw, Head of the Australian Mission in Japan, 'The Emperor's Visit to Hiroshima', despatch no.45/1947, Department of External Affairs.

SP1148/2. Manifests Passenger – Outwards Ships (Forms P1) and Manifests Passenger – Outwards Aircraft (Forms P1), Collector of Customs, Sydney.

SP42/1 C1934/4618. Ichiro Kagiyama [Applicant for Exemption from the Dictation Test under the Immigration Act and for Admission of his Wife into the Commonwealth] [Box 300], Collector of Customs, Sydney.

National Library of Australia

MS 1538. Papers of William Morris Hughes.

MS 3092. Papers of D.C.S. Sissons.

NSW State Archives and Records

1127/1932 and 73/1933, Divorce papers Cecilia Howard Kagiyama – Ichiro Kagiyama.

Published Sources

Ackland, Michael and Pam Oliver, eds. *Unexpected Encounters: Neglected Histories Behind the Australia-Japan Relationship*. Clayton: Monash Asia Institute, 2007.

Akami, Tomoko. 'Frederic Eggleston and Oriental Power, 1925-1929'. In *Relationships: Japan and Australia*, edited by Paul Jones and Vera Mackie, 101–32. Melbourne: University of Melbourne, 2001.

Alcock, Rutherford. *The Capital of the Tycoon: A Narrative of a Three Years' Residence in Japan*. London: Longman, Green, Longman, Roberts & Green, 1863.

Anderson, Fay. 'Chasing the Pictures: Press and Magazine Photography'. *Media International Australia* 150, no. 1 (February 2014): 47–55. doi.org/10.1177/1329878X1415000112.

Andriotis, Konstantinos and Misela Mavric. 'Postcard Mobility: Going Beyond Image and Text'. *Annals of Tourism Research* 40 (2013): 18–39. doi.org/10.1016/j.annals.2012.07.004.

Ang, Ien, Yudhishthir Raj Isar and Phillip Mar. 'Cultural Diplomacy: Beyond the National Interest?' *International Journal of Cultural Policy* 21, no. 4 (2015): 365–81. doi-org.ezproxy.lib.monash.edu.au/10.1080/10286632.2015.1042474.

Annear, Judy. 'Kiichiro Ishida and the Sydney Camera Circle'. *Look*, December 2003, 18–19.

Aoki-Okabe, Maki, Yoko Kawamura and Toichi Makita. 'Germany in Europe, Japan and Asia: National Commitments to Cultural Relations within Regional Frameworks'. In *Searching for a Cultural Diplomacy*, edited by Jessica C.E. Gienow-Hecht and Mark C. Donfried, 212–40. New York: Berghann, 2010.

Armstrong, J. 'Aspects of Japanese Immigration to Queensland before 1900'. *Queensland Heritage* 2, no. 9 (1979): 3–9.

Arndt, Richard. *The First Resort of Kings: American Cultural Diplomacy in the Twentieth Century*. Washington: Potomac, 2005.

Ashikari, Mikiko. 'The Memory of Women's White Faces: Japaneseness and the Ideal Image of Women'. *Japan Forum* 15, no. 1 (2003): 55–79. doi.org/10.1080/0955580032000077739.

Australia-Japan Foundation. *Annual Report 2002–03*. Canberra: Australian Government. dfat.gov.au/people-to-people/foundations-councils-institutes/australia-japan-foundation/Documents/ajf-annual-report-2002-03.pdf.

Axell, Albert and Hideaki Kase. *Kamikaze: Japan's Suicide Gods*. Harlow: Longman, 2002.

Bærenholdt, Jørgen Ole, Michael Haldrup, Jonas Larsen and John Urry. *Performing Tourist Places*. Aldershot: Ashgate, 2004.

Bain, May Albertus. *Full Fathom Five*. Perth: Artlook Books, 1982.

Barnes, Carolyn and Simon Jackson. 'Creature of Circumstance: Australia's Pavilion at Expo '70 and Changing International Relations. Panorama to Paradise 1'. In *Panorama to Paradise: Proceedings of the XXIVth International Conference of the Society of Architectural Historians, Australia and New Zealand, Adelaide, 21–24 September 2007*, 1–16. Adelaide: Society of Architectural Historians, 2007.

Blum, Ron. *George Rose: Australia's Master Stereographer*. Oaklands Park: Ron Blum, 2008.

Blumann, Sigismund. 'Monte Luke. An Artist Who Illuminates Australia's Fame'. *Asahi Camera*, May 1926, 120.

Bollen, Jonathan. 'Here and There—travel, television and touring revues: internationalism as entertainment in the 1950s and 1960s'. *Popular Entertainment Studies* 4, no. 1 (2013): 64–81.

Braw, Monica. *The Atomic Bomb Suppressed: American Censorship in Japan 1945–1948*. Tokyo: Liber Forlag, 1986.

Brennan, Niall. *Damien Parer: Cameraman*. Carlton: Melbourne University Press, 1994.

Broinowski, Alison. 'The Butterfly Phenomenon'. *The Journal of the Asian Arts Society of Australia* 1, no. 3 (1992): 10–11.

Broinowski, Alison. 'About Face: Asian Representation of Australia'. PhD diss., The Australian National University, Canberra, 2001.

Bullard, Steve. *Blankets on the Wire: The Cowra Breakout and its Aftermath*. Canberra: Australian War Memorial, 2006.

Bullard, Steven. 'A Japanese Invasion?'. *Wartime*, no. 77 (Summer 2017): 44–49.

Burchett, Wilfred. *Shadows of Hiroshima*. London: Verso, 1983.

Burgess, Chris. 'National Identity and the Transition from Internationalization to Globalization: "Cool Japan" or "Closed Japan"'. In *Languages and Identities in a Transitional Japan: From Internationalization to Globalization*, edited by Ikuko Nakane, Emi Otsuji and William S. Armour, 15–36. London: Routledge, 2016.

Burke, Janine. *The Eye of the Beholder: Albert Tucker's Photographs*. Melbourne: Museum of Modern Art at Heide, 1998.

Callas, Peter. 'Editorial'. Special issue on contemporary Japanese art. *Art Network*, Spring 1984, 23–24.

Carroll, Alison. *Sun Gazing: The Australia-Japan Art Exhibitions Touring Program, 2002–04*. Carlton: Asialink, 2004.

Carroll, Alison. 'Art to Life: 20 Years in the Australia-Asian Arts Atmosphere'. *Art Monthly Australia*, no. 235 (November 2010): 5–7.

Carver, S.R. *Demography Bulletin* no. 75. Canberra: Commonwealth Bureau of Statistics, 1957.

Castle, Terry. *Masquerade and Civilization: The Carnivalesque in Eighteenth-Century English Culture and Fiction*. Stanford: Stanford University Press, 1986.

Catalogue of an Exhibition Camera Pictures by the Photographic Society of N.S.W., 1922. Sydney: Photographic Society of New South Wales, 1922, plate V.

Cazneaux, Harold. 'A Review of the Pictures'. In *Cameragraphs of the Year 1924*, edited by Cecil W. Bostock. Sydney: Harringtons, 1924.

Clements, Bill. 'An Old Brown Overcoat: Kyoto in the Mid-Sixties'. *Kyoto Journal* 76 (Summer 2011): 10–16.

Clifton, Allan S. *Time of Fallen Blossoms*. London: Cassell, 1950.

Clune, Frank. *Ashes of Hiroshima*. Sydney: Angus & Robertson, 1950.

Colless, Edward. 'World Vision'. *Australian Art Collector*, July–September 2007, 109–17.

Collins, Darryl. 'Emperors and Musume: China and Japan "on the Boards" in Australia, 1850s–1920s'. *East Asian History* 7 (1994): 67–92.

Collins, J.G. *The War of the Veterans*. Toowoomba: J.G. Collins, 2001.

Crockett, Lucy Herndon. *Popcorn on the Ginza: An Informal Portrait of Postwar Japan*. London: Victor Gollancz, 1949.

Crombie, Isobel and Luke Gartlan. *Shashin: Nineteenth-Century Japanese Studio Photography*. Melbourne: National Gallery of Victoria, 2005.

D'Aliesio, Susanna. 'Arles 2017: Tokyo Is Yours by Meg Hewitt'. *British Journal of Photography*, 6 July 2017. www.bjp-online.com/2017/07/photobook-tokyo-is-yours-by-meg-hewitt/#closeContactFormCust00.n%20.

Davies, George. *The Occupation of Japan*. St Lucia, Brisbane: University of Queensland Press, 2001.

de Matos, Christine. 'Occupation Masculinities: The Residues of Colonial Power in Australian Occupied Japan'. In *Gender, Power and Military Occupations: Asia Pacific and the Middle East since 1945*, edited by Christine de Matos and Rowena Ward, 23–42. New York: Routledge, 2012.

de Matos, Christine. *Encouraging Democracy in a Cold War Climate*. Canberra: Australia-Japan Research Centre, 2001.

Dee, Moreen. *Friendship and Co-operation: The 1976 Basic Treaty Between Australia and Japan*. Canberra: Commonwealth of Australia, 2006.

Dennis, Peter, Jeffrey Grey, Ewan Morris, Robin Prior and Jean Bou. *The Oxford Companion to Australian Military History*. Melbourne: Oxford University Press, 1995.

Department of Information. *War in New Guinea*. Sydney: F.H. Johnston Publishing, 1943.

Dower, John. *War Without Mercy: Race and Power in the Pacific War*. New York: Pantheon Books, 1986.

Dower, John. *Embracing Defeat: Japan in the Aftermath of World War II*. Harmondsworth: Penguin, 2000.

Ebury, Francis. 'Making Pictures: Australian Pictorial Photography as Art 1897–1957'. PhD diss. University of Melbourne, 2001.

Edwards, Elizabeth. 'Postcards—Greetings from Another World'. In *The Tourist Image: Myths and Myth Making in Tourism*, edited by Tom Selwyn, 197–221. Chichester: John Wiley and Sons, 1996.

Elliott, Murray. *Occupational Hazards: A Doctor in Japan and Elsewhere*. Brisbane: Griffith University, 1995.

Evans, Gareth. 'Australia and Asia: The Role of Public Diplomacy'. Address by the Minister for Foreign Affairs and Trade, Senator Gareth Evans, to the Australia-Asia Association, Melbourne, 15 March 1990. www.gevans.org/speeches/old/1990/150390_fm_australiaandasia.pdf.

Farrell, J.T. 'Our Illustrations'. *Harrington's Photographic Journal*, 15 October 1919, 312.

Finch, Lynette. 'Knowing the Enemy: Australian Psychological Warfare and the Business of Influencing Minds in the Second World War'. *War & Society* 16, no. 2 (October 1998): 71–91. doi.org/10.1179/072924798791201336.

Finck, Henry T. *Lotus-Time in Japan*. New York: Charles Scribner's and Sons, 1895.

Fitzhardinge, L.F. 'Australia, Japan and Great Britain, 1914–18: A Study in Triangular Diplomacy'. *Historical Studies* 14, no. 54 (1970): 250–59. doi.org/10.1080/10314617008595422.

FitzSimons, Peter. *Kokoda*. Sydney: Hodder Headline, 2005.

Foster, Kevin. 'Deploying the Dead: Combat Photography, Death and the Second World War in the USA and the Soviet Union'. *WLA: An International Journal of the Humanities* 26 (2014): 1–32.

Fraser, Karen M. *Photography and Japan*. London: Reaktion Books, 2011.

Frei, Henry. *Japan's Southward Advance and Australia*. Carlton: Melbourne University Press, 1991.

Fukuoka, Maki. 'Selling Portrait Photographs: Early Photographic Business in Asakusa, Japan'. *History of Photography* 35, no. 4 (2011): 355–73. doi.org/10.1080/03087298.2011.611425.

Fussell, Paul. *The Boy Scout's Handbook and Other Observations*. New York: Oxford University Press, 1982.

Gartlan, Luke. 'Types or Costumes? Reframing Early Yokohama Photography'. *Visual Resources* 22, no. 3 (2006): 239–63. doi.org/10.1080/01973760600807812.

Gartlan, Luke. 'Japan Day by Day? William Henry Metcalf, Edward Sylvester Morse and Early Tourist Photography in Japan'. *Early Popular Visual Culture* 8, no. 2 (2010): 125–46. doi.org/10.1080/17460651003693360.

Gartlan, Luke. *A Career of Japan: Baron Raimund Von Stillfried and Early Yokohama Photography*. Leiden: Brill, 2016.

Gerster, Robin, ed. *Hotel Asia*. Ringwood: Penguin, 1995.

Gerster, Robin. *Travels in Atomic Sunshine: Australia and the Occupation of Japan*. Melbourne: Scribe, 2008.

Gerster, Robin. 'Bomb Sights in Japan: Photographing Australian-Occupied Hiroshima'. *Meanjin* 74, no. 4 (2015): 88–103. meanjin.com.au/essays/bomb-sights-in-japan/.

Gienow-Hecht, Jessica C.E. 'What Are We Searching For? Culture, Diplomacy, Agents and the State'. In *Searching for a Cultural Diplomacy*, edited by Jessica C.E. Gienow-Hecht and Mark C. Donfried, 16–25. New York: Berghann, 2010.

Gillen, Julia and Nigel Hall. 'The Edwardian Postcard: A Revolutionary Moment in Rapid Multimodal Communications'. Paper presented at the British Educational Research Association Annual Conference, University of Manchester, 2–5 September 2009.

Gillen, Julia and Nigel Hall. 'Any Mermaids? Early Postcard Mobilities'. In *Mobile Methods*, edited by Monika Buscher, John Urry and Katian Witchger, 20–35. London and New York: Routledge, 2010.

Goldstein-Gidoni, Ofra. 'Kimono and the Construction of Gendered and Cultural Identities'. *Ethnology* 38, no. 4 (Autumn 1999): 351–70. doi.org/10.2307/3773912.

Goldsworthy, David and Peter Edwards. *Facing North Volume 2: 1970s to 2000*. Carlton: Melbourne University Press, 2001.

Govett, Neville. *The Story of the B.C.O.F. Tourist Club*. Hiroshima: Hiroshima Publishing Co., 1950.

Graves, Christopher. 'Cool Is Not Enough'. In *Reimagining Japan: The Quest for a Future That Works*, edited by Clay Chandler, Heang Chhor and Brian Salsberg, 411–16. San Francisco: VIZ Media, 2011.

Green, Philip M. *Memories of Occupied Japan*. Blackheath, NSW: Philip Maxwell Green, 1987.

Green, Steven H. 'The Soft Power of Cool: Economy, Culture and Foreign Policy in Japan'. *Toyo Hogaku* 58, no. 3 (2015): 221–42.

Griffis, William Elliot. *The Mikado's Empire*. New York: Harper and Brothers, 1895.

Guth, Christine M.E. 'Charles Longfellow and Okakura Kakuzo: Cultural Cross-Dressing in the Colonial Context'. *Positions: East Asia Cultures Critique* 8, no. 3 (2000): 605–35.

Ham, Paul. *Kokoda*. Sydney: Harper Collins, 2005.

Hamilton, Walter. *Children of the Occupation: Japan's Untold Story*. Sydney: NewSouth Publishing, 2012.

Hariman, Robert and John Louis Lucaites. 'The Iconic Image of the Mushroom Cloud and the Cold War Optic'. In *Picturing Atrocity: Photographs in Crisis*, edited by Geoffrey Batchen, Mick Gidley, Nancy K. Miller and Jay Prosser, 135–46. London: Reaktion, 2012.

Hayashi, Tadahiko. *Kastori no jidai*. Tokyo: Pie Bukkusu, 2007.

Hewitt, Meg. 'Tokyo is Yours'. *Lens Culture*, 2016. Accessed 25 January 2018. www.lensculture.com/articles/meg-hewitt-tokyo-is-yours.

Hewitt, Meg. 'Tokyo Is Yours: Seeking Sense Through Street Photography'. *Lens Culture*, 2017. Accessed 25 January 2018. www.lensculture.com/articles/meg-hewitt-tokyo-is-yours-seeking-sense-through-street-photography.

Hickey, Gary. 'Impressions of Japan'. *Art Monthly Australia*, no. 236 (December 2010): 20–22.

Hill, Paul and Thomas Cooper, eds. *Dialogue with Photography*. New York: Farrar, Straus and Giroux, 1979.

Hilvert, John. *Blue Pencil Warriors: Censorship and Propaganda in World War II*. St Lucia, Brisbane: University of Queensland Press, 1984.

Hise, Beth and Pam Oliver. 'Kiichiro Ishida'. *Insites*, Summer 2003, 4–5.

Inglis, Ken. 'Young Australia 1870–1900: The Idea and the Reality'. In *The Colonial Child*, edited by Guy Featherstone, 1–23. Melbourne: Royal Historical Society of Victoria, 1981.

Iriye, Akira, ed. 'The Making of the Transnational World'. In *Global Interdependence: The World After 1945*, edited by Akira Iriye, 679–847. Cambridge, MA: Harvard University Press, 2014.

Iwabuchi, Koichi. 'Pop-Culture Diplomacy in Japan: Soft Power, Nation Branding and the Question of "International Cultural Exchange"'. *International Journal of Cultural Policy* 21, no. 4 (2015): 419–32. doi.org/10.1080/10286632.2015.1042469.

Jackson, Ian. '"Duplication, Rivalry and Friction": The Australian Army, the Government and the Press during the Second World War'. In *The Information Battlefield: Representing Australians at War*, edited by Kevin Foster, 74–85. North Melbourne: Australian Scholarly Publishing, 2011.

John, Major A.W. *Duty Defined, Duty Done: A Memoir*. Cheltenham, Vic.: The Gen Publishers, 2004.

Johnson, Paddy. 'Matthew Sleeth'. *Art and Australia* 45, no. 4 (2008): 646–47.

Johnston, George H. *The Toughest Fighting in the World*. New York: Duell, Sloan and Pearce, 1943.

Johnston, Mark. *Fighting the Enemy: Australian Soldiers and their Adversaries in World War II*. Cambridge: Cambridge University Press, 2000.

Jones, Lyndal. 'The Continuum Symposium on Australian Art'. Special issue on contemporary Japanese art. *Art Network*, Spring 1984, 49.

Jones, Noreen. *Number 2 Home: A Story of Japanese Pioneers in Australia*. Fremantle: Fremantle Arts Centre Press, 2002.

Jones, Paul and Pam Oliver, eds. *Changing Histories: Australia and Japan*. Clayton: Monash Asia Institute, 2001.

Kanamori, Mayu and Vera Mackie. 'You've Mistaken Me for a Butterfly'. *Japanese Studies* 37, no. 3 (2017): 387–94. doi.org/10.1080/10371397.2017.1363678.

Kazue, Morisaki. *Karayuki-San*. Tōkyō: Asahi Shimbunsha, 1976.

Keat, Connie, ed. *Amy's Diaries: The Travel Notes of Elizabeth Amy Cathcart Payne 1869–1875*. Morwell: LaTrobe Valley U3A, 1995.

Keehan, Reuben. 'Hello Tokyo! Good to See You Again'. *Artlink* 28, no. 4 (2008): 55–56.

Kersten, Rikki. 'Japan and Australia'. In *Japanese Foreign Policy Today*, edited by Inoguchi Takashi and Purnendra Jain, 283–96. Basingstoke: Palgrave, 2000.

Kirmess, C.H. *The Australian Crisis*. Melbourne: George Robertson, 1909.

Kociumbas, Jan. 'The Spiritual Child: Child Death and Angelic Motherhood in Colonial Women's Writing'. *Journal of the Royal Australian Historical Society* 85, no. 2 (1999): 85–104.

Kondo, Dorinne. *About Face: Performing Race in Fashion and Theatre*. New York and London: Routledge, 1997.

Lakin, Shaune. *Contact: Photographs from the Australian War Memorial Collection*. Canberra: Australian War Memorial, 2006.

Lambourne, Lionel. *Japonisme: Cultural Crossings between Japan and the West*. London and New York: Phaidon, 2005.

Larsen, Jonas. 'Geographies of Tourist Photography'. In *Geographies of Communication: The Spatial Turn in Media Studies*, edited by J. Falkheimer and A. Jansson, 241–57. Goteborg: Nordicom, 2006.

Littlewood, Ian. *The Idea of Japan: Western Images, Western Myths*. Chicago: Ivan R. Dee, 1996.

Loti, Pierre. *Madame Chrysanthème*. London: George Routledge and Sons, 1897.

Low, Morris. *Japan on Display: Photography and the Emperor*. Abingdon: Routledge, 2006.

Low, Morris. 'American Photography during the Allied Occupation of Japan: The Work of John W. Bennett'. *History of Photography* 39, no. 3 (August 2015): 263–78. doi.org/10.1080/03087298.2015.1064613.

Lowe, Peter. 'The British Empire and the Anglo-Japanese Alliance 1911–1915'. *History* 54, no. 181 (1969): 212–25. doi.org/10.1111/j.1468-229X.1969.tb01245.x.

Mackie, Vera and Paul Jones, eds. *Relationships: Japan and Australia*. Melbourne: University of Melbourne, 2001.

Manchester, William. *American Caesar: Douglas MacArthur 1880–1964*. New York: Dell Publishing, 1978.

Matsuoka, Seigow. *Roots of Japan(s): Unearthing the Cultural Matrix of Japan*. Tokyo: Ministry of Economy, Trade and Industry, 2011.

Matsurra, Toshio. 'Notes of a Traveller: Continuum '83 Reviewed'. *Bijutsu Techo* 35, no. 517 (1983): 174–79.

Mayer, Tara. 'Cultural Cross-Dressing: Posing and Performance in Orientalist Portraits'. *Journal of the Royal Asiatic Society* 22, no. 2 (2012): 281–98. doi.org/10.1017/S1356186312000168.

McDonald, Neil. *The Story of Damien Parer*. Port Melbourne: Lothian 1994.

McDonald, Neil and Peter Brune. *200 Shots: Damien Parer, George Silk and the Australians at War in New Guinea*. St Leonards: Allen & Unwin, 1998.

McFarlane, Kyla. 'Kristian Häggblom'. *Un Magazine* 7 (2006): 5–9.

McGray, Douglas. 'Japan's Gross National Cool'. *Foreign Policy* 130 (May–June 2002): 583–84.

McLaren, Sally. 'Made in Cool Japan: Delights and Disasters'. *Griffith Review* 49 (2015): 165–73.

McLelland, Mark. *Queer Japan from the Pacific War to the Internet Age*. Lanham, MD: Rowman and Littlefield, 2005.

Meaney, Neville. *The Search for Security in the Pacific 1901-1914*. Sydney: Sydney University Press, 1976.

Meaney, Neville. *Towards a New Vision: Australia and Japan through 100 Years*. East Roseville: Kangaroo Press, 1999.

Meaney, Neville. *Towards a New Vision: Australia and Japan Across Time*. Sydney: UNSW Press, 2007.

Meaney, Neville. *Australia and World Crisis 1914–1923*. Sydney: Sydney University Press, 2009.

Menpes, Mortimer. *Japan: A Record in Colour*. New York: Macmillan, 1901.

Miles, Melissa. 'Through Japanese Eyes: Ichiro Kagiyama and Australian-Japanese Relations in the 1920s and 1930s'. *History of Photography* 38, no. 4 (2014): 356–58.

Miles, Melissa. *The Language of Light and Dark: Light and Place in Australian Photography*. Montreal: McGill Queen's University Press, 2015.

Miles, Melissa. 'Ichiro Kagiyama in Early Twentieth Century Sydney'. *Japanese Studies* 37, no. 1 (2017): 89–116.

Miles, Melissa and Jessica Neath. 'Staging Japanese Femininity: Cross-Cultural Dressing in Australian Photography'. *Fashion Theory* 20, no. 4 (2016): 545–73. doi.org/10.1080/1362704X.2015.1125695.

Miles, Melissa and Kate Warren. 'The Japanese Photographers of Broome: Photography and Cross-Cultural Encounter'. *History of Photography* 41, no. 1 (2016): 3–24. doi.org/10.1080/03087298.2017.1280903.

Mitchell, Greg. 'The Great Hiroshima Cover-Up—And the Greatest Movie Never Made'. *Japan Focus*, 8 August 2011. apjjf.org/2011/9/31/Greg-Mitchell/3581/article.html.

Mitchell, J.M. *International Cultural Relations*. London: Allen and Unwin, 1986.

Mitsuda, Yuri. *Modernism/Japonism in Photography 1920s–40s. Kiichiro Ishida and Sydney Camera Circle*. Tokyo: Shoto Museum of Art, 2002.

Mizuta, Miya Elise. '"Fair Japan": On Art and War at the Saint Louis World's Fair, 1904'. *Discourse* 28, no. 1 (2006): 28–52.

Mōri, Yoshitaka. 'The Pitfall Facing the Cool Japan Project: The Transnational Development of the Anime Industry under the Condition of Post-Fordism'. *International Journal of Japanese Sociology*, no. 20 (2011): 30–42. doi.org/10.1111/j.1475-6781.2011.01146.x.

Murakami, Yuichi. 'Australia's Immigration Legislation, 1893–1901: The Japanese Response'. In *Relationships: Australia and Japan*, edited by Vera Mackie and Paul Jones, 45–70. Parkville: University of Melbourne, 2001.

Murphy, Michael David. 'Ten Series/106 Photographs'. *Foto8*, 14 November 2008. www.foto8.com/live/ten-series106-photographs/.

Myers, Ted. *Family Japan: Two Families from Tokyo*. Sydney: Qantas Airways and the Asian Studies Coordinating Committee, 1974.

Nagata, Yuriko. *Unwanted Aliens: Japanese Internment in Australia*. St Lucia, Brisbane: University of Queensland Press, 1996.

Nagata, Yuriko. 'Gendering Australia-Japan Relations: Prostitutes and the Japanese Diaspora in Australia'. *Ritsumeikan Journal of Asia Pacific Studies* 11 (March 2003): 71–84.

Nakamura, I. and M. Onouchi. *Nippon No Poppupawaa (Japanese Popular Power)*. Tokyo: Nihon Keizai Shimbunsha, 2006.

Newton, Gael. *Silver and Grey: Fifty Years of Australian Photography 1900–1950*. Sydney: Angus and Robertson, 1980.

Nish, I.H. 'Australia and the Anglo-Japanese Alliance, 1901–1911'. *Australian Journal of Politics and History* 9, no. 2 (1963): 201–12. doi.org/10.1111/j.1467-8497.1963.tb01063.x.

Norman, Henry. *The Real Japan: Studies of Contemporary Japanese Manners, Morals, Administration, and Politics*. London: FT Unwin, 1891.

Nye, Joseph. 'Soft Power and American Foreign Policy'. *Political Science Quarterly* 119, no. 2 (June 2004): 255–70. doi.org/10.2307/20202345.

Ogoura, Kazuo. 'From Ikebana to Manga and Beyond'. *Global Asia* 7, no. 3 (2012): 24–28.

O'Lincoln, Tom. *Australia's Pacific War: Challenging a National Myth*. Melbourne: Interventions, 2011.

Oliver, Pam. 'Interpreting "Japanese Activities" in Australia, 1888–1945'. *Journal of the Australian War Memorial* (online) 36 (2002). www.awm.gov.au/journal/j36/oliver.asp.

Oliver, Pam. 'Japanese Relationships in White Australia'. *History Australia* 4, no. 1 (2007): 5.1–5.20.

Ozaki, Y. 'Misunderstood Japan'. *The North American Review* 171, no. 527 (1900): 556–76.

Okakura, Kakuzo. *The Awakening of Japan*. New York: The Century Co., 1905.

Pham, P.L. 'On the Edge of the Orient: English Representations of Japan, Circa 1895–1910'. *Japanese Studies* 19, no. 2 (1999): 163–81. doi.org/10.1080/10371399908727675.

Photograms of the Year 1923. London: Iliffe & Sons Ltd, 1924.

Piel, Lizbeth Halliday. 'The Ideology of the Child in Japan 1600–1945'. PhD diss., University of Hawaii, 2007.

Popham, Peter. *Tokyo: The City at the End of the World*. Tokyo: Kodansha International, 1985.

Porter, Hal. *The Actors: An Image of the New Japan*. Sydney: Angus Robertson, 1968.

Queale, Alan. 'Japan Diary'. In *As You Were: A Cavalcade of Events with the Australian Services from 1788 to 1947*, 189–95. Canberra: Australian War Memorial, 1947.

Raftery, Judith. '"Mainly a Question of Motherhood": Professional Advice-Giving and Infant Welfare'. *Journal of Australian Studies* 19, no. 45 (1995): 66–78. doi.org/10.1080/14443059509387228.

Riding, Christine. 'Travellers and Sitters: The Orientalist Portrait'. In *The Lure of the East*, edited by Nicholas Tromans, 48–81. London: Tate Gallery, 2008.

Rittner, Geo. *Impressions of Japan*. New York: James Pott and Co., 1904.

Rix, Alan. *Coming to Terms: The Politics of Australia's Trade with Japan 1945–1957*. Sydney: Angus & Robertson, 1986.

Rix, Alan, ed. *Intermittent Diplomat: The Japan and Batavia Diaries of W. Macmahon Ball*. Carlton: Melbourne University Press, 1988.

Rix, Alan. *The Australia-Japan Political Alignment 1952 to the Present*. London: Routledge, 1999.

Roberts, Mary. 'Cultural Crossings: Sartorial Adventures, Satiric Narratives, and the Question of Indigenous Agency in Nineteenth-Century Europe and the near East'. In *Edges of Empire*, edited by Jocelyn Hackforth-Jones, 70–94. Malden: Blackwell, 2005.

Ryan, James R. *Picturing Empire: Photography and the Visualization of the British Empire*. London: Reaktion Books, 1997.

Said, Edward W. *Orientalism*. 1978. Reprint, New York: Vintage, 1994.

Sass, Alek. 'Old Friends and New: A Ramble through the Exhibition of Camera Pictures by the Photographic Society of New South Wales'. *Australasian Photo Review* 29, no. 11 (1922): 553–56.

Scarlett, Ken. 'Australia, Japan and "Continuum '83"'. In *Continuum '83: The 1st Exhibition of Australian Contemporary Art in Japan*. Tokyo: Japan-Australia Cultural & Art Exchange Committee, 1983.

Scherer, James A.B. *Japan Today*. Philadelphia and London: J.B. Lippincott Co., 1905.

Schwartz, Joan M. 'The Geography Lesson: Photographs and the Construction of Imaginative Geographies'. *Journal of Historical Geography* 22, no. 1 (1996): 16–45. doi.org/10.1006/jhge.1996.0003.

Seligmann, Ari. 'Tokyo Tropes, the Poetics of Chaos'. In *Fabulation: Myth, Nature, Heritage: The Proceedings of the 29th Annual Conference of the Society of Architectural Historians Australia & New Zealand*, edited by Stuart King, Anuradha Chatterjee and Stephen Loo, 979–93. Launceston, Tas.: Society of Architectural Historians Australia & New Zealand, 2012.

Shiga, Shigetaka. *Nan'yō Jiji (Current Affairs in the South Seas)*. Tokyo: Maruzen, 1887.

Shindo, Utako. *Imminent Landscape*. Sydney: Japan Foundation, 2010.

Simpson, Colin. *The Country Upstairs*. Sydney: Angus and Robertson, 1956.

Sissons, D.C.S. 'Attitudes to Japan and Defence, 1890–1923'. MA diss., University of Melbourne, 1956.

Sissons, D.C.S. 'Karayuki-San: Japanese Prostitutes in Australia, 1887–1916 —II'. *Historical Studies* 17, no. 69 (1977): 474–88. doi.org/10.1080/10314617708595566.

Sladen, Douglas and Norma Lorimer. *More Queer Things About Japan*. London: Anthony Treherns and Co., 1905.

Sladen, Douglas. *Queer Things About Japan*. 1904. Reprint, London: Kegan Paul, Trench, Trübner & Co., 1913.

Smith, H.A. *The Official Year Book of New South Wales 1922*. Sydney: NSW State Government, 1924.

Smyth, Diana. 'Baby Face'. *British Journal of Photography*, 19 December 2007, 16–17.

Sobocinska, Agnieszka. *Visiting the Neighbours: Australians in Asia*. Sydney: NewSouth Publishing, 2014.

Sontag, Susan. *On Photography* (1977). New York: Anchor Books Doubleday, 1990.

Sontag, Susan. *Regarding the Pain of Others*. New York: Picador/Farrar, Straus and Giroux, 2003.

Sperling, Joy. 'From Magic Lantern Slide to Digital Image: Visual Communities and American Culture'. *The Journal of American Culture* 31, no. 1 (2003): 1–6. doi.org/10.1111/j.1542-734X.2008.00659.x.

Stakelon, Pauline. 'Travel through the Stereoscope: Movement and Narrative in Topological Stereoview Collections of Europe'. *Media History* 16, no. 4 (2010): 407–15. doi.org/10.1080/13688804.2010.507476.

Sterry, Lorraine. 'Constructs of Meiji Japan: The Role of Writing by Victorian Women Travellers'. *Japanese Studies* 23, no. 2 (2003): 167–83. doi.org/10.1080/1037139032000129702.

Struk, Janina. *Private Pictures: Soldiers' Inside View of War*. London: I.B. Tauris, 2011.

Sugiyama, T. *Kūru Japan. Sekai Ga Kaitagaru Nippon* (*Cool Japan. The Japan the World Wants to Buy*). Tokyo: Shoutensha, 2006.

Sylvester, David. *Interviews with Francis Bacon*. London: Thames and Hudson, 1975.

Takemae, Eiji. *The Allied Occupation of Japan*. Translated by Robert Ricketts and Sebastian Swann. New York: Continuum, 2003.

Tamura, Keiko. 'Shooting an Invisible Enemy: Images of Japanese Soldiers in Damien Parer's New Guinea Newsreels'. *The Journal of Pacific History* 45, no. 1 (2010): 117–33. doi.org/10.1080/00223344.2010.484176.

Taylor, John. *Body Horror: Photojournalism, Catastrophe and War*. New York: New York University Press, 1998.

Terada, Takashi. 'The Australia-Japan Partnership in the Asia-Pacific: From Economic Diplomacy to Security Co-Operation?' *Contemporary Southeast Asia* 22, no. 1 (April 2000): 175–98. doi.org/10.1355/CS22-1G.

Thomas, Julia Adeney. 'Power Made Visible: Photography and Postwar Japan's Elusive Reality'. *The Journal of Asian Studies* 67, no. 2 (May 2008): 365–94. doi.org/10.1017/S0021911808000648.

Thoral, Marie-Cecile. 'Sartorial Orientalism: Cross-Cultural Dressing in Colonial Algeria and Metropolitan France in the Nineteenth Century'. *European History Quarterly* 45, no. 1 (2015): 57–82. doi.org/10.1177/0265691414556060.

Tilney, F.C. 'American Work at the London Exhibitions'. *American Photography* 21, no. 12 (December 1927): 666–74.

Tooth, Nevil A. 'A Camera in Japan'. *Harrington's Photographic Journal*, 22 December 1911, 381.

Torney, Prue. '"Renegades to their Country": The Australian Press and the Allied Occupation of Japan 1946–1950'. *War & Society* 25, no.1 (May 2006): 89–110. doi.org/10.1179/072924706791601973.

Torney-Parlicki, Prue. *Somewhere in Asia: War, Journalism, and Australia's Neighbours 1941–75*. Sydney: UNSW Press, 2000.

Tsuchikawa, Shūzō. 'Episodes from the War's End (Shusen Kobanashi)'. *Hida Shunju*, August 1978, 434.

Tsurumi, Wataru. *Kanzen jisatsu manyuaru (The Complete Manual of Suicide)*. Tōkyō: Ōta Shuppan, 1993.

Ure Smith, Sydney. 'The Story of the Home'. *The Home*, March 1930, 60.

Urry, John. *The Tourist Gaze*. 2nd ed. London: Sage, 2002.

Valaskivi, Katja. *Cool Nations: Media and the Social Imaginary of the Branded Country*. London and New York: Routledge, 2016.

Wakamatsu, Torao. *Farewell Message to Australian People*. Sydney: New Century Press, c. 1938.

Wakita, Mio. *Staging Desires: Japanese Femininity in Kusakabe Kimbei's Nineteenth Century Souvenir Photograph*. Berlin: Reimer, 2013.

Waley, Paul. 'Re-Scripting the City: Tokyo from Ugly Duckling to Cool Cat'. *Japan Forum* 18, no. 3, (November 2006): 361–80.

Walker, David. 'Shooting Mabel: Warrior Masculinity and Asian Invasion'. *History Australia* 2, no. 3 (December 2005): 89.1–89.11.

Watanabe, Toshio. *High Victorian Japonisme*. Berlin and New York: Peter Lang, 1991.

Watanabe, Yasushi. *Bunka to Gaikō: Paburikku Dipuromashii No Jidai* (*Culture and Diplomacy: The Age of Public Diplomacy*). Tokyo: Chukōshinso, 2011.

Webster, D.J. 'Mr K. Ishida'. *Harrington's Photographic Journal*, 1 September 1922, 23.

Webster, D.J. 'Photographic Society of New South Wales'. *Harrington's Photographic Journal* 31, no. 366 (1922): 11–15.

Weisenfeld, Gennifer S. 'Touring "Japan-As-Museum": Nippon and Other Japanese Imperialist Travelogues'. *Positions: East Asia Cultures Critique* 8, no. 3 (Winter 2000): 747–93.

White, Richard. 'The Retreat from Adventure; Popular Travel Writing in the 1950s'. *Australian Historical Studies* 28, no. 109 (1997): 101–02

White, Robert. *Discovering Cameras, 1945–1965*. London: Shire Discovering, 1968.

Williams, Robert J. 'Australia's International Cultural Relations: Some Domestic Dimensions'. *Australian Journal of Political Science* 30, no. 1 (1995): 56–73. doi.org/10.1080/00323269508402323.

Wilson, Sandra. 'Exhibiting a New Japan: The Tokyo Olympics of 1964 and Expo '70 in Osaka'. *Historical Research* 85, no. 227 (February 2012): 159–78.

Woods, Jennie. *Which Way Will the Wind Blow?* North Sydney: Jennie Woods, 1994.

Yahagi, H. 'Pictorial Photography in Japan'. In *Photograms of the Year 1915*, 27–29. London: Dawbarn & Ward, 1916.

Yano, Christine. 'Hello Kitty and Japan's Kawaii Diplomacy'. *East Asia Forum*, 10 October 2015. www.eastasiaforum.org/2015/10/10/hello-kitty-and-japans-kawaii-diplomacy/.

Yoshihara, Mari. *Embracing the East: White Women and American Orientalism*. Oxford: Oxford University Press, 2003.

Zelizer, Barbie. *Remembering to Forget: Holocaust Memory Through the Camera's Eyes*. Chicago: University of Chicago Press, 1998.

www.ingramcontent.com/pod-product-compliance
Lightning Source LLC
Chambersburg PA
CBHW040520220526
45473CB00013B/2927